JOE CASAD
WAYNE DALTON

MCSE
Training GUIDE

WINDOWS NT
SERVER 4

New
Riders

MCSE Training Guide: Windows NT Server 4

By Joe Casad with Wayne Dalton

Published by:
New Riders Publishing
201 West 103rd Street
Indianapolis, IN 46290 USA

Copyright © 1997 by New Riders Publishing

Printed in the United States of America 1 2 3 4 5 6 7 8 9 0

Library of Congress Cataloging-in-Publication Data

```
***CIP data available upon request***
```

ISBN: 1-56205-768-5

Warning and Disclaimer

This book is designed to provide information about **Windows NT Server 4**. Every effort has been made to make this book as complete and as accurate as possible, but no warranty or fitness is implied.

The information is provided on an "as is" basis. The author(s) and New Riders Publishing shall have neither liability nor responsibility to any person or entity with respect to any loss or damages arising from the information contained in this book or from the use of the disks or programs that may accompany it.

Publisher	*Don Fowley*
Associate Publisher	*David Dwyer*
Publishing Manager	*Emmett Dulaney*
Marketing Manager	*Mary Foote*
Managing Editor	*Carla Hall*
Director of Development	*Kezia Endsley*

Acquisitions Editor
Nancy Maragioglio

Senior Editors
Sarah Kearns
Suzanne Snyder

Development Editor
Scott Parker

Project Editors
Theresa Matthias
Amy Bezek

Copy Editor
Theresa Matthias

Technical Editor
Bob Reinch

Software Specialist
Steve Flatt

Assistant Marketing Manager
Gretchen Schlesinger

Acquisitions Coordinator
Amy Lewis

Administrative Coordinator
Karen Opal

Manufacturing Coordinator
Brook Farling

Cover Designer
Karen Ruggles

Cover Production
Nathan Clement

Book Designer
Glenn Larsen

Director of Production
Larry Klein

Production Team Supervisors
Laurie Casey
Joe Millay

Graphics Image Specialists
Kevin Cliburn, Sadie Crawford,
Tammy Graham

Production Analyst
Erich J. Richter

Production Team
Lori Cliburn, Tricia Flodder,
Christopher Morris,
Maureen West

Indexer
Kevin Fulcher

About the Author

Joe Casad is a freelance writer and editor who specializes in programming and networking topics. He was the managing editor of the short-lived but well-received *Network Administrator Magazine,* a journal of practical solutions for network professionals. Mr. Casad received a B.S. in engineering from the University of Kansas in 1980 and, before becoming a full-time writer and editor, spent ten years in the computer-intensive areas of the structural engineering profession. He now lives in Lawrence, Kansas with wife Barb Dineen and a pair of pint-sized hackers named Xander and Mattie.

Trademark Acknowledgments

Contents at a Glance

Chapter 1, Planning *4*

Chapter 2, Installation and Configuration *49*

Chapter 3, Managing Resources *225*

Chapter 4, Connectivity *341*

Chapter 5, Monitoring and Optimization *387*

Chapter 6, Troubleshooting *429*

Appendix A, Overview of the Certification Process *489*

Appendix B, Study Tips *499*

Appendix C, What's on the CD-ROM *503*

Appendix D, All About Test Prep *505*

Index *509*

Table of Contents

1 Planning   **4**

Windows NT Among Microsoft Operating Systems 5
    Windows 95 6
    Windows NT Workstation 6
    Windows NT Server 8
Workgroups and Domains 11
    Workgroups 12
    Domains 13
Choosing a Disk Configuration 14
    Partitions 15
    Primary and Extended Partitions 16
    Boot and System Partitions 18
    Windows NT File Systems 19
    Fault-Tolerance Methods 24
Choosing a Windows NT Network Protocol 27
    TCP/IP 28
    NWLink 31
    NetBEUI 32
    Planning for Network Clients 32
Exercise Section 35
Review Questions 39
    Review Answers 45

2 Installation and Configuration   **49**

Installing Windows NT Server 50
    Hardware Requirements 51
    Intel Requirements 52
    Other Hardware 53
    Multiboot Requirements 53
    Choosing a Server Type 55
    Installation Procedure 56
    The Installation Phases 61
    Uninstalling Windows NT 75
    Client Administrator Installation Aids 76
Windows NT and the Registry 80
    How Windows NT Uses the Registry 82
    How Users Use the Registry 83

How Administrators Use the Registry 83
Using the Registry Editor 84
Navigating the Registry 86
Editing the Registry 97
Searching the Registry 98
Windows NT Control Panel 99
Startup/Shutdown 100
Hardware Profiles 102
Environment 103
Performance 105
General 105
Configuring Protocols and Protocol Bindings 106
Installing and Configuring NWLink 110
Working with TCP/IP 113
Configuring Network Adapters 126
Windows NT Core Services 127
The Services Application 128
Network Services 130
Directory Replication 131
Windows NT Client Licenses 139
Computer Browser Service 142
Configuring Peripherals and Devices 144
Devices 145
Multimedia 147
Ports 147
Configuring Hard Disks 158
Customizing the Display 159
Partitioning 160
Stripe Sets 163
Marking Partition as Active 165
Committing Changes 166
Deleting Partitions 167
Saving and Restoring Configuration Information 167
Tools 168
Fault Tolerance 171
Securing System Partition on RISC Machines 173
Configuring Printing 174
Windows NT Printing Architecture 174
Printers Folder 181
Adding a Printer on Your Own Machine 183
Adding a Network Print Server 185
Configuring Printers 186
Sharing Printers 200
Setting Up a Printer Pool 200
Printing from MS-DOS Applications 202

Configuring Windows NT Server for Client Computers 202
Exercise Section 204
Review Questions 207
    Review Answers 221

3 Managing Resources   225

Managing User and Group Accounts 226
    Users and Groups 226
    Built-In User Accounts 234
    User Manager for Domains 235
    User Environment Profiles 240
    Account Administration Tasks 251
Managing Policies and Profiles 255
    User Profiles 256
Hardware Profiles 260
Managing System Policy with System Policy Editor 262
    Registry Mode 262
    Policy File Mode 268
Managing Windows NT Server from Client Machines 271
Managing Disk Resources 273
Working with Windows NT File Resources 273
The Universal Naming Convention (UNC) 274
    Copying and Moving Files 276
    Long File Names 276
    Compressing and Uncompressing Files, Directories, and Drives ... 281
    COMPACT.EXE 283
    Special Notes About Compressed Directories 284
Sharing Directories 285
    Sharing with Explorer and My Computer 286
    Sharing from the Command Prompt 289
Monitoring and Managing Shares 291
Synchronizing Files 294
Working with NTFS File Permissions and Security 297
    Ownership of NTFS Resources 297
    Auditing NTFS Resources 299
    Securing NTFS Resources 301
Exercise Section 318
Review Questions 323
    Review Answers 338

4 Connectivity   341

Interoperating with NetWare 342
    Gateway Services for NetWare (GSNW) 342
    Client Services for NetWare (CSNW) and the GSNW Client 347

File and Print Services for NetWare (FPNW) 352

Directory Service Manager for NetWare (DSMN) 352

Migration Tool for NetWare 353

Server and Client/Server Applications 354

NetWare Connectivity 355

Configuring Remote Access Service (RAS) 356

RAS Security 357

RAS Line Protocols 358

Routing with RAS 360

The Telephony API 360

Installing and Configuring RAS 361

Changing the RAS Configuration 366

Dial-Up Networking 366

Exercise Section 374

Review Questions 378

Review Answers 384

5   Monitoring and Optimization   387

Performance Optimization 388

Performance Objectives 388

Windows NT Tunes Itself 389

Reasons to Monitor Performance 390

Configuration Changes That Affect Performance 391

Before You Change Anything 401

Performance Monitor 402

Bottleneck—The Limiting Resource 404

Overall Performance Indicators 405

Establishing Baseline Performance Data 409

Exercise Section 410

Review Questions 421

Review Answers 425

6   Troubleshooting   429

General Troubleshooting Techniques 430

Document It 430

Back It Up 431

Test One Thing at a Time 431

Fix the Problem, Don't Remove It 431

Troubleshooting Installation 431

Troubleshooting Boot Failures 432

Booting Up 433

Troubleshooting the Boot Process 443

The Emergency Repair Process 444

Troubleshooting Configuration Errors 448
    Event Viewer 449
Windows NT Diagnostics 455
    System Recovery 457
    Backing Up the Registry 458
    Backing Up Individual Keys 461
Troubleshooting Printer Problems 461
    Spooling Problems 462
    Printing from Non-Windows-Based Applications 463
    Handling the Computer Crashing 464
    Printing Too Slow or Workstation Too Sluggish 464
Troubleshooting RAS 465
Troubleshooting Connectivity Problems 466
    Network Monitor 467
Troubleshooting Access and Permission Problems 471
Recovering from Fault-Tolerance Failures 472
    Backing Up Files and Directories 473
    Restoring Files and Directories 474
    Breaking a Mirror Set 476
    Regenerating a Stripe Set with Parity 476
    Troubleshooting Partitions and Disks 477
Exercise Section 478
Review Questions 480
    Review Answers 487

A **Overview of the Certification Process**   **489**
    How to Become a Microsoft Certified
      Product Specialist (MCPS) 490
    How to Become a Microsoft Certified
      Systems Engineer (MCSE) 491
    How to Become a Microsoft Certified Solution Developer
      (MCSD) 496
    Becoming a Microsoft Certified Trainer (MCT) 497

B **Study Tips**   **499**
    Pre-testing Yourself 500
    Hints and Tips for Doing Your Best on the Tests 501
      Things to Watch For 501
      Marking Answers for Return 502
      Attaching Notes to Test Questions 502

C **What's on the CD-ROM**   **503**
    New Riders' Exclusive TestPrep 503
    New Riders' Exclusive FLASH! Electronic Flash Card Program 503
    Transcender Corporation's Certification Sampler 504

MCP Endeavor Sampler 504

Exclusive Electronic Version of Text 504

Copyright Information and Disclaimer 504

D All About TestPrep   505

Question Presentation 505

Scoring 506

Non-Random Mode 506

Instructor Mode 506

Flash Cards 507

Index   509

Test Yourself

Stop! Before reading this chapter, test yourself to determine how much study time you will need to devote to this section.

1. Which of the following Windows NT machines can participate in a workgroup?

    A.   A Windows NT Server Primary Domain Controller (PDC).

    B.   A Windows NT Server Backup Domain Controller (BDC).

    C.   A Windows NT Server stand-alone server.

    D.   None of the above.

2. The _____ partition holds the files needed to boot your computer.

    A.   Primary

    B.   System

    C.   Boot

    D.   None of the above

3. The NTFS file system is generally more efficient for partitions larger than _____ MB.

    A.   50

    B.   100

    C.   400

    D.   800

4. The principal disadvantage of the NetBEUI protocol is: _____.

    A.   NetBEUI is slow

    B.   NetBEUI is difficult to configure

    C.   NetBEUI is not routable

    D.   NetBEUI is not compatible with Microsoft Client for MS-DOS.

Answers

1. C (see "Workgroups")
2. B (see "Boot and System Partitions")
3. C (see "NTFS")
4. C (see "NetBEUI")

Chapter 1

Planning

This chapter will help you prepare for the "Planning" section of Microsoft's Exam 70-67, "Implementing and Supporting Microsoft Windows NT Server." Microsoft provides the following objectives for the "Planning" section:

Test Objectives

> ▶ Plan the disk drive configuration for various requirements. Requirements include choosing a file system and choosing a fault-tolerance method.
>
> ▶ Choose a protocol for various situations. Protocols include TCP/IP, NWLink IPX/SPX Compatible Transport, NetBEUI.

Microsoft grew up around the personal computer industry and as of this writing has established itself as the preeminent maker of software products for computers. Microsoft has a vast portfolio of software products, but is best known for its operating systems.

Microsoft's current operating system products, listed here, are undoubtedly well known to anyone studying for the MCSE exams:

- ▶ Windows 95
- ▶ Windows NT Workstation
- ▶ Windows NT Server

Some older operating system products—namely, MS-DOS, Windows 3.1, and Windows for Workgroups—are still important to the operability of Windows NT Server, so don't be surprised if you hear them mentioned from time to time in this book.

Windows NT is the most powerful, the most secure, and perhaps the most elegant operating system Microsoft has yet produced. It languished for a while after it first appeared (in part because no one was sure why they needed it or what to do with it), but Microsoft has persisted with improving interoperability and performance. With the release of Windows NT 4 and the arrival of a new Windows 95-like user interface, Windows NT seems destined to assume a prominent place in today's world of network-based computing.

This chapter introduces you to Windows NT Server and Windows NT Workstation—the two flavors, you might say, of Windows NT. This chapter compares NT to Windows 95 and also compares the workgroup and the domain, the two basic network archetypes of Windows NT networking. This chapter also examines some planning issues you need to address before you set up your Windows NT network: specifically, choosing a disk configuration and choosing a network protocol.

Windows NT Among Microsoft Operating Systems

As already mentioned, Microsoft has three operating system products now competing in the marketplace—Windows 95, Windows NT Workstation, and Windows NT Server. Each of these operating system products has advantages and each has some disadvantages. These three operating systems have begun to look very much alike with the arrival of Windows NT 4. Each comes with the familiar Windows 95 user interface, featuring the Start button, the Recycling Bin, My Computer, and the ever-useful Explorer, but each is a specific product designed for specific situations. The following sections describe these Microsoft operating systems and delineate their similarities and differences.

Windows NT Server and Windows NT Workstation are essentially the same under the hood, though they include some different utilities and are optimized for different purposes. The term *Windows NT* is a collective name for these two very similar products.

Windows 95

Windows 95 is Microsoft's everyday, workhorse operating system. It provides a 32-bit platform and is designed to operate with a great variety of peripherals. Here are the minimum hardware requirements for Windows 95:

▶ 386DX/20 processor or better

▶ 4 MB RAM (8 MB is recommended)

▶ 40 MB of free disk space

Like Windows NT, Windows 95 supports preemptive multitasking, but unlike Windows NT, doesn't support multiple processors. Windows 95 supports Plug and Play, not to mention a vast number of hardware devices and device drivers (more than Windows NT).

Windows 95 supports 16-bit and 32-bit Windows and MS-DOS applications, including applications that access the hardware directly.

Windows 95 only runs on Intel platforms.

Windows 95 uses the FAT files system, which is less secure than the NTFS file system that Windows NT supports. Windows NT also supports FAT, but NT does not support the FAT32 file system that is supported by recent versions of Windows 95 (OEM Release 2).

You can network a Windows 95 computer in a workgroup (described later in this chapter in the section "Workgroups"), and you can use a Windows 95 computer as a client in a domain-based Windows NT network. However, Windows 95 alone cannot provide a network with centralized authentication and security.

Windows NT Workstation

The original Windows NT operating system has now evolved into a pair of operating system products—Windows NT Workstation and Windows NT Server. These two products are very similar; some might say they are virtually the same except that they include some different tools and are tuned and configured for different roles. NT Server, discussed in the next section, is designed to operate as a network server and domain controller. NT Workstation, like Windows 95, is designed to serve as a network client and desktop operating system.

When Windows 95 first appeared, it seemed that Microsoft planned for Windows 95 to inherit the market of Windows 3.1 (general-use desktop computing for business and consumer), and for Windows NT to focus on the specialty market of professionals, such as programmers who require extra processing power. Now it seems that Windows NT Workstation (with its stability, portability, and airtight security) is poised to assume a large share of the corporate desktop market.

Windows NT Workstation can serve as a stand-alone operating system, act as a client in a domain-based NT network, or participate in a workgroup.

The most striking difference between Windows NT Workstation and Windows 95 is their security. Windows NT Workstation is an extremely secure operating system, and for almost every facet of Windows NT administration and configuration, there are security implications. Windows NT provides security for files, directories, printers, and nearly everything else; in fact, a user must be authenticated to even use Windows NT at all.

Windows NT Workstation requires somewhat more powerful hardware than does Windows 95. Windows NT Workstation's minimum hardware requirements are as follows:

▶ 486DX/33 or better processor

▶ 12 MB of RAM (16 MB recommended)

▶ 120 MB of free disk space

Windows NT is designed to provide system stability; each application can run in its own memory address space. Windows NT supports preemptive multiprocessing and as well as true multiprocessing (more than one processor).

Windows NT doesn't support as many devices as Windows 95 and seems a bit more myopic when it comes to detecting and installing new hardware.

Although Windows NT doesn't support the vast array of devices Windows 95 supports, it supports more processor platforms. Because Windows NT is written mostly in C, it can be compiled separately for different processors. In addition to the Intel platform, versions of Windows NT are available for RISC, MIPS, DEC Alpha, and PowerPC-based systems.

Microsoft designed Windows NT for backward-compatibility with MS-DOS 5.0, Windows 3.1x, OS/2 1.x, and lateral-compatibility with POSIX-based applications. No other operating system supports such a broad spectrum of applications. For security and stability reasons, however, Windows NT doesn't allow applications to directly access the hardware; MS-DOS applications and other legacy applications that attempt to access the hardware directly will run into trouble with Windows NT.

Windows NT Server

When Windows NT 3.1 and Windows NT Advanced Server 3.1 debuted, the marketplace experienced quite a bit of confusion over what the distinction was between the two products. Windows NT Server had some clear advantages, however; unlike Windows NT 3.1, it supported Macintosh clients, for example, and availed its users of RAID fault tolerance. Still, if you just needed a file or print server, Windows NT 3.1 performed just as well as Windows NT Advanced Server 3.1, a situation which resulted in a potentially unprofitable situation for Microsoft.

With the introduction of Windows NT Workstation 3.5 and Windows NT Server 3.5, the two operating systems were tweaked in such a way as to make them different from each other in terms of performance and capacity and features. With version 4, NT Server and NT Workstation continue to differentiate themselves as they adapt to their respective markets. The next few sections go over the major (along with some minor) differences between Windows NT Workstation and Server.

Features

The following features are available on Windows NT Server but not on Windows NT Workstation:

- ▶ Services for Macintosh

- ▶ RAID fault tolerance

- ▶ Domain logon validation

- ▶ Directory replication

- ▶ Windows NT Directory Services (NTDS)

- ▶ Multiprotocol routing and advanced network services, such as DNS, DHCP, and WINS

Capacity

The following facets of Windows NT differ in capacity on Workstation and Server:

- ▶ **Concurrent Client Sessions.** Windows NT Server supports an unlimited number of inbound sessions; Windows NT Workstation supports no more than 10 active sessions at the same time.

- ▶ **Remote Access Sessions.** Windows NT Server accommodates an unlimited number of Remote Access connections (although Microsoft only supports up to 256); Windows NT Workstation supports only a single Remote Access connection.

- ▶ **Multiprocessors.** Although both Windows NT Workstation and Server can support up to 32 processors in an OEM (Original Equipment Manufacturer) configuration, Windows NT Workstation can only support two processors out-of-the-box, whereas Windows NT Server can support four.

- ▶ **Internet Service.** Both NT Workstation and NT Server come with Internet-type server applications, but the NT Server application (Internet Application Server) is more powerful and better suited to the open Internet than is the

NT Workstation application (Peer Web Services), which is designed primarily for in-house intranets. (Personal Web server software packages are available for Windows 95 systems.)

▶ **BackOffice Support.** Both NT Workstation and NT Server provide support for the Microsoft BackOffice family of software products (SQL Server, Systems Management Server, SNA Server, Exchange Server), but NT Server provides a higher level of support for BackOffice products.

Performance

Microsoft did some performance tuning to both Windows NT Workstation and Server to help them function more appropriately for their intended purposes. Some of the differences are as follows:

▶ Windows NT Workstation preloads a Virtual DOS Machine (VDM), the 32-bit MS-DOS emulator that supports legacy applications. Because older applications are more likely to run on a workstation than a server, the preloading of the VDM speeds up the load time of the first DOS or Win16 application started, at the expense of the RAM used by the VDM, which most likely would need to be loaded anyway. Windows NT Server devotes that RAM to caching and other server operations, because it is not as likely that an MS-DOS- or Win16-based application will be run on a server. This is not to imply that servers cannot run these applications, only that the first such applications executed are slower to load.

▶ Caching is handled differently on workstations and servers, enabling better network throughput on Windows NT Server and better local disk access time on Windows NT Workstation.

▶ Windows NT Server includes a configurable server service that enables you to tune the server as an application server or as a file/print server. Windows NT Workstation does not provide this feature, because it is limited to 10 inbound sessions.

▶ The server files system driver used in both Windows NT Workstation and Server (SRV.SYS) is more subject to paging under Windows NT Workstation than under Windows NT

Server. When Windows NT Workstation runs out of physical RAM, it pages the server code out to disk, which means its network sharing performance takes a hit, but local application performance gets a boost. Windows NT Server does not ever page much of the server code out; it is designed as a server, so it would not make much sense to impair that side of its functionality.

Minimum Hardware Requirements

The minimum requirements for NT Server and NT Workstation are roughly the same, but NT Server needs a little more RAM and a little more disk space, namely:

▶ 486DX/33 processor

▶ 16 MB of RAM

▶ 130 MB of disk space

Workgroups and Domains

Every networked Windows NT-based computer participates in a workgroup or a domain. The difference between a workgroup and a domain boils down to the question of where the user accounts will be stored.

Users must—and it should be stressed that this logon process is completely mandatory—log on to Windows NT to use a Windows NT-based computer.

When a user successfully logs on to Windows NT, it generates an access token, which contains the user's security identifier and group identifiers, as well as the user rights granted through the User Rights policy in User Manager or User Manager for Domains.

The access token identifies the user and all processes spawned by the user. No action can take place on a Windows NT system without somebody's access token attached to it.

Workgroups

A workgroup is a collection of computers in which each computer is like a sovereign state with its own set of security policies and accounts. The security information necessary to verify the user's credentials and generate the access token resides on the local machine. Thus, every Windows NT computer in a workgroup must contain accounts for each person who might ever need to access the workstation (see fig. 1.1). This involves a great deal of administration in workgroups that consist of more than a few members. If a user changes her password on her own workstation, for example, the administrator must connect to every other workstation in the workgroup and change the user's password on those computers as well; otherwise, the user can't access resources beyond her own computer.

Figure 1.1

In a workgroup, each computer is responsible for its own security and each computer maintains its own accounts database.

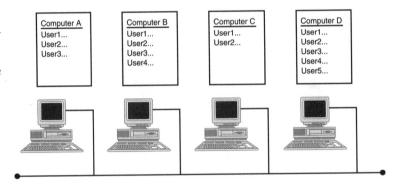

A workgroup is, however, simpler than a domain and easier to install. A workgroup does not require an NT Server machine acting as a domain controller, and the decentralized administration of a workgroup can be an advantage in small networks because it does not depend on the health of a few key server and controller machines.

Unless a Windows NT Server computer is configured as a stand-alone server, it cannot participate in a workgroup (see Chapter 2, "Installation and Configuration" Windows NT Server"). Windows NT Workstation computers, Windows 95 computers, and older networkable Microsoft systems, such as Windows for Workgroups, can participate in workgroups.

When you log on to a Windows NT machine in a workgroup, you are logging on to that specific machine; the local security database verifies your credentials. The local machine performs the following steps when you log on directly to a Windows NT computer:

1. WinLogon asks for your user name and password, which it then sends to the Local Security Authority (LSA).

2. The LSA sends the user name and password to the Security Accounts Manager (SAM), which looks for the user name and password in the directory database and notifies the LSA whether they are approved.

3. The LSA creates an access token with the user's assigned rights, and passes it to the WinLogon process.

4. The WinLogon process completes the logon, and then starts a new process for the user (usually Explorer.exe). The user's access token is attached to the new process.

Domains

In a domain environment, all nodes must authenticate logon requests with a domain controller that contains the central accounts database for the entire domain (see fig. 1.2). A password needs to be changed only one time to be usable on any member computer of the domain. Likewise, a user needs only a single account to access resources anywhere in the domain. Only Windows NT Server machines can serve as domain controllers in a Windows NT network.

Figure 1.2

In a domain, security and account information resides on one or more domain controllers, and logon requests pass across the network to the domain controller for authentication.

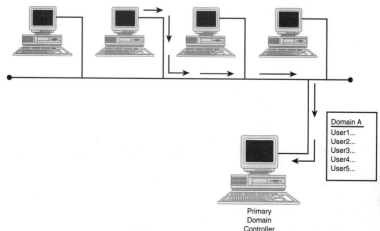

The logon process is somewhat more complicated for a domain because logon information must pass from the local machine (where the user is sitting) to the domain controller, and back again. This network logon process requires the NetLogon service.

The procedure is as follows:

1. WinLogon sends the user name and password to the Local Security Authority (LSA).

2. The LSA passes the request to the local NetLogon service.

3. The local NetLogon service sends the logon information to the NetLogon service on the domain controller.

4. The NetLogon service on the domain controller passes the information to the domain controller's Security Accounts Manager (SAM).

5. The SAM asks the domain directory database for approval of the user name and password.

6. The SAM passes the result of the approval request to the domain controller's NetLogon service.

7. The domain controller's NetLogon service passes the result of the approval request to the client's NetLogon service.

8. The client's NetLogon service passes the result of the approval request to the LSA.

9. If the logon is approved, the LSA creates an access token and passes it to the WinLogon process.

10. WinLogon completes the logon, thus creating a new process for the user and attaching the access token to the new process.

Choosing a Disk Configuration

One of the first tasks in planning a network is deciding on a disk configuration for each of the computers that will make up the network. Each computer will have its own disk configuration, but this book (and the Windows NT Server exam) targets the disk configuration options available in Windows NT Server systems.

The following sections highlight some specific planning issues related to disk configuration under Windows NT, as follows:

- ▶ Partitions

- ▶ Extended and primary partitions

- ▶ The boot and the system partitions

- ▶ Windows NT file systems

- ▶ Windows NT fault-tolerance methods

The topic of hard disks in Windows NT arises again in Chapter 2, which looks at disk configuration issues, and in Chapter 3, "Managing Resources," which looks at managing disk resources. The following sections concentrate on planning issues and provide the background you need to understand the later material.

Microsoft lists the following objective for the Windows NT Server exam:

Plan the disk drive configuration for various requirements. Requirements include choosing a file system and choosing a fault-tolerance method.

Partitions

A *partition* is a logical organization of a physical disk. Such an operating system as Windows NT can subdivide a disk drive into several partitions. Each partition is formatted separately. Windows NT assigns a different drive letter to each of the partitions, and users interact separately with each partition as if each partition were a separate disk drive.

Partitioning is the act of defining a partition and associating that partition with an area (or areas) of free space from a hard disk.

You must partition an area of free space before you can format it with a file system. After you have formatted the partition with a supported file system, you can use the partition for storing files and directories.

As you plan your Windows NT configuration, you must make some decisions about the arrangement of partitions on your disk drive. You must choose whether each partition will be a *primary partition* or an *extended partition*. You also need to designate a *system partition* and a *boot partition* for your Windows NT installation. The following sections discuss some of these concepts.

Primary and Extended Partitions

Windows NT provides the following two types of partitions:

▶ **Primary partitions.** A primary partition cannot be subdivided and is capable of supporting a bootable operating system. One hard disk can contain up to four primary partitions. Thus, you can assign up to four drive letters to a disk if you use only primary partitions.

▶ **Extended partitions.** An extended partition can be subdivided into smaller logical drives (see fig. 1.3). This feature enables you to assign more than four drive letters to the disk. An extended partition does not support a bootable operating system. The system partition therefore cannot reside on an extended partition (see next section). One hard disk can contain only one extended partition.

If you choose to use an extended partition of a hard disk, you are limited to three (rather than four) primary partitions for that disk.

MS-DOS 5.0 and earlier MS-DOS systems cannot recognize more than one primary partition per disk.

Figure 1.3

A physical disk can consist of up to four primary partitions or up to three primary partitions and one extended partition. An extended partition can be subdivided into logical drives.

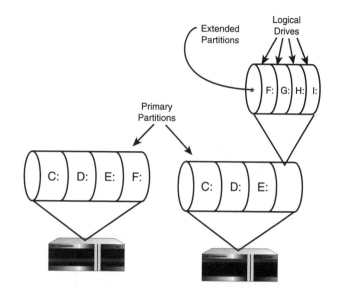

 You do not ever absolutely need to create an extended partition. If you do create one, however, remember that there can never be more than one on each physical disk under any circumstances.

On an Intel-based computer, one primary partition must be marked *active*. The active partition is then used to boot the computer (see the next section). Because any primary partition of sufficient size can support a bootable operating system, one advantage of using multiple primary partitions is that you can isolate different operating systems on different partitions.

 For file-management reasons, it may be advantageous to place the alternative operating system on a separate primary partition. You can, however, also achieve a dual-boot capability with both operating systems on the same partition.

If you install Windows NT on a computer with another operating system in place, the active partition does not change. If you install Windows NT on a new computer, the partition created by Setup becomes the active partition.

Boot and System Partitions

The *system* partition is the partition that contains the files necessary to boot the operating system. (See Chapter 2 for a description of which files these are.) The system partition does not have to be the partition on which Windows NT is installed.

The partition that holds the Windows NT operating system files is called the *boot partition.* If your system boots from drive C, and you install Windows NT on drive D, then drive C is your system partition and drive D is your boot partition (see fig. 1.4). If you boot from drive C, and Windows NT is installed on drive C, then drive C is both the system partition and the boot partition.

Figure 1.4

The partition that boots the computer is the system partition; the partition that holds the Windows NT directory is the boot partition. Note that these names are counter-intuitive.

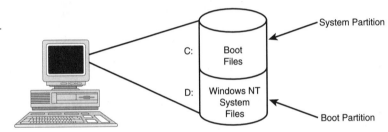

Recall from the preceding section that the active partition is the partition used to boot the system. The system partition must therefore be the active partition.

Yes, it sounds backward, but it is true: Windows NT boots from the system partition and then loads the system from the boot partition.

By the way, active partitions are only a relevant concept for Intel-based computers; RISC-based computers use a hardware configuration utility to designate the system partition.

Windows NT File Systems

After a partition has been created, it must be formatted with a supported *file system*. A file system is a system for organizing and managing the data on a disk. Windows NT supports three file systems: FAT (File Allocation Table), NTFS (NT File System), and CDFS (Compact Disk File System). CDFS is a read-only file system for CD-ROMs, so you can immediately rule it out for hard disk partitions. Each partition must use either the FAT file system or the NTFS file system. You need to understand the advantages and limitations of each file system before you can decide which is best for your system. The following sections introduce you to the FAT and NTFS file systems. Chapter 2 explains more about these file system.

FAT

The venerable File Allocation Table (FAT) file system was originally invented for MS-DOS. FAT is now supported by Windows NT, Windows 95, and OS/2, making it the most universally accepted and supported file system (see fig. 1.5). For this reason alone, you should seriously consider using FAT for your partitions.

Figure 1.5

The FAT file system is accessible from more operating systems than NTFS, but FAT doesn't provide the NTFS advantages.

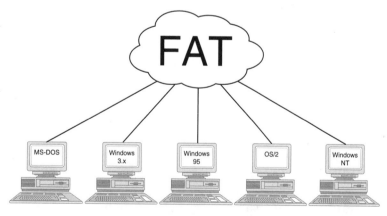

Earlier versions of FAT forced users to use short file names (eight characters plus a three-character extension), but Windows NT overcomes the 8.3 limitation on FAT partitions. Users

continues

can create files with up to 255 characters, as well as spaces and even multiple extensions in the file name. (Short file names are still maintained for compatibility with legacy applications and dual-boot systems.)

FAT has a lower overhead than its high-tech counterpart NTFS (less than 1 MB, compared to an average of 5–10 MB for NTFS), and FAT is typically the more efficient file system for small partitions (under 200 MB).

Some of the disadvantages of FAT are as follows:

▶ FAT is generally slower than NTFS. It takes longer to find and access files. For partitions greater than 200 MB, FAT performance degrades quickly.

▶ The maximum file, directory, or partition size under FAT is only 4 GB. Also, because Windows NT does not support any FAT compression software, including Microsoft's own DriveSpace and DoubleSpace, you cannot conserve space by compressing files on a FAT partition.

▶ FAT does not offer the security features offered by NTFS (see the following section).

▶ If the power fails during a disk transaction, the FAT file system may be left with cross-linked files or orphan clusters.

You should use the FAT file system if you will be dual-booting your computer with another operating system and you wish to access the partition from the other operating system.

MS-DOS and Windows 95 provide no native support for NTFS; however, software aids that read NTFS partitions, such as the NTFSDOS file system driver, have begun to emerge. These aids are not full implementations of NTFS. They do not, for example, support NTFS security.

If your Windows NT computer is a RISC-based system, your C drive should be FAT-formatted with at least 2 MB free space.

NTFS

For an exercise testing this information, see end of chapter.

The New Technology File System (NTFS) is designed to fully exploit the features and capabilities of Windows NT. For partitions larger than the range of 200–400 MB, the NTFS file system far outshines the FAT file system. The biggest drawback with using NTFS is that only the Windows NT operating system can access NTFS partitions (see fig. 1.6). If you plan to sometimes boot your computer under a different operating system, such as MS-DOS or Windows 95, you should be aware that the other operating system cannot access an NTFS partition.

Figure 1.6

The NTFS file system is accessible only from Windows NT—it provides a number of advantages for Windows NT users.

When partitions exceed 400 MB (on average), NTFS is your most reasonable choice. Remember that 400 MB is only an average; actual performance owes more to the number of files than to the size of the files.

NTFS is generally faster than FAT, and NTFS supports bigger partitions. (NTFS files and partitions can be up to 16 exabytes—an exabyte is one billion gigabytes, or 2^{64} bytes.) NTFS is also safer. NTFS supports sector sparing, also known as hot fixing, on SCSI hard drives. If a sector fails on an NTFS partition of a SCSI hard drive, NTFS tries to write the data to a good sector (if the data is still in memory) and map out the bad sector so that it is not reused. NTFS keeps a transaction log while it works. If the power fails, leaving NTFS in a possibly corrupt state, the CHKDSK command that executes when the system boots attempts to redo the transaction (in the case of a delete, for example), or undo the transaction (in the case of a file write where the data is no longer in memory). Two other principal advantages of NTFS are as follows:

▶ **File-level security.** NTFS enables you to assign specific permissions to individual files and directories.

▶ **File compression.** Windows NT provides the capability to compress NTFS files. Traditional FAT compression utilities, including Microsoft's own DriveSpace and DoubleSpace, won't work under Windows NT.

You should use NTFS if you wish to preserve existing permissions when you migrate files and directories from a NetWare server to a Windows NT Server system. Also, if you wish to allow Macintosh computers to access files on the partition through Windows NT's Services for Macintosh, you must format the partition for NTFS.

Like FAT, NTFS can handle long file names, up to 255 unicode characters. (Unicode is a method of including all foreign language characters in a single character set.) NTFS also maintains a short 8.3-compliant file name for compatibility with legacy applications.

Because NTFS has a higher overhead, somewhere between 4.5 and 10 MB for the file system itself, you cannot use the NTFS file system for floppy disks.

Choosing a File System

Here's a quick summary of the differences between file systems:

Feature	FAT	NTFS
File name length	255	255
8.3 file name compatibility	Yes	Yes
File size	4 GB	16 EB
Partition size	4 GB	16 EB
Directory structure	Linked list	B-tree
Local security	No	Yes
Transaction tracking	No	Yes
Hot fixing	No	Yes
Overhead	1 MB	>2 MB (avg. 4.5–10)
Required for RISC-based computers	Yes	No
Accessible from MS-DOS/ Windows 95	Yes	No
Accessible from OS/2	Yes	No
Case-sensitive	No	POSIX only
Case preserving	Yes	Yes
Compression	No	Yes
Efficiency	<200 MB	>400 MB
Windows NT formattable	Yes	Yes
Convertible	To NTFS only	No
Fragmentation level	High	Low
Floppy disk formattable	Yes	No
Extensible attributes	No	Yes
Creation/modification/ access dates	Yes	Yes

Windows NT provides a utility called `Convert.exe` that converts a FAT partition to NTFS. There is no utility for directly converting an NTFS partition to FAT. To Change an NTFS partition to FAT, back up all files on the partition, reformat the partition, and then restore the files to the reformatted partition (see Chapter 3).

Fault-Tolerance Methods

Fundamentally, *fault tolerance* is the system's capability to compensate in the event of hardware disaster. The standard for fault tolerance is known as Redundant Array of Inexpensive Disks (RAID). RAID consists of several levels (or categories) of protection that offer a mixture of performance, reliability, and cost. One of the steps in planning your Windows NT system may be to decide on a RAID fault-tolerance method. Windows NT Server offers the following two RAID fault-tolerance methods:

▶ **Disk mirroring (RAID Level 1).** Windows NT writes the same data to two physical disks. If one disk fails, the data is still available on the other disk.

▶ **Disk striping with parity (Raid Level 5).** Windows NT writes data across a series of disks (3 to 32). The data is not duplicated on the disks (as it is with disk mirroring), but Windows NT records parity information that it can use to regenerate missing data if a disk should fail.

The following sections introduce you to disk mirroring and disk striping with parity. Chapter 3 explains more about these important fault-tolerance methods.

It is important to note that the fault-tolerance methods available through Windows NT are software-based RAID implementations. Several hardware vendors offer hardware-based RAID solutions. Hardware-based RAID solutions, which, by the way, can be quite expensive, are beyond the scope of this book and beyond the scope of the Windows NT Server exam.

Disk Mirroring (RAID Level 1)

Disk mirroring calls for all data to be written to two physical disks (see fig. 1.7). A mirror is a redundant copy of a disk partition. You can use any partition, including the boot or system partitions, to establish a mirror.

Figure 1.7

How disk mirror-ing works.

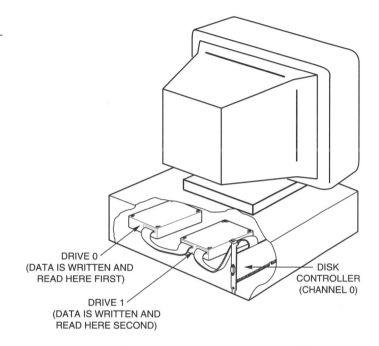

DRIVE 0
(DATA IS WRITTEN AND
READ HERE FIRST)

DRIVE 1
(DATA IS WRITTEN AND
READ HERE SECOND)

DISK
CONTROLLER
(CHANNEL 0)

You can measure the utilization of a fault-tolerance method by the percent of the total disk space devoted to storing the original information. Fifty percent of the data in a disk-mirroring system is redundant data. The percentage utilization is thus also 50 percent, making disk-mirroring less efficient than disk striping with parity. The startup costs for implementing disk mirroring are typically lower, however, because disk mirroring requires only two (rather than 3–32) physical disks.

Disk mirroring slows down write operations slightly (because Windows NT has to write to two disks simultaneously). Read operations are actually slightly faster, because NT can read from both disks simultaneously.

In a typical disk mirroring scenario, a single disk controller writes to both members of the mirror set. If a mirrored disk fails, the user can keep working. If the disk controller fails, however, Windows NT cannot access either disk. *Disk duplexing* is a special kind of disk mirroring that provides a solution for this potential pitfall. In a disk duplexing system, each of the mirrored disks has its own disk controller. The system can therefore endure either a disk failure or a controller failure. Disk duplexing also has some performance advantages, because the two disk controllers can act independently (see fig. 1.8).

Figure 1.8

Disk duplexing.

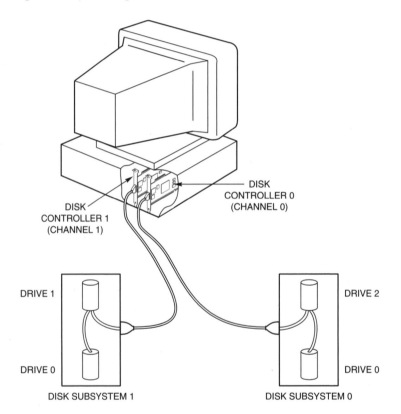

Disk Striping with Parity (RAID Level 5)

A stripe set with parity writes information in *stripes* (or rows) across 3 to 32 disks. For each stripe, there is a parity stripe block on one of the disks. If one of the disks fails, Windows NT can use the parity stripe block to regenerate the missing information. The parity stripe block is the only data that is additional to what the system would need to record the original data without fault tolerance. Disk striping with parity is therefore more efficient than disk mirroring. The percentage of disk space available for storing data is:

$$\% \text{ Utilization} = (\text{no. of disks} - 1) \,/\, \text{no. of disks} \times 100\%$$

If you have five disks, 80 percent of your disk space is available for storing data. This compares with 50 percent for a disk mirroring system. The more disks you add, the more efficient your fault-tolerance becomes. But at the same time, your setup costs also increase as you add more disks.

Windows NT must perform the parity calculations as it writes data to a stripe set with parity. Write operations therefore take three times as much memory if you are using a stripe set with parity. If all disks are working properly, read operations are faster under a stripe set with parity than they are under a mirror set. If a disk fails, however, Windows NT must backfigure the missing data from the parity information, and read operations will slow down considerably.

Any partition except the boot partition and the system partition can be part of a stripe set with parity, provided you have enough other partitions on 3–32 other physical disks.

Choosing a Windows NT Network Protocol

A network protocol is a collection of rules and procedures governing communication among the computers on the a network. In a sense, a protocol is a language your computer uses when speaking to other computers. If two computers don't use the same protocols, they cannot communicate. Windows NT includes several protocols designed for different situations and different networking environments. Later chapters discuss these protocols in more detail. This chapter examines some planning issues relating the three principal Windows NT networking protocols, as follows:

▶ **TCP/IP.** A widely-used, routable protocol that is the basis for communication on the Internet.

▶ **NWLink IPX/SPX Compatible Transport.** Microsoft's rendition of Novell's proprietary IPX/SPX protocol suite. NWLink is a routable protocol designed to enable Windows NT computers to interoperate with Novell NetWare networks.

▶ **NetBEUI.** A very fast but non-routable protocol used on Microsoft networks. Because NetBEUI is non-routable, it is only suitable for Local Area Networks (LANs).

You should learn the advantages and disadvantages of each of these protocols and understand when to use each.

Microsoft lists the following objective for the Windows NT Server exam:
Choose a protocol for various situations. Protocols include TCP/IP, NWLink IPX/SPX Compatible Transport, and NetBEUI.

Protocols and RAS

Windows NT Remote Access Service (RAS) can perform some interesting routing functions. These functions are likely to make their way into the Windows NT Server exam. Chapter 4, "Connectivity," examines RAS in more detail, but for the purposes of preparing for the "Planning" section, keep in mind that RAS can act as a NetBIOS gateway. A RAS client using the Net-BEUI protocol can connect to a RAS server and, using the NetBIOS gateway on the RAS server, can gain access to the remote LAN beyond the gateway regardless of which protocol the LAN is using.

RAS can also act as a TCP/IP or IPX router.

TCP/IP

For an exercise testing this information, see end of chapter.

Transmission Control Protocol/Internet Protocol (TCP/IP) is the default protocol for the Intel version of Windows NT. TCP/IP is the only protocol supported on the Internet (which is why it is rocketing toward becoming a global standard protocol).

Windows NT's version of the TCP/IP protocol, Microsoft TCP/IP, is a 32-bit native suite of protocols. It requires more configuration than other protocols, but Microsoft also provides some excellent configuration tools. The end result is a cross-platform, industry-standard, routable network implementation that you can expect only to grow in popularity.

The important things to remember about TCP/IP are as follows:

- ▶ **TCP/IP is routable.** Because TCP/IP packets can be forwarded through routers, you can use TCP/IP on Wide Area Networks (WANs). (The NetBEUI protocol, by contrast, can only be used on Local Area Networks.)

- ▶ **TCP/IP is the language of the Internet.** If your Windows NT computer will be connected to the Internet, you need to use TCP/IP.

- ▶ **TCP/IP is a widely accepted standard.** You can interconnect with more networks worldwide if you are using TCP/IP.

- ▶ **TCP/IP accommodates a wide range of network hardware, operating systems, and applications.**

TCP/IP comes with a number of useful utilities that facilitate network configuration and administration. Chapter 2 explains more about those TCP/IP utilities.

You implement TCP/IP on your network with the help of three important services: Dynamic Host Configuration Protocol (DHCP), Domain Name System (DNS), and Windows Internet Name Service (WINS). To plan your TCP/IP network, you need a basic understanding of these services, especially if you plan to connect your local LAN with a Wide Area Network or with the Internet.

The Internet Protocol (the IP in TCP/IP) sends packets using a computer's IP Address—a unique 32-bit binary number that no other computer on the network can possess. (More precisely, it is not every computer but rather every network adapter card that requires its own IP Address.)

The 32-bit IP address usually is expressed as four octets, or 8-bit numbers, which then are represented in decimal form. An 8-bit number can have a value of anywhere from 0 to 255, so an IP address consists of four numbers between 0 and 255 separated by decimal points (for example, 111.12.3.141).

Every computer on a TCP/IP network must have an IP address. You can configure a permanent IP address for each computer or you can configure each computer to receive a dynamically assigned IP address from a Dynamic Host Protocol (DHCP) server. (See Chapter 2 for more information on configuring TCP/IP.) A DHCP server is assigned a range of IP addresses. The DHCP server then "leases" (assigns for a limited duration) these IP addresses to DHCP clients in the subnet. A computer running Windows NT Server can act as a DHCP server, a DHCP client, or a DHCP relay agent. A DHCP relay agent forwards DHCP broadcast messages across an IP router to a DHCP server on a different subnet.

The decimal octet form of an IP address is easier to remember than its binary equivalent, but even such a number as 111.12.3.141 is not really very easy to remember. The Domain Name System (DNS) is a feature of TCP/IP networks that enables you to map an IP address to an alphanumeric name that is theoretically even easier for humans to remember than the decimal octet. (Internet domain names, such as *newriders.mcp.com*, are now easily recognizable in this age of e-mail.) Windows NT Server's Microsoft DNS Server service can map IP addresses to domain names on a TCP/IP network.

Windows NT's WINS service is similar to DNS except that, rather than mapping IP addresses to domain names, WINS maps IP addresses' NetBIOS names. NetBIOS names are used to identify resources on Microsoft networks. NetBIOS names follow the familiar Universal Naming Convention (UNC) format you use to locate resources from the Windows NT command prompt:

```
\\computername\sharename\path
```

The WINS service is also dynamic. Whereas DNS requires a static listing of all domain name-to-IP-address mappings, the WINS service can automatically associate NetBIOS names with IP addresses.

NWLink

The primary purpose of Microsoft's NWLink/SPX Compatible Transport protocol is to provide connectivity with the many thousands of Novell NetWare networks. NWLink is, however, a fully functional and fully routable protocol. You can use NWLink to network Windows NT machines with or without the involvement of NetWare resources. Because TCP/IP is Internet-ready (and more universally accepted) and NetBEUI is faster and simpler for Microsoft LANs, however, the chances are that if you are using NWLink you will be connecting to NetWare. Chapter 2 describes how to configure NWLink on your Windows NT Server system, and Chapter 4 discusses some issues related to NetWare connectivity.

NWLink provides compatibility with IPX/SPX-based networks, but NWLink alone does not necessarily enable a Windows NT computer to interact with NetWare networks. Windows NT includes several services that provide connectivity with NetWare services after NWLink is in place. Refer to Chapter 4 for more on connecting to NetWare resources using NWLink. Some important points to remember are as follows:

▶ The NWLink protocol provides compatibility with Novell NetWare IPX/SPX networks.

▶ A Windows NT Workstation computer running Client Services for NetWare (CSNW) and the NWLink protocol or a Windows NT Server computer running Gateway Services for NetWare (GSNW) and the NWLink protocol can connect file and print services on a NetWare server.

▶ A Windows NT computer using the NWLink protocol can connect to client/server applications on a NetWare server (without requiring additional NetWare-connectivity services).

▶ Any Microsoft network client that uses Server Message Block (Windows NT, Windows 95, or Windows for Workgroups) can access NetWare resources through a NetWare gateway on a Windows NT Server computer running Gateway Services for NetWare. The NetWare resources will appear to the Microsoft network client as Windows NT resources.

NetBEUI

NetBEUI is the fastest protocol that comes with Windows NT, but it cannot be routed. This means that the NetBEUI protocol is generally only useful for what Microsoft calls "department-sized LANs." The recent emphasis on internetworking means that, in all but the smallest and most isolated networks, NetBEUI is usually not the ideal choice for a primary network protocol. That is why NetBEUI has not been a default protocol for Windows NT since version 3.1 (although Windows NT Server 3.5 and RISC version 3.51 included it for backward-compatibility purposes).

> You cannot use NetBEUI with a router, but you can use a bridge to connect LAN segments operating with the NetBEUI protocol.

NetBEUI was designed for Microsoft networks, and one of the advantages of NetBEUI is that it enables Windows NT machines to interact with older Microsoft network machines that use NetBEUI (for instance, Windows for Workgroups 3.1 or Microsoft LAN Manager).

NetBEUI is also extremely easy to implement. It is self-tuning and self-configuring. (If you try to configure NetBEUI through the Protocols tab of Windows NT's Network application, you receive a message that says, `Cannot configure the software component`.) Because NetBEUI was designed for an earlier generation of lower-performance computers, it also comes with a smaller memory overhead.

The speed and simplicity of NetBEUI comes with a downside, however: NetBEUI relies heavily on network broadcasts, which can degrade performance on large and busy subnets.

Planning for Network Clients

The Windows NT CD-ROM includes client software for a number of operating systems that are not as naturally networkable as

Windows NT or Windows 95. Some of those client software packages are as follows:

▶ Microsoft Network 3.0 for MS-DOS

▶ LAN Manager 2.2c for MS-DOS client

▶ LAN Manager 2.2c for OS/2 client

Microsoft Network Client 3.0 for MS-DOS enables MS-DOS machines to participate in Windows NT networks. An MS-DOS client using Microsoft Client 3.0 for MS-DOS configured with the full director can perform the following tasks on a Windows NT network:

▶ Log on to a domain

▶ Run logon scripts

▶ Access IPC mechanisms, such as RPCs, named pipes, and WinSock

▶ Use RAS (version 1.1)

A Microsoft Client 3.0 for MS-DOS client cannot browse the network unless a Windows NT computer or a Windows for Workgroups computer is in the same workgroup.

The Windows NT CD-ROM also includes a pair of network client packages that help connect LAN Manager 2.2c systems with Windows NT. Those client packages are LAN Manager 2.2c for MS-DOS client and LAN Manager 2.2c OS/2 client. The LAN Manager 2.2c for MS-DOS client includes some features not found in the OS/2 version, including support for the Remoteboot service (described later in this chapter) and the capability to connect to a NetWare server.

Table 1.1 describes which network protocols and which TCP/IP services each of the client systems supports.

Table 1.1

Network Protocol and TCP/IP Service Support for Various Windows NT Client Systems

Network Protocol	TCP/IP DNS Service	IPX-Compatible	IPX/SPX Compatible	NetBEUI	TCP/IP	DLC	DHCP	WINS
Network Client for MS-DOS	X	X		X	X	X		
LAN MAN 2.2c for MS-DOS	X			X	X	X		
LAN MAN 2.2c for OS/2	X			X				
Windows 95	X		X	X		X	X	X
Windows NT Workstation	X		X	X	X	X	X	X

Exercise Section

Each chapter of this book contains some exercises that give you first-hand knowledge of the chapter's topics. This chapter does not offer the same opportunities for first-hand exploration that later chapters provide, but the following exercises provide a glimpse of two very important concepts: NTFS file permissions and IP addresses. If you are an experienced NT administrator, you have probably undertaken these exercises many times, and you may want to move on to Chapter 2. If you are just starting to explore Windows NT and its features, try the following exercises.

Exercise 1.1:   Exploring NTFS

Exercise 1.1 will help you explore NTFS file permissions—one of the principal features that distinguishes FAT from NTFS.

Estimated Time: 10 minutes

1. Log on as an administrator to a Windows NT Server system.

2. Right-click on the Start button (start Explorer).

3. Scroll to an NTFS partition on your system.

4. Find a file on the NTFS partition and right-click on the file icon. Choose Properties. The File Properties dialog box appears.

5. Click on the Security tab (see fig. 1.9). You will see separate buttons for file Permissions, Auditing, and Ownership. (You will learn more about how to manage and configure file security in later chapters.)

6. Click on the Permissions button. The File Permissions dialog box appears (see fig. 1.10). From within the File Permissions dialog box, you can specify which type of access to the file each user or group will receive. Clicking on the Add button enables you to add new users and groups to the access list.

Figure 1.9

The Security tab of the File Properties dialog box.

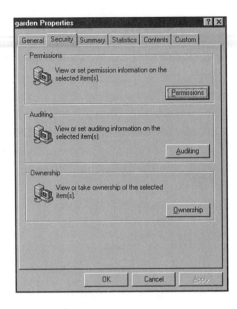

Figure 1.10

The File Permissions dialog box.

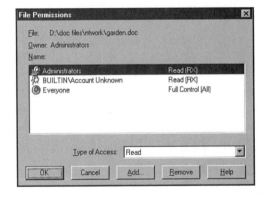

7. Close the File Permissions dialog box and the File Properties dialog box. You return to Explorer. Make sure the file you selected in step 4 is still selected.

8. Pull down the Explorer Edit menu and choose Copy.

9. Scroll the left window of Explorer to a directory on a FAT partition. Select the directory.

10. Pull down the Edit menu and select Paste. A copy of the file you selected in step 4 appears in the FAT directory.

11. Right-click on the new file icon and choose Properties.

12. Examine the File Properties dialog box for the new file. Notice that the Security tab is missing. Because the FAT file system does not enable you to set user and group access to files, you cannot craft a specific security environment for the file as you can through the Security tab and the File Permissions dialog box of the NTFS file. File-level security is one of the biggest advantages of NTFS files.

Exercise 1.2: PING and IPCONFIG

In Exercise 1.2, you will learn how to use the important TCP/IP utilities IPCONFIG and PING to verify your TCP/IP configuration.

Estimated Time: 10 minutes

1. Make sure TCP/IP is installed on your network.

2. Choose Start, Programs, Command Prompt.

3. From the command prompt, type **IPCONFIG**. The IPCONFIG command tells you the IP address, subnet mask, and default gateway for all network adapters to which TCP/IP is bound. (Chapter 2 explains more about TCP/IP configuration and adapter bindings.)

4. If TCP/IP is working properly on your system, the IPCONFIG utility outputs the IP address, subnet mask, and default gateway for your network adapter(s). If your computer obtains an IP address from a DHCP that is not working at this time—for instance, if you have a dial-up adapter that you use to access the Internet with an Internet service provider and you are not presently connected—the IP address and subnet mask appears as 0.0.0.0. If you have a duplicated IP address, the address appears, but the subnet mask appears as 0.0.0.0. Write down your IP address.

continues

5. Type **PING 127.0.0.1**. The Ping utility (Packet INternet Groper) tests your TCP/IP connection. You can specify the IP address of another computer with the command, and Ping makes sure your connection with the other computer is working. The format for the Ping command is:

   ```
   ping <IP address>
   ```

   The address you just typed (127.0.0.1) is a special address called the *loopback address*. The loopback address verifies that TCP/IP is working correctly on your system.

6. Ping the IP address of your own computer. This confirms that your IP address is configured correctly and informs you as to whether any duplicate IP addresses are on your network.

7. Ping the address of another computer on your subnet. If a system has a default gateway (see step 4), it is a common practice to ping the default gateway to ensure that your connection to the gateway is working.

8. If you know the IP address of a computer beyond the gateway, ping the IP address of the remote to ensure that you can connect to remote resources.

Review Questions

The following questions will test your knowledge of the information in this chapter. For additional questions, please see MCP Endeavor and the Microsoft Roadmap/Assessment exam on the CD-ROM that accompanies this book.

1. What are the minimum hardware requirements to run Windows 95?

    A. Intel 286 CPU, 4 MB RAM, 40 MB of disk space

    B. Intel 386 CPU, 4 MB RAM, 40 MB of disk space

    C. Intel 386 CPU or RISC-based processor, 8 MB RAM, 40 MB of disk space

    D. Intel 386 CPU, 8 MB RAM, 45 MB of disk space

2. You need to select an operating system that enables you to run your MS-DOS–based legacy applications. You have been told by your MIS department that these applications are written for speed, and hence sometimes directly access the hardware device. Which of the following operating system(s) should you choose to run these applications? Choose all that apply.

    A. Windows NT Workstation

    B. Windows NT Server

    C. Windows 95

    D. Windows for Workgroups

3. You need an operating system that supports multiple CPUs for a multithreaded database application that your company is developing. Which of the following operating systems support multiple processors? Choose all that apply.

    A. Windows 95

    B. Windows NT Workstation

    C. Windows NT Server

    D. Windows for Workgroups

4. Charles comes to you and says he needs to run a Windows 95 application on his DEC Alpha computer. He wants to know under what circumstances this is possible. Select the best response from the following answers.

    A. It is possible. Windows 95 runs on any RISC-based computer.

    B. It is not possible with his current configuration. He needs to purchase the Windows 95 emulator from Microsoft. After installation, he will be able to run Windows 95 programs on his Alpha.

    C. It is not possible to run Windows 95 on anything but an Intel platform.

    D. Although he can run Windows 95 on a DEC Alpha computer, it violates the license agreement.

5. Your boss comes to you and asks you why, when the company moved to Windows NT, you decided to put Windows NT Workstation rather than Windows NT Server on his computer. What would your explanation be?

    A. Windows NT Workstation is for the average user, whereas NT Server is for power users, such as CAD/CAM users and engineers.

    B. Windows NT Workstation is required on his machine because he is using an Intel-based computer, and NT Server requires a RISC-based CPU for more power.

    C. Windows NT Workstation is specifically tuned for workstation usage, whereas NT Server is tuned more toward being a file and print server.

    D. Tell him that you made a mistake and will load NT Server on his computer as soon as possible.

6. What are the system requirements for running Windows NT Workstation?

    A. Intel CPU, 8 MB of RAM, 120 MB free disk space

    B. Intel CPU, 12 MB of RAM, 85 MB free disk space

    C. Intel CPU or RISC-based computer, 12 MB of RAM, 120 MB free disk space

    D. RISC-based computer, 12 MB of RAM, 120 MB free disk space

7. You need the capability to have Macintosh users connect to and store files on a computer. Which of the following operating systems can serve this purpose? Choose all that apply.

    A. Windows NT Workstation

    B. Windows 95 with the computer to MAC and Back third-party add-on

    C. Windows for Workgroups

    D. Windows NT Server

    E. No version of any Microsoft operating system supports this because of software license issues

8. You get a call from a user stating that he is trying to share a directory with all the users in his office. But not all users can connect to his NT Workstation. His office consists of 15 users all running a mix of NT Workstation and Windows for Workgroups. What could be the potential problem?

    A. The users running Windows for Workgroups need to upgrade to NT Workstation before they can attach his computer.

    B. If he intends on sharing resources, he really should upgrade to NT Server.

    C. He has used up all his licensed sessions. NT Workstation only allows 10 simultaneous sessions.

    D. Tell him to restart his computer and the problem should go away.

9. You are evaluating operating systems for a mission-critical application that your MIS department is in the process of developing. You must choose an operating system that gives you basic data protection features, such as disk mirroring, RAID support, and the capability to secure the data against unauthorized individuals. Which of the following operating systems must you choose? Choose all correct answers.

    A. Windows NT Server

    B. Windows NT Workstation

    C. Windows 95

    D. MS-DOS

10. At a weekly management meeting, the director of the sales department relays concerns from her salespeople that whenever they try to dial in to the network they usually get busy signals. Currently, 10 salespeople are out in the field, but this number is expected to double in the next six months. Currently, all the sales people are accessing the network via RAS (Remote Access Service) running on a dedicated Windows NT Workstation computer. What can you suggest to enable more simultaneous connections?

    A. Nothing more can be done.

    B. Upgrade the dial-in computer to Windows NT Server, which can support up to 256 RAS users. NT Workstation only supports one RAS user at a time.

    C. You must set up a bank of 10 computers all running NT Workstation so that you can provide an adequate number of connections. When the new salespeople are hired, you must purchase an additional 5 to 10 computers.

11. What are the minimum hardware requirements to run Windows NT Server 4?

    A. 386 DX/33 or higher CPU, 16 MB of RAM, 130 MB of disk space

    B. 386 DX2/66 or higher CPU, 12 MB of RAM, 130 MB of disk space

    C. Pentium or higher CPU, 16 MB of RAM, 130 MB of disk space

    D. 486 DX/33 or higher CPU, 16 MB of RAM, 130 MB of disk space

12. Users of the HR workgroup come to you and complain that every time someone joins or leaves their department, they have to delete and re-create user IDs on each one of their 10 workstations. They are running Windows NT Workstation on all their computers. One user asks why this has to be done. Which of the following best describes why this is so?

    A. In a workgroup model, account information is stored on each machine participating in the workgroup. To access a resource on another machine in the workgroup, a user must have an account on the workgroup. To use a single user ID and password for all computers, you must install NT Server in a domain model.

    B. This is known problem in NT Workstation and is easily remedied by downloading a bug fix from Microsoft.

    C. The user needs to designate one of the NT Workstations as the master controller for the workgroup and then transfer all the user account information to that machine. After this is done, users are authenticated by that dedicated workstation and only need one user ID and password.

13. To organize your users and groups in a domain, which type of operating system must you install? Choose all that apply.

    A. NT Workstation—running in dedicated mode

    B. Windows 95

    C. Windows for Workgroups

    D. Windows NT Server

14. You are planning to install Windows NT in a dual-boot configuration on a computer currently running Windows 95. The network users are accustomed to using long file names. The other computers on the network are a mixture of Windows NT and Windows 95 computers, and you have opted for the dual-boot configuration so that users can access file resources from either operating system. Which file system should you use?

   A. NTFS

   B. FAT

   C. HPFS

   D. Either A or B

15. You plan to collect several large directories on to a single partition. The directories require a total of 5 GB in a uncompressed state. You should _____.

   A. Format the partition for the FAT file system

   B. Format the partition for FAT and use DriveSpace file compression

   C. Format the partition for NTFS

   D. Either B or C

   E. All of the above

16. You have a Windows NT Server system with three physical disks. One disk has a single partition that serves as the boot and system partition. The second disk has two partitions of approximately equal size—one formatted for FAT and one for NTFS. The third disk is currently free space. What fault-tolerance method(s) could you use?

   A. Disk mirroring

   B. Disk striping with parity

   C. All of the above

   D. None of the above

17. Users on your Windows NT network occasionally have to exchange messages with users on a Novell NetWare 4.0 network via the Internet. You must use the _____ protocol.

    A. TCP/IP

    B. NWLink

    C. Both A and B

    D. None of the above

18. Your network is a collection of Windows NT machines, Windows 95 machines, and MS-DOS machines running LAN MAN 2.2c Client for MS-DOS. The network, which uses the NetBEUI protocol, used to perform reasonably well, but you recently added additional nodes and noticed a sharp decline in performance. Now you are planning to add to the network again. Which of the following steps might improve network performance?

    A. Keep NetBEUI, but subdivide the network using a bridge

    B. Switch to NWLink

    C. Switch to TCP/IP

    D. A or C

    E. All of the above

Review Answers

1. B	6. C	11. D	16. A
2. C D	7. D	12. A	17. A
3. B C	8. C	13. D	18. D
4. C	9. A	14. B	
5. C	10. B	15. C	

Test Yourself

Stop! Before reading this chapter, test yourself to determine how much study time you will need to devote to this section.

1. To change a member server into a backup domain controller, you must _____.

   A. change the Registry SERVER_TYPE setting in the HKEY_LOCAL_MACHINE Hardware subkey.

   B. change the server type configuration using Server Manager.

   C. configure a domain account database for the server using User Manager for Domains.

   D. reinstall Windows NT Server.

2. The_____helps you upgrade from a previous version of Windows NT.

   A. WINNT.EXE

   B. WINNT32.EXE

   C. UPGRADE.EXE

   D. WINNTUP.EXE

3. Change the IRQ for a network adapter using the Control Panel _____ application.

   A. System

   B. Adapters

   C. Network

   D. None of the above

4. Which three of the following can act as a directory replication import server?

   A. Windows NT Server

   B. Windows NT Workstation

   C. Windows 95

   D. LAN Manager OS/2 Server

Answers

1. D (see "Choosing a Server Type")
2. B (see "Network Installs")
3. C (see "Configuring Protocols and Protocol Bindings")
4. A B D (see "Directory Replication")

Chapter

Installation and
Configuration

This chapter will help you prepare for the "Installation and Configuration" section of Microsoft's Exam 70-67, "Implementing and Supporting Windows NT Server 4.0." Microsoft provides the following objectives for the "Installation and Configuration" section:

Test Objectives

▶ Install Windows NT Server on Intel-based platforms.

▶ Install Windows NT Server to perform various server roles. Server roles include: primary domain controller, backup domain controller, member server.

▶ Install Windows NT Server by using various methods. Installation methods include: CD-ROM, Over the network, Network Client Administrator, Express versus Custom.

▶ Configure protocols and protocol bindings. Protocols include: TCP/IP, NWLink IPX/SPX Compatible Transport, NetBEUI.

▶ Configure network adapters. Considerations include: changing IRQ, I/O base, memory address, configuring multiple adapters.

▶ Configure Windows NT Server core services. Services include: Directory Replicator, License Manager, other services.

▶ Configure peripherals and devices. Peripherals and devices include: communications devices, SCSI devices, tape device drivers, UPS and UPS service, mouse drivers, display drivers, and keyboard drivers.

▶ Configure hard disks to meet various requirements. Requirements include: allocating disk space capacity, providing redundancy, improving performance, providing security, formatting.

▶ Configure printers. Tasks include: adding and configuring a printer, implementing a printer pool, setting print priorities.

▶ Configure a Windows NT Server computer for various types of client computers. Client computer types include: Windows NT Workstation, Microsoft Windows 95, Microsoft MS-DOS-based.

Installation and configuration is a major thrust of the Windows NT Server exam, so it is a good idea for you to devote time to exploring the installation prerequisites, precautions, and procedures. This chapter traces the installation process start to finish and explains each option you encounter along the way. You will also learn how to configure various components of Windows NT Server—such as protocols, network adapters, services, peripherals, hard disks, and printers—for various situations. Along the way, this chapter will examine some important Windows NT concepts, such as server roles, browser elections, and directory replication.

Installing Windows NT Server

To install Windows NT efficiently, it is best to do some planning in advance. Be prepared with answers to the questions the setup program will ask. And take the time to determine which installation method will work best for you. The following section discusses Windows NT Server installation.

Microsoft lists the following objectives for the Windows NT
Server exam:

▶ Install Windows NT Server on Intel-based platforms

▶ Install Windows NT Server to perform various server
  roles. Server roles include: primary domain controller,
  backup domain controller, member server.

▶ Install Windows NT Server by using various methods.
  Installation methods include: CD-ROM, Over the network, Network Client Administrator, Express vs. Custom

Hardware Requirements

Before you install Windows NT, you need to ensure that your
hardware can support it. Windows NT doesn't approach the sheer
number of devices that Windows 95 supports, so don't assume
that Windows NT can support the hardware you currently use for
MS-DOS or Windows 95.

You receive lots of advice in this chapter; first and foremost of that
advice is to consult the Hardware Compatibility List (HCL) before
you try to install Windows NT—certainly before you purchase any
new hardware on which to run Windows NT. The HCL includes
the vendor and model names for all systems and devices tested
and approved for use with Windows NT.

You should know a few things about the HCL, including the following:

▶ The HCL that ships with the product is now obsolete; the
  HCL is frequently updated and can be found in more recent
  form on TechNet, Microsoft's monthly product support CD-
  ROM, as well as on Microsoft Network, CompuServe, the
  Internet, and other online services.

▶ Just because a product is listed on the HCL doesn't mean it's
  fully 100 percent compatible. Check the fine print; usually
  you can find a footnote or endnote that certain caveats apply
  to supporting a device under Windows NT.

▶ Just because a product isn't listed on the HCL doesn't mean it isn't fully 100 percent compatible. It may just mean it hasn't been tested yet. Before giving up hope, ask the vendor if any drivers are available for Windows NT 4. Recognize, however, that when the device isn't on the HCL, Microsoft probably will just refer you back to the vendor for technical support issues.

▶ If a product isn't on the HCL and the vendor doesn't have a Windows NT 4 driver, ask the vendor if any compatible drivers are available. For instance, the modem may be Hayes-compatible, or the network card may be NE2000-compatible. Should a problem arise down the road, however, chances are you won't be able to rely on Microsoft or the vendor for technical support.

The specific hardware requirements differ depending on the platform on which you intend to install Windows NT.

Intel Requirements

Intel-based computers form the largest segment of the Windows NT installed base, owing to the worldwide predominance of Intel-based computers. If you plan to install Windows NT on an Intel-based computer, make sure that your hardware meets the following minimum requirements:

▶ **Processor.** Intel-based computers require a 32-bit Intel or Intel-compatible CPU (80486 DX-33 or higher); Pentium CPUs give optimal performance.

▶ **Memory.** Windows NT Workstation will install with as few as 8 MB of RAM, but Microsoft's official box specs (and therefore the MCP exam) require 12 MB. Realistically, don't go with less than 16 MB, and expect great performance gains with memory increases up to 32 MB.

▶ **Hard disk.** Windows NT Workstation installation requires at least 110 MB free disk space on the hard drive for Intel-based machines; Windows NT Server installation requires at least 125 MB free. On RISC-based machines, Windows NT

Workstation requires 110 MB and Windows NT Server requires at least 160 MB.

On any platform, cluster size also is important. Microsoft recommends that a Windows NT Server with 32 KB clusters have at least 200 MB free space.

> Any supported hard disk suffices, but Windows NT may have a problem addressing IDE drives roomier than 540 MB. If your IDE controller is compatible with the Western Digital WD1003 standard, Windows NT can handle your EIDE drive, but if it isn't, you need to take additional steps. A BIOS upgrade should solve the problem. A utility for MS-DOS called Disk Manager (published by OnTrack Systems) also might do the trick; it alters the BIOS on the hard disk so that MS-DOS (and Windows NT) can correctly handle the drive.

Other Hardware

You need a 3 ½-inch disk drive if you install Windows NT on an Intel-based computer, because Microsoft no longer supplies 5 ¼-inch Setup disks for Windows NT. You also need a VGA (or higher) video card. Other devices, while not mandatory, certainly are quite valuable; for example, a mouse or similar pointing device is hard to get by without these days, as are a CD-ROM drive (optional on Intel only, required for RISC) and a network adapter card. If you're using a PowerPC with an NE-2000 compatible network card, make sure that the computer's firmware is version 1.24 or later.

Multiboot Requirements

You can install Windows NT alongside another operating system on the same machine. You would use a dual boot configuration if you have two operating systems you want to use. If you decide you need or want to do so, you should read the following sections according to the operating systems you want to use.

Windows NT Server

An unlimited number of Windows NT variants can coexist on the same workstation. Be careful to install each operating system in a separate directory. Windows NT-based operating systems will automatically create and update a boot loader menu if other operating systems are found on the system.

Windows 95

Windows 95 and Windows NT can coexist on the same machine, but not in the same directory root, because each OS has files that differ in content but not in name or location. Win95 applications, therefore, must be reinstalled under Windows NT Workstation before you can use them under both operating systems. Again, Windows NT will detect Windows 95 if present and create or update the boot loader menu.

Because Windows 95 and Windows NT have different Registries, and because they support different hardware, no option for upgrading from Windows 95 to Windows NT presently is available; you must perform a full installation.

MS-DOS

If your MS-DOS installation includes Windows 3.x or Windows for Workgroups, you can install Windows NT in the existing Windows root directory. The benefit of this arrangement is a synchronized desktop environment. Also, such an arrangement frees you from having to reinstall your Windows applications before you can use them under Windows NT.

OS/2

You can install Windows NT on a system that currently runs OS/2, but doing so disables OS/2's Boot Manager in favor of the Windows NT Boot Loader. If you want to use the OS/2 Boot Manager, you must re-enable it through Disk Administrator by marking the Boot Manager active after Windows NT successfully installs. When Boot Manager is active, you can boot to Windows NT by choosing MS-DOS from the Boot Manager menu. Choosing MS-DOS invokes the Windows NT Boot Loader, from which you can boot either Windows NT or MS-DOS.

Early versions of OS/2 (version 1.x) don't have Boot Manager. Instead, you must use the BOOT command: type BOOT /DOS from inside OS/2 and reboot to bring up the Windows NT Boot Loader, or type BOOT /OS2 from MS-DOS and reboot to bring up OS/2.

Choosing a Server Type

If you installing Windows NT Server, you must make an important choice; you have to decide on a server role for the computer on which you install Windows NT. You must choose one of three server roles:

▶ **Primary Domain Controller (PDC).** Contains the master copy of the directory database (which contains information on user accounts) for the domain. There can be only one primary domain controller per domain, and the primary domain controller must be the first machine installed.

▶ **Backup Domain Controller (BDC).** Helps the primary domain controller. The primary domain controller copies the directory database to the backup controller(s). The BDC can authenticate users just as the PDC can. If the PDC fails, the BDC is promoted to a PDC, but if a BDC is promoted, any changes to the directory database since the last time it was copied from the old PDC are lost. A domain can have more than one BDC.

▶ **Member or Stand-alone Server.** A stand-alone server is a Windows NT Server machine that doesn't participate in the system of domain controllers of the domain. A stand-alone server can provide all Windows NT Server function (file service, print service, Internet service, or whatever) but it doesn't maintain a copy of a domain accounts database, and cannot authenticate domain users.

A stand-alone server can be part of a domain or a workgroup. Stand-alone servers that are parts of domains are called member servers, which are useful because keeping a file or print servers free from the overhead of authenticating users often proves cost-effective. You cannot change a stand-alone server into a domain controller after installing it; your only option under such circumstances is to reinstall Windows NT and change the server type to domain controller during the installation process.

After you install a PDC or BDC into a domain, it must remain in that domain unless you reinstall Windows NT, because you can't change the Security Identifier (SID) for the domain after setting it during installation. You can, however, change the name of a domain; change the domain name first on the PDC, then on the other network machines. Windows NT simply maps the new domain name with the old SID for the domain.

Installation Procedure

The user documentation that accompanies Windows NT 4 includes detailed instructions for installing and upgrading to Windows 4.

The following are two possible sources of Windows NT 4 installation files:

▶ The Windows NT Installation CD-ROM (with three setup floppies)

▶ A network sharepoint (with three setup floppies)

Most installation procedures consist of two distinct phases: a file copying phase that takes place under a minimal text-mode version of Windows NT and a configuration phase that runs under the full GUI Windows NT Setup wizard.

The details of the Windows NT installation process depend on the details of your system; different prompts and dialogs may ask you for additional information depending on the devices on your system and the components you want to install.

CD-ROM

The Windows NT Installation CD-ROM, the easiest and most common method for installing NT, comes with three startup floppy disks. To begin the CD-ROM installation process, boot from Setup Disk 1. Setup asks for all three of the setup disks before it asks for the CD-ROM. (You learn how to regenerate these disks should the need arise later in this chapter.)

You also can begin the installation by starting the CD-ROM (from within your existing operating system) and double-clicking on Windows NT Setup. Setup copies the installation files from the CD-ROM to your hard drive and asks you to restart your computer. Don't throw away your Setup floppy disks, however. Even if you initiate the installation from the CD-ROM, Setup asks for Setup Disk 2. (You learn more about the three Windows NT Setup disks later in this chapter.)

If you are initiating the installation from the Setup disks, you must boot from the Setup disks; don't type the standard run a:\setup. Setup is a Windows NT program, so to run it requires that Windows NT be running. When you boot from the initial setup disk, a minimal version of Windows NT loads and initializes.

Network Installs

If you have to roll out many Windows NT Workstations in a short time frame, a CD-ROM-based installation may be impractical. Perhaps not all of your workstations have CD-ROM drives; perhaps you don't have as many copies of the CD-ROM as you do workstations. A network install is really a CD-ROM install; an initial preinstallation phase is added in which the contents of the CD-ROM are copied across the network from the server to the client computer. After all the installation files have been copied, the client computer reboots from the setup disks and proceeds with the installation as if it were a CD-ROM install (in this case, the "CD-ROM" is the hard drive). You can use Windows NT's Client Administrator application to create a network installation startup disk that will enable you to boot the client machine and connect to the shared directory with the installation files. The Client Administrator startup disk is described later in this chapter.

When many workstations are simultaneously downloading the installation files, performance isn't great, but you can still set up many clients at once and let them run while you do other things.

To improve performance, copy the contents of the CD-ROM to the hard drive and share the hard disk's copy rather than the CD's. Hard disks are much faster than CD-ROM drives.

To start an installation across the network, you must first redirect an MS-DOS drive letter to the network sharepoint containing the installation files. From a NetWare client, you use the MAP command; from a Windows 95 client, you utilize the Network Neighborhood and connect to a drive; from an MS-DOS client, you use the NET USE command; from a Windows for Workgroups client, you choose Disk, Connect Network Drive in File Manager. In short, establish network connections however you ordinarily do it.

If you have questions about net commands, type **net help** at the prompt. If you require assistance on the specific command, type **net help** followed by the command, such as **net help view** or **net help logoff**.

After you map a drive to the installation share, change to the drive and run a program called WINNT.EXE. (If you install from a previous version of NT, the system prompts you to run WINNT32.EXE instead of WINNT.EXE.) WINNT.EXE is an MS-DOS program that generates the three necessary Setup disks and copies the Windows NT installation files from the server to the local hard drive. After all the files are copied, WINNT.EXE prompts you to insert Setup Disk 1 so it can reboot the computer and begin the installation process.

One interesting quirk about WINNT.EXE: When it asks you to insert each of the three blank, formatted disks necessary to create the setup disks, it does so in reverse order. It asks for Disk 3 first, then Disk 2, and finally Disk 1. Microsoft did this for your convenience, believe it or not: one less disk swap occurs in this scenario—try it and see. Still, it confuses many first-time installers who try to reboot their machine from Disk 3, believing it to be Disk 1.

WINNT.EXE Switches

The following switches enable you to customize how WINNT.EXE begins the setup process.

/B No Boot Floppies

The /B switch instructs WINNT.EXE not to create the three setup disks. Instead, WINNT.EXE creates images of these disks on your system partition, requiring an extra 4 or 5 MB of disk space. The boot sector of the hard disk is modified to point to the temporary directory that contains the images (WIN_NT.~BT).

The /B switch can significantly speed up the installation process. If the computer crashes during Setup, however, you may not be able to reboot to your old operating system. Keeping an MS-DOS or Windows 95 bootable disk around should solve that problem. Simply enter the SYS command for the C drive; your system should boot normally.

/S Source File Location

When WINNT.EXE executes, it immediately asks the user for the location of the Windows NT source files, even if the user is in the same directory from which WINNT.EXE was run. To avoid answering this question, supply the information up-front using the syntax WINNT.EXE /S:<path>.

/U Unattended Installation

The Unattended Installation option automates the installation or upgrade process so you don't have to sit at the keyboard and respond to Setup prompts. Because you're present, you must tell WINNT.exe in advance where to find the installation files, so you must use the /u switch with the /s switch. Normally, the unattended installation only operates unattended through the copy phase, the text mode portion of Setup, and the initial reboot; Setup requires a user to enter the computer name, network settings, and so on. You can, however, enter a colon and a file name after the /u switch, as follows:

```
winnt /u:c:\answer.txt
```

The file answer.txt is an answer file, a file that contains responses to the final Setup prompts. Using the /u switch with an answer file, you can automate the entire installation.

You can use the Setup Manager utility to create an answer file, or you can use any text editor to edit the answer file template unattend.exe (found on the Windows NT installation CD-ROM). You can save the answer file to any legal name.

You can use an answer file in conjunction with the (Uniqueness Database File) /UDF switch.

/UDF Uniqueness Database File

A Uniqueness Database File (UDF) lets you tailor an unattended installation to the specific attributes of specific machines. The UDF contains different sections, each identified with a string called a *uniqueness ID*. Each section contains machine-specific information for a single computer or a group of computers. You can then use a single answer file for all the network installations, and reference machine-specific information by providing the uniqueness ID with the /UDF switch.

/T:drive_letter Temporary Drive

This switch tells winnt or winnt32 to put the installation files on the specified drive.

/OX Only Make Boot Diskettes (Local Install)

Essentially the same command as the /O switch, /OX also creates boot disks. The only difference is that /O creates disks that require the installation files to be in the hard disk's WIN_NT.˜LS temporary directory, and /OX requires the installation files to be on disk or CD-ROM.

The difference between the resulting setup disks is just a single byte on Disk 2. The WINNT.SIF file on Disk 2 is a text file which has an entry of MsDosInitiate= which is set to 1 if the /O command is used, and set to 0 if the /OX command is used. You can actually convert local install disks to network install disks simply by changing this entry in WINNT.SIF.

/F Don't Verify Files

You can shave a bit of time off the installation process by skipping the verification of the files copied to the boot disks, but the savings are negligible. It doesn't take that much time to verify the files, and it certainly takes much longer to restart the installation if the disks are corrupt. Still, such corruption during file copying is rare, so if you aren't averse to the occasional odds-favorable risk, go for it.

/C Don't Check for Free Space

This switch tells WINNT.EXE not to check for the required free space on the setup boot disks. You should not use this switch for two reasons:

▶ The disks are pretty packed; if you have other files on the disks, you probably won't be able to fit all of the required Setup files anyway.

▶ The amount of time you can save by using this switch is approximately equal to the amount of time it takes to type the switch.

The Installation Phases

Microsoft divides the Windows NT installation process into four phases:

▶ Phase 0: Preinstallation

▶ Phase 1: Gathering information about your computer

▶ Phase 2: Installing Windows NT Networking

▶ Phase 3: Finishing Setup

The following sections guide you through these installation phases.

Phase 0: Preinstallation

During preinstallation, Setup copies the necessary installation files to your hard drive and assembles the information it needs for the install by detecting hardware and also by asking the user for configuration information. Before you begin studying the installation process, you should look at what's on the three Windows NT Setup disks.

Setup Disk One

When your computer boots from this disk, the Master Boot Record loads and passes control to NTLDR, the Windows NT Boot Loader. NTLDR, in turn, loads the kernel (NTKRNLMP.EXE). Next, one of three Hardware Abstraction Layers (HAL) is loaded—HAL486C.DLL, HALMCA.DLL, or HALAPIC.DLL—depending on the platform detected.

Setup Disk Two

This disk contains a minimal registry used by Setup, SETUPREG.HIV. This registry contains single entry instructs that tell Windows NT to load the main installation driver, SETUPDD.SYS. After loading SETUPDD.SYS, Windows NT loads generic drivers for video (VIDEOPRT.SYS), keyboard (I8042PRT.SYS, KBDUS.DLL), floppy drive (FLOPPY.SYS), and the FAT file system (FASTFAT.SYS). This disk also includes the setup font (VGAOEM.FON), locale-specific data (C_1252.NLS, \C_437.NLS and L_INTL.NLS), and the first of many SCSI port drivers, which continue on the third Setup disk.

Setup Disk Three

Disk three contains additional SCSI port drivers, of which only one or two are typically loaded (depending on what SCSI adapters are installed, if any). Windows NT loads additional file system drivers, such as NTFS.SYS, from this disk. This disk also includes drivers for specific types of hard disks, specifically ATDISK.SYS for ESDI or IDE and ABIOSDSK.SYS for Micro Channel.

At this point, the SCSI drivers have been loaded, so Windows NT should recognize supported SCSI CD-ROM drives. Windows NT also detects IDE CD-ROM drives, but may not detect proprietary Mitsumi or Panasonic drives; you must manually inform Windows NT of their presence.

The Phase 0 Process

Phase 0 is the same for both Windows NT Server and Windows NT Workstation. In Phase 0, Setup loads a minimal version of Windows NT into memory, and asks if you want to perform an installation or an upgrade.

Between Setup disks two and three, the Welcome screen appears, informing you of your options: installing Windows NT, repairing an existing installation, or learning more about the setup process. Take a moment to read the online help if you want. When you're ready to begin, press Enter to begin the installation.

During this phase of the installation, Setup asks you to verify certain information about your hardware and your hardware-related software components. The following sections describe the questions Setup asks.

Mass Storage Devices

Setup asks if you want it to attempt to detect the mass storage devices attached to your computer. A note informs you that Setup can automatically detect floppy controllers and standard ESDI/ IDE hard disks. (Some other mass storage devices, such as SCSI adapters and certain CD-ROM drives can cause the computer to malfunction or become unresponsive.)

Press Enter to let Setup detect mass storage devices on your computer.

Press S to skip mass storage device detection and manually select SCSI adapters, CD-ROM drives, and special disk controllers.

Setup asks for Setup Disk 3 and attempts to detect the mass storage devices. Setup then asks you to verify the list.

Press Enter if you have no additional devices.

Type **S** to specify an additional device.

Hardware and Components

Setup looks for certain hardware and software components, such as a keyboard, a mouse, a video screen, and the accompanying drivers. Setup presents a list of components and asks if you want to make any changes.

Press Enter to accept the list.

To change an item, select the item using the arrow keys and press Enter to see alternatives.

Partitions

After you identify your SCSI adapters and CD-ROM drivers, Windows NT Setup needs to know on which partition it should install Windows NT. Setup displays a screen showing the existing partitions on your hard drive and the space available for creating new partitions.

Press Enter to install Windows NT on the highlighted partition or unpartitioned space.

Type **C** to create a new partition in unpartitioned space.

Type **D** to delete a partition.

NTFS

Setup then presents the following options:

- ▶ Format the partition using the FAT file system.

- ▶ Format the partition using the NTFS file system.

- ▶ Convert the partition to NTFS.

- ▶ Leave the current file system intact.

Specifically designed for Windows NT, NT File System (NTFS) offers some advantages, including better performance and increased security, but NTFS isn't compatible with Windows 95 or earlier versions of DOS and Windows. The other optional file systems for NT hard drives is FAT (for MS-DOS and Windows systems). If you choose FAT, you lose the data currently on the partition.

The conversion to NTFS isn't performed during installation, but rather, after Windows NT is completely installed and the computer reboots for the first time. The end result is the same: before the user can log on to Windows NT, the partition has been converted.

The default choice is to leave the current file system intact. If your system is now running MD-DOS, Windows 3.x, or Windows 95, the current file system is the FAT file system. If you plan on ever accessing the partition from MS-DOS or Windows, select the FAT file system.

See Chapter 3, "Managing Resources," for more on the file systems that Windows NT supports.

NT Root Directory

Setup asks what name you want to give the Windows NT root directory. By default, Setup suggests \WINNT of the system partition as the installation directory.

> Windows NT can peacefully coexist with Windows 3.x in the same directory tree, but do not, under any circumstance, install Windows NT in the same directory as Windows 95; currently the two operating systems cannot coexist in the same directory structure.

If Setup detects an installation of Windows NT already in the selected directory, you are given the options to replace the existing installation or choose another location.

Hard Disk Corruption

Setup examines your hard disk(s) for corruption. It automatically performs a basic examination. You can choose whether you want Setup to perform an exhaustive secondary examination, which may take several minutes, by pressing Enter. Press Esc to skip the secondary examination.

Reboot

A progress bar appears as Setup copies files to your hard disk. This may take several minutes.

The last text-mode screen announces that this portion of Setup is complete and asks that you remove the disk from your floppy drive and restart your computer.

Press Enter to restart your computer.

Phase 1: Gathering Information

After your computer restarts, Setup asks you to approve the licensing agreement and begins copying file from the disks, CD-ROM, or network to the Windows NT root directory. The Windows NT Setup Wizard then appears, announcing the three remaining parts of the setup process:

1. Gathering information about your computer.

2. Installing Windows NT Networking

3. Finishing Setup

Name and Company Name

For legal and registration reasons, Setup then asks for your name and organization, which it then uses as the defaults for additional software installed under Windows NT. You must enter a value in the Name field but you can leave the Company Name blank.

Setup also asks for your Product ID number, which is a sticker attached to the CD-ROM sleeve. You must enter this number before you can continue with the installation.

Licensing Mode (NT Server Only)

If you're installing Windows NT Server, you must specify a licensing mode. These are your options:

▶ **Per server license.** Clients are licensed to a particular server, and the number of concurrent connections to the server cannot exceed the maximum specified in the license. When the maximum number of concurrent connections is reached, Windows NT returns an error to a connecting user and prohibits access. An administrator can still connect after the maximum is reached, however.

▶ **Per seat license.** Clients are free to use any server they want, and an unlimited number of clients can connect to a server.

If you can't decide which mode to select, choose Per Server mode. You have a one-time chance to convert the per server license to a per seat license using the Control Panel Licensing application.

Computer Name

Every networked Windows NT-based computer must have a unique computer name, even if the computers are split among multiple domains. The computer name is a typical NetBIOS name: that is, it consists of up to 15 characters. Because workgroup and domain names also use NetBIOS names, the computer name must be unique among all of these names as well. NetBIOS names aren't case-sensitive; they always appear in uppercase.

Server Type (NT Server Only)

If you're installing Windows NT Server, you must specify whether the computer is a primary domain controller, a backup domain controller, or a stand-alone server. These server type options are discussed earlier in this chapter.

Administrator Password

Setup asks you to enter a password for the Administrator account. The length of the password should be 14 characters or less. See Chapter 3, for more on Windows NT accounts. You need the Administrator account to create and manage other accounts within Windows NT.

Don't forget to write down the Administrator account password and store it in a safe place.

Emergency Disk

The Setup Wizard asks if you want to create an emergency repair disk. Chapter 6, "Troubleshooting," discusses the Emergency Repair Disk (ERD) in detail. It's essentially a clone of the information stored in the \REPAIR directory in case that directory or even the hard disk becomes corrupt or inaccessible. Creating an ERD for every computer in your company is a good idea. Label each ERD with the serial number of the computer to which it is paired.

The Wizard then asks whether you want the most common components installed or whether you would prefer to choose the components from a list. (Note that the Microsoft Exchange messaging client may not be in the list of common components.)

If you want to view the list of components, you can always choose the Choose Components option to view the list and then click on Next (leaving the list unchanged and accepting the defaults).

Optional Components

If you're installing Windows NT Server, or if you're installing Windows NT Workstation using the Custom Setup option, Setup asks you to specify which optional components you want to install.

Phase 2: Installing Windows NT Networking

The Wizard then announces that it is ready to begin installing Windows NT Networking. The following sections describe the Networking phase of the setup.

Network Participation

The next screen asks if your computer will participate in a network, and if so, whether it will be wired to the network or whether it will access the network through a modem. If you intend to connect via both a modem and an ISDN adapter or network adapter, check both boxes.

If you click in the No button (your computer will not participate in a network) the Wizard proceeds to Phase 3, "Finishing Setup."

Internet/Intranet Service

If you're installing Windows NT Server, Setup asks if you want to install Internet Information Server (IIS).

If you're installing Windows NT Workstation, Setup asks if you want to install Peer Web Server (PWS).

Network Adapter Card

The next screen asks if you want Setup to search for your network adapter card. Click on Start Search if you want Setup to find your card. Setup stops after it finds the first card and the Start Search button changes into a Find Next button. If you have another network adapter card, choose Find Next. Alternatively, you can choose Select from List to select your Adapter card from a list. The Have Disk button in the Select Network Adapter dialog box enables you to install the software for the adapter card. You need to obtain a Windows NT 4 driver from your vendor and supply the path to the driver in the dialog box.

If Setup successfully autodetects your network adapter card, it displays its findings so that you can confirm the network adapter card and its settings. If it cannot detect the card, Setup expects you to manually select a network adapter card from a list of drivers supplied with Windows NT.

After selecting or confirming your network adapter card, you may see a dialog box with card configuration options. These options may include Interrupt Request (IRQ), Base I/O Address, Transceiver Type, and other card-specific parameters. Confirm these options before proceeding because Windows NT doesn't always pick all of these up correctly, especially if you added your card manually, skipping detection.

If you don't have a network card, you can still install the networking services on top of the remote access service (RAS). You'll only be prompted to install RAS during Setup if you do not select a network card at all. See Chapter 4, "Connectivity," for more information about RAS.

Network Protocols

The next screen enables you to specify networking protocols for your network. You can check TCP/IP, NWLink IPX/SPX Compatible Transport, or NetBEUI. Click on Select from List for a new window with some additional options, including AppleTalk, DLC, Point to Point Tunneling Protocol, and Streams Environment. This new window also provides a Have Disk option you can use if you want to install your own protocol software.

By default, only TCP/IP is installed on an Intel-based computer.

Carefully consider your current network configuration and needs before accepting the default protocols. If your network currently runs mostly NetWare, you may want to use NWLink rather than TCP/IP. If your network uses both NetWare and Unix, you may want both NWLink and TCP/IP. If your network is a small, self-contained workgroup, you may want to use NetBEUI only. See Chapter 1, "Planning," for more information about network transport protocols.

If your clients already use TCP/IP, then you know how easy it is to misconfigure TCP/IP when installing it, especially the subnet mask and default gateway. If you are installing over the network and have copied the install directory (that is, I386) to the hard drive, you can modify IPINFO.INF. This file is a template for TCP/IP configuration parameters. It's a fairly large file, but you're only interested in the section that begins with [De-faultIPInfo]. The file consists of mostly comment lines, so make sure that you have found the section that does not have each line preceded by a semicolon (the comment indicator).

After you find the [DefaultIPInfo] section, you can modify the following parameters:

▶ NumberOfIPAddress = x, in which x is the number of IP Addresses o be assigned. For most workstations, this should simply be set to 1.

▶ IPAddress1 = 'xxx.xxx.xxx.xxx'. Because this parameter will change from client to client, you might not want to fill this in.

▶ SubnetMask1 = 'xxx.xxx.xxx.xxx'. All of your clients will probably use the same subnet mask, so this is a smart default to set.

▶ DefaultGateway = 'xxx.xxx.xxx.xxx'. Again, all of your clients on a particular subnet should use the same default gateway (router), so this is another smart default.

Of course, users can still override this information during an installation, but at least they won't be guessing parameters out of the blue.

Network Services

If you're installing Windows NT Server, Setup asks what optional network services you want to install.

The other chapters of this book discuss many of the network service options. If you don't install a particular service during Setup, you can always add it later using the Services tab of the Control Panel Network application.

Network Components

Setup then asks if you want to change any of your previous choices, and then proceeds to install your networking components. Depending on the components and options you select, various dialog boxes may appear as the components are installed. The Setup Wizard may try to find your modem, for example, or you may be asked whether you want to use Dynamic Host Configuration Protocol (\DHCP). You also may be prompted for the IP address and default gateway.

After installing the network components, Setup announces that it's ready to start the network so you can complete the network installation. Setup asks for the name of the workgroup or domain to which your computer will belong. (Select Workgroup or Domain, and type the name.) If Setup successfully starts the network, Setup immediately begins to copy additional files for a few minutes. If unsuccessful, Setup asks if you want to change your network adapter card's configuration parameters. It's a good idea not to proceed any further until the network starts correctly, particularly if you're doing a network installation: if your computer doesn't have a CD-ROM drive, you may find yourself unable to load additional drivers after Windows NT restarts. If you cannot get the network to start after multiple attempts, you may proceed with installation, but you can't join a domain until the network services successfully begin at some point.

You must join either a domain or a workgroup, or neither. You cannot join both.

Joining a workgroup requires nothing more than the name of that workgroup. The workgroup doesn't have to exist prior to this point; you can create it just by joining it. In a workgroup, everyone's a chief. Every Windows NT-based computer has its own account database, and sharing resources between computers requires an immense amount of administration or a significant lack of security.

If you're installing a Windows NT workstation or member server and you elect to join a domain, a domain must already exist; that is, a primary domain controller (PDC) must be defined and available on the network. If Setup cannot find a Windows NT Server acting as a primary domain controller for that domain on the network, you can't join the domain.

If the primary domain controller does exist and is available, then an account must be created at the PDC for your workstation or member server. This can occur if the domain administrator manually adds an account for this workstation using the Server Manager application, or if you create the account yourself during workstation installation. Before you can do so, you must know the username and password of the domain administrator or have the user right "Create computer accounts in the domain."

Phase 3: Finishing Setup

After the network components are installed, Setup is almost complete. The Wizard announces that you are ready for Phase 3: Finishing Setup. The following sections describe the Phase 3 installation steps.

Time Zone

You can set your computer's current date and time and select the appropriate time zone through a Setup dialog box. Specify the date and time in the Date & Time tab. Specify a time zone in the Time Zone tab. If you choose a time zone that switches from standard time to daylight savings time and back, you may elect to have Windows NT automatically make this change for you. If so, select the Automatically Adjust Clock for Daylight Savings Changes check box.

Note that certain separate time zone entries for certain individual states simply don't fit within a time zone profile. Arizona, for instance, geographically belongs to the Mountain Standard time zone but, unlike other Mountain Standard time states, does not switch to Daylight Savings Time in the summer. Arizona has a separate entry in the Time Zone list.

Exchange Configuration

If you choose to install Microsoft Exchange as an optional component in Phase 1, Setup requests some information for configuring Exchange.

Display Settings

Setup detects the video display adapter. If the adapter uses a chipset for which Windows NT includes a driver, the name of the chipset appears on-screen.

If this setting is correct, confirm it. If not, choose another driver by choosing Have Disk and supplying the path to the third-party driver; or just choose the standard VGA driver. For best performance, use a card-specific driver rather than the standard VGA driver. Contact your card's vendor for a Windows NT driver if Windows NT does not detect it correctly.

Setup doesn't let you proceed unless you test the settings you have selected. Because Windows NT cannot detect your monitor settings, you could pick a resolution or refresh rate that your card but not your monitor supports. When you click on the Test button, the screen briefly goes blank, to be quickly replaced by a test pattern. If all looks well, confirm the settings for the card when the Windows NT Setup interface returns. Otherwise, choose a new setting and test again. If your test is unsuccessful, odds are that Windows NT doesn't work right under that setting. A few monitors go blank and stay blank during testing, even though the chosen settings are supported. If this is the case with your installation, and you're sure that both adapter card and monitor support your configuration, you can lie and tell Setup that the test was successful. If Windows NT restarts in an unusable video state when you reboot, reboot again and choose Boot Loader, Windows NT Server 4.0 [VGA mode].

Pentium Patch

The last bit of detection that Setup performs is for the presence of the Intel Pentium floating-point division error. If you get this error, Setup asks you if you want to disable the floating-point hardware and enable floating-point emulation software.

Disabling the hardware makes your floating-point calculations much more accurate, at the expense of performance (because the software isn't as fast as the native floating-point hardware). The nice thing about this software solution, however, is that Windows NT continues to detect the hardware error every time it boots. If and when the processor is upgraded to an error-free Pentium or higher processor, the emulation software will be automatically disabled and the floating-point hardware re-enabled.

Emergency Repair Directory and Disk

Installation is almost complete. Setup copies files to your Windows NT root directory. The screen then clears, except for a progress gauge called Saving Configuration. At this point, Setup has created a \REPAIR directory in the Windows NT root directory to which it is backing up the configuration registry files. This procedure may take a few minutes, but when it is complete the \REPAIR directory will contain the information necessary to repair most damaged Windows NT installations.

If you previously told Setup you wanted to create an Emergency Repair Disk (refer to the section, "Emergency Disk," earlier in this chapter), Setup now creates an Emergency Repair Disk. Insert a disk into the floppy drive. The disk you supply does not have to be blank or formatted. Setup automatically formats the disk to ensure that it has no media errors. After the disk finishes, Setup informs you that installation is complete and prompts you to reboot.

Uninstalling Windows NT

Uninstalling Windows NT is relatively painless. In most cases, you can remove the operating system without damaging the other applications and documents on your system.

To remove Windows NT from your computer, follow these steps:

1. Boot to another operating system, such as Windows 95 or MS-DOS.

2. Delete the Windows NT installation directory tree.

3. Delete pagefile.sys.

4. Turn off the hidden, system, and read-only attributes for NTBOOTDD.SYS, and then delete them. You might not have all of these on your computer, but if so, you can find them all in the root directory of your drive C.

If you are dual-booting Windows NT and another operating system (such as MS-DOS or Windows 95), create a startup disk for the other operating system before you uninstall Windows NT. If MS-DOS, Windows 3.x, or Windows 95 doesn't boot properly after you remove NT, boot to the startup disk and type **SYS C:** to reinstall your system files onto the hard drive.

To create a startup disk in Windows 95, go to the Add/Remove Programs applet in Control Panel and select the Startup Disk tab.

Client Administrator Installation Aids

The Network Client Administrator application, in the Administrative Tools group, lets you configure your Windows NT Server system to assist you with the process of installing client machines on the network. Figure 2.1 shows the Network Client Administrator.

Figure 2.1

Network Client Administrator.

The first two options are designed to help with installing network clients, as follows:

▶ **Make Network Installation Startup Disk.** Shares the client installation files on the network and creates an installation startup disk you can use to connect to the server from the client machine and to download the installation files.

▶ **Make Installation Disk Set.** Creates a set of floppies you can use to install network client software on a client computer.

The following sections discuss these two installation options.

Network Installation Startup Disk

For an exercise testing this information, see end of chapter.

The Make Network Installation Startup Disk option in the Network Client Administrator enables you to set up a share containing installation files and then a create a network startup floppy disk that will enable you to connect to the installation files from the client machine. Client Administrator adds the necessary files to an MS-DOS system disk so that you can boot from the disk and connect to the network share.

You can use this option to create a network startup disk for any of the following operating systems:

▶ Windows NT Server v3.5, 3.51, 4.0

▶ Windows NT Workstation v3.5, 3.51, 4.0

▶ Windows 95

▶ Windows for Workgroups v3.11

▶ Microsoft Network Client for MS-DOS v3.0

The installation files for Windows 95 and Microsoft Network Client for MS-DOS are included on the Windows NT Server CD-ROM, and you'll have the option of copying them to the share you create through Client Administrator. If you plan to install a Windows NT Server, Windows NT Workstation, or Windows for Workgroups system, copy the installation files from the appropriate CD-ROM to to the shared directory on the installation server.

Although Windows 95 installation files are included on the Windows NT Server CD-ROM, you still have to purchase a license for each Windows 95 client you install. The same applies to Windows NT Server, Windows NT Workstation, or Windows for Workgroups installation files that you copy from the appropriate CD-ROM to the installation drive. As with any Windows installation, you are limited to one install per license. You are, however, at liberty to install Microsoft Client for MS-DOS.

The Windows NT Server and Workstation startup disks work only for Intel computers.

To create a network installation startup disk:

1. Select the Make Network Installation Startup Disk radio button in the Network Client Administrator dialog box. The Share Network Client Installation Files dialog box appears (see fig. 2.2).

Figure 2.2

The Share Network Client Installation Files dialog box.

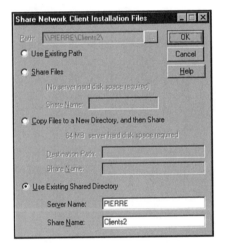

You can either copy the files to your hard disk and share them or share them directly from the Windows NT Server CD-ROM.

The Share Files radio button shares the files directly from the CD-ROM, which doesn't require any hard disk space. Choose the Copy Files to a New Directory, and then Share radio button to copy the files to your hard disk: you'll need 64 MB of hard disk space. The Use Existing Shared Directory radio button tells Client Administrator to set up the

installation disk to use an existing share. You can specify a
server name and a share name.

When you have configured the location of the installation
files, click OK.

2. The Target Workstation Configuration dialog box appears
    (see fig. 2.3). Specify the size of the floppy disk, the type of
    network client software, and a network adapter card for the
    client machine. Click on OK.

Figure 2.3

*The Target Work-
station Configura-
tion dialog box.*

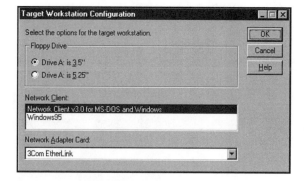

3. The Network Startup Disk Configuration dialog box appears.
    Specify a computer name, user name, domain, and network
    protocol for the client machine plus any TCP/IP settings.
    The Destination Path is the path to the floppy drive.

4. Insert a formatted, high-density MS-DOS system disk in the
    destination drive and click on OK.

5. You now can use the network installation startup disk to boot
    the client machine and connect to the installation files.

Make Installation Disk Set

The Make Installation Disk Set radio button in the Network Client
Administrator dialog box enables you to create a set of floppy
installation disks you can use to install the following network client packages:

▶ Microsoft Network Client 3.0 for MS-DOS and Windows

▶ Microsoft LAN Manager 2.2c for MS-DOS

▶ Microsoft LAN Manager 2.2c for OS/2

▶ Microsoft Remote Access Service Client v1.1 for MS-DOS

▶ Microsoft TCP/IP for Windows for Workgroups

1. Select the Make Installation Disk Set radio button and click on Continue. The Share Network Client Installation Files dialog box appears (refer to fig. 2.2 and discussion in the preceding section).

2. After that, you'll see the Make Installation Disk Set dialog box (see fig. 2.4). Choose the network software you want to install on the client, choose a destination drive, and click on OK.

Figure 2.4

The Make Installation Disk Set dialog box.

Windows NT and the Registry

The Registry is Windows NT's storehouse for configuration information. In order to understand Windows NT, you certainly must have an understanding of what the Registry is and how it works. And yet, direct references to the Registry are conspicuously absent from Microsoft's exam objectives for the Windows NT Server exam. It could be that Microsoft finds it impossible to write an exam question on the hundreds of Registry keys, subkeys, and values that is anything other than pure memorization. Whatever the reason, it is important to know that *any* configuration you do in Windows NT somehow finds its way into the Registry and, because this is a chapter on Windows NT Configuration, it wouldn't be complete without a discussion of the Registry itself.

The Registry is a configuration database, replacing the plethora of INI files used to configure both the operating system and applications under other versions of Windows. Unfortunately, Windows 95, which is on its way to becoming Registry-based, is not quite there yet. The Registry has several advantages over the older system:

▶ **Centralized.** Instead of a PROGMAN.INI, CPANEL.INI, and a host of other such files for your applications, Windows NT stores all its configuration data in the Registry. As a result, all Windows NT components and Windows NT-based applications can easily find information about any other aspect of the computer. In addition, the Registry supports remote administration: an administrator, sitting at her own workstation, can alter another computer's configuration by remotely editing its Registry.

▶ **Structured.** The Registry can contain subsections within sections, something that was impossible with INI files. The end result is a much more orderly, logical record.

▶ **Flexible.** INI files contained ASCII text. The Registry can contain text as well, but it also can hold binary and hexadecimal values. It can even hold executable code or entire text files. The Registry also contains preferences and restrictions for individual users, something that INI files never have done. This provides a configuration database that stores not only computer-specific information but also user-specific information.

▶ **Secure.** You can protect the Registry just like any object in Windows NT. An access control list can be defined for any Registry key, and a special set of permissions exists specifically for dealing with the Registry.

When viewed from this perspective, one wonders how users survived without the Registry. However, the Registry has its drawbacks:

▶ **Cryptic.** Unlike INI files, the assumption with many parts of the Registry seems to be: humans just don't go here. It isn't always easy to determine why certain entries are present or how to effectively configure them.

▶ **Sprawling.** Imagine all the INI files on an average Windows 3.x-based computer merged into a single file, with some additional hardware information as well. The Registry begins its life big, and it only gets bigger. Searching for a specific entry is further complicated by the fact that you cannot search for a specific value in the Registry (which of course you could always do in a plain-text INI file).

▶ **Dangerous.** If you make a mistake when editing an INI file, or if you aren't sure about the potential effect of a change, you can always exit the text editor without saving the file. Even a fatal change to an INI file can be fixed by booting to MS-DOS and using a text editor to alter the problematic file. Not so the Registry: Direct changes to the Registry are often dynamic and potentially irreversible.

Windows NT provides the following three tools for editing and managing Registry information:

▶ Registry Editor

▶ Control Panel

▶ System Policy Editor

Later in this chapter, you'll learn more about the Registry Editor and some of the Control Panel applications. (For a guided tour of Control Panel applications, see Appendix B.) Chapter 3 describes System Policy Editor.

How Windows NT Uses the Registry

You now know what the Registry is, at least conceptually. But when and how is it used? The when is easy: constantly. The how is a bit harder to answer, only because the scope of the Registry is so broad.

Windows NT accesses the Registry in the following situations:

▶ **Control Panel.** All changes to values in the Control Panel are written to the Registry. Even when the Control Panel serves merely to confirm values already in place, the information is read from the Registry.

▶ **Setup.** The main Windows NT Setup program or a setup program for a Win32 application always examines the Registry for existing configuration information before entering new configuration information.

▶ **Administrative Tools.** User Manager, Event Viewer, and other Administrative Tools all read and write their information to various parts of the Registry.

▶ **Booting.** When Windows NT boots, hardware information is fed into the Registry. In addition, the kernel reports its version and build number to the Registry and extracts the name and order of the device drivers that must be loaded. These device drivers communicate with the Registry as well, reporting the resources they're using for the current session.

How Users Use the Registry

They don't. Although users can read entries in the Registry, they should not change any of them, and frankly, the Registry should be transparent to them. User settings can be modified indirectly through the Control Panel. Only experienced administrators should work directly with the Registry.

How Administrators Use the Registry

Just because administrators can directly modify the Registry doesn't mean they should do so. Continue to use the Control Panel, Windows NT Setup, and the other front ends whenever possible. Only edit the Registry directly when there is no other option to accomplish the configuration task at hand (which sadly is too often the case). The Registry is so delicate that Microsoft always includes a disclaimer with any instructions about making changes. Edit the Registry only with the specific steps spelled out and only after creating a current emergency repair disk (ERD). For more on the Windows NT Emergency Repair Disk, see Chapter 6.

Using the Registry Editor

REGEDT32.EXE enables you to directly edit the Registry (see fig. 2.5). You can find REGEDT32.EXE, also known as the Registry Editor, in the System32 subdirectory of your Windows NT root directory. The Registry Editor is installed on every Windows NT-based computer, although an icon for it is not placed in any of the program groups, not even Administrative Tools.

Figure 2.5

The Registry Editor REGEDT32.EXE

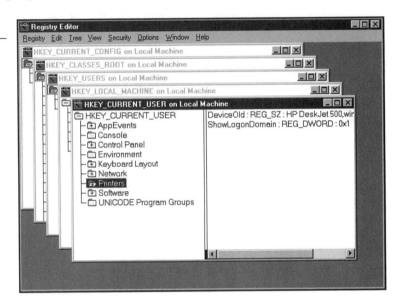

The absence of a Registry Editor icon is your first clue that you just don't toy with the Registry.

Don't confuse Registry Editor with Registry Editor. Unfortunately, two applications have this name in Windows NT. This chapter discusses REGEDT32.EXE. However, Windows 3.x has a Registry Editor, too, retained in Windows NT for compatibility. The old Registry Editor is called REGEDIT.EXE and was used solely for recording file association and OLE information, which information is now contained within a branch of the Windows NT Registry.

Launching the Registry Editor opens a screen similar to the screen shown in figure 2.5.

Before exploring the Registry in the next sections, you should know about a couple of recommendations and one major warning:

▶ From the Registry Editor Options menu, select Read Only Mode. If a check mark precedes the option on the menu, the option is already selected. Working in Read Only mode prevents changes from being recorded to the Registry— which is the safest way to explore the Registry.

▶ Choose Options, Confirm on Delete. As with Read Only Mode, a check mark precedes the option on the menu when it has been selected. If the option isn't selected, pressing the Delete key irretrievably erases the selected Registry key and all its subkeys. By default, Confirm on Delete is selected, and it's automatically enabled when working in Read Only mode. In fact, in Read Only Mode, you cannot turn off Confirm on Delete.

▶ If you're using a production computer to explore the Registry, back up Registry files before you go any further.

Before you change anything using Registry Editor, you should understand that Microsoft washes its hands of its technical support responsibility if you edit the Registry directly. In other words, you're on your own. If after altering the Registry your computer does not boot, you can call Microsoft's Product Support Service Engineers, and they probably will do their best to help you. But their best may not be good enough. You may have to reinstall the operating system, or, at the very least, undertake the emergency repair process described in Chapter 6. Because the Registry Editor writes binary, ASCII, hex, or executable code directly into the Registry, a simple mistyped character can have disastrous consequences.

Navigating the Registry

Refer to the Registry Editor main window shown in figure 2.5 and examine it for a minute. Refer to it as you read the next section, which introduces some important MCSE terminology.

Notice that Registry Editor contains five child windows. If you conceptualize the Registry as a giant tree with branches and sub-branches and leaves, then these five windows are the roots of the tree. In Windows NT-parlance, these roots are called subtrees (and occasionally, predefined key handles). The five subtrees are as follows:

▶ **HKEY_LOCAL_MACHINE.** Stores all the computer-specific configuration data.

▶ **HKEY_USERS.** Stores all the user-specific configuration data.

▶ **HKEY_CURRENT_USER.** Stores all configuration data for the currently logged on user.

▶ **HKEY_CLASSES_ROOT.** Stores all OLE and file association information.

▶ **HKEY_CURRENT_CONFIG.** Stores information about the hardware profile specified at startup.

Before delving into a discussion of these subtrees, take a closer look at the foreground window in the Registry Editor. You might find it somewhat similar in appearance to Explorer. This is intentional: conceptually, it helps to picture the Registry as a series of directories, subdirectories, and files. Unfortunately, the Registry doesn't really work that way.

Several files collectively comprise the Registry, but they don't break down as evenly as they do in the interface. In fact, they hardly break down below the top level at all. Some of the data in the Registry actually never gets written to disk: it's dynamically collected every time the system boots and is stored in memory until the system is shut down.

Each of the folders that you see in the left pane of the subtree windows represents a key. A key is a category, a fitting abstraction, because keys don't really exist anywhere outside Registry Editor. As you also can see from the diagram, keys can contain subkeys (or subcategories); there is no limit to how far a branch can reach.

Eventually, however, branches sprout leaves. In the Registry, keys produce values. A value has three components: a name by which it is referenced in the Registry, a data type (text, binary, and so on), and the data itself.

The types of data that can be stored in the Registry have been defined, but look at how these data types are referenced in the Registry Editor:

- ▶ **REG_BINARY.** Indicates that binary data follows. The binary data, however, actually is stored as a string of hexadecimal pairs, which represent byte values (2 hex digits gives a range of 0 to 255 for each byte).

- ▶ **REG_DWORD.** Indicates that the data is stored in a word, a term applied to a four-byte number. Words can range in value from 0 to 4,294,967,295 (a 4 GB range, enough to accommodate the full address range of a 32-bit operating system).

- ▶ **REG_SZ.** Denotes a string value. A string is simply text.

- ▶ **REG_MULTI_SZ.** Denotes a multiple string, which actually appears as a list in the Registry, with each list item separated by a null character.

- ▶ **REG_EXPAND_SZ.** Indicates an expandable string, which really is a variable. For instance, %SystemRoot% is an expandable string that Windows NT would interpret as the actual root directory for the operating system.

HKEY_LOCAL_MACHINE

HKEY_LOCAL_MACHINE contains all configuration information relevant to the local machine (see fig. 2.6). Every piece of information that applies to the local computer, regardless of who (if anyone) is logged on, gets stored somewhere in this subtree.

This subtree has five subkeys: HARDWARE, SAM, SECURITY, SOFTWARE, and SYSTEM.

Figure 2.6

The Registry HKEY_LOCAL_MACHINE key.

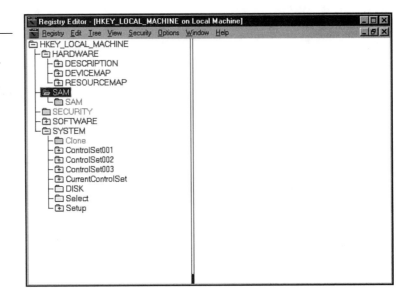

HARDWARE

The Hardware key is the only volatile key in HKEY_LOCAL_MACHINE—its data is never saved to or read from a file. Instead, Windows NT automatically detects the current hardware every time the operating system is booted and stores that information under the Hardware key under the following three subkeys: Description, DeviceMap, and ResourceMap (see fig. 2.7).

Description

The Description subkey contains the hardware database as detected by Windows NT during system boot. On Intel-based computers, the Windows NT hardware recognizer (NTDETECT.COM) autodetects this information. On RISC-based computers, the computer's firmware reads this information.

Figure 2.7

The HKEY_LOCAL_MACHINE Hardware key.

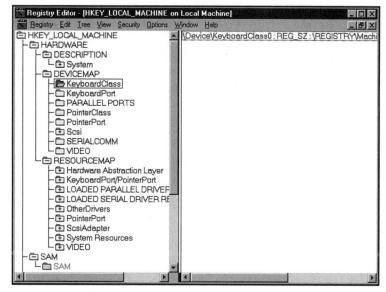

Entries for the CPU (CentralProcessor), math coprocessor (FloatingPointProcessor), and <multifunction_adapter>, which is usually called Multifunction Adapter (except in EISA computers, where it is called EisaAdapter) are listed at the top of the following tree:

```
HKEY_LOCAL_MACHINE\HARDWARE\DESCRIPTION\System
```

The <multifunction_adapter> entry enumerates the rest of the devices on the system, including the hard disk controller and serial and parallel ports.

Each device key has an Identifier value, which contains the "name" of each detected device—information that can prove helpful when troubleshooting hardware information.

DeviceMap

The subkeys of this subkey enumerate the Windows NT device drivers currently in use with pointers to the configuration information for each driver contained elsewhere in the Registry; to be exact:

```
HKEY_LOCAL_MACHINE\SYSTEM\CurrentControlSet\Services
```

ResourceMap

The ResourceMap key tracks IRQ, DMA, and other resource allocation for and by each driver. If two devices are competing for a specific resource, the information in ResourceMap can tell you which devices are conflicting—although the information isn't readable; you need to use another front-end, like Windows NT Diagnostics (WINMSD.EXE) to view it in a readable form. (See Chapter 6 for more information on WINMSD.)

SAM

SAM, Security Accounts Manager, is the Registry key that contains the entire user and group account database. As such, it sure is tempting to poke around in it a bit. Unfortunately for would-be techno-predators, but fortunately for administrators, this key is off-limits even to administrators. The only way to modify the data that SAM contains is to use the User Manager utility (or User Manager for Domains on a Windows NT Server domain controller). SAM is actually a subkey of the SECURITY key:

```
HKEY_LOCAL_MACHINE\SECURITY\SAM
```

SECURITY

Besides mirroring the SAM key, SECURITY also contains all the policy information discussed in Chapter 3, well as local group membership information. As with SAM, this key is off-limits to all users (including administrators). To modify this information, an application such as User Manager must make a call to the Windows NT Security API.

SOFTWARE

SOFTWARE is a particularly busy key: it defines and maintains configuration data for all Win32 software on the computer, including Windows NT itself (see fig. 2.8). At least five, and often more, subkeys are available here: Classes, Microsoft, Program Groups, Secure, Windows 3.1 Migration Status, and perhaps additional subkeys for other software vendors besides Microsoft.

Figure 2.8

The HKEY_LOCAL_ MACHINE Soft- ware key.

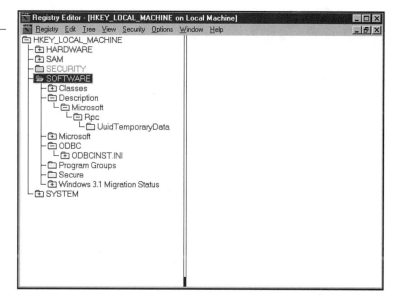

Classes

File association and OLE information is stored in this subkey (see fig. 2.9), which evolved from the old Windows 3.x configuration registry. In fact, to maintain compatibility with the old Win3.x registry addressing scheme, this information is mirrored in the HKEY_CLASSES_ROOT subtree. The applications themselves handle OLE configuration, and file association using File Manager hasn't changed since Windows 3.1.

Microsoft

This is one of the more populated keys in the Registry: it contains subkeys for all Microsoft software installed on the Windows NT-based computer (see fig. 2.10). Most of these entries are for Windows NT itself and its related components (Browser, Clipbook Server, Mail, and so on), but others are for Microsoft Office, Cinemania 96, or whatever Microsoft applications you may have installed.

This key sets the rule for other vendors' keys as well. Typically, you can expect to find one key at this level for each software vendor with subkeys for each installed title published by that vendor.

Figure 2.9

First page of the HKEY_LOCAL_ MACHINE\Software\ Classes subkey.

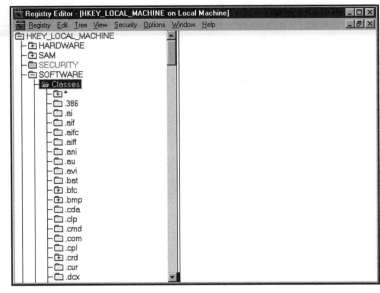

Figure 2.10

The first page of the HKEY_ LOCAL_ MACHINE\ SOFTWARE\ Microsoft subkey.

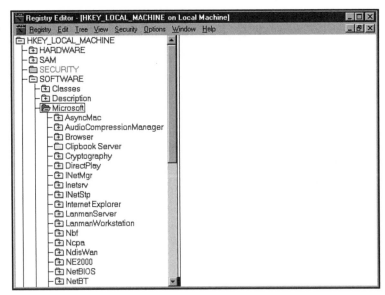

Of particular interest is the following key:

```
HKEY_LOCAL_MACHINE\SOFTWARE\Microsoft\Windows NT\CurrentVersion
```

You can find various useful items under this key, such as the name and company of the user who installed the operating system (which you can change from here), the current build number, the current service pack, and other items specific to Windows NT.

Program Groups

In Windows NT, the program groups in the Programs menu can be personal, in which case they appear only on the desktop of the user that created them, or common, in which case they appear on the desktop of anyone who logs on at the computer. The HKEY_LOCAL_MACHINE\SOFTWARE\Program Groups Registry subkey contains a list of just the common program groups for this computer (the personal program groups are stored under HKEY_USERS because it's user-specific information).

Secure

This key actually goes completely unused by Windows NT, although other applications (such as Microsoft Exchange Server) use it to maintain configuration data restricted to administrator access.

Windows 3.1 Migration Status

If you installed Windows NT Workstation in the same directory as an old copy of Windows 3.x or Windows for Workgroups 3.x, certain computer-specific configuration items from Win3.x were migrated to Windows NT when the system rebooted for the first time. These items include the REG.DAT file and certain WIN.INI settings. The presence of this key indicates that the migration is complete. To force the migration to occur again, you can simply delete this key.

SYSTEM

The critical HKEY_LOCAL_MACHINE\SYSTEM subkey maintains information about the device drivers and services installed on a Windows NT-based computer (see fig. 2.11). The SYSTEM key contains numerous subkeys, most of which are called ControlSets because they contain configuration settings used to control the devices and services on the computer. Each ControlSet contains four subkeys: Control, Enum, Hardware Profiles, and Services.

The Control key maintains information necessary to control the computer, such as the current time zone, the list of drivers to load during system boot, and the name of the computer as seen on the network. The Services key configures background processes that control hardware devices, file systems, network services, and so on.

Figure 2.11

The HKEY_LOCAL_ MACHINE\ SYSTEM\ CurrentControlSet subkey.

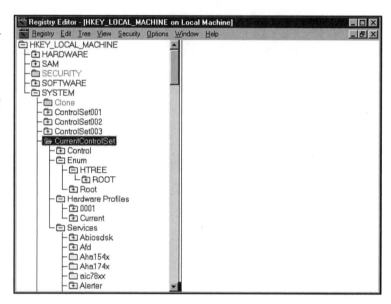

Typically, you see a ControlSet001 and ControlSet002. You also might see a ControlSet003 and even a ControlSet004. Potentially, the four possible ControlSets are as follows:

▶ **Current.** The ControlSet used to successfully boot the computer for the current session.

▶ **Default.** The ControlSet to be used to boot the system the next time the computer reboots.

▶ **Failed.** The ControlSet that attempted but failed to boot the system for this current session.

▶ **LastKnownGood.** The ControlSet that was used to successfully boot the computer for the current session and has been backed up in case the Default ControlSet fails the next time the system is rebooted.

Each of the ControlSet00x entries maps to at least one of these four types of ControlSets. You can view the mappings by examining the HKEY_LOCAL_MACHINE\SYSTEM\Select key. The values for this key are entries for each of the preceding ControlSets. The data for each value is the x in a ControlSet00x entry.

Typically, only two ControlSet00x entries appear. One of these maps to both Current and Default, and because the Current ControlSet was successful, it's used as the Default ControlSet for the next reboot. The other ControlSet00x entry maps to LastKnownGood.

If you do see a third ControlSet00x entry, it most likely indicates a configuration change made during the current session. Because the Current ControlSet (the one used to boot the system) no longer is the Default ControlSet (the one used to boot the system next time), a separate ControlSet00x entry must exist for Current and Default.

A fourth ControlSet00x entry should exist only if your computer failed to restart and had to resort to the LastKnownGood configuration. In this case, the ControlSet that was Default and would have been Current becomes Failed, and LastKnownGood becomes Current.

The Clone subkey of the SYSTEM key is a temporary holding area that Windows NT uses for creating the LastKnownGood ControlSet, and the CurrentControlSet subkey is a mirror of whichever ControlSet00x entry contains the Current ControlSet. The final subkey is the Setup key, which the Windows NT Setup program uses. Administrators and users have no need to go here.

HKEY_CLASSES_ROOT

As mentioned earlier, the HKEY_CLASSES_ROOT subtree is a mirror of HKEY_LOCAL_MACHINE\SOFTWARE\Classes. It's mirrored here to provide compatibility with the Windows 3.x registration database, which also is accessed using the HKEY_CLASSES_ROOT handle.

HKEY_CURRENT_USER

The HKEY_CURRENT_USER subtree contains the user profile for the currently logged-on user (refer to fig. 2.5). Profiles contain all user preferences and restrictions, including Control Panel settings, personal program groups, printer connections, network drive connections, bookmarks in WinHelp, and even the most recently accessed documents in Microsoft Word. User profiles are discussed in-depth later in this chapter.

HKEY_CURRENT_USER maps to HKEY_USERS\<SID_of_current_user>, in which SID is the lengthy Security Identifier associated with the user. Occasionally, keys in this subtree duplicate keys found in HKEY_LOCAL_MACHINE but with different values. HKEY_CURRENT_USER almost always overrides HKEY_LOCAL_MACHINE.

HKEY_USERS

HKEY_USERS can potentially contain the user profiles for all users defined in the accounts database, although in practice it usually contains only the default user profile (HKEY_USERS\.DEFAULT) and the profile for the currently logged on user (HKEY_USERS\<SID_of_current_user>, mapped also to HKEY_CURRENT_USER) (see fig. 2.12).

People frequently ask why Microsoft chose not to load all the user profiles in this subtree. The answer is that it isn't necessary and probably disadvantageous. Remember that the Registry resides in memory. The more data in the Registry, the more memory the Registry uses. Because the only user profile required in memory at any given time is the profile in use by the current user, loading the other users' profiles as well is unnecessary. If you do need to alter another user's profile, however, you can do so.

HKEY_CURRENT_CONFIG

The HKEY_CURRENT_CONFIG subtree contains information about the current hardware profile for the system. You learn more about hardware profiles later in this chapter.

Figure 2.12

*The
HKEY_USERS
subtree.*

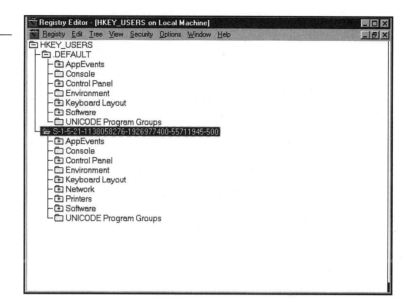

Editing the Registry

To edit any value in the Registry, simply double-click on the value
in Registry Editor. A dialog box appears with the current value
selected. You may enter the data for a new value at this point.
Choosing OK effectively enters the value in the Registry. Don't
look for a "save settings?" prompt message when you close Registry Editor; your changes are saved as soon as you make them.

You must leave Read Only mode to add a Registry value or
key. Choose the Options menu and deselect Read Only
Mode.

To add a value to an existing key, use the following procedure:

1. Select the key for which you want to add a value.

2. Choose Edit, Add Value to open the Add Value dialog box
    (see fig. 2.13).

Figure 2.13

*Adding a value to
an existing key.*

3. In the Value Name text box, enter the name of the new value.

4. Select the appropriate data type from the Data Type combo box and choose OK.

5. In the String Editor dialog box, enter the data for the new value.

To add a new key to the Registry, use this procedure:

1. Select the key under which you want to insert the new key.

2. Choose Edit, Add Key.

3. In the Add Key dialog box, enter a name for the new key in the Key Name box and then choose OK.

To delete a key or a value, simply select the key or value and press Delete. Again, be cautious: you cannot undo deletions any more than you can undo additions or changes. Every action taken in Registry Editor is irreversible (except through manual intervention). Therefore, you should enable Confirm on Delete from the Options menu. If it's already activated, a check mark appears immediately to its left.

Searching the Registry

Unfortunately, Microsoft hasn't included a thorough search utility for use with the Registry (odd, considering the nice facility available for the Windows 95 Registry). Here are your options:

▶ **Find Key.** (Accessed via the View menu.) Searches only the Registry Keys for the desired search string. You can't search for specific values using Find Key. Also, the Find Key command works only in the selected subtree, and in that subtree only from the current key onward. You can't search more than one subtree using a single Find Key command.

▶ **Save Subtree As.** (Accessed via the Registry menu.) Saves up to an entire subtree in a text file that any ASCII text editor or word processor can view. Before choosing this command, choose the key you want to use as the top level of your subtree. Registry Editor populates the text file with that key and its children. From the file, you can then perform a search using a word processor or text editor.

▶ **Print Subtree.** (Accessed via the Registry menu.) Converts the selected key and its descendants into text. Instead of saving it to a text file, however, this command directs its output to a printer.

True masters of Windows NT are true students of the Windows NT Registry, and the best way to study the Registry is to print a copy of each subtree using the Print Subtree command. Armed with a hard copy of your Registry, begin to peruse the Windows NT Resource Guide, which thoroughly documents the major (and most of the minor) Registry entries. Whatever the Resource Guide misses, the REGENTRY.HLP file, which accompanies the Resource Guide on CD-ROM, more than picks up the slack. REGENTRY.HLP is an excellent hypertext guide to the Registry. You can download REGENTRY.HLP free from Microsoft's FTP server: `ftp.microsoft.com`.

Windows NT Control Panel

The Windows NT Control Panel is a collection of small applications that each provide an interface to the Registry for the purpose of editing some specific Windows NT component (see fig. 2.14). The Control Panel is usually the first place to look if you need to make a change to your Windows NT configuration.

Figure 2.14

The Control Panel window.

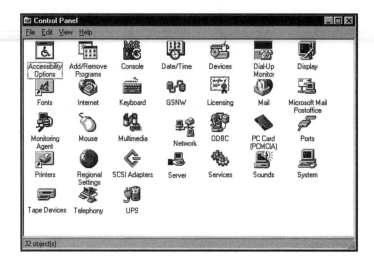

To open the Control Panel, choose Start, Settings, Control Panel. The Control Panel applications each have a specific purpose, and you'll hear them described throughout this book. This section will introduce you to the Control Panel System application. In later sections, you'll learn about the Network application, the Licensing application, and the various Control Panel applications that let you install and configure peripherals and other devices. Refer to Appendix B for a guided tour of Control Panel applications.

The System application is a typical Control Panel application. The System application is a smorgasbord of system-wide configuration parameters. Because the System application is a fairly important configuration tool, and because it doesn't fall very neatly into any of the later section in this chapter, I'll describe it for you here as an example of a Control Panel application.

Double-click on the System application in Control Panel. The System Properties dialog box will appear. The System Properties dialog box tabs are discussed in the following sections.

Startup/Shutdown

The Startup/Shutdown tab enables you to set the default boot menu option for the system startup (see fig. 2.15). It also enables you to define some recovery options in case the system encounters a STOP error.

Figure 2.15

The System Properties Startup/ Shutdown tab.

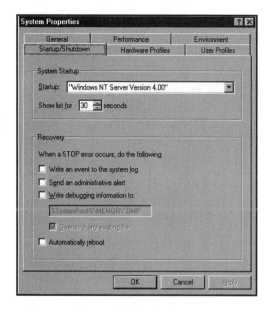

When a Windows NT-based computer is booted, the information in BOOT.INI is used to build the Boot Loader menu that appears before Windows NT loads. Boot Loader menu options typically include Windows NT Workstation 4, Windows NT Workstation 4 [VGA mode], and any other operating system set up to dual-boot with Windows NT. Although BOOT.INI is a text file, you take a risk when you edit it directly; a mistyped character can have disastrous results. The Startup/Shutdown tab provides a safe way to configure the default operating system and the length of time the Boot Loader waits for a selection before proceeding to load the default operating system(the Startup selection).

The Recovery section of the Startup/Shutdown tab determines what happens in the event of a system crash. Any one or all of the four options can be used at any given time:

▶ **Write an event to the system log.** This option records an event that can be viewed using Event Viewer.

▶ **Send an administrative alert.** If the Alerter and Messenger services are running, alerts are sent to designated users and workstations if the system crashes.

▶ **Write debugging information to.** This option launches a program called SAVEDUMP.EXE whenever a system crash occurs. SAVEDUMP.EXE writes the entire contents of the computer's memory to the pagefile and flags it so that when the system reboots, the pagefile will be copied to the file specified in this option. Note that you can overwrite an existing file which may have been generated by an old crash dump. The dump file can then be sent to a debugger or a PSS Engineer for analysis. Before this option can work, your computer's boot partition must have a pagefile of at least the size of your computer's memory.

▶ **Automatically reboot.** This option may be useful if a power surge or an errant application causes a crash (although the latter is extremely unlikely). If the problem is hardware-related, however, the same problem is likely to occur after you restart the system.

Hardware Profiles

The Hardware Profiles tab enables you to create new hardware profiles and change the order of precedence among hardware profiles (see fig. 2.16). Click on the Properties button to define a docking state for a portable computer or to enable/disable network hardware.

To create a new hardware profile, select an existing profile and click on the Copy button. In the subsequent Copy Profile dialog box, enter a name for the new hardware profile. The new hardware profile will appear in the Available Hardware Profiles list.

If you have defined more than one hardware profile, Windows NT displays a menu of hardware profiles at startup and asks which profile you want to use. The profile you specify becomes the active hardware profile. Any changes to your hardware configuration affect the active hardware profile.

Figure 2.16

The System Properties Hardware Profiles tab.

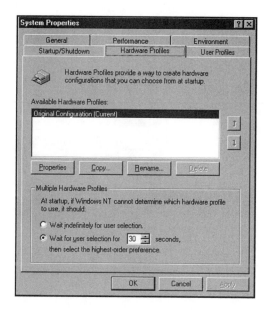

The up and down arrows to the right of the Available Hardware Profiles list let you change the preference order of the hardware profiles. The radio buttons at the bottom of the Hardware Profiles tab let you specify whether Windows NT waits indefinitely for you to choose a hardware profile, or whether the choice defaults to the highest-preference profile after a specific time interval.

Environment

The Environment tab enables you to define system and user environment variables (see fig. 2.17). The system environment variables are written to the following key:

```
HKEY_LOCAL_MACHINESYSTEM\CurrentControlSetControl\Session
Manager\Environment
```

You have to be an administrator before you can alter the System environment variables using Control Panel.

The User Variables section is the only area of this application that non-administrators can access and configure.

To set or change a user environment variable, follow these steps:

Figure 2.17

The System Properties Environment tab.

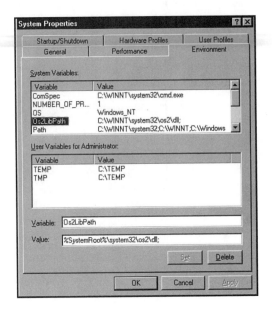

1. Select the environment variable you want to change. (The variable and value appear in the Variable and Value text boxes.)

2. Position the cursor at (or tab down to) the Variable or the Value text box.

3. Change the variable or value (or both).

4. Click on the Set button.

To create a new environment variable and set its value, do these steps:

1. Click in the System Variables list box if you want to add a system variable; click in the User Variables for Administrator list box if you want to add a user variable.

2. Click in the Variable text box and enter the name of the new variable.

3. Click in the Value text box and enter the value for the new variable.

4. Click on the Set button.

To delete an environment variable, follow these steps:

1. Select the variable in the System Variables list or User Variables for Administrator list.

2. Click on the Delete button.

Performance

The Application Performance setting of the Performance tab enables you to boost the response time for the foreground application (see fig. 2.18). Click on the Change button in the Virtual Memory section to open the Virtual Memory dialog box, which maintains settings for Paging file sizes and Registry size (see fig. 2.19).

Figure 2.18

The System Properties Performance tab.

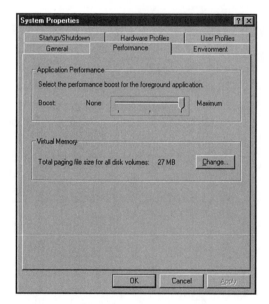

General

The System Properties General tab displays some basic information about your computer: the operating system and version number, the processor type and the amount of RAM, and the registration names from NT Setup.

Figure 2.19

The Virtual Memory dialog box.

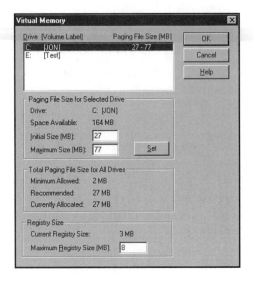

Configuring Protocols and Protocol Bindings

The Control Panel Network application is a central spot for entering and altering network configuration information. The five tabs of the Network application are as follows:

▶ **Identification.** The Identification tab specifies the computer name for the computer and the domain to which it belongs (see fig. 2.20). Click on the Change button to change the values. If your Windows NT computer is a domain controller, you cannot move to a different domain, but you can change domain's name using the Change button. If your Windows NT computer is a workstation or a member server, the Change button offers several alternatives (see fig. 2.21). You can join a workgroup or domain, or you can set up an account for the computer in the domain's security database.

Figure 2.20

The Network application Identification tab.

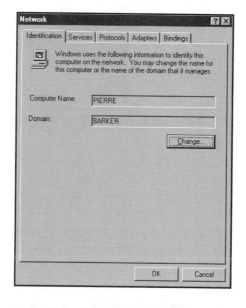

Figure 2.21

The Identification Changes dialog box for a non-domain controller, invoked from the Network application Identification tab.

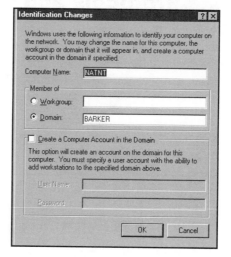

▶ **Services.** The Services tab lets you add, remove, or configure network services (see fig. 2.22). Network services were described earlier in this chapter. Click on the Add button to view a list of available network services. Click on the Properties button to view and configuration information for the service.

Figure 2.22

The Network application Services tab.

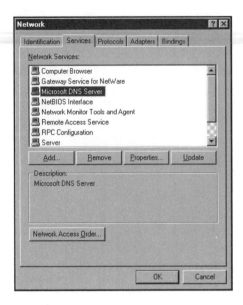

▶ **Protocols.** The Protocols tab lets you add, remove, and configure network protocols (see fig. 2.23). Some of the protocol configuration options are discussed later in this chapter.

Figure 2.23

The Network application Protocols tab.

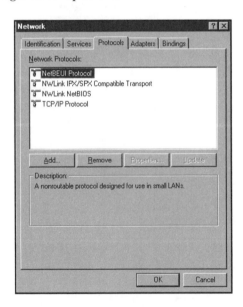

▶ **Adapters.** The Adapters tab lets you add, remove, and configure network adapter cards for the system (see fig. 2.24).

Click on Add to view a list of available network adapter card drivers. The Properties button lets you configure the IRQ and the Port address for the adapter.

Figure 2.24

The Network application Adapters tab.

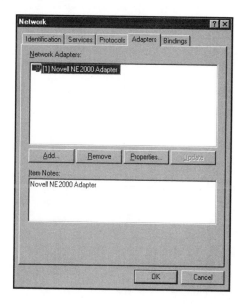

▶ **Bindings.** A binding is a potential pathway from a particular network service to a network protocol to a network adapter. The Bindings tab tabulates the bindings for the system. In figure 2.25, the Workstation service is bound to the Net-BEUI, WINS Client (TCP/IP), and NWLink NetBIOS protocols. Click on the plus sign beside the protocol to reveal the adapters that are bound to the protocol for the particular service. Much of the binding configuration takes place automatically. If you install Remote Access Service and enable TCP/IP, for example, the Remote Access WAN Wrapper appears beneath the WINS Client (TCP/IP) protocol.

Microsoft lists the following objective for the Windows NT Server exam:

Configure protocols and protocol bindings. Protocols include: TCP/IP, NWLink IPX/SPX Compatible Transport, NetBEUI.

Figure 2.25

The Network application Bindings tab.

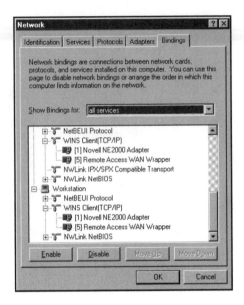

Installing and Configuring NWLink

For an exercise testing this information, see end of chapter.

All Windows NT networking components are installed and configured in the Control Panel Network application. If you want to install the NWLink protocol, choose the Protocols tab and click on the Add button. The message Building Network Protocol Option List appears briefly, and then you are prompted to select a networking component.

Select NWLink IPX/SPX Compatible Transport. You need to steer Setup toward the original source files at this point. (You might need to point Setup to the Microsoft Windows NT Workstation CD-ROM.) If Remote Access Services is installed on your system, Setup asks if you want to configure RAS to support NWLink. After the NWLink files finish installing, an icon labeled NWLink IPX/SPX Compatible Transport appears in the Network Protocols list of the Protocols tab. You must shut down and restart your computer before the changes can take effect.

Figure 2.26 shows the NWLink IPX/SPX Properties dialog box. To reach the NWLink IPX/SPX Properties dialog box, select NWLink IPX/SPX Compatible Transport in the Network application Protocols tab and click on the Properties button. Windows

NT automatically detects your network adapter at Startup. If you know which frame type is in use on your network, you can use this dialog box to manually set Windows NT to match it. By default, Windows NT is configured to autodetect the frame type, which it does by sending out a Routing Information Protocol (RIP) request on all frame types when NWLink is initialized. One of the following scenarios will occur:

Figure 2.26

The NWLink IPX/ SPX Properties dialog box.

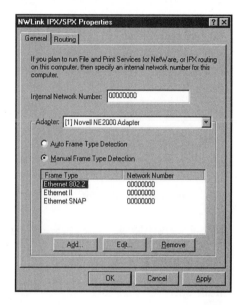

▶ **No response from any of the frame types.** NWLink uses the default frame type, which is 802.2 when Windows NT is first installed.

▶ **A response from one of the frame types.** NWLink uses this frame type, which also becomes the default protocol the next time autodetection occurs.

▶ **Multiple responses are received.** NWLink steps through this list (in order) until it finds a frame type that was one of the multiple responses:

   ▶ Ethernet 802.2

   ▶ Ethernet 802.3

▶ Ethernet II

▶ SNAP

You can configure both Windows NT Workstation and Windows NT Server for multiple frame types, but you can use Control Panel Network to do so only for Server. If you want Windows NT Workstation to use multiple frame types, you must edit the registry directly with RegEdit. Find the following key and change the PktType value (which is of type REG_MULTI_SZ) to any combination of the following numbers:

```
HKEY_LOCAL_MACHINE\SYSTEM\CurrentControlSet\Services\NWlnkIpx\
~NetConfig\<NIC_Driver>
```

▶ 0 Ethernet II

▶ 1 Ethernet 802.3

▶ 2 Ethernet 802.2

▶ 3 Ethernet SNAP

▶ 4 ARCnet

Make sure you're using the correct frame type for your network; an incorrect frame type can cause an immense slowdown in network performance. If, because Auto Detected is selected, you cannot determine what frame type your Windows NT-based computer is using, use the IPXROUTE CONFIG command from the command prompt. You get an instant report of the frame type(s) in use.

If you're not sure which frame type(s) your other servers and clients are using, here is a list of which frame types particular servers use:

▶ **802.2.** Windows NT Workstation 3.5x, Windows NT Server 3.5x, NetWare 4.x, NetWare, 3.12, Windows for Workgroups 3.11 from the Windows NT Server CD, Microsoft Network Client 3.0

▶ **802.3.** Windows NT 3.1, Windows NT Advanced Server 3.1, NetWare 3.11 and below, Windows for Workgroups 3.x retail.

The preceding are the defaults for the listed operating systems; your mileage, as they say, may vary. To verify the frame type on a NetWare server, check its AUTOEXEC.NCF file.

The Network Number field at the bottom of the NWLink IPX/SPX Properties dialog box reveals one additional configuration parameter, the Internal Network Number.

The Internal Network Number is similar to a subnet address on a TCP/IP network; that is, it determines which servers are considered "local" and which ones are considered "remote." The default setting here is 0, which forces Windows NT to send out a RIP request and wait for the closest NetWare server to respond with the proper internal network number.

Working with TCP/IP

Of all the protocols that ship with Windows NT, TCP/IP requires the most configuration by the administrator. Nevertheless, TCP/IP is an integral part of the Internet, and it's becoming an increasingly popular protocol for private networks as well. The section defines some important TCP/IP concepts, describes how to configure TCP/IP on a Windows NT machine, and looks at some of the important commands and tools that will assist you in implementing TCP/IP on your network. This discussion is by no means complete or exhaustive; NRP's *MCSE Study Guide: TCP/IP and SMS* furnishes a thorough discussion of TCP/IP addressing and configuration. This book discusses the basics, the parameters that are necessary to install any TCP/IP network client.

TCP/IP is one of those broad topics that is difficult to position in either the MCSE Server or Enterprise exam. Microsoft's exam objectives include TCP/IP protocols and bindings with the Server exam but reserve TCP/IP-related topics such as DHCP, WINS, and DNS for the Enterprise exam. Nevertheless, it is difficult to even describe how to configure TCP/IP without at least touching on DHCP, WINS, and DNS. Microsoft's Windows NT Core Technologies course includes material on DHCP, WINS, and DNS, and these services are an important component of even smaller Microsoft networks.

IP Address

In any type of network, communication between computers is possible only when you have a bulletproof way for uniquely identifying any computer on the network. At the lowest level, packets are sent from one network card to another, and it's the serial numbers burned into the card itself that serve to identify the sender and receiver.

Most networks cannot see that far down, however, so they apply another level (or perhaps more than one level) of addressing to ensure compatibility across different platforms. The Internet Protocol (the IP in TCP/IP) sends packets using a computer's IP Address (a unique 32-bit binary number that no other computer on the network can possess). Actually, it's about time to stop speaking in terms of computers and begin speaking in terms of network interface cards (NICs): each NIC requires its own IP Address.

Because a 32-bit binary address isn't any easier to remember than the hexadecimal NIC address burned into the card (try 10000011011010110000001011001000 on for size), the 32-bit address usually is expressed as four octets, or eight-bit numbers, which then are represented in decimal form. An eight-bit number can have a value of anywhere from 0 to 255, so an IP address consists of four numbers between 0 and 255 separated by decimal points. The 32-bit binary address in the beginning of this paragraph can also be written like this: 131.107.2.200.

Subnet Mask

Each IP address consists of a netid and a hostid. The netid is the left-most portion of the address and assigns an address every NIC on the same physical network shares. If other physical networks are interconnected via routers (these physical networks are called subnetworks or simply, subnets), each of these networks must have its own unique netid. The hostid is the right-most portion of the IP address, and a unique hostid must be assigned to every network adapter that shares a common netid.

The netid/hostid split isn't always fifty-fifty; a parameter called the Subnet Mask determines how many bits are devoted to each field. The Subnet Mask also is a 32-bit number, and each bit set to 1 denotes a bit assigned to the netid; each bit set to 0 denotes a bit assigned to the hostid.

Some platforms' implementations of TCP/IP do not require the administrator to configure a subnet mask. That doesn't mean that the subnet mask isn't required, just that the operating system is using default subnet masks.

Default subnet masks are defined by the three Internet classes of IP Addresses:

▶ **Class A.** The first octet belongs to the netid and the others to the hostid. Class A netids can range from 0 to 127 (although both 0 and 127 are excluded—see the section "The Rules," later in this chapter), which means that there can only be 126 class A networks in the entire Internet, and because three octets are available for the hostid, each of these 126 networks can host more than 16 million NICs. Odds are, you probably won't be using one of these.

▶ **Class B.** The first two octets define the netid, and the next two octets define the hostid. The first octet of the netid can range from 128 to 191. Combined with the unrestricted second octet, there is room for more than 16,000 Class B networks, each with the capacity for more than 65,000 NICs. These are more common than Class A networks, but still a bit of overkill for most networks.

▶ **Class C.** The first three octets define the netid, and the last octet is the hostid. The first octet of the netid can range from 192 to 223, and combined with the second and third octets, you can have more than two million Class C networks on the Internet. Each of these is restricted to only 254 hosts, however (the extremes in either field are always excluded). This is the most common type of IP address the InterNIC assigns.

You can see that the problem of relying on the default subnets is that if you have more than 254 NICs to support on a single network, you either need to segment your network, or move to a Class B address and probably waste many of the 65,000 hostids that cannot be assigned elsewhere.

That's why the subnet mask comes in handy. Here are the subnet masks for the various classes of networks:

▶ Class A: 255.0.0.0

▶ Class B: 255.255.0.0

▶ Class C: 255.255.255.0

Defaults are an all or nothing deal, but by borrowing some bits from the hostid and tacking them on to the netid, you can take a Class B address and share it among multiple physical networks. You would be well advised to check out the TCP/IP study guide because unless you are already a TCP/IP administrator, you need more depth than this book can devote.

Default Gateway

A default gateway is a router, a device that sends packets on to a remote network. A router can be a device created for that purpose, such as Cisco or 3Com makes, or it can be a Windows NT-based computer that has at least two network cards (for spanning two networks). When a packet is sent to a remote netid, IP forwards the packet to the default gateway in the hopes that it knows where to send the packet. Although strictly speaking, default gateways are optional parameters, without one, communications are limited to the local subnet.

Putting It Together

An important point to remember is that every computer on the internetwork must have a unique IP address. When your internetwork is the Internetwork, that's pretty hard to ensure. Here are a few things to keep in mind:

▶ If you're on the public Internet, apply for a range of addresses from the Internet Network Information Center (InterNIC). The InterNIC is the closest thing the Internet has to a governing body, and it's the organization responsible for tracking and assigning the usage of IP addresses. You can reach the InterNIC via e-mail at hostmaster@internic.net and via the U.S. Postal Service at 505 Huntmar Park Drive, Herndon, VA 22070.

▶ If you aren't on the public Internet, consider applying to the InterNIC anyway. Odds are, you'll be on the Internet sooner or later.

▶ If you're absolutely sure that you don't need Internet connectivity (most likely because you plan to use a proxy server such as Microsoft's forthcoming Catapult project), you may use any IP addresses you like, as long as they're unique within your private internetwork, and as long as they follow the rules.

The Rules

This section doesn't pretend to be a complete discussion of IP addressing requirements, but it does lay out a couple cardinal rules that every TCP/IP administrator must know.

▶ **Rule #1.** Don't go to extremes. Hostids cannot be set to all zeroes or all ones, because these denote broadcast messages rather than a specifically targeted message. An easy rule of thumb is to stay away from 0 and 255 when assigning octets.

▶ **Rule #2.** Don't use 127 as a netid. When 127 is used as the first octet of a netid, TCP/IP recognizes the address as a special diagnostic address called the *loopback address*, so called because any message to this address is returned to its sender. 127 addresses are used to test the configuration of a TCP/IP-based computer.

▶ **Rule #3.** All netids on a subnet must match. If an NIC doesn't have the same netid as the rest of the NICs on its subnet, the host can't communicate with the other hosts on the subnet. Likewise, if a host on a remote subnet is configured using the netid of the local subnet, communication between the two subnets becomes impossible because the packets are never routed because they appear to the local host as the local netid.

▶ **Rule #4.** All hostids in a subnet must be unique. If, on a subnet, two hosts share a hostid, the results are unpredictable—and certainly unwanted. If a Windows NT-based computer attempts to join the network with a duplicate hostid, Windows NT doesn't let it join the network; it sends a message to both the usurper and the usurpee explaining the problem. If a non-Windows NT-based host joins the network with a duplicate hostid, the results can range from the intercepting of the other host's packets, to the locking up of the usurper's computer (and perhaps the usurpee's as well if it isn't a Windows NT-based computer). In short, keep careful tabs on your IP addresses, or use the DHCP protocol described later in this chapter.

Installing TCP/IP

To install TCP/IP, start from the Control Panel Network application. Choose the Protocols tab and click on the Add button. Select TCP/IP Protocol. Choose OK.

Installing and Configuring TCP/IP with DHCP

When you install TCP/IP, Setup asks if you want to use DHCP to dynamically provide IP addresses. DHCP stands for Dynamic Host Configuration Protocol; rather than keep tabs yourself on where your IP addresses have been assigned at any given moment, a Windows NT Server running DHCP can do it for you. A DHCP server leases addresses to clients when they join the network.

If you have a DHCP server on your subnet, or if your routers can forward DHCP packets (ask your vendor if the router is RFC 1542 compliant if you aren't sure) consider choosing Yes for the prompt shown in figure 2.27. The DHCP client is assigned an IP address automatically when it restarts.

Figure 2.27

The DHCP prompt in TCP/IP.

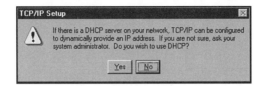

Selecting the DHCP option enables DHCP for all network interface cards in the computer. To selectively assign DHCP to individual NICs in a multihomed computer (a computer with more than one NIC), don't select DHCP at this time. Choose No. You can configure each NIC separately in the Microsoft TCP/IP Properties dialog box.

If Remote Access Services (RAS) is installed on your system, Setup asks if you want to configure RAS to support the TCP/IP protocol. After the installation finishes, choose Close in the Network application main window and the Microsoft TCP/IP Properties dialog box appears (see fig. 2.28).

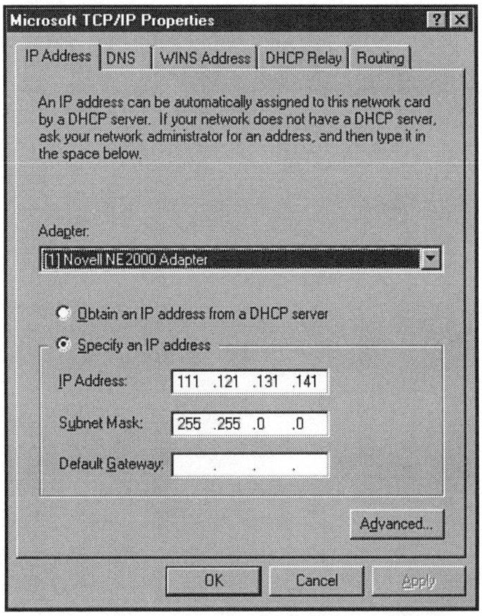

Figure 2.28

The Microsoft TCP/IP Properties dialog box.

In the Adapter drop-down list in the IP Address tab of the Microsoft TCP/IP Properties dialog box, you may select any of the network adapters you have installed on your computer. After you select a network adapter, you have one more chance to Enable Automatic DHCP Configuration. If you enable the Obtain an IP address from a DHCP server radio button, the IP Address and Subnet Mask for this network adapter becomes grayed out, because that information henceforth comes from a DHCP server. You may still specify a Default Gateway by clicking on the Advanced button, but this information can come from a DHCP server as well. Any information you enter at this screen overrides the DHCP-assigned information.

The Advanced button opens the Advanced IP Addressing dialog box (see fig. 2.29). The Advanced IP Addressing dialog box lets you enter multiple IP addresses for a single network adapter, which enables administrators to create logical networks within a single physical network; virtual subnets, you might say. Each IP Address also requires its own Subnet Mask entry. You also may enter multiple Default Gateways for each network adapter. The arrow buttons allow you to adjust the order in which the gateways are tried. If the gateway at the top of the list fails, the second one is used unless it too fails, in which case the third one is used, and so on down the list.

Figure 2.29

The Advanced IP Addressing dialog box.

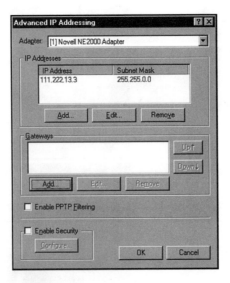

Select the Enable Security check box and click on the Configure button to open the TCP/IP Security dialog box, which lets you selectively enable TCP ports, UDP ports, and IP protocols.

Installing and Configuring TCP/IP Manually

If you really want to configure TCP/IP manually, you must enter an IP Address and Subnet Mask for each NIC. Although Windows NT doesn't consider the Default Gateway mandatory, you probably should enter your router's IP address here (that is, if you want to communicate with remote subnets). To enable IP routing, select the Routing tab in the Microsoft TCP/IP Properties dialog box and enable the Enable IP Routing check box.

What Is WINS?

The WINS Address tab in the Microsoft TCP/IP Properties dialog box lets you specify IP addresses for Primary and Secondary WINS Servers (see fig. 2.30). Although WINS is another service included only with Windows NT Server, as with DHCP, Windows NT Workstations can act as clients to a WINS server.

Figure 2.30

The WINS Address tab of the Microsoft TCP/IP Properties dialog box.

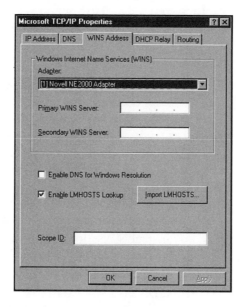

WINS stands for Windows Internet Name Service. WINS is a service that maps NetBIOS names to IP addresses. Four decimal octets rather than the full 32-bit binary number are used for configuring IP addresses because it's easier to remember the four decimal octets. Of course, that is a relative concept; it isn't all that easy to remember 131.107.2.200, either.

To make things more user-friendly as well as to maintain the UNC convention across the board, Windows NT includes a NetBIOS layer that resides just above TCP/IP. This component, called NetBT, allows communication using standard Microsoft NetBIOS computer names, such as \\NTServer.

This is great news for users, but it doesn't change the fact that TCP/IP requires IP addresses to communicate. To resolve the NetBIOS names to IP addresses, Windows NT must broadcast the name of the server and wait for it to respond with its IP address. This takes time, causes network broadcast traffic, and generally doesn't work across subnets (because most routers do not forward broadcast messages).

Here's where WINS comes in. WINS maintains a database of active names on the network. When a WINS client needs to contact another server, the WINS server resolves the NetBIOS name, and responds with the server's IP address.

If you have a WINS server on your network, you may enter its IP address in the Primary WINS Server field. If you have more than one WINS server, you may enter another server's IP address in the Secondary WINS Server field. Again, however, you also can assign this information via DHCP.

The bottom of the WINS Address tab has three Windows Networking parameters:

▶ **Enable DNS for Windows Resolution.** Selecting this check box instructs Windows NT to look up NetBIOS names against a Domain Name Server, which is usually a service running on Windows NT Server, or a daemon running on Unix. DNS is a static database usually reserved for TCP/IP hostnames, such as ftp.microsoft.com, but NT 4.0 provides WINS/DNS integration so that you can use DNS for NetBIOS resolution as well.

▶ **Enable LMHOSTS Lookup.** This check box incorporates a text database mapping of NetBIOS names to IP addresses into the name resolution process. This name resolution technique predates WINS, and although it's harder to keep up-to-date, it causes less network traffic than WINS, because name resolution occurs on the client itself before it attempts to use network name resolution resources.

▶ **Scope ID.** Enables administrators to create logical IP networks that are invisible to each other. Hosts must belong to the same NetBIOS scope before they can communicate.

DNS

To configure DNS, select the DNS tab in the Microsoft TCP/IP Properties dialog box. Enter your domain name. Click on the Add button under the DNS Service Search Order box and enter the addresses of the DNS servers on your network. You can change the search order of the DNS servers using the Up and Down buttons to the right of the box. The DNS tab also allows you to enter a domain suffix search order.

TCP/IP Diagnostics

A host of TCP/IP utilities are included with Windows NT. Some of the more useful ones are IPConfig, Ping, and TRACERT.

IPConfig

IPConfig displays the TCP/IP configuration parameters of the local host. The /ALL switch can be used to display every field, including DHCP and WINS information.

Ping

Ping is a diagnostic utility used to test the connection between two hosts on an internetwork. It uses the Internet Control Message Protocol (ICMP) echo and reply functions to send messages to and from a remote host. If the connection is successful, Ping returns four responses similar to the following:

```
Pinging ftp.microsoft.com [198.105.232.1] with 32 bytes of data:
Reply from 198.105.232.1: bytes=32 time=227ms TTL=51
Reply from 198.105.232.1: bytes=32 time=221ms TTL=51
Request timed out.
Reply from 198.105.232.1: bytes=32 time=205ms TTL=51
```

Note that the third attempt timed out. This can happen on the Internet during busy periods, which is why Ping makes four attempts at a connection. Four timeouts would indicate that a connection is unlikely for the time being.

TRACERT

The TRACERT utility traces the hops that packets take on their way from the local host to a remote host. Here's the route from the Portland, OR MSN, connection, to Microsoft's FTP Server:

```
Tracing route to ftp.microsoft.com [198.105.232.1]
over a maximum of 30 hops:
1    161 ms    154 ms    156 ms   Max3.Seattle.WA.MS.UU.NET
➥[204.177.253.3]
2    198 ms    190 ms    160 ms   Cisco2.San-Francisco.CA.MS.UU.Net
➥[137.39.2.63]
3    185 ms    184 ms    214 ms   San-Jose3.CA.ALTER.NET
➥[137.39.100.17]
4    195 ms    192 ms    213 ms   mae-west.SanFrancisco.mci.net
➥[198.32.136.12]
5    264 ms    191 ms    346 ms   borderx2-hssi2-
➥0.SanFrancisco.mci.net [204.70.158.117]
6    *         212 ms    218 ms   core2-fddi-1.SanFrancisco.mci.net
➥[204.70.158.65]
7    220 ms    229 ms    202 ms   core1-hssi-2.Sacramento.mci.net
➥[204.70.1.146]
8    253 ms    435 ms    269 ms   core-hssi-3.Seattle.mci.net
➥[204.70.1.150]
9    236 ms    263 ms    205 ms   border1-fddi-0.Seattle.mci.net
➥[204.70.2.146]
10   *         204 ms    *        nwnet.Seattle.mci.net
➥[204.70.52.6]
11   242 ms    242 ms    234 ms   seabr1-gw.nwnet.net
➥[192.147.179.5]
12   197 ms    209 ms    199 ms   microsoft-t3-gw.nwnet.net
➥ [198.104.192.9]
```

```
13    *       259 ms   232 ms   131.107.249.3
14   220 ms   245 ms   228 ms   ftp.microsoft.com [198.105.232.1]
Trace complete.
```

Armed with these three utilities, you can troubleshoot connectivity problems between two hosts. Say, for instance, you're trying to reach Microsoft as FTP server, but the connection fails.

First, use IPConfig to confirm that you do indeed have TCP/IP correctly initialized on your computer. Also check the Default Gateway and name resolution information, because incorrect configuration of these items affects your ability to connect to remote hosts.

If everything looks okay, Ping 127.0.0.1, a loopback diagnostic address, and it will confirm that TCP/IP is correctly initialized and bound on your computer. If this step isn't successful, shut down and restart your computer, and try again. If this step still isn't successful, check the network bindings using the Bindings tab of the Control Panel Network application.

Next, ping your own IP address to confirm that your computer is configured with the correct address and to ensure that no other hosts on the network have your IP address. If this step is unsuccessful, use IPCONFIG to check for a typo in your IP address. If the address looks fine but you still cannot ping yourself, check the Event Viewer for a message that indicates another host has your IP address. A message always appears when you do this, but it's easy to dismiss without reading it.

If you successfully ping yourself, try pinging your default gateway. If the router is down, you can't communicate with any remote hosts. If this step is successful, move on to the next step.

Ping the remote host. If this step is successful, you should be able to form a connection. If this step is unsuccessful, a router probably is down somewhere between your default gateway and the remote host. Confirm that by using the TRACERT utility to see where the communication breakdown is occurring.

Configuring Network Adapters

The Adapters tab of the Control Panel Network application lets you add and configure network adapters for your system (refer to fig. 2.24).

To add a new network adapter, click on the Add button. The Select Network Adapter dialog box that appears lets you select an adapter from a list (see fig. 2.31). Click on Have Disk to install an adapter that isn't on the list.

Figure 2.31

The Select Network Adapter dialog box.

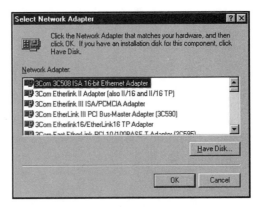

Microsoft lists the following objective for the Windows NT Server exam:

Configure network adapters. Considerations include: changing IRQ, I/O base, memory address, configuring multiple adapters.

To configure the IRQ and/or I/O port address (base-memory I/O address—expressed in decimals), double-click on an adapter in the Network application Adapters tab or select an adapter and click on the Properties button. The Network Card Setup dialog box lets you configure an IRQ and I/O port address (see fig. 2.32).

Figure 2.32

The Network Card Setup dialog box.

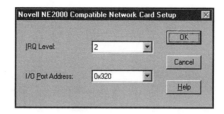

Windows NT Core Services

A service is a built-in application that provides support for other applications or other components of the operating system. Windows NT inlcudes dozens of services, each performing a highly specialized function. Many of Windows NT's services support NT's networking capabilities.

Examples of Windows NT services include:

▶ Windows Internet Name Service (WINS), which maps IP addresses to NetBIOS names.

▶ UPS service, which interacts with an Uninterruptible Power Supply system to prevent your system from abruptly shutting down.

▶ Server service, which accepts I/O requests from the network and routes the requested resources back to the client.

▶ Workstation service, which accepts I/O requests from the local system and redirects the requests to the appropriate computer on the network.

Services are background processes that perform specific functions in Windows NT. Typically, services don't interact with the user interface in any way (including appearing in the Task List), so users shouldn't be aware of their existence. Think of a Windows NT service as the equivalent of Unix daemon, or if you are more comfortable with NetWare, the equivalent of a NetWare Loadable Module (NLM).

This section will take a closer look at some important Windows NT services and how to configure them.

Microsoft lists the following objective for the Window NT Server exam:

Configure Windows NT Server core services. Services include: Directory Replicator, License Manager, other services.

The Services Application

The Control Pandel Services application manages the services on your system.

For an exercise testing this information, see end of chapter.

The Services application writes directly to the following key, where configuration data for Windows NT services is maintained:

HKEY_LOCAL_MACHINE\SYSTEM\CurrentControlSet\Control\Services

Double-click on the Services icon in Control Panel to open the Services dialog box (see fig. 2.33). The Services dialog box lists the services on your system, as well as the Status (whether the service is started or not) and the Startup type. The Startup type setting describes whether the service will start automatically or manually, or whether it is disabled. Automatic services start at the very end of the boot process, after the "Welcome: Press Ctrl+Alt+Del to log on" window appears. (Because services are Win32 programs, they require a fully functional operating system before they can be opened.) Manual services start when you select the service in the Services dialog box and click on the Start button.

Figure 2.33

The Control Panel Services application

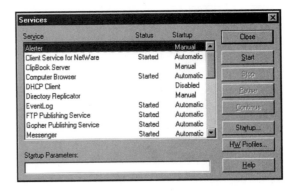

Note that the Services dialog also includes buttons that stop a service, pause a service, or continue a service that has been paused. Pausing a service causes the service to continue handling the processes it's currently serving but not take on any new clients. For example, the Server service is required to run on a server before it can accept connections from a client. Stopping the Server service causes all connections to be immediately dropped, but pausing the service preserves existing connections while rejecting new connection attempts.

To enable a service for a given hardware profile, click on the HW Profiles button in the Services dialog, select a profile, and click on OK.

Double-click on a service to open a configuration dialog box—called the Service dialog (as opposed to the Services dialog)—that enables you to configure a startup type and define a logon account for the service.

The logon account defines a security context for the service. Because services are Win32 programs, they must run under the aegis of a user account. The problem is, services continue to execute even when nobody is logged on to the computer, so the administrator must configure the service to use a specific user account. Here are two options:

▶ **System Account.** An internal account, called SYSTEM, can be used either by the operating system or by the service. This method isn't recommended, however, because you can't fine-tune rights and permissions without possibly affecting the performance and stability of the operating system and other services that may use this account.

▶ **This Account.** You may designate any user account from your account database here. You should create a separate account for each service for which you want to configure rights and permissions.

Network Services

The Services tab of the Control Panel Network application lets you add, configure, and remove services that support network functions (refer to fig. 2.22). The Add button opens the Select Network Service dialog box, which provides a list of available Windows NT network services. Select a service and click OK to add the service to your configuration. Or, click the Have Disk button if you are attempting to install a new service from a disk.

Some of the services in the Network Services list are configurable through the Network application and some are not. Select a service and click on the Properties button to open a configuration dialog box for the service (if there is one). Figure 2.34 shows the configuration dialog box for the Server service.

Figure 2.34

The Server dialog box.

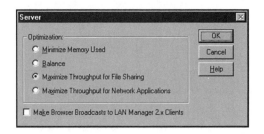

Many of the network components you'll read about elsewhere in this book (DHCP, WINS, DNS, RAS, and Gateway Services for NetWare) are actually services that, though often configured elsewhere, can still be added, started, stopped, and managed through the Network Services tab and the Control Panel Services application. For the most part, anything you do on the network occurs through some form of network service.

The following sections examine some important topics relating to Windows NT services, as follows:

▶ Directory replication

▶ Client license management

▶ The browser process

Directory Replication

For an exercise testing this information, see end of chapter.

Directory Replication is a facility that lets you configure Windows NT Servers to automatically transmit updated versions of important files and directories to other computers on the network.

The purpose of Directory Replication is to simplify the task of distributing updates for logon scripts, system policy files, Help files, phone lists, and other important files. The network administrator updates the file(s) on a single server (called the export server) and the export server automatically distributes the file(s) to other network servers or even to network workstations. The computer receiving the update is called the import computer. A Windows NT Server, a Windows NT Workstation, or a LAN Manager OS/2 server can act as an import computer.

Directory Replication is performed by the Directory Replicator service. You can start and stop the Directory Replicator service from the Control Panel Services application. The parameters for the Directory Replicator service are found in the Registry key:

```
HKEY_LOCAL_MACHINE\SYSTEM\CurrentControlSet\Services\Replicator\
Parameters
```

Most of the parameters in the Registry key HKEY_LOCAL_MACHINE\SYSTEM\CurrentControlSet\Services\Replicator\Parameters can be configured within Server Manager (described later in this chapter). Two important exceptions are:

Interval. A REG_WORD value that defines how often an export server checks for updates. The range is from 1 to 60 minutes and the default is 5 minutes.

GuardTime. A REG_WORD value that defines how long a directory must be stable before its files can be replicated. The range is 0 to one half of the Interval value. The default is 2 minutes. See the "Configuring the Export Computer" section later in this chapter for a discussion of the Wait Until Stabilized check box.

The export directory on the export server holds the files and directories are replicated across the network. The default export directory is

```
\<winnt_root>\System32\Repl\Export
```

For each group of files that set for replication, create a subdirectory in the export directory. When the Directory Replicator service starts, NT shares the export directory with the share name Repl$.

Each import computer has a directory called the import directory, and the default directory is

```
\<winnt_root>\System32\Repl\Import
```

The Directory Replicator service copies files from the export server's export directory to the import directories of the import computers. In addition to copying files, the Directory Replicator service automatically creates any necessary subdirectories in the import directory so that after each replication the directory structure of the import directory matches the export directory's directory structure.

The process occurs as follows:

1. The export server periodically checks the export directory for changes and, if changes have occurred, sends update notices to the import computers.

2. The import computer receives the update notices and calls the export computer.

3. The import computer reads the export directory on the export server and copies any new or changed files from the export directory to its own import directory.

The following sections describe how to set up the export and import computers for directory replications.

Configuring the Export Computer

To set up the export server for directory replication:

1. Double-click on the Control Panel Services application to start the Directory Replicator service.

2. Create a new account for the Directory Replicator service. (See Chapter 3 for more on creating accounts using User Manager for Domains.) The Directory Replicator account must be a member of the Backup Operator group or the Replicator group for the domain. When you set up the new account, be sure to enable the Password Never Expires option and disable the User Must Change Password at Next Logon option. Also, make sure the account has logon privileges for all hours.

3. Start the Server Manager application in the Administrative Tools program group (see fig. 2.35). Server Manager is a tool for managing network servers and workstations from a single location.

Figure 2.35

The Server Manager main screen.

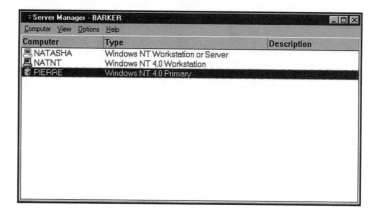

4. In the Server Manager, double-click on the export server to open the Server Properties dialog box (see fig. 2.36).

5. Click on the Replication button to open the Directory Replication dialog box (see fig. 2.37).

Figure 2.36

The Server Properties dialog box

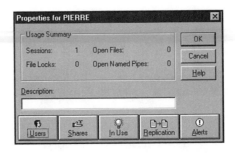

Figure 2.37

The Directory Replication dialog box.

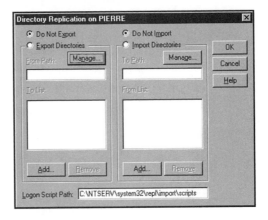

A Windows NT server can serve as an export server, an import computer, or both. The left side of the Directory Replication dialog box defines export properties. The right side of the Directory Export dialog box defines import properties.

6. In the Directory Replication dialog box, select the Export Directories radio button. The default path to the export directory appears in the From Path box. Click on the Add button to open the Select Domain dialog box (see fig. 2.38). Click on a domain to select it. Double-click on a domain to display the computers within that domain (see fig. 2.39). If you select a whole domain, all import servers in the domain receive the replicated data. If you choose a specific computer, only that computer receives the replicated data. You can choose any combination of domains and specific computers.

Figure 2.38

*The Select Do-
main dialog box.*

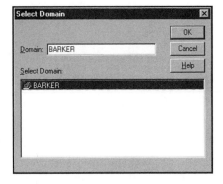

Figure 2.39

*The Select Do-
main dialog box
displaying spe-
cific computers
within the do-
main.*

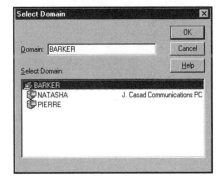

7. Click on the Manage button to open the Manage Exported
   Directories dialog box (see fig. 2.40). Subdirectories within
   the export directory appear in the Sub-Directory list. You
   can add or remove subdirectories from the list by clicking on
   the Add or Remove buttons. Note the check boxes at the
   bottom of the screen. Enabling the Wait Until Stabilized
   check box tells the Directory Replicator service to wait at
   least two minutes after any change to the selected subdirectory tree before exporting. Enabling the Entire Subtree
   check box tells the Directory Replicator service to export all
   subdirectories beneath the selected subdirectory. The Add
   Lock button lets you lock the subdirectory so it can't be exported. More than one user can lock a subdirectory. (Consequently, a subdirectory can have more than one lock.) To
   remove a lock, click on the Remove Lock button.

Figure 2.40

The Manager Exported Directories dialog box.

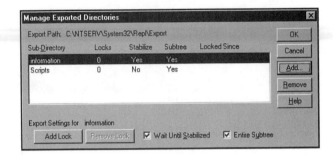

8. Click on OK in the Manage Exported Directories dialog box, the Directory Replication dialog box, and the Server Properties dialog box.

Configuring the Import Computer

To set up the import computer for directory replication:

1. Double-click on the Services icon in the Control Panel. Select the Directory Replicator service and click on the Startup button to open the Service dialog box (see fig. 2.41).

Figure 2.41

The Service dialog box.

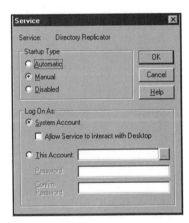

2. In the Startup Type frame, select the Automatic radio button. Select the This Account radio button and enter a username and password for the replicator account you created on the export server.

If the import computer and the export server aren't part of the same domain or a trusting domain, you must create a replication user account on the import computer and give that account permission to access the Repl$ share on the export server. Enter this account and password in the Service dialog box in step 2.

3. Start Server Manager, select the computer you're now configuring, and click on the Replication button in the Properties dialog box. The Directory Replication dialog box appears. This time, you're concerned with the import side (the right side) of the dialog box, but the configuration steps are similar to steps for configuring the export side. The default import directory appears in the To Path box. Click on the Add button to add a domain or a specific export server (see step 6 in the preceding section). Click on the Manage button to open the Manage Imported Directories dialog box, which lets you manage the import directories (see fig. 2.42).

Figure 2.42

The Managing Imported Directories dialog box.

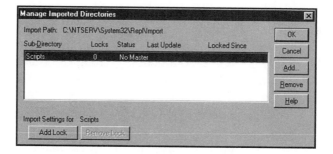

4. In the Manage Imported Directories dialog box, click on Add or Remove to add or remove a subdirectory from the list. Click on Add Lock to add a lock to the subdirectory (see preceding section).

Troubleshooting Directory Replication

The Status parameter in the Manage Exported Directories and the Manager Imported Directories dialog boxes gives the status of the directory replication for a subdirectory. The possible values are as follows:

▶ **OK.** The export server is sending regular updates, and the import directory matches the export directory.

▶ **No Master.** The import computer isn't receiving updates, which means the export server may not be running, or the Directory Replicator service on the export server may not be running.

▶ **No Sync.** The import directory has received updates, but the data in the updates isn't what it should be, which means there could be an export server malfunction, a communication problem, open files on either the import of the export computer, or a problem with the import computer's access permissions.

▶ **(Blank).** Replication has never occurred. The cause could be improper configuration on either the import or the export computer.

When the Directory Replication service generates an error, check Event Viewer to learn what you can about the cause.

Microsoft recommends the following solutions for some common replication errors:

▶ **Access Denied.** The Directory Replicator service might not be configured to log on to a specific account. Check Event Viewer. Check the Startup dialog box in the Control Panel Services application to see if an account is specified, and use User Manager for Domains to check the permissions for the logon account.

▶ **Exporting to Specific Computers.** Designate specific export servers for each import server and specific import computers for each export server. If you just choose a domain in the dialog box opened by clicking on the Add button in the Directory Replication dialog box, every domain computer receives replicated data and every import computer receives updates from every export server in the domain.

▶ **Replication over a WAN link.** When transmitting replication data across a WAN link, specify the computer name rather than just the domain name when you click on the Add button in the Directory Replication dialog box.

▶ **Logon Scripts for Member Servers and Workstations.** NT Workstations and non-controller NT Servers must use the default logon script directory:

```
C:\<winnt_root>\System32\Repl\Import\Scripts
```

Windows NT Client Licenses

Microsoft requires that every client accessing a resource on a computer running Windows NT Server have a Client Access License (CAL). The Client Access License is separate from the license for the client's operating system. Your Windows 95 or Windows NT Workstation doesn't include implied permission to access resources on a Windows NT Server—to access NT Server resources you must have a CAL.

Microsoft provides two options for purchasing Client Access Licenses, as follows:

▶ **Per Server mode.** Client Access Licenses are assigned to each server. A Windows NT Server might be licensed for, say, 10 simultaneous client connections. No more than 10 clients will be able to access the server at one time—additional clients will not be able to connect.

▶ **Per Seat mode.** Client Access Licenses are assigned to each client machine. You purchase a CAL for every client computer on the network. If the total number of simultaneous connections on all Windows NT Servers exceeds the number of per seat licenses, a client can still connect.

Microsoft allows a one-time switch from Per Server to Per Seat licensing mode. If you aren't sure which option to choose, you can choose Per Server mode and change later to Per Seat mode if you determine that Per Seat mode is more cost effective.

If your network has only one server, Microsoft recommends that you choose Per Server licensing mode. If you have more than one server on your network, Microsoft suggests the following formulas:

A=Number of servers

B=number of simultaneous connections to each server

C=total number of seats (clients) accessing computers

If A * B < C use Per Server licensing. Number of CALs=A*B

IF A * B > C use Per Seat licensing. Number of CALs=C

Windows NT Server includes the following tools for managing client licenses:

▶ The Licensing application

▶ License Manager

The following sections describe these Windows NT license-managing tools.

The Licensing Application

The Control Panel Licensing application opens the Choose Licensing Mode dialog box (see fig. 2.43). The Choose Licensing Mode dialog box lets you add or remove client licenses or switch from Per Server to Per Seat licensing mode.

Figure 2.43

The Choose Licensing Mode dialog box.

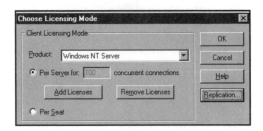

The Replication button opens the Replication Configuration dialog box (see fig. 2.44). The Replication Configuration dialog box lets you configure license replication.

Figure 2.44

The Replication Configuration dialog box.

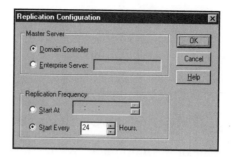

License replication is a convenient feature that lets individual servers send their licensing information to a master server. The master server creates and updates a database of licensing information for the entire network. This provides a single central location for licensing information.

License Manager

License Manager, a tool in the Administrative Tools program group, displays licensing information for the network (see fig. 2.45). You can maintain a history of client licenses, examine your networks Per Server and Per Seat licenses by product, and browse for client license information on particular network clients. You also can monitor server usage by Per Seat clients, and even revoke a client's permission to access a server.

Figure 2.45

The License Manager window.

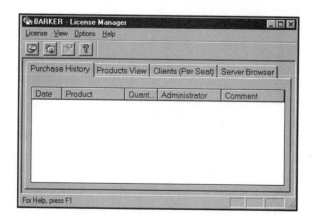

You also can use License Manager to add or edit license groups. A license group is a group of users mapped to a group of Per Seat licenses. License groups are a means of tracking per seat license usage in situations where an organization has more users than computers (or in some cases, more computers than users). For example, a retail outlet may have 10 employees sharing three Per-Seat-licensed computers.

Computer Browser Service

One of the most important network services is the Computer Browser service. The Computer Browser service oversees a hierarchy of computers that serve as browsers for the network. A browser is a computer that maintains a central list of network servers. (In this case, a server is any computer that makes resources available to the network.) That list then becomes available to clients who are "browsing" the network looking for remote computers, printers, and other resources. The list that appears when you open the Network Neighborhood application, for instance, comes from a network browser list.

The advantage of the browser process is that it allows a small number of network computers to maintain browse lists for the whole network, thereby minimizing network traffic and eliminating duplication of efforts. (The alternative would be for all computers to constantly poll the network in order to maintain their own lists.) Before the browser process can function efficiently, however, it must be highly organized so that clients know where to find a list and so that contingencies can take effect when a browser fails.

In a Windows NT domain, each computer assumes one of five browser roles:

▶ **Master browser.** Each workgroup or domain subnet must have a master browser. At startup, all computers running the Server service (regardless of whether they have resources available for the network) register themselves with the master browser. The master browser compiles a list of available servers on the workgroup or subnet and forwards the list to the Domain Master Browser. Master browsers then receive a complete browse list for the entire domain from the domain master browser.

▶ **Domain master browser.** The domain master browser requests subnet browse lists from the master browsers and merges the subnet browse lists into a master browse list for the entire domain. It also forwards the domain browse list back to the master browsers. The Primary Domain Controller (PDC) serves as the domain master browser for a Windows NT domain.

▶ **Backup browsers.** The backup browser gets a copy of the browse list from the master browser (on the subnet) and distributes the browse list to subnet clients who request it. If the master browser fails, a backup browser can serve as the master browser for the subnet.

▶ **Potential browser.** A potential browser is a computer that isn't presently serving as a browser but can become a browser at the request of the master browser or as a result of a browser election (described later in this section).

▶ **Non-browser.** A non-browser is a computer that cannot serve as a browser.

The first time a client computer attempts to access the network, it obtains a list of backup browsers for the subnet or workgroup from the master browser. It then asks a backup browser for a copy of the browse list.

If a master browser fails, a new master browser is chosen automatically in what is known as a browser election. A browser election can occur if a client or backup browser cannot access the master browser. A browser election isn't exactly an election; it's really more of a contest. The browsers and potential browsers rank themselves according to a number of criteria, and the machine with the highest ranking becomes the new master browser. Some of the criteria used in a browser election are as follows:

▶ **Operating system.** Windows NT Server gets a higher score than Windows NT Workstation, which gets a higher score than Windows 95.

▶ **Version.** Windows NT Server 4 gets a higher score than Windows NT Server 3.51, and so forth.

> ▶ **Present browser role.** A backup browser scores higher than a potential browser.

You can configure a Windows NT computer to always, never, or sometimes participate in browser elections, using the Maintain-ServerList parameter in the registry key:

`HKEY_Local_Machine\System\CurrentControlSet\Services\Browsr\Parameters`

The possible values are as follows:

> ▶ **Yes.** Always attempt to become a browser in browser elections (default for Windows NT Server domain controllers).

> ▶ **No.** Never attempt to become a browser in browser elections.

> ▶ **Auto.** The Auto setting classifies the computer as a potential browser (default for Windows NT Workstations and Windows NT Servers that aren't acting as domain controllers).

To make other domains available to the browser service, select the browser service in the Network application's Services tab and click on the Properties button. The Browser configuration dialog box appears. Enter a domain name in the box on the left and click the Add button; then click on OK.

Configuring Peripherals and Devices

Control Panel includes several applications that help you install and configure peripherals and devices. You should be familiar with how to use these applications to install drivers and configure peripherals and hardware. The following sections examine these applications:

> ▶ Devices

> ▶ Multimedia

> ▶ Ports

> ▶ UPS

- ▶ SCSI

- ▶ Tape Devices

- ▶ PC Card

- ▶ Modems

- ▶ Keyboard

- ▶ Mouse

- ▶ Display

You should be familiar with how to use these applications for installing and configuring peripherals and devices. Some of the following sections also appear in the full discussion of Control Panel applications in Appendix A.

Microsoft lists the following objective for the Windows NT Server exam:

Configure peripherals and devices. Peripherals and devices include: communications devices, SCSI devices, tape device drivers, UPS and UPS service, mouse drivers, display drivers, and keyboard drivers.

Devices

The Devices application (SRVMGR.CPL) writes to HKEY_LOCAL_MACHINE\SYSTEM\CurrentControlSet\Services. You can start, stop, or disable device drivers in this Control Panel applet (see fig. 2.46).

Figure 2.46

The Devices application.

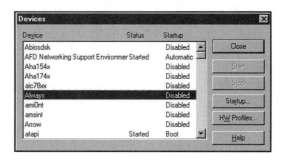

The three columns in the Control Panel Devices main display area are labeled Device, Status, and Startup. The Device column identifies the name of the device driver as it appears in the Registry; the Status column reads "Started" if the driver is active, and otherwise appears blank; the Startup column denotes when each driver is configured to initialize.

To set the Startup value, select the device driver you want to modify and choose the Startup button. In the Device dialog box, shown in figure 2.47, choose one of the following Startup Types:

Figure 2.47

The Device dialog box.

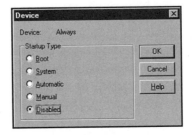

- ▶ **Boot.** These devices start first, as soon as the kernel is loaded and initialized (see Chapter 6, "Troubleshooting," for more details about the boot process). These devices have a Start value of 0 in the Registry. Atdisk, the hard disk driver, is an example of a boot device.

- ▶ **System.** These devices start after the boot devices and after the HKEY_LOCAL_MACHINE subtree has begun to be built. These devices have a start value of 1 in the Registry. The video driver is a system device.

- ▶ **Automatic.** These devices start late in the boot process, after the Registry is almost entirely built, just before the Winlogon screen appears. These devices have a start value of 2 in the Registry. Serial, the serial port driver, is an automatic device.

- ▶ **Manual.** These devices are never started without administrator intervention. They may be manually started through the Control Panel Devices menu. These devices have a start value of 3 in the Registry.

> ▶ **Disabled.** These devices cannot be started at all unless their startup Type is changed to something other than Disabled. These devices have a start value of 4 in the Registry. File system drivers are disabled by default (although file system recognizers are started with the system devices; if any file systems are "recognized," the Startup Type of the file system drivers is changed to System as well).

To start a device that isn't active, select the device and choose the Start button. If the Start button is greyed out, the device is already started or disabled.

To stop a device that's active, select the device and choose the Stop button. A greyed out stop button indicates that the device already is inactive.

To enable or disable a device for a given hardware profile, select the device, click on HW Profiles, select enable or disable to change to the desired status, and click on OK. You learn more about hardware profiles later in this chapter.

Multimedia

The Multimedia application (MMSYS.CPL) writes to HKEY_LOCAL_MACHINE\SYSTEM\CurrentControlSet\Services. Multimedia device drivers are added and configured from this Control Panel applet. The Multimedia application also provides settings for CD music, audio, video, and MIDI.

Ports

The Ports application (PORTS.CPL) writes directly to the following key:

```
HKEY_LOCAL_MACHINE\SYSTEM\CurrentControlSet\Services\Serial
```

This Control Panel interface lists only the serial ports that are available but not in use as serial ports. In other words, if a mouse is connected to your COM1 port, COM1 doesn't show up in the

Control Panel Ports dialog box. All serial ports, regardless of whether they appear in Control Panel Ports, are logged in the Registry under the following key:

```
HKEY_LOCAL_MACHINE\HARDWARE\Description\System\<multifunction_
adapter>\0\~SerialController\<COM_port_number>
```

The Settings button displays values for the port's baud rate, data bits, parity, stop bits, and flow control.

If you need an additional port for use under Windows NT, choose the Add button. You may assign a different COM port number, base I/O port address or IRQ, or enable a First In-First Out (FIFO) buffer for that port (see fig. 2.48).

Figure 2.48

Adding a new port using the Ports application's Add button.

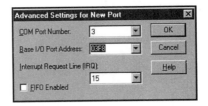

To remove a port, simply select it and click on the Delete button.

UPS

The UPS application (UPS.CPL) writes to the following key:

```
HKEY_LOCAL_MACHINE\SYSTEM\CurrentControlSet\Services\UPS
```

If your computer is equipped with a Universal Power Supply (UPS), Windows NT can be configured to communicate with it. The specific voltages requested in the UPS Configuration area depend on the UPS manufacturer and model. You may need to consult with your vendor to get these values. Armed with the correct information, Windows NT can recognize the following:

▶ **Power failure signal.** The point when an event is logged and the Server service paused. No new connections to this server can be made, but existing connections still function.

▶ **Low battery signal at least 2 minutes before shutdown.**
As the name implies, Windows NT recognizes when the UPS
battery is about to be exhausted.

▶ **Remote UPS Shutdown.** Signals Windows NT that the UPS
is shutting down.

The Execute Command File option enables an administrator to
specify a batch or executable file that runs immediately preceding
a shutdown. The program has 30 seconds before the system shuts
down. The program cannot open a dialog box because that would
require an attendant user.

If no Low Battery Signal is configured, the administrator can enter the Expected Battery Life and the Battery Recharge Time Per
Minute of Run Time in the lower left corner of the dialog box.

After the initial PowerOut alert is raised (the power failure signal
has been received), Windows NT waits until the Time Between
Power Failure and Initial Warning Message has elapsed, and then
sends an alert to all interactive and connected users. Windows NT
continues to send these alerts every time the Delay between Warning Messages elapses.

If the UPS is about to run out of steam, the system shuts down
safely. If power is restored, users are notified, an event is logged,
and the Server service resumes.

SCSI Adapters

This application is one of the great misnomers in Windows NT. As
it suggests, this application opens the SCSI Adapters dialog box,
which is used to install SCSI adapter drivers. However, this dialog
box also is used to install and remove IDE CD-ROM drivers as well
as drivers for CD-ROM drives that use proprietary interfaces, such
as Mitsumi or Panasonic drives. The dialog box should refer to
both SCSI adapters and CD-ROM drives; currently the interface is
completely counter-intuitive.

To add a SCSI adapter or CD-ROM device driver, follow these
procedures:

1. Double-click in the SCSI Adapters application in the Control Panel.

2. In the SCSI Adapters dialog box, choose the Drivers tab and click on the Add button.

3. Select the driver from the list of available drivers in the Install Driver dialog box. If your driver isn't listed but you have a disk from the manufacturer with a Windows NT driver, click on the Have Disk button.

4. Choose OK. You must point Windows NT toward the original installation files (or the disk that contains the driver) and restart the computer in order for the new driver to initialize.

To remove a SCSI adapter or CD-ROM device driver, perform these instructions:

1. Select the Drivers tab in the SCSI Adapters dialog box.

2. Select the driver you want to remove.

3. Choose the Remove button.

Tape Devices

Almost identical to the SCSI Adapter Setup dialog box in both appearance and function, this dialog box allows the installation and removal of tape drives for use with a Windows NT Backup program.

To add a tape drive device driver, use these steps:

1. Double-click on the Tape Devices icon in Control Panel.

2. Select the Drivers tab.

3. Click on the Add button.

4. Select the driver from the list of available drivers. If your driver isn't listed but you have a disk from the manufacturer with a Windows NT Driver, click on the Have Disk button.

5. Choose OK. You must point Windows NT toward the original installation files (or the disk that contains the driver) and restart the computer in order for the new driver to initialize.

To remove a tape drive device driver, do these steps:

1. Select the driver from the list of installed drivers in the Tape Devices dialog box of the Drivers tab.

2. Choose the Remove button.

PC Card (PCMCIA)

The PC Card application helps you install and configure PCMCIA device drivers. Select a PC card and click on Properties. Select the Drivers tab and then choose Add, Remove, or Configure as necessary.

A red X next to a device in the PC card list indicates that NT doesn't support the device.

Modems

The Modems application enables you to add or remove a modem. You can ask NT to detect your modem, or you can select a modem from a list.

To add a modem:

1. Double-click on the Modems application in the Control Panel.

2. Click on Add in the Modem Properties dialog box (see fig. 2.49).

3. In the Install New Modem dialog box, click on Next if you want NT to try to detect your modem. If you want to select your modem from the list, or if you're providing software for a modem not listed, enable the check box and then click on Next (see fig. 2.50).

Figure 2.49

The Modem Properties dialog box.

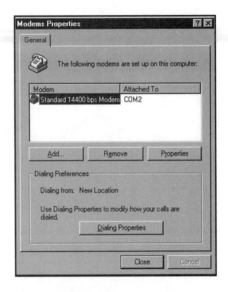

Figure 2.50

The Install New Modem dialog box.

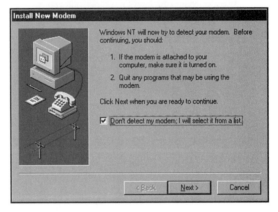

4. Select a manufacturer and a model, and click on Next. Or click on the Have Disk button if you're installing software for a modem not shown on the list.

5. Select a port for the modem, or select All ports. Click on Next.

Select a modem in the Modems list and click on Properties to change the parameters for that modem. A new dialog box opens, with two tabs, General and Connection. The General tab enables you to set the port number and the maximum speed. The Connection tab enables you to define some connection preferences, such as the Data bits, Stop bits, and Parity. Click on Advanced for additional settings.

The Dialing Properties button in the Modem Properties dialog box calls up the My Location tab, which is also in the Telephony application. The My Locations tab enables you to set the dialing characteristics for the modem. If you have a portable computer, you can define additional locations and configure a complete set of dialing properties for each location. If you sometimes travel to a certain hotel in Paris, for instance, you can define a location called Paris and specify the dialing properties you want to use for the Paris hotel. The next time you're in Paris, you only have to change the location setting in the I Am Dialing from box at the top of the My Location tab. The other settings automatically change to the settings you defined for Paris.

To add a new location, follow these steps:

1. Click on the New button at the top of the My Locations tab. (NT announces that a new location has been created.)

2. The new location has the name New Location (followed by a number if you already have a location called New Location). Click on the name and change it if you want to give your location a different name. (NT might not let you erase the old name completely until you add your new name. Add the new name and then backspace over the old text if necessary.)

3. Change any dialing properties. The new properties will apply to your new location.

Keyboard

The Keyboard application opens the Keyboard Properties dialog box, which enables the user to set the keyboard repeat rate, the repeat delay, the cursor blink rate, and the keyboard layout properties. The keyboard driver appears in the General tab in the Keyboard Type text box (see fig. 2.51). To select a new driver, click on the Change button. The Select Device dialog box appears (see fig. 2.52). The Show All Devices radio button will cause a list of available drivers to appear in the Models list. Choose the keyboard model that matches your hardware. If your keyboard comes with its own installation disk for a model that isn't in the list, click on the Have Disk button.

Figure 2.51

The Keyboard Properties dialog box.

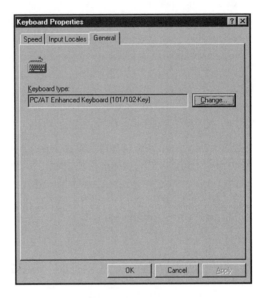

Figure 2.52

The Select Device dialog box.

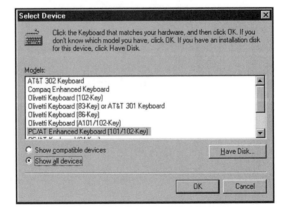

Mouse

The values for this key control the mouse speed, sensitivity, and left- or right-handedness. The one new setting added to this dialog box's Win3.x predecessor is the Snap to Default option in the Motion tab, which instantly positions the pointer over the default button in the active dialog box. In the Pointers tab, you can select a pointer type. The General tab lets you install a new mouse driver. The procedure for selecting a mouse driver is similar to the procedure for selecting a keyboard driver (described in the preceding section).

Display

The Display application configures the values in the following key, including the video driver, screen resolution, color depth, and refresh rate:

```
HKEY_LOCAL_MACHINE\SYSTEM\CurrentControlSet\Services\<video_driver>\
Device0\
```

The five tabs of the Display Properties dialog box, shown in figure 2.53, are as follows:

Figure 2.53

The Display Properties dialog box.

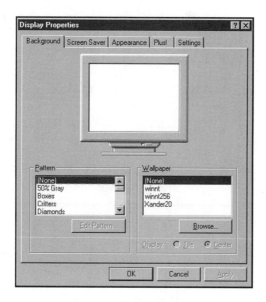

▶ **Background.** Defines the wallpaper for the Desktop.

▶ **Screen Saver.** Defines the screen saver for the Desktop.

▶ **Appearance.** Defines window properties.

▶ **Plus!.** The Visual Enhancements tab from the Microsoft Plus! package for Windows 95 lets you configure the desktop to use large icons or stretch the wallpaper to fit the screen.

▶ **Settings.** Defines desktop colors, refresh frequency, and other screen-related settings.

The Settings tab contains a Test button. You should always test new display settings before making changes permanent. Although Windows NT can detect the capabilities of your video card, it can't do the same with your monitor. Testing these settings before applying them ensures that both video card and monitor can support the new settings.

Unlike Windows 95, Windows NT doesn't let you change video resolution on the fly. The computer must be restarted for the changes to take effect.

All hardware breaks sooner or later, including monitors. When a monitor dies, you often can dig up an older model to use temporarily. Often, however, such a resurrected monitor isn't as advanced as the one that just died, and when you restart Windows NT, such video card settings as the resolution and refresh rate aren't supported. The typical result is that you no longer can view anything on-screen.

If this happens, reboot the computer using the [VGA mode] option on the Boot Loader menu. Windows NT boots using the standard VGA driver at 640x480 resolution. When the system is fully loaded, log on and go to the Settings tab of the Control Panel Display application, so that you can choose optimal settings for your temporary monitor.

To change the video display adapter:

1. Start the Control Panel Display application and click on the Settings tab (see fig. 2.54).

2. Click on the Display Type button. The Display Type dialog box appears (see fig. 2.55).

Figure 2.54

*The Display
Properties Set-
tings tab.*

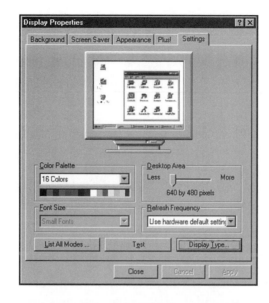

Figure 2.55

*The Display Type
dialog box.*

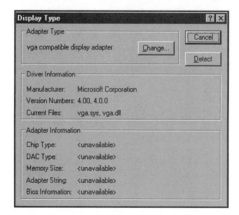

3. Click on the Change tab in the Adapter Type frame. The
   Change Display dialog box appears (see fig. 2.56). Select an
   adapter from the list and click on OK. Or, if you have a manufacturer's installation disk, click on Have Disk.

Figure 2.56

*The Change
Display dialog
box.*

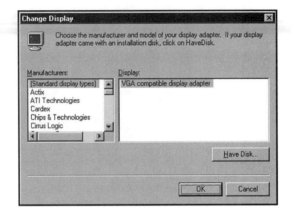

Configuring Hard Disks

Chapter 1 discussed some important concepts related to disk configuration, such as file systems, primary partitions, extended partitions, and fault-tolerance. This section describes how to apply those concepts to an actual disk configuration using Windows NT's Disk Administrator disk utility. To access Disk Administrator, you must be using an administrator account.

Microsoft lists the following objective for the Windows NT Server exam:

Configure hard disks to meet various requirements. Requirements include: allocating disk space capacity, providing redundancy, improving performance, providing security, formatting.

To start the Disk Administrator, choose Start, Programs, Administrative Tools (common), Disk Administrator.

When using the Disk Administrator for the first time, a message box appears, telling you the following:

```
No signature found on Disk 0.access this disk from other operat-
➥ing systems, such as DOS.
If you choose not to write a signature, the disk will be inacces-
➥sible to the Windows NT Disk Administrator program.
```

```
Do you want to write a signature on Disk 0 so that the Disk Ad-
➥ministrator can access the drive?
```

Choosing Yes has a 32-bit signature that uniquely identifies the disk written to the primary partition. This function makes possible recognition of the disk as the original, even if it is has been used with a different controller or its identification has changed.

If you select any modifications to be performed on a disk(s), a message appears warning that certain changes, such as deleting a partition, are irreversible and require user approval. The changes don't become permanent until you exit the program or choose Partition, Commit Changes Now.

Customizing the Display

The status bar at the bottom of the Disk Administrator's main window displays basic disk information (see fig. 2.57). Along with the status bar, a color-coded legend displays the different representations for partition colors and patterns. When working with multiple disks, hiding one or both of these two options gives you a larger area for viewing information. To do so, choose Options and then select Status Bar or Legend, or both.

Figure 2.57

The Disk Administrator main window.

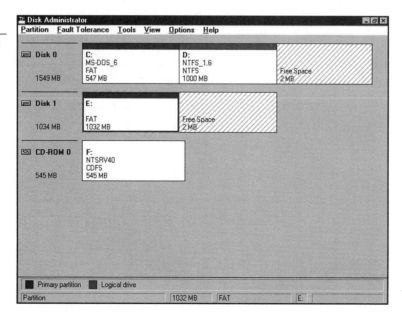

You also can set different colors and patterns to distinguish between different disks and disk characteristics for the primary partition, logical drive, mirror set, and volume set. To change the default settings, choose Options, Colors and Patterns. The Colors and Patterns dialog box appears (see fig. 2.58).

Figure 2.58

Disk Administrator's Colors and Patterns dialog box.

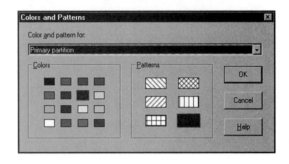

Initially, each disk represented in the display window is sized proportionately. By choosing Options, Region Display, you get several choices in the Region Display Options dialog box for customizing the appearance of each region (see fig. 2.59).

Figure 2.59

Disk Administrator's Region Display Options dialog box.

Partitioning

Partitioning refers to the method in which hard disks are made usable. Windows NT includes four options for creating partitions with the Disk Administrator.

To create primary partitions using the Disk Administrator, follow these steps:

1. Select an area of free space on a disk.

2. Choose Partition, Create.

   A message box appears indicating the possible minimum and maximum sizes for a new primary partition.

3. In the Create Primary Partition dialog box, enter the size of the partition you want to create and choose OK.

To create an extended partition using the Disk Administrator, follow these steps:

1. Select an area of free space on a disk.

2. Choose Partition, Create Extended.

   A message box appears indicating the possible minimum and maximum sizes for a new extended partition.

3. In the Create Extended dialog box, enter the size of the extended partition you want to create and choose OK.

To create a logical drive within an extended partition, select the extended partition and choose Partition, Create. If this command is unavailable, you probably have selected another partition rather than the extended one.

To create a volume set using the Disk Administrator, follow these steps:

1. Select the areas of free space you want to include with a volume set.

2. Choose Partition, Create Volume Set.

   A message box appears indicating the possible minimum and maximum sizes for a new extended partition.

3. In the Create Volume Set dialog box, enter the size of the volume set you want to create and choose OK.

After you create a volume set, you must format it before you can use it (NTFS and FAT are both supported). To format the new volume, you must save the changes by choosing Partition menu, Commit Changes Now, or by responding to the prompts when exiting the Disk Administrator. You also must restart the system before formatting.

Before you can reclaim any of the disk space that a volume set uses, you must delete the volume set entirely (although, if formatted with NTFS, you can extend a volume set using other drives without doing additional formatting or losing data).

> If NT is configured to support multiple operating systems (such as DOS) when a volume set or stripe set is created, the other systems cannot see the set and, therefore, cannot access it.

The only differences between configuring volume sets and ordinary partitions are as follows:

▶ The system and boot partitions cannot be part of a volume set. Windows NT must be running before these volume sets can be addressed; if Windows NT itself is on a volume set, there is no way to address the volume set.

▶ You can extend an NTFS volume set (but not a FAT volume set) by selecting the volume set in Disk Administrator and simultaneously selecting at least one area of free space (hold down the Ctrl key to select more than one area at a time). Choose the Partition, Extend Volume Set to get a chance to enter a new size for the volume set.

▶ You can never shrink a volume set; after creating or extending it, it's set in stone. You can delete the entire volume set, but not any individual area within it.

If you choose to implement a volume set, be aware of the following drawbacks and dangers:

▶ Only Windows NT supports volume sets; if you're booting between Windows NT and Windows 95, MS-DOS, or another operating system, your volume set is inaccessible if Windows NT isn't active.

▶ Your volume set will break because all drives fail sooner or later, and combining free space from multiple drives increases the chances of a disaster. Be sure to back up your data frequently. If a single member of the volume set fails, you lose a good portion of your data. The rest of the volume set may still be addressable, but don't count on being able to retrieve your data intact. Shut down the system, replace the bad drive, reformat the volume set, and restore your data from backup.

To extend a volume set, both the existing set and the volume you're adding must be formatted with NTFS. To extend a volume set using the Disk Administrator, follow these steps:

1. Select an NTFS volume, then select the area(s) of free space you want to add. (Hold down the Ctrl key while you select the areas of free space.)

2. Choose Partition, Extend Volume Set.

   A dialog box appears indicating the possible minimum and maximum sizes for the creation of an extended partition.

3. In the Create Extended Volume Set dialog box, enter the size of the volume you want to create and choose OK.

Stripe Sets

Stripe sets are similar to volume sets in that they also combine anywhere from 2 to 32 areas of free space into a single logical drive. Stripe sets differ from volume sets in that the free space areas must all be equally sized areas from separate physical disks. Data is read from and written to the stripe set in 64 KB blocks, disk by disk, row by row. If multiple controllers service your stripe set, or if your single controller can perform concurrent I/O requests, you can improve performance dramatically because you can then use multiple drives simultaneously.

Be careful, however—not only do the same dangers apply to stripe sets as apply to volume sets, the potential disaster is even more dire. If any single member of a stripe set fails, the entire volume becomes inaccessible to the point that—because your data is contiguous only for 64 KB at a time—not even a disk editor can help you. If you didn't back up, your data is gone for good.

If all of this scares you, good; preferable alternatives to volume or stripe sets usually are available. Windows NT Server has a more robust method of improving performance while maintaining fault tolerance, called stripe sets with parity. Use a stripe set with parity if you really want the performance boost from striping. If you're using Windows NT Workstation rather than Server, you don't have that option, but you can go with a hardware implementation of striping that offers some method of parity maintenance. This fault tolerant technology is called Redundant Array of Inexpensive Disks (RAID).

The same rules apply for both stripe sets and volume sets—no limits on drive types, no limit for the file system, and no system and boot partitions. You cannot extend a stripe set the way you can volume sets, however, and you cannot shrink one either.

A stripe set can support IDE, EIDE, and SCSI drive types.

When creating a stripe set, the space on each disk must be the same size (see fig. 2.60); if not, the Disk Administrator approximates the sizes for each to make them equal.

To create a stripe set using the Disk Administrator, follow these steps:

1. Select at least two areas of free space on different hard drives.

2. Choose Partition, Create Stripe Set.

   A dialog box appears indicating the possible minimum and maximum sizes for the creation of an extended partition.

3. In the Create Stripe Set dialog box, enter the size of the stripe set you want to create and choose OK.

Figure 2.60

Figure 2.60

*The Disk Admin-
istrator main
window display-
ing stripe set
information.*

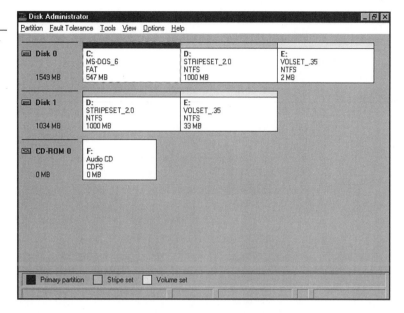

As with a volume set, you must format the stripe set before you
can use it. To format the new volume, save the changes by choosing Partition, Commit Changes Now option or by responding to
the prompts when exiting the Disk Administrator. You also must
restart the system before formatting.

Marking Partition as Active

On a disk(s) using a Windows NT computer, the areas that contain the startup files are called the system and boot partitions. The
system partition contains the boot files, and the boot partition
contains the system and support files. These denotions appear
backwards by conventional terminology, but they accurately describe Windows NT.

With an I386 computer, the system partition is located on the first
disk, is marked active, and is designated as the primary partition.
You can have only one active partition at a time. To boot between
multiple operating systems, you must set the partition as active
before restarting the computer.

On RISC-based systems, hard disks aren't marked as active; rather, a manufacturer-supplied hardware configuration utility controls them.

To mark a partition as active using the Disk Administrator, follow these steps:

1. Select a primary partition that contains startup files for a particular OS you want to make active.

2. Choose Partition, Mark Active.

   A dialog box appears indicating that the new partition is active and will be used on startup.

3. Choose OK in the Disk Administrator dialog box.

Notice the asterisk that now appears in the color bar of the new active partition (see fig. 2.61).

Figure 2.61

The Disk Administrator main window depicting active stripe sets (indicated with colored bars).

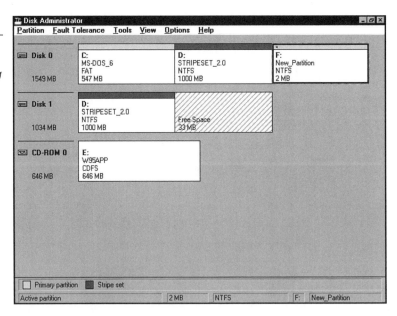

Committing Changes

After you create a partition, you may format it from within Disk Administrator, but only if you choose Partition, Commit Changes Now.

Until you commit changes, your commands aren't actually carried out, so you can change your mind if necessary. If you exit Disk Administrator without first choosing the Commit Changes Now command, Disk Administrator asks you whether it should save your changes (which is the same thing as committing them). That's the last chance you get to back out gracefully.

Deleting Partitions

You can delete any partition except for the system and boot partitions (and you can't delete those because Windows NT is using them) from Disk Administrator. Simply select the partition you want to delete, then choose Partition, Delete. Confirm your action to officially remove the partition from the interface. Again, until you commit changes, nothing officially happens. If you make a mistake, just exit Disk Administrator without saving or committing changes.

Saving and Restoring Configuration Information

The Configuration command on Disk Administrator's Partition menu enables you to save or restore a disk configuration using a floppy disk. You can save the disk configuration to a blank floppy, a floppy with a previous disk configuration, or an emergency repair disk.

You can use the Configuration Save option if you want to change your disk configuration but think you may someday want to return to the configuration you have now. Also, Microsoft recommends that you save a copy of your disk configuration before upgrading Windows NT.

The Configuration Restore option restores a saved disk configuration from a floppy.

The Configuration command includes a third option, Search, which searches your hard drive for other Windows NT installations. If you find any, you can then choose to update your disk configuration to match the configuration of one of the other Windows NT installations on the list.

Both the Restore and Search options come with a warning that you are about to overwrite your disk configuration. The Restore and Search operations don't create or delete partitions, but they do affect drive letters, volume sets, stripe sets, parity stripes, and mirrors.

Tools

The Disk Administrator Tools menu provides some options for further defining and protecting hard disks. The next few sections discuss these options in turn.

Format

A hard disk is divided into logical sections that enable a disk to locate data in a systematic fashion. This process is called formatting.

To format a partition using the Disk Administrator, follow these step:

1. Select the newly created partition you want to format.

2. Choose Partition, Commit Changes Now. Click on Yes to save the changes.

3. Choose Tools, Format.

4. In the Format dialog box, enter the volume label to identify the partition.

5. Select the type of file system to use, then choose OK.

   If you enable the Quick Format check box, the Disk Administrator doesn't scan for bad sectors during the format process. This option isn't available when you format mirror sets or stripe sets with parity.

6. Choose Yes from the Confirmation dialog box to begin the process.

   A dialog box appears indicating the current progress of the format. The format progress window lets you cancel the process, although if you do cancel it, you can't be sure that the volume will be returned to its original state.

You also can format partitions from the command prompt using the syntax

```
FORMAT <drive_letter>: /FS:FAT¦NTFS
```

Assigning a Drive Letter

Normally, Windows NT assigns drive letters starting with the first primary partition on the first physical drive, followed by the logical drives, and finally the remaining primary partitions. After Disk 0 is complete, Windows NT begins assigning drive letters to the partitions on the next physical drive in the same fashion.

If you want to override the normal drive-naming algorithm, choose Tools, Assign Drive Letter. You may change the drive designation to any other unused letter, or you may simply remove the drive letter altogether. The latter option may seem of dubious value, but it allows an administrator to "hide" a partition and its files by not providing the computer a "handle" (drive letter) by which to access it. If the administrator needs to recover the data, the partition can be reassigned a drive letter. This procedure is secure because only Administrators can work with Disk Administrator.

You can manually configure the drive letter of any volume by using the option on the Tools menu. To change a drive letter using the Disk Administrator, follow these steps:

1. Select the partition or logical drive that you want to assign a drive letter.

2. Choose Tools, Assign Drive Letter.

   A message box appears indicating the remaining drive letters for assignment.

3. In the Assign Drive Letter dialog box, select the letter to use and choose OK.

Certain programs make references to a specific drive letter, so be careful when changing drive letter assignments, especially to the active primary partition.

Properties

If you click on a volume and choose Tools, Properties, the Volume Properties dialog box appears (see fig. 2.62). (The Volume Properties dialog box is the same dialog box that will appear if you right-click on the disk in Explorer and choose Properties.) The General tab presents a graphical representation of the free and used space on the volume.

Figure 2.62

The Volume Properties dialog box.

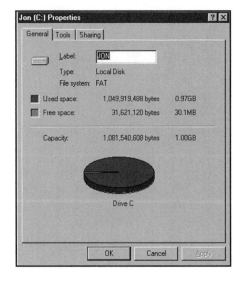

The Sharing tab of the Disk Properties dialog box lets you create and configure a network share for the volume. The Tools tab lets you back up or defragment the volume or check the volume for errors (see fig. 2.63).

Figure 2.63

The Volume Properties Tool tab.

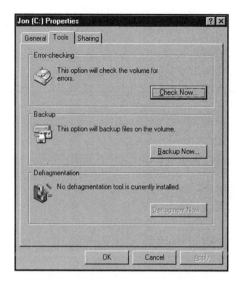

In contrast to earlier versions of NT, in which the only way to scan a volume for errors was to use CHKDSK (which you had to execute from a VDM), NT 4 provides a graphical method of checking hard disks for errors.

To check for disk problems from Disk Administrator, select the partition you want to check, choose Tools, Properties, and select the Tools tab from the Properties dialog box. Click on the Check Now button to open the Check Disk dialog box, which offers the following options:

▶ Automatically fix file system errors

▶ Scan for and attempt recovery of bad sectors

Choose either or both options and click on the Start button to begin checking the partition.

Fault Tolerance

Fundamentally, fault tolerance is the system's ability to recover in the event of hardware disaster.

The standard for fault tolerance is known as Redundant Array of Inexpensive Disks (RAID). Chapter 1 introduced the two RAID fault-tolerance methods available with Windows NT, as follows:

▶ Disk Mirroring

▶ Disk Striping with Parity

The following sections describe how to configure these fault-tolerance methods through Disk Administrator.

Creating a Mirror

Disk mirroring is a RAID level 1 fault tolerance method. A mirror is a redundant copy of another disk partition, and it uses the same or a different hard disk controller. You can use any partition, including the boot or system partitions, to establish a mirror.

In the past, disk mirroring was one of the more expensive solutions of protecting against disk failure. However, because a mirror requires only two hard disks for implementation, if you take into account global reductions in pricing, this method now is an effective alternative to other forms of fault tolerance.

To create a mirror using the Disk Administrator, follow these steps:

1. Select at least two areas of free space on different hard drives.

2. Choose Fault Tolerance, Establish Mirror.

The Disk Administrator then creates spaces of equal size on both disks and assigns a drive letter to them.

Creating a Stripe Set with Parity

A stripe set with parity is considered a RAID level 5 fault tolerance method; it differs from other approaches by writing information across all disks in the array. It accomplishes fault tolerance by keeping the data and parity on separate disks.

Parity information exists as a stripe block in each row that spans the array, so three rather than two drives must be used. In the event a single drive fails, enough information is distributed across the drives for it to be completely reconstructed. When creating a stripe set with parity, you may use all partitions except for the boot or system partition. To create a stripe set with parity, follow these steps:

1. Select between 3 and 32 areas of free disk space on each drive.

2. Choose Fault Tolerance, Create Stripe Set with Parity.

   A dialog box appears indicating the possible minimum and maximum sizes for a new extended partition.

3. In the Create Stripe Set with Parity dialog box, enter the size of the stripe set to create and choose OK.

The Disk Administrator calculates the stripe set with parity's total size, based on the number of disks selected, and creates a space that is equal on each disk. It then combines the drives into one logical volume. If you have selected free areas that are disproportionate, the Disk Administrator rounds to the closest value.

As you must with other new volumes, you must format the stripe set before it can be used. To format the new volume, save the changes by choosing Partition, Commit Changes Now or answer the prompts when exiting the Disk Administrator. You also must restart the system before formatting.

Securing System Partition on RISC Machines

The system partition on a RISC computer must be a FAT partition. Because Windows NT cannot provide the same security for a FAT partition that it provides for an NTFS partition, the RISC version of Windows NT includes a special Secure System Partition command that provides an extra layer of security for RISC-based system partitions. This command specifies that only members of the local Administrators group have access to the system partition.

Configuring Printing

The printing process is an important part of an operating system, and network administrators spend a significant amount of time chasing down printing problems. For the NT Server exams, you should become familiar with the following printer-related topics:

- ▶ Understanding Windows NT printing architecture

- ▶ Installing printers

- ▶ Configuring printers

- ▶ Sharing printers

- ▶ Setting up a printer pool

- ▶ Printing from MS-DOS applications

This chapter examines how printing works under Windows NT, both locally and remotely, and examines each of these topics.

Microsoft lists the following objective for the Windows NT Server exam:

Configure printers. Tasks include: adding and configuring a printer, implementing a printer pool, setting print priorities.

Windows NT Printing Architecture

Most of us visualize a printer as a device that receives data from the computer and converts it into a rendered hard copy. In Windows NT, however, the term printer refers to the software that controls a specific printing device or devices.

Windows NT uses the term printing device to refer to the hardware that produces the actual output.

Other operating systems—NetWare, for example—use the term print queue for what Windows NT calls a printer. Windows NT also uses the term print queue, but in NT, a print queue is simply the list (queue) of documents waiting to print.

It's interesting to note that under Windows NT, a single printer can control more than one printing device. When a single printer (software) controls more than one printing device (hardware), the resulting configuration is called a printer pool. Printer pools are discussed in more detail later in this chapter.

You should become familiar with the components of the Windows NT printing process for the MCSE exam. The process goes roughly as follows:

1. When an application on an NT client sends a print job, Windows NT checks to see if the version of the printer driver on the client is up-to-date with the version on the print server. If it isn't, Windows NT downloads a new version of the printer driver from the print server to the client.

2. The printer driver sends the data to the client spooler. The client spooler spools the data to a file, and makes a remote procedure call to the server spooler, thus transmitting the data to the server spooler on the print server machine.

3. The server spooler sends the data to the Local Print Provider.

4. The Local Print Provider passes the data to a print processor, where it's rendered into a format legible to the printing device. Then, if necessary, the Local Print Provider sends the data to a separator page processor, where a separator page is added to the beginning of the document. The Local Print Provider lastly passes the rendered data to the print monitor.

5. The print monitor points the rendered data to the appropriate printer port and, therefore, to the appropriate printing device.

The following sections discuss the components of the NT printing process.

Printer Drivers

In the first step of the printing process, Windows NT checks to see if the printer driver on the print client is current; if it isn't, Windows NT downloads a new copy of the printer driver from the print server.

> This automatic update of the printer driver on the client is a fundamental element of Windows NT printing. When you set up a Windows NT printer, the Setup wizard asks for the operating systems and hardware platforms of all client machines that are going to access the printer. The wizard then places the appropriate printer drivers on the server so they will be available for downloading.

Because the printer driver is responsible for generating the data stream that forms a print job, the success of the print job relies on the printer driver's health. The Windows NT printer driver is implemented as a combination of two dynamic link libraries (or DLLs) and a printer-specific minidriver or configuration file.

Typically, Microsoft supplies the two dynamic link libraries with Windows NT, and the original equipment manufacturer of the printer supplies the minidriver or configuration file. The following list describes these three files:

- ▶ **The Printer Graphics Driver DLL.** This dynamic link library consists of the rendering or managing portion of the driver; it's always called by the Graphics Device Interface.

- ▶ **The Printer Interface Driver.** This dynamic link library consists of the user interface or configuration management portion of the printer driver; it's used by an administrator to configure a printer.

- ▶ **The Characterization File.** This component contains all the printer-specific information, such as memory, page protection, soft fonts, graphics resolution, paper orientation and size, and so on; it's used by the other two dynamic link libraries whenever they need to gather printer-specific information.

These three components of a printer driver (printer graphics driver, printer interface driver, and configuration file) are all located in the following directory, according to their Windows NT platforms (w32x86, w32mips, w32alpha, and w32ppc) and version numbers (0 = version 3.1, 1 = version 3.5x, 2 = version 4.x):

```
winnt_root\system32\spool\drivers.directory
```

The printer driver is specific to both the operating system and the hardware platform. You can't use a Windows 95 printer driver with Windows NT, and you can't use an Intel Windows NT printer driver on an Alpha Windows NT machine (see fig. 2.64).

Figure 2.64

*Choosing a
printer driver in
the printer Prop-
erties Sharing
tab.*

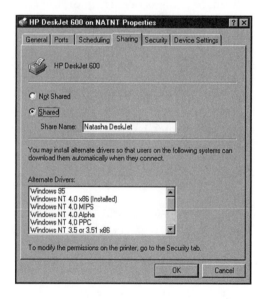

Spooler

The Spooler is a Windows NT service that operates in the background to manage the printing process. The spooler consists of a series of DLLs that work together to accept, process, and distribute print jobs.

You need to understand that the spooler really runs the show. Specifically, the spooler service is responsible for the following functions:

▶ Keeping track of what jobs are destined for which printers

▶ Keeping track of which ports are connected to which printers

▶ Routing print jobs to the correct port

▶ Managing printer pools

▶ Prioritizing print jobs

The NT Spooler service must be running on both the client and the print server machines for the printing process to function properly. Logically, however, you can think of the print spooler as a single process occurring on the client and on print server machines.

By default, the spool file folder is the `winnt_root\system32\spool\PRINTERS` directory. You can change the spool folder by using the Advanced tab of the printer server Properties dialog box. (The print server Properties dialog box gets more attention later in this chapter.) You also can use Registry Editor to set the spool directory, like so:

For all printers:

```
HKEY_LOCAL_MACHINE\SYSTEM\CurrentControlSet\Control\Print\Printers
DefaultSpoolDirectory:REG_SZ:<New Spool Path>
```

On a per-printer basis:

```
HKEY_LOCAL_MACHINE\SYSTEM\CurrentControlSet\Control\Print\Printers\
<printer>SpoolDirectory:REG_SZ:<New Spool Path>
```

In the event that a print job gets stuck in the spooler to the point that an administrator or print operator cannot delete or purge it, you can stop the Spooler service and restart it using the Control Panel Service application.

You also can start or stop the Spooler service using the following commands at the command prompt:

```
net start spooler
net stop spooler
```

Router

The print router receives the print job from the spooler and routes it to the appropriate print processor.

The Print Processor

The process of translating print data into a form that a printing device can read is called rendering. The rendering process begins with the printer driver. The print processor is responsible for completing the rendering process. The tasks performed by the print processor differ depending on the print data's data type.

The primary Windows NT print processor is called WINPRINT.DLL, and is located in

```
winnt_root\system32\spool\prtprocs\platform
```

WINPRINT.DLL recognizes the following data types:

▶ **Raw data.** Fully rendered data that is ready for the printer. A postscript command, for instance, reaches the print processor as raw data.

▶ **Windows NT Enhanced Metafile (EMF).** A standard file format that many different printing devices support. Instead of the raw printer data being generated by the printer driver, the Graphical Device Interface generates NT EMF information before spooling. After the NT EMF is created, control returns to the user. The NT EMF is then interpreted in the background on a 32-bit printing subsystem spooler thread and sent to the printer driver. This process returns control to the user in significantly less time than waiting for the printer calls to be directly interpreted by the printer driver.

▶ **TEXT.** Raw text with minimal formatting. The TEXT data type is designed for printing devices that don't directly accept ASCII text. The print processor sends TEXT data to the graphics engine.

If you're running Services for Macintosh on a Windows NT server, you also have access to the print processor SFMPSPRT.DLL, which supports the PSCRIPT1 data type. The PSCRIPT1 data type is for print data sent from Macintosh clients to non-PostScript printing devices.

Print Monitors

Print Monitors controls access to a specific device, monitors the status of the device, and communicates this information back to the spooler, which relays the information via the user interface. The print monitor essentially controls the data stream to one or more printer ports; its responsibilities include writing a print job to the output destination and taking care of port access (opening, closing, configuring, reading from, writing to, and acquiring or releasing ports).

To install a new print monitor, click on Add Port in the Ports tab of the printer Properties dialog box. Click on the New Monitor button in the Printer Ports dialog box that appears (see fig. 2.65).

Figure 2.65

The Printer Ports dialog box.

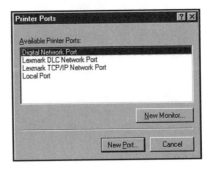

In addition, the print monitor has the following duties:

▶ Detect unsolicited errors (such as Toner Low).

▶ Handle true end-of-job notification. The print monitor waits until the last page has been printed to notify the spooler that the print job has finished and can be discarded.

▶ Monitor printer status to detect printing errors. If necessary, the print monitor notifies the spooler so that the job can continue or be restarted.

Windows NT provides some standard print monitors. These include print monitors for the following:

▶ Local output to LPTx, COMx, remote printer shares and names pipes (\WINNT_ROOT\SYSTEM32\ LOCALMON.DLL).

▶ Output to Hewlett-Packard network interface printing devices (\WINNT_ROOT\SYSTEM32\HPMON.DLL), which can support up to 225 (configured for 64) Hewlett-Packard network interface printing devices. This print monitor requires the DLC protocol.

▶ Output to Digital network port printers (DECPSMON.DLL), supporting both TCP/IP and DECnet protocols. The DECnet protocol doesn't ship with Windows NT.

▶ Output to LPR (Line Printer) Ports (LPRMON.DLL), allowing Windows NT to print directly to UNIX LPD print servers or network interface printing devices over the TCP/IP protocol.

▶ Output to PJL Language printing device (PJLMON.DLL).

▶ Output to Apple Macintosh postscript printers (SFMMON.DLL), for Windows NT servers with services for the Apple Macintosh installed.

Printers Folder

The Printers folder is the Windows NT printing system's primary user interface. The Printers folder replaces Print Manager, the printing interface in previous versions of NT. You can reach the Printers folder through Control Panel, or through the Settings item in the Start menu.

From the Printers folder, you install, configure, administer, and remove printers. You also supervise print queues; pause, purge and restart print jobs; share printers; and set printer defaults. The following sections discuss two of the principal activities managed through the Printers folder: adding printers and configuring printers.

You can install printers on your Windows NT workstation in two ways: install a printer on your own workstation, or connect to a remote printer. Installing your own printer is much more involved than connecting to a remote printer, and it requires Administrative or Power User-level rights. You add a new printer or connect to a remote printer using the Add Printer icon in the Printers folder. You also can connect to a remote printer via Network Neighborhood.

From the Printers folder, double-click on the Add Printer icon to open the Add Printer Wizard (see fig. 2.66).

Figure 2.66

The Add Printer Wizard screen.

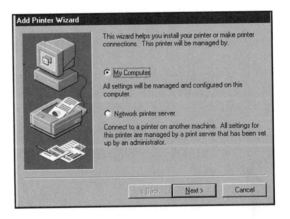

The first screen of the Add Printer Wizard asks if the new printer will be attached to your computer (the My Computer option) or connected to another machine and accessed via the network (the Network printer server option). The My Computer option requires Administrator or Power User rights, whereas the Network printer server option does not; you don't have to be an Administrator or a Power User to connect to a shared printer on another machine.

Adding a Printer on Your Own Machine

If you select the My Computer option from the Add Printer Wizard screen, and then click on Next, the Wizard asks you what port you want to use (see fig. 2.67). You must select a port for the new printer. The Wizard won't let you proceed until you have either checked one of the ports or added a new port.

Figure 2.67

The Add Port button enables you to add a new digital network port, local port, or PJL language monitor to your printing system.

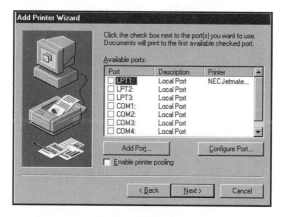

The next screen asks you to specify the manufacturer and model of the new printer (see fig. 2.68). Select a manufacturer, and a list of drivers for printers by that manufacturer appears. Or, if you want to install an unlisted printer driver from a disk, click on the Have Disk button.

Figure 2.68

The manufacturer and model options screen of the Add Printer wizard.

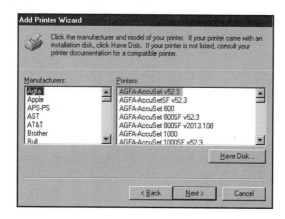

The next screen asks for a printer name, and whether you want the printer to become the default printer for Windows-based programs. As with all objects in Windows NT, a printer requires a name. The printer name can be as long as 32 characters and doesn't have to reflect the name of the driver in use. You should avoid using the full 32 characters, however, because you might sometimes need to type the printer name to connect to it from a remote computer.

The next screen asks if you want to share the printer (see fig. 2.69). If you want to share the printer with other computers on the network, you must also specify a share name (the default share name is the printer name specified in the preceding screen.) The wizard also asks you to specify the operating systems of all computers that will be sharing the printer. Your only choices are Windows 95 and a number of NT versions and platforms.

Figure 2.69

The Add Printer Wizard asks if you want to share the printer.

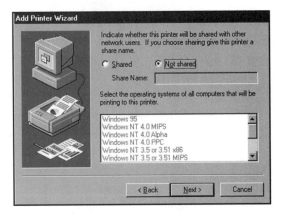

The Add Printer Wizard then attempts to install the printer driver. You may be asked to supply the Windows NT installation disk. (If you designate Windows 95 as the operating system of a computer sharing the printer, you may also be prompted to supply the Windows 95 installation CD-ROM.) The wizard then asks if you want to print a test page.

When the installation is complete, the Add Printer wizard opens the Properties dialog box for the new printer. You can read more about the Properties dialog box later in this chapter.

Adding a Network Print Server

If you choose the work printer server option in the first screen of the Add Printer Wizard, the Wizard opens the Connect to Printer dialog box (see fig. 2.70), which asks for the name of the shared printer to which you want to connect. Click on the workstation to which the printer is attached and then select the printer.

Figure 2.70

The Connect to Printer dialog box.

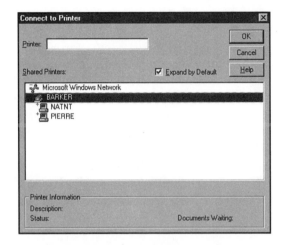

The Add Printer Wizard doesn't know enough to open a network connection for you; if you don't open a connection using the workstation you select in the Connect to Printer dialog box, the printers attached to that workstation don't display. If this situation occurs, double-click on the Network Neighborhood icon and then double-click on the icon for the workstation, to enter your username and password and establish a connection. As long as you're in Network Neighborhood, you might as well establish the printer connection through Network Neighborhood.

The Wizard then asks if you want the printer to serve as a default printer, and completes the installation. If the installation is successful, the icon for the printer appears in the Printers folder.

Configuring Printers

Almost all the configuration settings for a printer in Windows NT 4 are accessible through the following three options of the Printers folder File menu:

▶ Document Defaults

▶ Server Properties

▶ Properties

You also use the Sharing option in the File menu for configuration; specifically, to set up the printer as a shared printer on the network. It's actually just a different path to the Sharing tab of the Properties dialog box.

You find most of the configuration settings for a given printer in the Properties dialog box. The NT 4 printer Properties dialog box is designed to serve as a central location for printer configuration information.

The Server Properties dialog box holds information specific to the computer's print server activities. The Server Properties dialog box thus is independent of any particular printer (which is why Server Properties appears in the File menu regardless of whether a printer is selected.) The Document Defaults option opens the Default Document Properties dialog box, which holds page setup and document settings for a given printer.

You can reach most of the Printers folder File menu options easily; if you right-click on a printer icon in the Printers folder, the File menu options appear in a context menu.

Document Defaults

Choose File, Document Defaults to open the Default Document Properties dialog box (see fig. 2.71). The Default Document Properties dialog box contains document settings for the documents that are to print on the selected printer. A good example of a document setting you can control by using the Default Document Properties dialog box is the Orientation setting.

Figure 2.71

*Page Setup tab
of the Default
Document Prop-
erties dialog box.*

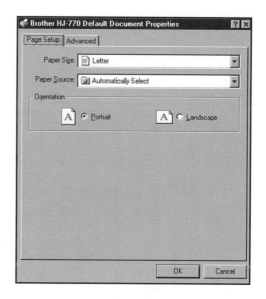

The Page Setup tab defines the Paper Size, Paper Source, and
Orientation options for controlling settings for the document you
want to print. You change the size, source, and orientation settings in the Advanced tab, which also contains settings for graphics resolution, color adjustment, and print quality (see fig. 2.72).

Figure 2.72

*The Advanced
tab of the Default
Document Prop-
erties dialog box.*

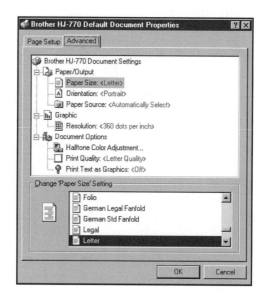

Server Properties

Choose File, Server Properties to open the Print Server Properties dialog box (see fig. 2.73). The following sections discuss the three tabs in the Print Server Properties dialog box.

Figure 2.73

The Forms tab of the Print Server Properties dialog box.

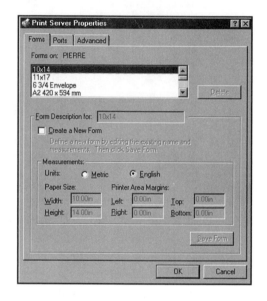

Forms

The Forms tab of the Print Server Properties dialog box defines the print forms available on the computer. Think of a print form as a description of a piece of paper that might be in a printer tray. A print form tells NT the size of the paper and where to put the printer margins. The Device Settings tab of the Properties dialog box lets you assign a print form to an actual tray. Thus, you can tell NT the size of the paper in each printer tray, and the size of the printer margins. This facility is useful when you have multiple printer trays with different sizes of paper in each, or when one of your printer trays contains a particular type of paper, such as corporate letterhead paper, which requires a different top or bottom margin from the standard tray.

You can create your own print forms from within the Forms tab. To create your own form, follow these steps:

1. Click on an existing form in the Forms On list.

2. Select the Create a New Form check box.

3. Change the name of the form, and change the form measurements to the new settings.

4. Click on the Save Form button.

Ports

The Ports tab of the Printer Server Properties dialog box maintains a list of available ports. You can add, delete, or configure a port. The Ports tab here is similar to the Add Printer Wizard Ports tab (discussed earlier in this chapter) and the printer Properties Ports tab (discussed later in this chapter) except that, in this case, you don't have to select a port because you aren't associating a port with a particular printer, but rather, are merely viewing the ports that are available for all printers.

Advanced

The Advanced tab of the Printer Server Properties dialog box provides the location of the spooler and an assortment of logging and notification options (see fig. 2.74).

Figure 2.74

The Advanced tab of the Print Server Properties dialog box.

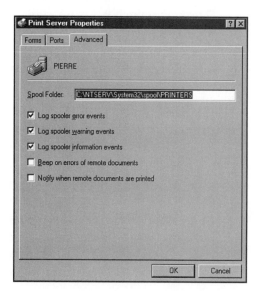

Properties

You can find most of the printer configuration settings in the printer Properties dialog box (see fig. 2.75). To open the printer Properties dialog box, select a printer in the Printers folder and choose File, Properties, or right-click on the printer and choose Properties. The following sections discuss the six tabs of the printer Properties dialog box.

Figure 2.75

The printer Properties dialog box.

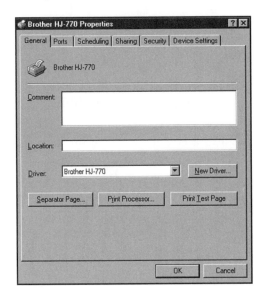

The Printer Properties General Tab

The General tab lets you install a new driver for the printer. The Print Test Page button provides a convenient method for testing whether a printer connection is working. The Separator Page and Print Processor buttons are a bit more complicated.

Separator File

By default, Windows NT doesn't separate print jobs with even a blank sheet of paper; to print a separator page between print jobs, you must configure a separator file, of which three are included with Windows NT. You may use one of these or create your own:

▶ **SYSPRINT.SEP.** Prints a separator page for PostScript printers; stored in the \<winnt_root>\SYSTEM32 directory.

▸ **PSCRIPT.SEP.** Switches Hewlett-Packard printers to Post-
  Script mode for printers incapable of autoswitching; located
  in the \<winnt_root>\SYSTEM32 directory.

▸ **PCL.SEP.** Switches Hewlett-Packard printers to PCL mode
  for printers not capable of autoswitching (and prints a separator page before each document); located in the
  \<winnt_root>\SYSTEM32 directory.

You also may choose to design your own separator page. If so, use
a text editor and consult the escape codes listed in table 2.1 . The
escape codes are special symbols that prompt Windows NT to
replace them with specific pieces of data. For instance, /N is the
escape code that instructs Windows NT to print the username of
the user who printed the job, and /D represents the date the job
was printed.

Table 2.1

Windows NT Printing Escape Codes	
Code	Instruction for Windows NT
\<number>	Skip specified number of lines (0–9)
\B\M	Print text in double-width block mode
\B\S	Print text in single-width block mode
\D	Print current date using Control Panel International format
\E	Eject the page
\F<filename>	Print a file
\H<code>	Send printer-specific hexadecimal ASCII code
\I	Print job number
\L<text>	Print the specified text (use another escape code to end)
\N	Print username of job owner
\T	Print time the job was printed. Use Control Panel International format.
\U	Turn off block mode (see \B\M and \B\S)
\W<width>	Set width of the page (<=256)

To specify a separator file, click on the Separator Page button in the printer Properties General tab and enter the name of the file, or click on Browse and locate the separator file.

Print Processor

Don't mess with the print processor; it's the component of the printing subsystem that actually performs the rendering. Typically, WINPRINT.DLL performs the print processor functions. If it becomes necessary to replace it, Windows NT does it for you.

WINPRINT.DLL supports the following five data types:

▶ Raw Fully rendered data ready for printing

▶ RAW (FF appended)

▶ RAW (FF auto)

▶ NT EMF (enhanced metafile format) A device-independent file format. An EMF file can be spooled directly to the print server and rendered at the server into the correct print format.

▶ TEXT Raw, unformatted ASCII text ready for printing as is.

Printer Properties Ports Tab

The printer Properties Ports tab lets you select a port for the printer, and add or delete a port from the tab (see fig. 2.76). The Configure Port button allows you to specify the Transmission Retry time (the amount of time that must elapse before NT notifies you that the printing device isn't responding). The Transmission Retry setting applies not just to printer you selected but to all printers that use the same driver.

Figure 2.76

The printer Properties Ports tab.

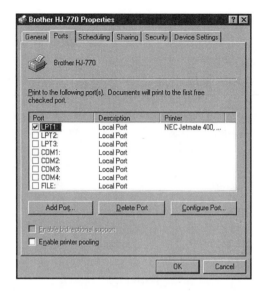

Printer Properties Scheduling Tab

The printer Properties Scheduling tab lets you designate when the printer is to be available, and to set the printer priority (see fig. 2.77). It also displays some miscellaneous settings that define how the printer processes print jobs. The next few sections discuss the important settings of the Scheduling tab.

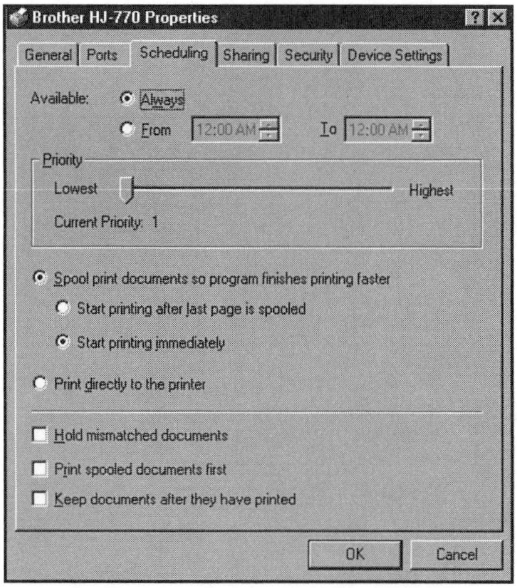

Figure 2.77

The printer Properties Scheduling tab.

Available

The Available setting lets you limit the availability of a printer to a specific period of time. Note that just because a printer is restricted to a certain period of time doesn't mean the device must be similarly restricted. To keep long monthly reports from monopolizing a device during business hours, for example, you could create two printers for the same printing device, one of which might be used for short print jobs and be available during the day, the other of which might be used for long reports and print only at night.

Priority

The default priority for a printer is 1, but it can be set as high as 99. Changing this setting from its default of 1 is useful in situations in which you have more than one printer printing to the same printing device, in which case the printer with higher priority (99 being the highest) prints before printers of lower priority (1 being the lowest). Note that the Printer Priority is not related to the Print job priority.

Spool Print Documents or Print Directly to Printer

If you spool print documents, the computer and the printer don't have to wait for each other. It's almost always more efficient to spool print documents; you rarely have reason to change this default. One advantage, however, of Print Directly to Printer is that printing directly to the printer might allow you to troubleshoot a problem with the spooler. If you can print to the printer but you can't print via the spooler, you may have a problem with your spooler.

Under the Spool print documents option, there are two other options:

▶ Start printing after the last page is spooled.

▶ Start printing immediately.

The first choice is (in part) a holdover from earlier versions on NT; NT used to wait until a job was completely spooled before beginning to print it. This wait could take a long time for reports hundreds of pages long, so more recent versions offered a "Job prints while spooling" option to let the printer start printing before the spooler finishes. In NT 4, "Start printing immediately" is the default option, but you still have the option of not printing until after the last page spools.

Hold Mismatched Documents

In other Windows-based operating environments, improperly configured print jobs—a print job, for example, requesting a paper tray that isn't present—can be sent to a printer, which usually causes the printer to hang with an error message. But with the Hold Mismatched Documents option selected, Windows NT examines the configuration of both the print job and printer to make sure that they are in agreement before it sends the job.

Print Spooled Documents First

Ordinarily, Windows NT prints documents on a first-come, first-served basis; the document at the top of the queue prints before the documents below it. If the document at the top of the queue takes a long time to spool, and if the Job Prints While Spooling option isn't selected, you might want to enable the Print Spooled Documents First setting. Windows NT always prints the first available completely spooled print job. If this setting is used in conjunction with Job Prints While Spooling, all the completely spooled documents ahead of the spooling document print first. The spooling document is processed next, even if completed documents are waiting behind it in the queue.

Keep Documents After They Have Printed

Normally, Windows NT cleans up after itself as it finishes printing each job. If you enable the Keep documents after they have printed option, however, Windows NT keeps the print document after it prints. One reason to check this box is if you want to have a record of completed print jobs that all users can access. Although you may choose to have completed print jobs recorded in the event logs, non-administrative users cannot view the event logs.

The Printer Properties Sharing Tab

The Sharing tab lets you share the printer with other computers on the network (see fig. 2.78). If you didn't install the printer as a shared printer but decide later to share it, you can change the printer to a shared printer.

Figure 2.78

The printer Properties Sharing tab.

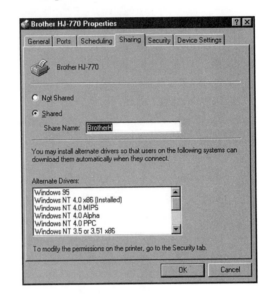

To share a printer, follow these steps:

1. Select Sharing tab in the printer Properties dialog box.

2. Specify a share name (or accept the default, which is the first eight characters of the printer name).

3. Specify what operating systems the other workstations will be using (so NT can automatically download the necessary print drivers to the connecting computers).

4. Click on OK.

You access the Sharing tab directly by clicking on a printer and choosing File, Sharing in the Printers folder, or by right-clicking on a printer and choosing Sharing.

The Printer Properties Security Tab

The Security tab lets you configure permissions, auditing, and ownership for the printer (see fig. 2.79).

Figure 2.79

The printer Properties Security tab.

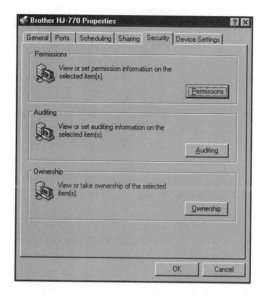

Windows NT printers are Windows NT resources, and Windows NT resources are Windows NT objects. Windows NT objects are protected by the Windows NT security model; that is, they have owners and Access Control Lists that owners can use to protect the printers.

To set or change permissions, a user must be the owner, an Administrator, a Power User, or a user who has Full Control permissions on the printer's ACL.

To set permissions for a printer, select the Security tab in the printer Properties dialog box and click on the Permissions button. You see the Printer Permissions dialog box, which displays common user groups and the permission levels granted to each group for the use of selected printer (see fig. 2.80).

Figure 2.80

The printer Per-missions dialog box.

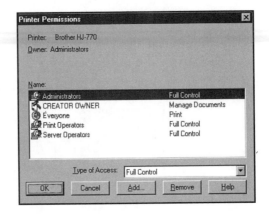

The four possible permission levels are as follows:

▶ **No Access.** Completely restricts access to the printer.

▶ **Print.** Allows a user or group to submit a print job, and to control the settings and print status for that job.

▶ **Manage Documents.** Allows a user or group to submit a print job, and to control the settings and print status for all print jobs.

▶ **Full Control.** Allows a user to submit a print job, and to control the settings and print status for all documents as well as for the printer itself. In addition, the user or group may share, stop sharing, change permissions for, and even delete the printer.

These permissions affect both local and remote users. By default, permissions on newly created printers comply with the following scheme:

Administrators	Full Control
Creator/Owner	Manage Documents
Everyone	Print
Power Users (workstations only)	Full Control and servers
Print Operators (domain only)	Full Control controllers
Server Operators (domain only)	Full Control controllers

To change the permission level for a group, select the group in the Name list and enter a new permission level in the Type of Access combo box, or open the Type of Access combo box and select a permission level. To add a group or user to the permissions list, click on the Add button. The Add Users and Groups dialog box opens (see fig. 2.81).

Figure 2.81

The Add Users and Groups dialog box.

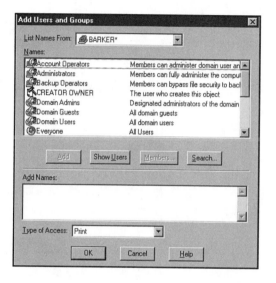

To add a group to the permissions list, select a group in the Names list of the Add Users and Groups dialog box and click on Add. The name of the group appears in the Add Names box. Click on OK to add the name to the permissions list.

To add an individual user to the permissions list, click on the Show Users button in the Add Users and Groups dialog box. This adds users to the Names list. Select the user and click on Add. The name of the user then appears in the Add Names box. Click on OK to add the name to the permissions list.

After you add the group or user to the permissions list, you can change the permission level for that group or user, as described earlier in this section.

The printer Properties Security tab also enables you to set up auditing for the printer and to take ownership of the printer.

Printer Properties Device Settings Tab

The printer Properties Device Settings tab maintains settings for the printing device (see fig. 2.82). These settings differ depending on your printing device. The Form To Tray Assignment setting allows you to associate a print form with an actual paper tray on the printing device.

Figure 2.82

The printer Properties Device Settings tab.

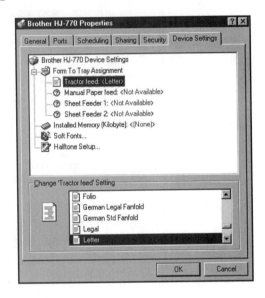

Sharing Printers

As you install a new printer, you can designate as a printer to share over the network. The section "Adding a Printer on Your Own Machine" earlier in this chapter describes how to do this.

You can share a printer that already has been installed using the Sharing tab in the printer Properties dialog box. See the section "The Printer Properties Sharing Tab," earlier in this chapter.

Use the Security tab in the printer Properties dialog box to set or change permissions for printers.

Setting Up a Printer Pool

A printer pool presents interesting possibilities for some office environments. A printer pool is essentially a single logical printer that prints to more than one printing device; it prints jobs sent to it to the first available printing device (and therefore provides the throughput of multiple printing devices with the simplicity of a single printer definition).

The user has no control over which device prints the job; therefore, printer pools are incredibly annoying if the printing devices aren't located at the same place.

If a printer controls a printer pool, Windows NT ensures that no single device is ever sent more than one document at a time if other devices currently are available. This characteristic ensures the most efficient utilization of your printing devices.

Printer pools are an extremely efficient way of streamlining the printing process, although they don't necessarily fit every environment. Before your network can use a printer pool, it must meet the following criteria:

▶ You must have at least two printing devices capable of using the same printer driver because the entire pool is treated as a single logical device, and is managed by a single printer driver.

▶ The printing devices should be adjacent to each other. Users aren't notified of the actual device that prints their job; users should be able to check all the printing devices rapidly and easily.

To create a printer pool, configure the printer to print to more than one port, and make sure a printing device is attached to each of the ports that the printer is using. You can choose more than one port when you select a printer port at installation (as described earlier in this chapter). Or, you can designate a new port for an existing printer using the Ports tab in the printer Properties dialog box.

Printing from MS-DOS Applications

MS-DOS applications provide their own printer drivers and automatically render printer data to the RAW data type or to straight ASCII text. The print data is then intercepted by the client spooler and routed through the Windows NT printing system.

The MS-DOS application typically isn't equipped to process UNC names, so if it is printing to a remote printer, you should map a physical port to the remote printer, as follows:

```
net use LPTx: \\pserver\printer_name
```

Because the application itself renders the printer data, an MS-DOS application that prints graphics and formatted text must have its own printer driver for the printing device. An MS-DOS application can print ASCII text output without a vendor-supplied printer driver.

Configuring Windows NT Server for Client Computers

The Windows NT CD-ROM includes client software to assist with networking certain common operating systems with Windows NT. Chapter 1 (and the section on "Installing with Client Administrator," earlier in this chapter) discuss some of the client software packages included with Windows NT Server. When you are configuring networking protocols on your Windows NT Server system, it is important to remember that all these software packages don't support all the native Windows NT network protocols and network services.

Microsoft lists the following objective for the Windows NT Server exam:

Configure a Windows NT Server computer for various types of client computers. Client computer types include: Windows NT Workstation, Microsoft Windows 95, Microsoft MS-DOS-based.

Table 2.2 describes which network protocols and which TCP/IP services each of the client systems supports. This table also appears in Chapter 1, in the section entitled "Planning for Network Clients." You must ensure that the Windows NT configuration provides the appropriate protocols for whatever client systems you'll have running on your network. For more on these client system, see Chapter 1.

Table 2.2

Network Protocol and TCP/IP Service Support for Various Windows NT Client Systems

Network Protocol TCP/IP Service

	Net-BEUI	Com-patible	Com-patible	TCP/IP	DLC	DHCP	WINS	DNS
Network Client for MS-DOS	X	X	IPX	X	X	X		
LAN MAN 2.2c for MS-DOS	X		IPX/ SPX	X	X			
Lan MAN 2.2c for OS/2	X			X				
Windows 95	X		X	X		X	X	X
Windows NT Workstation	X		X	X	X	X	X	X

Exercise Section

Exercise 2.1:   The Server and Workstation Services

In Exercise 2.1, you learn about starting and stopping services using the Services application in the Control Panel, and you study the functions of the Server and Workstation services.

1. Start two Windows NT PCs on your network that each provide shared resources. This exercise will refer to those computers and as Computer A and Computer B.

2. Using Network Neighborhood, browse Computer B from Computer A. Then browse Computer A from Computer B. Make sure the shared resources are available.

3. Start the Control Panel Services application on Computer B. Shut down the Server service. Windows NT will ask if it's OK to shut down the Computer Browser service too. Click OK. Click Close to close the Services application.

4. Now try to browse Computer B from Computer A. You'll get a message that says, *"<\\computer_name>* is not accessible. The network path was not found."

5. Restart the Server service in the Control Panel Services application. Now try to browse Computer B from Computer A. The shared resources are now available.

6. In the Control Panel Services application, shut down the Workstation service. Notice that you can still browse Computer B from Computer A.

7. With the Computer B Workstation service stopped, try to browse Computer A from Computer B. You'll get a message that says "Unable to browse the network. The network is not present or not started.

8. Restart the Computer B Workstation service. You can now browse computer A from Computer B.

Exercise 2.2: Creating a Network Installation Disk

Exercise 2.2 will show you how to create a network installation disk using Network Client Administrator.

1. Prepare an MS-DOS system disk using the MS-DOS sys command on an MS-DOS machine.

2. Create a network installation startup disk as described in this chapter in the section entitled "Network Installation Startup Disk." Create a share for the installation files using the Share Files option in the Share Network Client Installation Files dialog box, which shares directly from the Windows NT CD-ROM and doesn't require disk space on the installation server.

3. Boot a network computer using the network installation startup disk and attempt to connect to the installation share you created in Step 2.

Exercise 2.3: Directory Replication

In Exercise 2.3, you learn how to set up directory replication on your network.

1. Set up the Windows NT Server export server for directory replication using the procedure described in the "Directory Replication" section of this chapter.

2. Set up an import computer using the procedure described in the "Directory Replication" section of this chapter.

3. Copy some files to the export directory of the export server.

4. Wait a few minutes. See if the files you copied to the export directory in step 3 appear in the import directory of the import computer.

Exercise 2.4: Network Bindings

Just because a protocol is properly installed, it doesn't mean you can use it with a particular network adapter. To use a protocol with an network adapter, a *binding* between the protocol and the adapter must exist. Exercise 2.4 studies the effect of removing a network binding.

1. Logon to a Windows NT Server system that uses the TCP/IP protocol and go to the command prompt.

2. Ping the loopback address: 127.0.0.1 (see Exercise 2 of Chapter 1). The loopback address verifies that TCP/IP is properly configured for your system. You should get four replies.

3. Ping the IP address of the computer you are now using. The IP address is actually associated with your network adapter. You should get four replies.

4. Start Control Panel Network application and select the Bindings tab.

5. In the Show Bindings for: box, select all adapters.

6. Expand the tree for your network adapter. Select the TCP/IP protocol.

7. Click on the Disable button. This will disable the TCP/IP binding for your network adapter card. Click OK.

8. Windows NT will ask if you want to restart your system. Click Yes.

9. Restart your system. Logon and go to the command prompt.

10. Ping the loopback address. You should still get four replies.

11. Ping the IP address of your own computer. You'll get a message that says "Destination host unreachable" four times. Your network adapter is "unreachable" because you have disabled the binding that associates you adapter with the TCP/IP protocol.

12. Ping another computer on your network. You should get the "Destination host unreachable" message for other PCs too, because disabling the binding has disrupted the pathway through which your computer communicates with the network.

13. Return to the Bindings tab of the Network application. In the box labeled Show Bindings for:, select *all adapters*. Expand the tree for your network adapter. Enable the the TCP/IP protocol. Shut down and restart your system.

Review Questions

1. You're considering purchasing a file server for the Accounting department to run Windows NT Server 4. What's the first thing you should do?

   A. Verify that all the hardware to be contained in the server is on Microsoft's Hardware Compatibility List (HCL).

   B. Purchase the parts and put the server together yourself so you know you're obtaining a quality computer.

   C. Buy the server hardware only from a reputable dealer licensed to sell Microsoft Windows NT Server.

   D. Contact Microsoft and ask them to direct you to a Microsoft Certified Hardware vendor in your area.

2. You installed Windows NT Server 4 on a machine that has an existing installation of OS/2. Now, after the final reboot of the installation program, you notice that the OS/2 boot manager menu isn't displaying. What could be the problem?

   A. When you installed NT you actually upgraded from OS/2 to NT, thus overwriting the OS/2 installation.

   B. Nothing, you can't boot OS/2 when Windows NT 4 is installed.

   C. Windows NT has disabled the boot manager and you need to re-enable it via Disk Administrator by marking the Boot Manager active.

   D. Nothing, but you need to install DOS and create a FAT partition and then reinstall OS/2.

3. You installed Windows NT Server 4, but during the installation process you selected Server as the type of installation. You now want to make the Server a backup domain controller. What must you do to convert the server?

   A. Nothing. The next time you restart the server simply select NT Server - Domain Controller from the boot menu.

B. Under Control Panel, System, change the server type to Domain Controller.

C. Under Control Panel, Network, change the server type to Domain Controller.

D. You cannot designate a member server to be a domain controller unless you reinstall NT Server.

4. A domain must have at least one of the following. Select all that apply.

A. A BDC and a PDC

B. Only a BDC

C. A PDC

D. A PDC and at least one BDC

5. What is the main difference between an NT Server acting as a domain controller and an NT Server not installed as a domain controller?

A. A domain controller maintains a copy of the directory database, whereas a non-domain controller does not.

B. A non-domain controller maintains a copy of the directory database, whereas a domain controller does not.

C. A non-domain controller validates user logons, whereas a domain controller does not.

D. NT Server 4 cannot be installed as a domain controller.

6. You want to install NT Server on four new servers simultaneously. Which installation method would provide you with the fastest installation?

A. Floppy disk

B. CD-ROM

C. Over the network

7. What must you do to perform an NT installation using the over the network method?

    A. Copy the entire CD-ROM contents to a web server and access the server installation files using a web browser installed on the new server.

    B. Take the CD-ROM and install it in an existing NT Server and then transfer the program files to the new server by using the NetTransfer program included on the CD-ROM.

    C. Copy the I386 directory to a share point on an existing server, connect to the share point using the MS-DOS client software, and then run the WINNT program.

    D. Purchase a CD-ROM drive that has an Ethernet card in it and share the CD-ROM over the network. Then run the client software on the computer on which you are going to install NT and run the WINNT program.

8. To save time, you want to install Windows NT without first making the three boot floppies. Which command line switch should you use with the WINNT program.

    A. /OX

    B. /NF

    C. /O

    D. /B

9. You're upgrading from Windows NT 3.5 to 4. How should you proceed with the installation?

    A. Restart the computer in DOS and run the WINNT program from the CD-ROM.

    B. Run the WINNT program from the Program Manager, File, Run command.

    C. Run the WINNT32 program from the Program Manager, File, Run command.

    D. You cannot directly upgrade to NT 4 because of the new user interface. You must install a fresh copy.

10. If you're installing NT Workstation and you want to be able to specify all the components that should be installed, which installation method should you choose?

    A. Custom

    B. Compact

    C. Typical

    D. Portable

11. While installing NT Server, you were prompted for a Computer Name. Which statement best describes the purpose of the computer name?

    A. The computer name is the NetBIOS name. It identifies the computer on the network. It's okay to have two computers with the same computer name as long as they are separated by a router.

    B. The computer name is the NetBIOS name. It identifies the computer on the network. Under no circumstances should two computers have the same name.

    C. The computer name identifies the computer to the domain controller. The computer name must be at least two characters and must include the domain name as part of the computer name.

    D. Computer names are case-sensitive and must be entered when the user logs on to the computer for the first time.

12. What is the default network protocol installed with Windows NT on an Intel-based platform?

    A. NetBEUI

    B. AppleTalk

    C. IPX/SPX

    D. TCP/IP

13. A user calls you and asks how he can make his NT Workstation a member of a workgroup and domain. He needs to share files with users in his department and access the file server at the same time. How does he make his server a member of the workgroup and the domain at the same time?

   A. He cannot. An NT Workstation computer cannot be a member of a domain and a workgroup at the same time.

   B. Under Control Panel, Network enter the workgroup name and the domain name and then restart the workstation.

   C. He can be a member of both only if the workgroup and domain name are the same.

14. A user calls you and states that during the course of installing NT Workstation, he tried to enter the domain name when prompted, but could not continue. The computer said something on the order of "You do not have sufficient authority to join the domain." What do you need to do so that he can join the domain?

   A. Nothing. A Windows NT Workstation cannot be a member of a domain, only a workgroup.

   B. Grant his domain userid the authority to create computer accounts in the domain and tell him to try it again.

   C. Give him the domain administrator's userid and password and tell him to try it again.

   D. Create a computer account for the user in Server Manager and ask him to try entering the domain name again.

15. You're trying to install Windows NT on a RISC-based computer. Which of the following requirements must you meet?

   A. A Microsoft Certified Hardware Reseller must supply the RISC-based computer and the vender must install NT on the computer.

   B. You must install NT from a SCSI CD-ROM and have at least a 2 MB FAT partition.

   C. You must install NT using the over the network installation method, because NT doesn't support SCSI CD-ROM devices on RISC-based computers.

   D. You must request the special RISC-based CD-ROM when ordering Windows NT.

16. Which of the following outlines the correct procedures for uninstalling Windows NT from a computer that does not have a FAT partition?

    A. You must low-level format the hard drive to remove NT.

    B. You must boot the computer with a DOS bootable disk and then run the SYS.COM program to restore the boot sector files.

    C. You can remove NT by deleting the NTFS partition by using the DOS 6.22 version of FDISK.

    D. You can remove NT by deleting the NTFS partition using a tool such as DELPART or OS/2 version of FDISK.

17. Which statement best describes the differences between a per server and a per seat license mode?

    A. In a per server license mode, a certain number of connections are assigned to the server and in a per seat mode, a license is assigned to each client connecting to the server.

    B. In a per seat mode, a certain number of connections are assigned to the server and in a per seat mode, a license is assigned to each client connecting to the server.

    C. You can convert from a per seat mode license to a per server mode license for a one time charge from Microsoft.

    D. You can convert from a per server license to a per seat license for a one time charge from Microsoft.

18. If you're installing multiple Windows NT Servers, which is the most cost-effective license mode to choose?

    A. Per server

    B. Per seat

    C. It doesn't matter which mode you choose as long as you have a special exemption from Microsoft.

    D. You can install the server in a per seat mode and then later covert to a per server mode if the need arises.

19. Which statement best describes the purpose of the Registry?

    A. The Registry is a configuration database that replaces the INI files used by previous versions of Windows.

    B. The Registry is a configuration database that Windows NT uses to keep domain account information (that is, registered information).

    C. Windows 3.x applications use the Registry rather than INI files to store their configuration information.

20. What is the name of the utility used to directly edit the Registry?

    A. REGEDIT.EXE

    B. EDITREG.EXE

    C. REGEDT32.EXE

    D. CHGREG.EXE

21. What five subtrees make up the Registry?

    A. HKEY_LOCAL_MACHINE; HKEY_ALL_USERS; HKEY_CURRENT_USER; HKEY_ROOT; HKEY_CURRENT_CONFIG

    B. HKEY_LOCAL_MACHINE; HKEY_COMMON; HKEY_CURRENT_USER; HKEY_CLASSES_ROOT; HKEY_CURRENT_CONFIG

    C. HKEY_MACHINE; HKEY_CLASSES_ROOT; HKEY_CURRENT_USER; HKEY_USERS; HKEY_CURRENT_CONFIG

    D. HKEY_LOCAL_MACHINE; HKEY_USERS; HKEY_CURRENT_USER; HKEY_CLASSES_ROOT; HKEY_CURRENT_CONFIG

22. Which Registry subtree contains the information about the current configuration of the computer?

    A. HKEY_CURRENT_USER

    B. HKEY_CURRENT_MACHINE

    C. HKEY_LOCAL_MACHINE

    D. HKEY_CLASSES_ROOT

23. The best way to back up the Registry is to _____.

   A. use the Windows NT Backup utility

   B. choose Registry, Save Key

   C. use the MS-DOS 6.22 Backup program

   D. simply copy the Registry files to a floppy disk using the XCOPY /n command

24. The preferred method of modifying the Registry is to use the _____ utility?

   A. Registry Editor (REGEDT32.EXE)

   B. Control Panel

   C. REGEDIT.EXE

   D. None of the above (The Registry is a system database and should never be directly edited by any users.)

25. A user calls you and tells you that he was trying to verify his hardware settings for his COM ports by looking at Control Panel, Ports, but he doesn't see any listing for his serial mouse, which is on COM1. Why is this?

   A. The user doesn't actually have a serial mouse. He has a bus mouse and that's why the port doesn't show up.

   B. The user is mistaken and probably doesn't have a mouse attached to his system.

   C. The user has a mouse, but needs to look under Control Panel, Mouse to see his device settings.

   D. Control Panel, Ports shows only available ports, not ones in use.

26. You have installed the Remote Access Service (RAS) on your Windows NT Workstation so that you may dial in to your network remotely. However, every time you restart your computer, you must manually restart the RAS service. How can you make this automatic?

   A. Place the RAS icon in the Startup group. This will launch the program every time the workstation is restarted.

B. There is no way to launch this application automatically because it's a system service.

C. Change the following Registry entry to 1 and restart your workstation:
HKEY_LOCAL_MACHINE\CurrentControlSet\Microsoft\ Software\LaunchRas

D. Go into Control Panel, Services and select the RAS service and configure it as an automatic service.

27. Your mission critical NT Server just crashed owing to a power failure. You purchase a UPS (Uninterruptible Power Supply) and attach it to the NT Server computer. How can you configure the operating system so that it shuts down gracefully before the UPS runs out of power?

A. You cannot. You must manually shut down the server before the UPS runs out of power.

B. Choose the Control Panel, System option, select UPS, and configure the estimated runtime of the UPS. Be sure to select a number of minutes less than the actual runtime of the UPS.

C. Use the Control Panel, UPS applet and configure the COM Port, Run Time, and signaling methods of the UPS.

D. Because NT is Plug-and-Play compatible, you don't need to configure the UPS. The next time you restart the Server, the device is automatically configured.

28. A user calls you and states that after installing a new hard disk in his computer and partitioning it, he cannot select Format from the Tools menu in Disk Administrator. What does he need to do to be able to format the drive?

A. He must reboot the computer in DOS and then use the Format command to format the hard disk.

B. He has to commit the changes in Disk Administrator before the partition can be formatted.

C. He has to use the low-level format program in the computer's BIOS to prepare the disk.

D. The disk must first be partitioned using FDISK and

then formatted with DOS and then converted to NTFS before it can be used.

29. You have installed a new hard disk in your NT Server computer and have partitioned it and formatted as a FAT partition. You want to add this disk space onto an existing volume to extend the disk space. However, when you attempt to extend the volume, you cannot. Why?

   A. The volume that you created must already include four primary partitions and cannot be extended any further.

   B. You must commit the changes before you can proceed.

   C. You can only extend a volume that has been formatted or converted to NTFS.

   D. You can only extend volumes that have been formatted or converted to FAT.

30. What is a disk partitioning scheme that allows equal areas of disk space to be combined from 2 to 32 physical drives into one logical drive?

   A. Stripe Set with Parity

   B. Volume Set

   C. NTFS volumes

   D. Stripe Set

31. What is a type of disk system that makes an exact copy of all data from one disk partition onto another disk partition?

   A. RAID

   B. Disk Saving

   C. Disk Mirroring

   D. Hot Fixing

32. What is the type of disk system that uses 3 to 32 disks and is also known as RAID level 5?

   A. Disk Striping with Parity.

   B. Disk Striping without Parity.

   C. Disk Mirroring.

D. Striping with Redundant Data.

33. The types of disk systems that are fault-tolerant are: Select all correct answers.

    A. Volume Sets
    B. Disk Striping with Parity
    C. Disk Striping without Parity
    D. Disk Mirroring
    E. RAID level 0

34. In a Windows NT environment, what is the term that refers to the object that performs the actual printing process?

    A. Printer
    B. Printing device
    C. Print queue
    D. Print server

35. A user states that she's trying to load a printer driver for her laser printer but cannot find one specifically written for Windows NT. She wants to know if the one she has for Windows 95 will work. Which statement best describes the relationship between printer drivers for different NT platforms?

    A. The Windows NT printer drivers are platform-specific. You cannot use a Windows 95 driver on an NT computer. You also must be sure to use the printer driver for the platform on which you're running NT.
    B. The NT printer drivers are interchangeable and can be used on any NT platform.
    C. The NT printer drivers and Windows 95 drivers are interchangeable because both operating systems are 32-bit. However, you cannot substitute 16-bit drivers for NT drivers.

36. If print jobs aren't printing properly and you cannot remove print jobs from the printer, what can you do to fix the problem?

A. Nothing.

B. Wait a couple hours; the spooler service will detect the problem and correct it.

C. Take the print server down and restart it.

D. Stop the spooler service on the print server and then restart it.

37. Which statement best describes the procedure for updating the printer driver on all your Windows NT computers?

A. Create a disk with the new printer driver on it and go to each computer and load the new version of the printer driver.

B. You must purchase and configure the SMS product from Microsoft if you want to automatically configure NT computers to update their printer drivers.

C. Load the new driver on the computer acting as the print server. The NT computers will automatically copy down the new printer driver the next time they print.

D. Put the printer driver in a shared directory and have your NT users install the new driver manually.

38. How do you install a new printer driver? Select all correct answers.

A. Choose Start, Settings, Printers. Run the Add Printer Wizard.

B. Start Print Manager and add the printer from the Printer menu.

C. Run Control Panel and click on the Printer icon; then double-click on the Add Printer Wizard.

D. Run the Windows NT Setup program and install the printer driver under the Configuration menu.

39. If you have a printer that has multiple paper trays, how can you make it easier for users to select the proper paper tray for the type of paper they want to print on?

A. Tell the users the type of paper that's in each of the paper trays so that they can select the proper tray when printing.

B. Assign a type of paper to the paper tray under the printer properties. The users can select the type of paper on which to print without knowing which tray the paper is in.

C. The users must select manual feed and then notify the printer operator when they're printing on non-standard paper types.

D. The users must select manual feed and then feed the correct type of paper when they print their documents.

40. If you have a printer set for use only by network users, only during after hours, what's the best way that you can set a schedule so that jobs print only between the hours of 6 p.m. and 6 a.m.?

A. Change the scheduling properties of the printer so that it prints only between the hours that you designate.

B. Only turn on the printer between the hours that you want it to print.

C. Pause the printer until the designated time. Then start the printer and the jobs will print. This way, users can print to the printer during the day and the jobs will accumulate in the printer until the pause is released.

D. Tell your users not to print to the printer until after the designated start time.

41. You have two groups of users who need to print to the same printer. However, one of the groups needs to have priority over the other groups print jobs. How best can you accomplish this arrangement?

A. You must install two separate printing devices and assign each group to print to one of the printing devices.

B. Make the users the higher printing priority printer operators so that they may adjust the order of their print jobs in the printer.

    C. Have the network administrator set up a printing pool with multiple printers.

    D. Install two printers that are connected to the same printing device. Assign different priorities and groups to each printer.

42. Some of the users on your network habitually select the incorrect printer driver when printing to your laser printer. How can you make sure that improperly formatted documents don't print on the printer, possibly causing it to hang?

    A. Tell the users to always check the printer driver selected before printing their documents.

    B. Install a printer that supports both PostScript and PCL printing definition languages.

    C. Select the Hold Mismatched Documents option in the printer properties. This way, the NT print server holds any documents that don't match the printer language.

    D. You shouldn't have to worry about it. The newer printer drivers can automatically translate the page formatting language to match the printer.

43. To set up a printing pool, which of the following criteria must be met? Select all correct answers.

    A. All the printers should be in the same general area.

    B. The printers should be of the same make and model.

    C. The printers must be connected to the same print server.

    D. The printers must be connected to the same type of port.

44. To print from a DOS application to a network printer under Windows NT, what two things must be done?

    A. The LPT device must be redirected to the network printer share using the NET USE command.

    B. The LPT device must be redirected to the network print queue using the CAPTURE command.

    C. The correct printer driver must be selected in Windows NT and it must be set as the default printer before printing from the DOS application.

D. The correct printer driver and LPT port must be selected in the DOS application before printing.

Review Answers

1. A	10. A	19. A	28. B	37. C
2. C	11. B	20. C	29. C	38. A C
3. D	12. D	21. D	30. D	39. B
4. C	13. A	22. C	31. C	40. A
5. A	14. D	23. A	32. A	41. D
6. C	15. B	24. B	33. B D	42. C
7. C	16. D	25. D	34. B	43. A B C
8. D	17. A	26. D	35. A	44. A D
9. C	18. B	27. C	36. D	

Test Yourself

Stop! Before reading this chapter, test yourself to determine how much study time you will need to devote to this section.

1. The capability to perform a particular action on the system without regard to a specific case is a _____.

    A. Permission

    B. Policy

    C. Right

    D. None of the above

2. To enter the roaming profile path, you must first click on the _____ button in the _____ of _____.

    A. Path...Environment Profile...Server Manager

    B. Profile...User Properties...User Manager for Domains

    C. Profile...User Options...Server Manager

    D. Profile...Account Policies...User Manager for Domains

3. Which three of the following are part of Windows NT Server's client-based network administration tools package for Windows 95?

    A. Event Viewer

    B. System Policy Editor

    C. User Manager for Domains

    D. File and Print Services for NetWare

4. If you _____ a file within the same partition, it will retain its original compression attribute.

    A. copy

    B. move

    C. copy or move

    D. None of the above

Answers

1. C (see "Assigning Rights to Groups by Assigning Groups to Rights")
2. B (see "User Environment Profiles")
3. A C D (see "Managing Windows NT Server from Client Machines")
4. B (see "Copying and Moving Files")

C h a p t e r

Managing Resources

This chapter will help you prepare for the "Managing Resources" section of Microsoft's Exam 70-67, "Implementing and Supporting Microsoft Windows NT Server." Microsoft provides the following specific objectives for the "Managing Resources" section:

Test Objectives

> ▶ Manage user and group accounts. Considerations include managing Windows NT groups, managing Windows NT user rights, managing Windows NT account policies, and auditing changes to the user account database.
>
> ▶ Policies and profiles for various situations. Policies and profiles include local user profiles, roaming user profiles, and system policies.
>
> ▶ Adminster remote servers from various types of client computers. Client computer types include Windows 95 and Windows NT Workstation.
>
> ▶ Manage disk resources. Tasks include copying and moving files between file systems, creating and sharing resources, implementing permissions and security, and establishing file auditing.

This chapter examines some important topics related to managing resources on a Windows NT network. *Managing resources* is of course a very broad topic, but Microsoft has narrowed it somewhat in its objectives for the Windows NT Server exam. This chapter considers user and group accounts and the important tool User Manager for Domains, which you will use to manage accounts on an NT domain. This chapter also discusses user profiles, hardware profiles, and system policies—three important features that help administrators define the user environment.

You will learn about the remote administration tools available through Windows NT Server to administer NT resources from client machines. And lastly, this chapter describes some issues relating to administering file and disk resources.

Managing User and Group Accounts

Windows NT users get their rights and permissions in either of two ways: They are explicitly assigned a right or permission through their accounts, or they are members of a group that has been given a right or permission.

When you boot Windows NT, your first interaction with the operating system is with the WinLogon process (see Chapter 1).

An administrator creates an account (maybe more than one) for each person who will use the system. When prompted by WinLogon, the user enters the assigned username and password and logs on to the system. Once on the system, Windows NT checks the user's credentials against the list of valid users and groups for each object to which he or she requests access.

Microsoft lists the following objective for the Windows NT Server exam:

Manage user and group accounts. Considerations include: managing Windows NT groups, managing Windows NT user rights, managing Windows NT account policies, and auditing changes to the user account database.

Users and Groups

Windows NT administrators can create two types of accounts: one for users and one for groups. *User accounts* belong to one person only; rights and permissions assigned to a user account affect only the person who uses that account to log on. A *group* is a collection of users who hold common rights and permissions by way of their association with the group. The number of people who can belong to a group is unlimited, and all members enjoy the rights and permissions (or rue the lack thereof) assigned to the group.

In practice, a group is a vehicle for assigning rights and permissions to an individual user. If you determine that a certain group of users in your environment requires a specific set of rights and permissions, you can create a group that has those rights and permissions and add the users to the new group. It is important to note that there is no order of precedence among user and group accounts. No one group takes priority over any other group, and groups do not take priority over user accounts (or vice versa).

For management purposes, it is easier to use group accounts when assigning rights and permissions. First, it's cleaner: users can be members of as many groups as desired, and group names can be more descriptive than user names. When looking at the permission list for a file, for example, you probably would understand why Vice Presidents have access to sensitive financial information before you would understand why JackS, JanetP, and BillG are allowed in. Second, it's simpler: if you need to give a user the right to back up files and directories, you can find a built-in group, called Backup Operators, specifically designed for that purpose. In fact, you rarely have to create a new group (unless you want to for oversight and management purposes) because Windows NT has built-in groups for almost anything anyone needs to do on the system.

Windows NT has two types of groups: local groups and global groups.

On a Windows NT Workstation or member server of a domain, a *local group* is an entity that exists for the purpose of assigning rights and permissions to resources on the local machine. Remember that these resources consist of drive space and printers on that specific computer. That local group exists only on that computer.

This changes slightly at the domain level—enough to cause quite a bit of confusion. A local group created on a domain controller appears on all domain controllers within that domain. A local group created on one Backup Domain Controller (BDC) appears on the Primary Domain Controller (PDC) and all the BDCs within that domain. You then can assign this local group rights and permissions. Keep in mind that the local share or printer might exist only on that first BDC where the local group was created—and that is where you get the confusion.

A *global group* is a collection of user accounts within the domain. These global groups have *no* power by themselves. These global groups must be assigned to local groups to gain any access to the local resources. You use a global group as a container of users that you then can add to local groups.

When a Windows NT workstation becomes part of a domain, the built-in domain global groups (described later in this chapter) join the corresponding local groups in the workstation's local security database. The global group Domain Admins, for example, becomes a member of the local group Administrators. Each user account in the domain database is a member of an appropriate global group. The Administrator account, for example, is a member of the Domain Admins global group. By nesting global groups in the local groups of individual machines, Windows NT provides users with seamless access to resources across the domain.

A global group must be a member of a local group, but a local group cannot be a member of a global group, nor can a global group be a member of another global group. A global group can contain only user accounts. A local group can contain user accounts and global groups, but putting users in local groups is not good domain management.

Built-In Groups on Domain Controllers

Windows NT domain controllers oversee eight built-in local groups and three built-in global groups. These groups create a wide range of access levels for network resources.

The Windows NT domain local groups are as follows:

- ▶ Administrators

- ▶ Users

- ▶ Guests

- ▶ Backup Operators

- ▶ Replicator

- ▶ Print Operators

- ▶ Server Operators

Administrators

Administrators is the most powerful group in Windows NT. Because Administrators has complete control over the entire Windows NT environment, use caution when adding users to this group. If you will be the administrator for a Windows NT machine, consider creating an ordinary user account as well for safety reasons. If an administrator walks away from a computer while still logged on, anyone can walk up to that computer and make unauthorized changes. Even if you are extremely conscientious, mistakes happen. An application that malfunctions and deletes files can wreak more havoc if it runs under an administrative account than if it runs under a user account. Use administrator-level accounts only when necessary.

In the following situations, it is necessary to use administrator-level accounts:

- ▶ To create other administrator-level accounts

- ▶ To modify or delete users, regardless of who created them

- ▶ To manage the membership of built-in groups

- ▶ To unlock workstations, regardless of who locked them

- ▶ To format a hard disk

▶ To upgrade the operating system

▶ To back up or restore files and directories

▶ To change the security policies

▶ To connect to administrative shares

Users

By default, new accounts become members of the Users group automatically. The Users group provides users everything needed to run applications safely and to manage their own local environment—local to the user, that is, not the computer. Users can

▶ Run applications

▶ Manage their own files and directories (but not share them)

▶ Use printers (but not manage them)

▶ Connect to other computers' directories and printers

▶ Save their settings in a personal profile

Because users cannot affect files to which they have not been granted access, and cannot format hard disks, delete accounts, and so on, it is safest to use the Users account unless you need to perform a task that only an administrator or power user has the right to do.

Guests

Windows NT also provides a relatively powerless group called Guests. Because Windows NT Workstation requires accounts for anyone and everyone who accesses the system, you can use the Guest account (described later in this chapter) and the Guests group to allow limited access to users who don't possess an account on your computer. Because the default Guest account does not require a password, it can pose a security risk. The actual extent of the access provided to the Guests group depends on how you implement it. If you are concerned about security, you can disable the Guest account.

Backup Operators

Backup Operators have a singular purpose: to back up files and directories and to restore them later. Although any user can back up and restore files to which he has been granted permissions, backup operators can override the security on resources, but only when using the NTBackup program.

Replicator

The Replicator group is a special group used by the Directory Replication Service. See Chapter 2, "Installing and Configuring Windows NT Server," for more information on this group.

Print Operators

Members of the Print Operators group waive the power to create, manage, and delete print shares on domain controllers.

Server Operators

The members of a Server Operators group have the power to administer primary and backup domain controllers. They can log on to and shut down servers, lock and unlock servers, change the system time, back up and restore files, and manage network shares.

Built-In Global Groups

Windows NT domain controllers also oversee the following three global groups:

▶ **Domain Admins.** Global group of administrator accounts. The Domain Admins group is a member of the Administrators local group for the domain, and is, by default, a member of the local group for every computer in the domain running Windows NT Server or NT Workstation. A domain administrator, therefore, can perform administrative functions on local computers.

▶ **Domain Users.** Global group of user-level accounts. During setup, the domain's Administrator account is part of the

Domain Users global group. All new domain accounts are automatically added to the Domain Users group.

▶ **Domain Guests.** Global group for users with guest-level accounts. The Domain Guest group is automatically a member of the domain's Guest group.

Built-In Groups on Workstations and Member Servers

Windows NT Server member servers (servers that are not domain controllers) and Windows NT Workstations have the following built-in local groups:

▶ Administrators

▶ Backup Operators

▶ Power Users

▶ Guests

▶ Replicator

▶ Users

The descriptions for these groups are the same as the descriptions for their domain-controller counterparts, except for the Power User group, which is not a built-in group on Windows NT domain controllers. Power Users live somewhere between the kingdom of Administrators and the masses of Users. Power users have considerably more power than ordinary users, but not nearly the amount of control that an administrator has. A similar principle applies here: Do not use or give out Power User accounts unless doing so is necessary for performing a task. Power User accounts are ideal for the following types of tasks:

▶ Sharing (and revoking) directories on the network

▶ Creating, managing, and sharing printers

▶ Creating accounts (but not administrator-level)

- ▶ Modifying and deleting accounts (but only the accounts that the power user has created)

- ▶ Setting the date and time on the computer

- ▶ Creating common program groups

Power users cannot touch any of the security policies on a Windows NT system, and their powers are limited in scope. It is best, therefore, to use a Power User account rather than an Administrator account if you can accomplish what you need to as a power user.

Windows NT member servers and workstations don't control any global groups, because global groups can be created and administered only on domain controllers. Global groups nevertheless play an important part in assigning local rights and permissions to server and workstations resources. The following section describes how global groups interact with local accounts.

Member Server and Workstations Accounts

Windows NT Server machines acting as member servers maintain local account databases and manage a set of local accounts and groups independent of any domain affiliations. You can understand the need for these local accounts when you consider the emphasis on security in Windows NT. A user must provide credentials to access a Windows NT system even if that system is not attached to a domain, or even if it has never been attached to a domain. The local account information controls access to the machine's resources.

Domain users can access resources on server and workstation machines logged into the domain because (by default) each domain user is a member of the global group Domain Users, and the global group Domain Users is a member of the machine's local group Users. In the same way, domain administrators are part of the global group Domain Admins, which is part of the machine's local Administrator's group.

Hard-Coded Capabilities

So far, only the hard-coded characteristics of the Windows NT built-in groups have been discussed; in other words, some things you can change and some things you can't. Everything, for example, previously mentioned in the group paragraphs are things that cannot be changed. Users cannot share directories, no matter how hard you might try to change that, and power users cannot be prevented from sharing directories (to which they have access, of course), no matter how hard you might try.

You cannot modify hard-coded capabilities, but you can change user rights. An administrator can grant or revoke a user right at any time. Only administrators have the hard-coded capability to manage this policy. At this point, it is important to clearly distinguish between user rights and resource permissions. *User rights* define what a user can and cannot do on the system. *Resource permissions* establish the scope where these rights can be used. In other words, user rights are stuff you can do, and resource permissions control where you can do it.

Built-In User Accounts

Groups are the center of power in Windows NT, but groups need members to have any effect at all. At least two accounts are created when you install Windows NT Workstation. These users and their group memberships are discussed next.

Administrator

The Administrator account, the first account created during an installation, is a member of the Administrators group. This is an important concept because the Administrator account by itself is powerless—you could remove it from the Administrators group and place it in the Guests group, and you would have a really wimpy administrator. Power in Windows NT comes not from who you are, but from who you know.

The Administrator account is also permanent. You cannot disable or delete it, although it might not be a bad idea to rename it.

Because a username and password are all that is necessary to log on to most Windows NT systems, if you do not rename the Administrator account, a cyber-delinquent has half the information necessary to break into the system.

Guest

The Guest account is another permanent account. It is a member of the Guests group, but this affiliation can be changed. Like the Administrator account, the Guest account itself has no inherent power or lack thereof; it is the group membership for the account that establishes its scope.

Unlike the Administrator account, however, you can disable the Guest account. You might want to disable the account if you are in a secure environment; otherwise, users who don't have an account on your system can log on as guests. At the very least, you should consider adding a password to the Guest account.

User Manager for Domains

Windows NT Server includes a tool called User Manager for Domains that you can use to administer User and Group accounts. User Manager for Domains is similar to the User Manager tool available with Windows NT Workstation, but, whereas User Manager is primarily designed to oversee local Workstation accounts, User Manager for Domains includes additional features that enable it to manage accounts at the domain level and even interact with other domains.

For an exercise testing this information, see end of chapter.

To reach User Manager for Domains, choose Programs in the Start menu, choose Administrative Tools (Common), and then select User Manager for Domains.

Figure 3.1 shows the main screen for User Manager for Domains.

User Manager for Domains enables you to administer any domain over which you have administrative rights. The Select Domain option in the User menu enables you to choose a different domain (see fig. 3.2).

Figure 3.1

Main screen for User Manager.

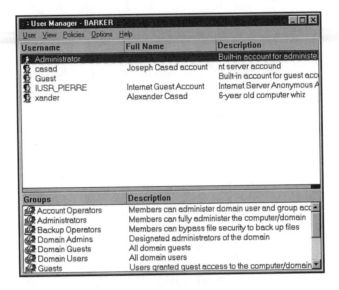

Figure 3.2

Select Domain option in the User menu.

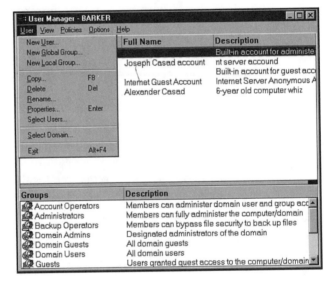

Some of the tasks you can perform with User Manager for Domains include the following:

▶ Creating new user and group accounts

▶ Viewing and configuring the properties of user and group accounts

▶ Adding new members to groups and removing members from groups

▶ Viewing and configuring account policy restrictions

▶ Adding user rights to users and groups

▶ Auditing account-related events

▶ Establishing, viewing, and configuring trust relationships

You can find most administration and configuration options on the User and Options menus.

Creating a User

Figure 3.2 shows the User menu for User Manager for Domains. To add a new user account, choose User, New User. The New User dialog box opens (see fig. 3.3).

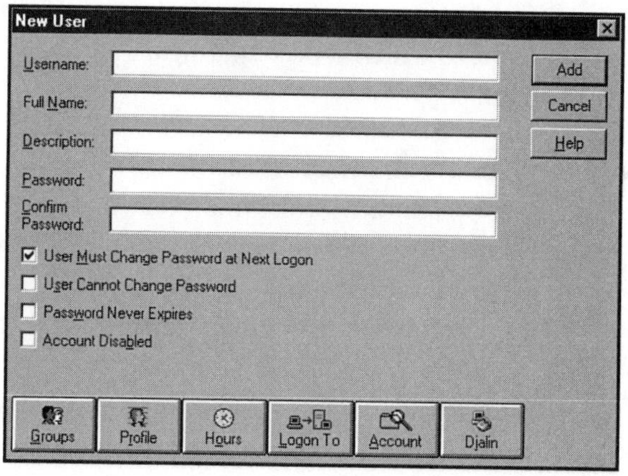

Figure 3.3

The New User dialog box.

Only two pieces of information are required to create an account: a username and a password. The username is a short "handle" used to identify the user to the system. The password is proof that the user account actually belongs to the person attempting to use it.

The name in the Username field must be unique. No other user or group can have the same username. The username can be as long as twenty characters and is not case-sensitive.

The password entered in the Password field is case-sensitive; in fact, the most common logon-related problem reported by Windows NT users is solved just by pressing the Caps Lock key. The Password field can be left blank (although not recommended for obvious reasons), or it can be as long as fourteen characters. It does not echo on-screen as anything other than asterisks, so you don't need to worry about someone looking over your shoulder. For this reason, however, you must confirm the password just to make certain that you did not mistype a character or two behind those asterisks.

The other parameters in this dialog box are optional but useful. The Full Name is a free text field that can be used for the full name, including spaces and initials, for a particular user. Having both a username and a full name enables users to log on quickly (using the username) but still be listed and available by their full name.

The Description field is also free text. Use it to track the department to which a user belongs, or maybe a location or project team.

Enabling the User Must Change Password at Next Logon check box option is useful when creating an account. Because a new account has a preset password picked by the administrator, this option forces the user to change the password immediately after logging on the first time after setting this option. When the user attempts to log on, the message `You are required to change your password at first logon` appears. After the user dismisses the message, a Change Password dialog box appears.

Enabling the User Cannot Change Password check box prevents users from making any change to their password at any time. You might want to use this for the Guest account and any other account that several people might share.

Enabling the Password Never Expires check box overrides any blanket password expiration date defined in the Account policy. Again, the Guest account is a likely candidate for this option.

Enabling the Account Disabled check box turns off the account but does not remove it from the database. In general, you should disable rather than remove user accounts. If a person leaves the organization and then later returns, you can reactivate the account. If the user never returns, you can rename the account and reactivate it for the new person replacing the former user. All rights and permissions for the original user are transferred to the new user.

Other serious implications when deleting and disabling accounts are covered later in this chapter; see the section entitled "Deleting versus Disabling."

Clicking on the six buttons at the bottom of the New User dialog box opens the following corresponding dialog boxes:

▶ **Groups.** Enables you to add and remove group memberships for the account. The easiest way to grant rights to a user account is to add that account to a group that possesses those rights.

▶ **Profile.** Enables you to add a user profile path, a logon script name, and a home directory path to the user's environment profile. You learn more about the Profile button in the following section.

▶ **Hours.** Enables you to define specific times when the users can access the account. (The default is always.)

▶ **Logon To.** Enables you to specify the workstations to which the user can log on. (The default is all workstations.)

▶ **Account.** Enables you to provide an expiration date for the account. (The default is never.) You also can specify the account as global (for regular users in this domain) or domain local.

Don't confuse a domain local account with a local group membership or a local account on a workstation. A domain local account is designed to enable individual users from untrusted domains to access to this domain. Unless a domain local account is explicitly granted logon permission, the user must log on normally to a workgroup or domain where he or she has a valid account and then connect to the domain controller that is home to the domain local account.

▶ **Dialin.** Enables you to specify whether the user can access the account via a dial-up connection. You also can call back Properties.

User Environment Profiles

The Profile button invokes the User Environment Profile dialog box, which consists of two frames: User Profiles and Home Directory (see fig. 3.4).

Figure 3.4

The User Environment Profile dialog box.

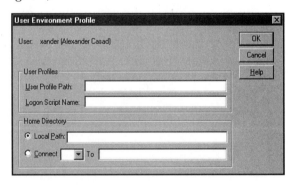

The User Profiles section of the User Environment Profile dialog box enables you to specify the user profile path and the logon script name. The user profile path is for cases in which a roaming or mandatory profile for the user will reside on another computer. If the user will log on to both Windows NT 3.x and Windows NT 4 computers, include the user profile file name in the user profile path. If the user will use only a computer running Windows NT 4, the user profile path should point to the user profile directory and should not include the file name. If the directory does not exist, Windows NT creates it when the roaming profile is created (see the discussion of roaming proiles later in this chapter), but note that the local machine must have access to the roaming profile directory by way of a network share.

The Logon Script Name text box enables you to specify a logon script for the user. *Logon scripts* are CMD or BAT files that contain a series of valid Windows NT commands. A logon script might reestablish a series of network drive connections or display a welcome message. Notice that the dialog box asks only for the name, not the full path. Windows NT already has a directory for logon scripts, but it is buried pretty deep:

```
<winnt_root>\SYSTEM32\REPL\IMPORT\SCRIPTS
```

Typically, logon scripts are not used on Windows NT workstations. User profiles can accomplish most things that logon scripts can.

The Home Directory section of the User Environment Profile dialog box is used whenever a user opens or saves a file in an application, or when the user opens a command prompt window. The default home directory is \USERS\DEFAULT; if a workstation will support more than one user, consider establishing separate home directories for each user. Note that users are not restricted to or from these home directories (unless you establish that security separately); this is just where they start by default when working with documents.

You do not have to create the home directory; User Manager will do it for you as long as you have it create only a single directory at a time. You might have User Manager create a home directory called c:\ken, for example, but it could not create c:\ken\home if the \KEN directory did not already exist. That is just a limitation of User Manager.

Click on the Local Path radio button to specify a local path for the home directory. To specify a home directory on the network, click on the Connect radio button, select a drive letter from the drop-down list, and enter the network path in the To box.

Here's a tip for home directory creation: If you would like the home directory name to be the same as the user's username, you can use a special environment variable in this dialog box: %USERNAME%. The actual username replaces %USER-NAME% after the account is created. This is not really any faster than just typing in the actual username, but it can really save time when copying accounts (described later in this chapter).

When you use User Manager for Domains to create a user's home directory on an NTFS partition, the default permissions for that directory grant that user Full Control and restrict access to all other users.

Creating a Group

You can create new global and local groups by using the New Global Group and New Local Group options on the User Manager for Domains User menu. Figure 3.5 shows the New Global Group dialog box. Note that, by default, the Administrator account is automatically a member of the new group. Only user accounts can be members of a global group. To add a member to the new global group, select a user in the Not Members list and click on the Add button to add the user to the Members list. Click on the Remove button to remove a user account from the Members list.

Figure 3.5

The New Global Group dialog box.

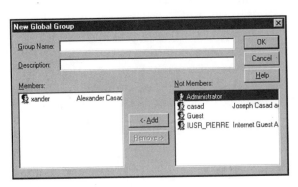

Figure 3.6 shows the New Local Group dialog box. To add additional members to the new local group, click on the Add button. Individual users and global groups both can join a local group.

Figure 3.6

The New Local Group dialog box.

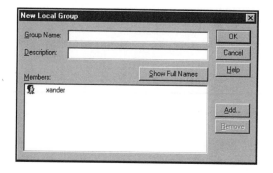

If you select one or more users in the User Manager for Domains main screen, those users automatically appear in the membership list for the new local group. This shortcut can save you a step, but you also need to be careful to make certain that no users are selected in the main screen if you don't want those users to be part of the new group.

You cannot directly add rights to a group. You have to add the group to the list of groups that have a particular right. To add groups to a right, use the User Rights option on the Policies menu (described later in this chapter).

User and Group Properties

The Properties command on User menu of the User Manager opens a Properties dialog box for the selected object. The User Properties dialog box resembles the New User dialog box (refer back to fig. 3.3) except that all the information is filled in. Use the User Properties dialog box to edit user properties after creating an account.

The group Properties dialog boxes for global and local groups also resemble their respective creation dialog boxes (see the preceding section).

Administering Account Policy

Figure 3.7 shows the Policies menu of User Manager for Domains.

Choose the Account option to open the Account Policy dialog box (see fig. 3.8).

Figure 3.7

The User Manager for Domains Policies menu.

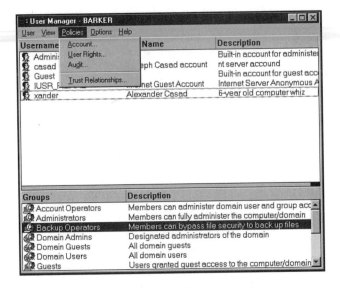

Figure 3.8

The Account Policy dialog box.

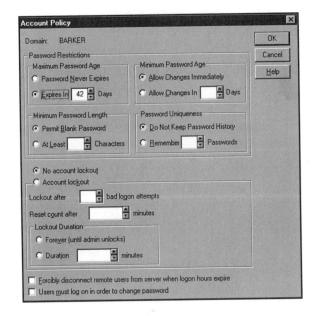

The Account Policy dialog box is pretty busy, but all the options revolve around a single concept: passwords.

Maximum Password Age

In a secure environment, the longer a password is in use, the greater the chance that an unauthorized user will discover it and break in repeatedly. Setting a maximum password age forces users to choose a new password periodically. You have a choice here: If you don't care about password ages, leave the setting at its default of Password Never Expires; if you do want a maximum password age, choose the Expires In radio button and enter the number of days to use as the limit. (The default is 42, but the value can range from 1–999.)

When a maximum password age is in effect, users get a warning 14 days before the password is set to expire.

At the onset of the first warning message, the user can change the password or choose to wait. The password expiration message appears each time the user logs on, until the maximum password age has been reached. At that point, the user cannot access the system until the password has changed. See the section entitled "User Must Log On in Order to Change Password" later in this section for more information.

Minimum Password Age

Users can get very attached to their passwords and resent having to change them. A classic user trick is changing the password when forced and then immediately changing it back, thereby retaining the old password. Setting a minimum password age circumvents this problem. The default, Allow Changes Immediately, enables users to perform the favorite-password sleight-of-hand just mentioned. Allow Changes In forces users to wait anywhere from 1–999 days (at the administrator's discretion) before making changes.

Minimum Password Length

Users also get tired of typing in long passwords. Given the opportunity, many users will use short 3- or 4- (or fewer) character passwords. Setting a minimum password length forces users to choose a longer password. Although you can require up to 14 characters, using 6 to 8 usually suffices.

Password Uniqueness

Even if you force users to set a longer password and wait a week or two before changing it, some tenacious users still swap between two passwords continuously. The Password Uniqueness setting tells Windows NT to remember each password (up to 24) that a user sets. As long as a password is in a user's password history cache, the user cannot reuse it. A Remember setting of 24 combined with a Minimum Password Age of seven days forces users to wait almost six months before reusing a password.

Even all these password options combined won't prevent a user from changing his or her password from "password" to "passworda," "passwordb," "passwordc," and so on. NT can do only so much; the rest is up to you as an administrator.

Account Lockout

The bottom half of the dialog box deals with unauthorized logon attempts.

Windows NT will lock out an account after a certain number of bad logon attempts (that is, an incorrect password for a valid username) within a certain period of time. You can enable this feature by choosing the Account lockout radio button. You must supply a couple of parameters: How many bad attempts should trigger the lockout, how long should the system wait following a bad logon attempt before resetting the counter, and how long should the account stay locked out? If you choose Forever for the last option, the administrator must manually unlock the account in User Manager; otherwise, you can elect to set a duration after which the account will be unlocked.

To set the Account Lockout Policy:

1. In User Manager, choose Policies, Account.

2. Choose the Account lockout radio button.

3. Enter the number of bad logons required to trigger the lockout in the Lockout after bad logon attempts field.

4. Enter the timeout period for resetting the bad logon count in the Reset count after field.

5. Choose a lockout duration: Forever (until admin unlocks) or a specific duration (in minutes).

To unlock an account at any time, perform the following steps:

1. Select the username in User Manager for Domains.

2. Choose User, Properties.

3. To unlock the account, clear the Account Locked Out check box.

Note that, by default, the account lockout feature is turned off. Windows NT has tight security as it is, and the potential is there for this feature to be misused. It is entirely possible, for example, that a user could deliberately lock out a coworker's or supervisor's account by purposefully entering bad passwords with that person's username. For this reason, the built-in Administrator account can never be disabled. Many Administrators don't care for this "out." The Administrator account is arguably the one you need to protect the most. Yet, if the Administrator account was locked out, it is possible that no one else could get on the system to unlock it. Therefore, you should rename the Administrator account after installation. Someone trying to break into the system will have to discover both username and password.

If a user attempts to log on with a locked account, the following message appears:

```
Unable to log you on because your account has been locked out,
please contact your administrator.
```

Forcibly Disconnect Remote Users from the Server After Logon Hours Expire

You can use the Hours button in the New User and User Properties dialog boxes to specify when the user is allowed to access the system. Enable this check box to have the user forcibly disconnected after the specified logon hours expire.

User Must Log On in Order to Change Password

This check box item relates to the password expiration settings
discussed earlier. When a user's password nears expiration, the
user is prompted at each logon to change it. If the user declines
and the password age is exceeded, the user cannot log on until
the password is changed. If this selection is cleared (the default),
the user is presented with the Change Password dialog box and
not allowed to proceed until changing the obsolete password. If
this selection is checked, users are allowed to change the password
only after logging on. Because an expired password cannot be
used to log on, the administrator must change the user's password
from within User Manager before the user can log on again. This
is a useful option in a secure environment, and the embarrass-
ment of calling the administrator should prompt users to pay
more attention to the warnings that precede a lockout.

Assigning Rights to Groups by Assigning Groups to Rights

Choose the User Rights option on Policies menu of User Manager
for Domains to open the User Rights Policy dialog box, which
enables you to assign groups to a particular right (see fig. 3.9).

Figure 3.9

*The User Rights
Policy dialog box.*

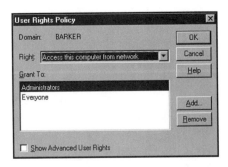

Here you face the most confusing part of User Manager's interface: You cannot view the rights assigned to a particular user. Instead, you must choose a right from the drop-down list so that you
can view the users assigned to it. You probably wonder why Microsoft implemented the interface this way. The answer is, "Probably to discourage people from messing with it."

Whereas a *permission* is targeted at a specific object (such as a directory or file), the term *right* refers to a general right to take a particular action on the system. Some Windows NT rights are as follows:

- ▶ Log on locally

- ▶ Shut down the system

- ▶ Restore files and directories

- ▶ Take ownership of files or other objects

The built-in groups described earlier in this chapter are automatically assigned appropriate user rights. Choose Restore files and directories from the Right combo box in the User Rights Policy dialog box (refer to fig. 3.9). You will see that administrators, backup operators, and server operators all have the right to restore files and directories.

The Add button in the User Rights Policy dialog box enables you to add a user or group to the list of accounts assigned to a particular right. To add a user or group to the rights list for a particular right, perform the following steps:

1. Choose the right from the Right combo box and click on the Add button. The Add Users and Groups dialog box appears (see fig. 3.10).

2. Select the name of a user or group from the Names list and click on the Add button. (By default, only group names appear in the Names list. Click on the Show Users button to include users in the list.)

3. The name(s) you selected appear in the Add Names list in the lower frame. Click on the OK button to add the selected user or group to the list of accounts assigned to the right.

The Remove button in the User Rights Policy dialog box removes an account from the rights list. To deny a right to a user or group account, perform the following steps:

Figure 3.10

The Add Users and Groups dialog box.

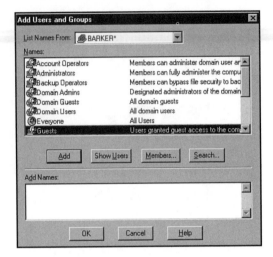

1. Choose the right from the Right combo box.

2. Select the user or group from the Grant to list.

3. Click on the Remove button.

You should not need to change user rights policy too often. The built-in groups already are assigned appropriate user rights for most situations. Before you modify the rights policy, make certain that you could not instead simply add or remove a user from an existing group to accomplish the same end.

Note the Show Advanced User Rights check box at the bottom of the User Rights Policy dialog box (refer to fig. 3.9). Advanced user rights are not shown by default, because you rarely need to change them. These rights include creating a pagefile, logging on as a service, and other rights that programs, but not people, need.

Auditing Account-Related Events

The Auditing option in the User Manager for Domains Policy menu invokes the Audit Policy dialog box, which enables you to track certain account-related events (see fig. 3.11). You can track either the success or the failure of the events shown in figure 3.11. Event information is stored in a security log. You can view the security log by using Event Viewer (see Chapter 6, "Troubleshooting").

Figure 3.11

The Audit Policy dialog box.

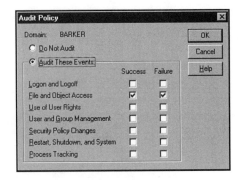

Trust Relationships

The Trust Relationships option on the User Manager for Domains Policy menu enables you to set up and modify trust relationships for the domain.

A trust relationship is a relationship between different domains in which one domain, the *trusting* domain, relinquishes control of its account database to another domain, called the *trusted* domain. Trust relationships are commonly used in Wide Area Network (WAN) situations, and you will get a heavy dose of them if you ever decide to prepare for the Windows NT Server Enterprise exam.

Account Administration Tasks

An administrator's job does not end after creating the accounts; in fact, it just begins. Changes and modifications inevitably are necessary in day-to-day operations. You can review the properties of any user account by double-clicking on the username in User Manager for Domains or by selecting the username and choosing User, Properties. The User Properties dialog box appears (see fig. 3.12). Although you can change most things about a user in the User Properties dialog box, you should be aware of a few separate commands that are launched from the User menu of the User for Domains main window (see fig. 3.13).

Figure 3.12

The User Properties dialog box.

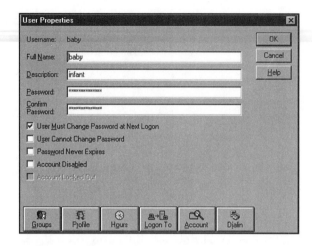

Figure 3.13

The User menu of the User Manager.

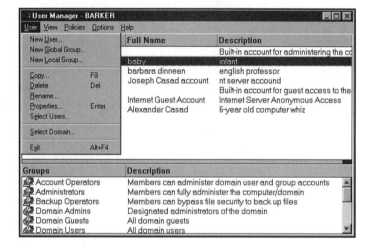

Renaming Users

The User Properties dialog box shows that although you can change a user's full name at any time, the username is fixed. To change the username (remember, the username is the logon name), you must choose User, Rename in the User Manager for Domains main window (refer to fig. 3.13).

When you rename an account, it retains all of its other properties, including user rights and resource permissions. Internally, Windows NT is no more fooled by the new moniker than your family would be if you legally changed your own name. This is because

Windows NT tracks users with an internally defined Security Identifier (SID), which is like a Social Security Number. Once created, an account's SID never changes, even if the account is renamed.

Copying Users

If you need to create many users at one time, consider creating a template account and copying it. When you copy an account by choosing User, Copy in the User Manager, you must enter a new username, full name, and password, but the other properties are retained, including the description, group memberships, and profile information. The only exception is the Account Disabled check box, which is cleared automatically.

Using the home directory tip mentioned earlier, if you copied an account called Ken with a home directory of c:\%USERNAME% and named the new account RyanC, a new directory would be created called \RyanC, in addition to the already existing \Ken directory.

Deleting Versus Disabling

Earlier, Security Identifiers (SIDs) were compared to Social Security Numbers. SIDs, however, go one step further than SSNs. When people die, their SSNs are recycled. SIDs are not recycled. When an account is deleted, that account's SID is never reused. If it were, it would be possible (in fact, probable) that a new account would inherit all the permissions and rights assigned to the account that had previously owned the SID.

This is a cautionary tale: Don't delete accounts if you can at all avoid it; you will have a hard time if you need to re-create it. Consider the following two different scenarios:

Scenario 1

Dan was a consultant with Acme Training Co., with a username of DanR. One day, Dan decided to leave Acme and strike out on his own, so the network administrator deleted Dan's account. Dan struck out, and came crawling back to Acme to his old job. The administrator re-created the account with the exact same name and password, and Dan was able to log back on to the network. Before too long, however, he noticed that he was no longer able to access the files to which he used to have permissions, even his own. Dan had to call each and every person in the company and ask them to please assign permissions to his new account for each file and directory he needed to use. Dan was not a popular person in the office that day.

Scenario 2

Dan tried one more time to make it on his own. This time, suspecting Dan might return, the administrator just disabled the account, leaving its entry in the account database but restricting it from being used to log on to the system. After a few days, Abby was hired to replace Dan. Rather than create a brand new account and face the same problems Dan had faced when he returned to the company in Scenario 1, the administrator just enabled the account and renamed it to AbbyR. Abby suddenly had all the access she needed to all the files, directories, and printers she needed to use. After a week or so, Dan returned and asked for his old job back again. Although the network administrator could have just renamed the account back to DanR, Abby was doing a much better job than Dan ever did, so Abby stayed.

The moral of these stories is that Dan is a loser, but you don't have to be. Disable accounts at least temporarily before you decide to delete them. If you need the account back, re-enable it. If someone else needs it, rename it. If time has passed, and you are certain that you really don't need it anymore, delete it. Life will be much easier.

To disable a user account, perform the following steps:

1. In the User Manager for Domains, select the username of the account you want to disable.

2. Choose User, Properties.

3. In the User Properties dialog box, enable the Account Disabled check box.

To enable a user account that has been disabled, perform the following steps:

1. In the User Manager, select the username of the account you want to enable.

2. Choose User, Properties.

3. In the User Properties dialog box, deselect the Account Disabled check box.

To delete an account, perform the following steps:

1. In the User Manager, select the username of the account you want to delete.

2. Choose User, Delete.

3. A warning message appears (see fig. 3.14). Click on OK to proceed with the deletion.

Figure 3.14

If you attempt to delete a user, you receive this warning.

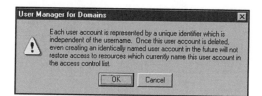

Managing Policies and Profiles

Policies and profiles are two powerful methods for defining the user environment. This section focuses on the following:

▶ User profiles

▶ Hardware profiles

▶ System policies

Microsoft lists the following objective for the Windows NT Server exam:

Create and manage policies and profiles for various situations. Policies and profiles include local user profiles, roaming user profiles, and system policies.

User Profiles

A user profile is the entire collection of configuration data that applies to a specific user and only to that user. Because profiles are maintained for each individual user, users can change their own environment without affecting the environment of other users.

Profiles contain quite a number of items, including the following:

- ▶ Settings for the user-specific Control Panel entries

- ▶ Persistent network drive connections

- ▶ Remote printer connections

- ▶ Personal program groups

- ▶ User environment variables

- ▶ Bookmarks in Help

- ▶ Preferences for Win32 applications

- ▶ Most recently accessed documents in Win32 applications

You can think of a user profile as a bundle of objects in an individual user profile subdirectory that collectively define a desktop environment for the user. The user's profile subdirectory generally consists of an ntuser.dat file (containing Registry information), a transaction log file called ntuser.dat.log (which provides fault tolerance for ntuser.dat), and a series of folders containing other items such as shortcuts and application-specific profile data.

Windows NT provides two types of user profiles: local profiles and roaming profiles. A local profile is stored on a local machine. Because a local profile resides on the local machine, it does not follow the user if the user logs on to the network from a different machine. A roaming profile is a profile that can follow the user to other computers on the network because it is stored at a central location that the other computers can access at logon.

Local Profiles

Unless you specify a roaming profile (see the following section), Windows NT obtains user-specific settings from a local user profile on the workstation the user is currently using. You can find a local user profile subdirectory for each workstation user in the <winnt_root>\profiles directory.

When a user logs on for the first time, the Windows NT logon process checks the user account database to see whether a roaming profile path has been specified for the account (see the following section). If the accounts database doesn't contain a profile path for the user, Windows NT creates a local user profile subdirectory for the user in the <winnt_root>\profiles directory and obtains initial user profile information from the local default user profile, which is stored in the subdirectory:

```
<winnt_root>\profiles\Default User
```

Windows NT saves all changes to the user profile in the new local user profile. The next time a user logs on at the workstation, Windows NT accesses the local user profile and configures all user-specific settings to match the information in the profile.

Roaming Profiles

A *roaming profile* is a centrally located user profile that other workstations on the network can access at logon. You specify a path to a roaming profile subdirectory in User Manager.

When a user logs on to the domain, the Windows NT logon process checks to see whether the account database contains a roaming profile path for the account.

If the account database contains a path to a roaming profile, Windows NT checks whether the user has changed the profile type to Local in the User Profile tab of the Control Panel System application (described later in this chapter). If the profile type is set to Local, Windows NT uses a version of the profile stored locally instead of downloading a new version from the path specified in the account database. If the user has not changed the type to Local in the Control Panel System application, Windows NT compares the local version of the profile with the roaming profile specified in the account database. If the local version is more recent, Windows NT asks whether you would like to use the local version rather than the roaming version. Otherwise, Windows NT downloads the roaming version.

At logoff, if the user is a guest or if the profile is a mandatory profile, Windows NT doesn't save the current user profile to the user profile subdirectory. If the user is not a guest, and if the profile isn't mandatory, Windows NT saves the current profile information. If the profile type has been set to Local in the User Profile tab of the Control Panel Systems application, Windows NT saves the current user profile to the local copy of the profile. If the profile type is set to Roaming, Windows NT saves the current profile information to both the local copy and the version specified in the account database.

A mandatory profile is a preconfigured roaming profile that the user cannot change. To create a mandatory profile, create a roaming profile subdirectory and specify the path to that directory in User Manager for Domains. Then, copy a user profile to the roaming profile subdirectory (using the Copy To command in the User profile tab of the Control Panel System application) and rename the ntuser.dat file to ntuser.man. The MAN extension makes the file a read-only file.

To configure a roaming profile for an account, perform the following steps:

1. Select the account in the User Manager for Domains and choose User, Properties. The User Properties dialog box appears (refer to fig. 3.12). (If you are creating a new

account, choose User, New User. The New User dialog box is similar to the User Properties dialog box.)

2. Click on the Profile button. The User Environment Properties dialog box appears (refer to fig. 3.4).

3. The User Profiles frame of the User Environment Profile dialog box enables you to specify the user profile path and a logon script name. The user profile path is for cases in which the account will use a roaming or mandatory profile. If the user will log on to both Windows NT 3.x and Windows NT 4 computers, include the user profile file name in the user profile path. If the user will use only a computer running Windows NT 4, the user profile path should point to the user profile directory and should not include the file name. If the directory does not exist, Windows NT creates it when the roaming profile is created. Note, however, that the local machine must have access to the roaming profile directory by way of a network share. The User Profile path should include the full UNC path to the profile, including a computer name, a share name, and the directory path. (See the section on the UNC naming convention later in this chapter.)

The User Profiles tab of the Control Panel System application will use a locally stored version of the profile, or whether the computer should download a roaming profile at logon. If you are logged on as an administrator, the user profile list in figure 3.15 displays all user profiles currently stored on the computer. If you are logged on as a user, the list displays only the profile you are currently using. The Change Type button enables you to specify whether to use the local version of the profile, or whether to download a roaming profile at logon. If you choose the roaming profile option, click on the box labeled Use cached profile on slow connections if you want Windows NT to use the local profile when the network is running slowly.

Click on the Copy To button box in the User Profiles tab to open the Copy To dialog box, which enables you to copy the user profile to another directory or to another computer on the network. If a different user will use the profile at its new location, you must give that user permission to use the profile. To add a user to the permissions list for the profile, click on the Change button in the Copy To dialog box.

Figure 3.15

The System Properties User Profiles tab.

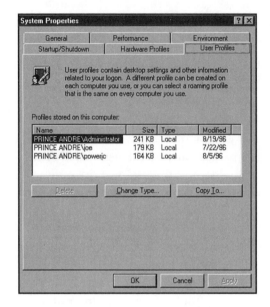

Hardware Profiles

Hardware profiles, a new addition to NT, refers to a collection of information about devices, services, and other hardware-related settings. Hardware profiles were designed for portable computers. The hardware configuration of a portable computer might change each time the portable is attached or removed from a docking station. A hardware profile enables the user to define a set of hardware conditions under which the computer will operate at a given time. A different hardware profile then can define a different set of conditions (see fig. 3.16).

Figure 3.16

Hardware profiles enable the user to predefine hardware configurations.

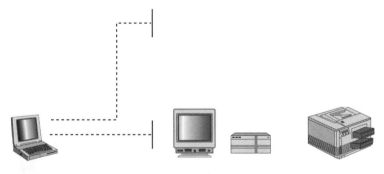

If you have more than one hardware profile, you are asked to specify a hardware profile at startup. The Registry key HKEY_CURRENT_CONFIG contains information about the hardware profile selected at startup.

The Control Panel System application's Hardware Profiles tab enables you to create new hardware profiles and change the order of precedence among hardware profiles (see fig. 3.17). Click on the Properties button to define a docking state for a portable computer or to enable/disable network hardware.

Figure 3.17

The Hardware Profiles tab.

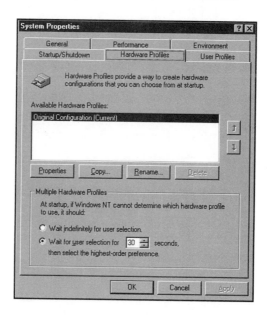

To create a new hardware profile, select an existing profile and click on the Copy button. In the Copy Profile dialog box that appears, enter a name for the new hardware profile. The new hardware profile will appear in the Available Hardware Profiles list in the Hardware Profiles tab.

If you have defined more than one hardware profile, Windows NT displays a menu of hardware profiles at startup and asks which profile you want to use. The profile you specify becomes the active hardware profile. Any changes to your hardware configuration affect the active hardware profile. You can enable or disable a device for a given hardware profile using the Control Panel

Devices application. You can enable or disable a service using the Control Panel Services Application.

The up and down arrows to the right of the Available Hardware Profiles list enable you to change the preference order of the hardware profiles (refer to fig. 3.17). The radio buttons at the bottom of the Hardware Profiles tab enable you to specify whether Windows NT waits indefinitely for you to choose a hardware profile, or whether the choice defaults to the highest-preference profile after a specific time interval.

Managing System Policy with System Policy Editor

System Policy Editor, a powerful configuration tool included with Windows NT Server, enables a network administrator to maintain machine and user configurations for the entire network from a single location.

System Policy Editor can operate in Registry mode or Policy File mode. The following sections discuss these two modes and the two distinct functions associated with both. The exam objectives for the "Managing Resources" section of the NT Server exam specifically mention *system policies*. This implies that, at least for the purposes of the "Managing Resources" section, the Policy mode functions of System Policy Editor are the more significant. The Windows NT Registry, however, is an extremely important part of Windows NT, and System Policy Editor Registry mode is an able and important interface to the Registry.

Registry Mode

For an exercise testing this information, see end of chapter.

In Registry mode, System Policy Editor enables whoever is using it to display and change Registry settings of either the local computer or another computer on the network. In form and function, System Policy Editor's Registry mode stakes out a niche somewhere between Control Panel and Registry Editor. It does not provide the complete Registry access provided that Registry

Editor affords, but it is much easier to use, and it provides powerful access to settings you cannot access via Control Panel. System Policy Editor has a hierarchical structure similar to the Registry, and though it isn't quite as GUI as Control Panel, it is remarkably simple and convenient when you consider its power.

You can use System Policy Editor for the following tasks:

- ▶ Set the maximum number of authentication retries

- ▶ Prohibit NT from creating 8.3 aliases for long file names

- ▶ Define a logon banner to appear prior to logon

- ▶ Enable or disable a computer's capability to create hidden drive shares

- ▶ Hide the Network Neighborhood icon

- ▶ Remove the Run command from the Start menu

- ▶ Require a specific desktop wallpaper

- ▶ Disable Registry editing tools

The best way to get a feel for the kinds of things you set using System Policy Editor is to browse through the Properties dialog boxes yourself (as described later in this section). As you study for the MCSE exam, spend some time familiarizing yourself with System Policy Editor settings.

You can find System Policy Editor in the Administrative Tools program group. Choose Programs in the Start menu, select Administrative Tools, and click on the System Policy Editor icon.

System Policy Editor's Registry mode displays a portfolio of Registry settings that enable the administrator to customize the configuration for a specific machine or a specific local user.

To change Registry settings by using System Policy Editor, follow these steps:

1. Choose File, Open Registry in the System Policy Editor. Figure 3.18 shows the System Policy Editor main screen in Registry mode.

2. Click on the Local Computer icon to configure Registry settings for the computer you are currently using. The Local Computer Properties dialog box appears, showing the hierarchy of the local computer (see fig. 3.19). Click on a plus sign to see settings within each of the categories (see fig. 3.20). Check or uncheck the leaf-level settings to enable or disable the option. If the option requires additional input (such as display text for a logon banner) additional boxes and prompts appear in the space at the bottom of the dialog box. Click on OK to return to the System Policy Editor main window.

Figure 3.18

System Policy Editor Registry mode.

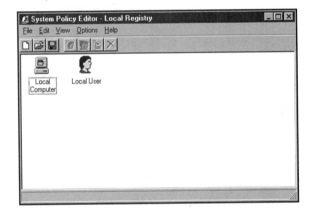

3. Click on the Local User icon to configure Registry settings for the user currently logged on to the computer. The Local User settings differ from the Local Computer settings, but the procedure is the same. Figure 3.21 shows the Local User Properties dialog box. Click on a plus sign to see settings within each of the categories (see fig. 3.22). Check or uncheck the leaf-level settings to enable or disable the option. If the option requires additional input, additional boxes and prompts then appear at the bottom of the dialog box.

Figure 3.19

The Local Computer Properties dialog box in System Policy Editor's Registry mode.

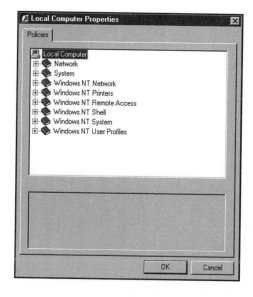

Figure 3.20

The Local Computer Properties dialog box with branches expanded.

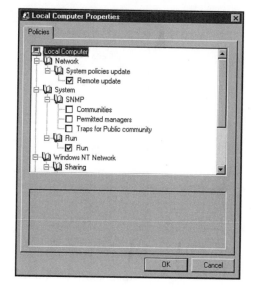

To configure another computer on the network, follow these steps:

1. Choose File, Connect in the System Policy Editor to open the Connect dialog box (see fig. 3.23).

Figure 3.21

The Local User Properties dialog box in System Policy Editor's Registry mode.

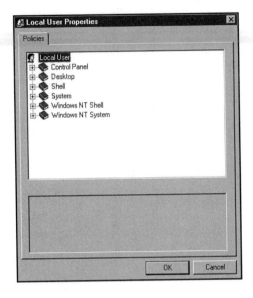

Figure 3.22

The Local User Properties dialog box with branches expanded.

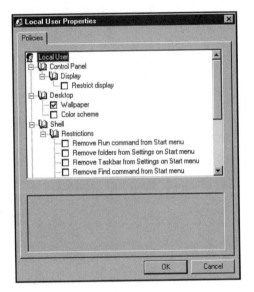

2. Enter the name of the computer you want to reach and click on OK. Another dialog box appears, asking which user account on the remote computer you want to administer. Select an account and click on OK.

Figure 3.23

*The Connect
dialog box.*

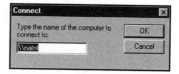

3. The System Policy Editor reappears, looking as it did in figure 3.18, except the name of the remote computer appears in the title bar.

4. Click on the Local Computer icon or the Local User icon, and change the settings as described in the preceding steps.

A typical use of System Policy Editor task is to customize the logon process. The following steps show you how to add a logon banner that appears before you log on to your system:

1. Start the System Policy Editor.

2. Choose File, Open Registry.

3. Double-click on the Local Computer icon.

4. Click on the plus sign next to Windows NT system.

5. Click on the plus sign next to Logon.

6. Select the Logon banner check box. Enter a caption and some text in the text boxes provided at the bottom of the dialog box (see fig. 3.24).

The Logon banner caption and text appears under the LegalNoticeCaption and LegalNoticeText values of the following subkey:

```
\HKEY_LOCAL_MACHINE\Software\Microsoft\Windows NT\
CurrentVersion\Winlogon
```

Figure 3.24

Enabling a logon banner.

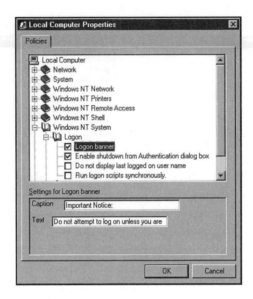

Figure 3.24 also shows another popular System Policy Editor setting. If you select the Do not display last logged on user name check box, Windows NT does not display the most recent user in the User Name text box of the Logon dialog box.

Policy File Mode

System Policy Editor's Policy File mode looks similar to Registry mode, but it is significantly different; System Policy is a kind of meta-Registry. The System Policy file can contain settings that override local Registry settings, you can therefore use System Policy Editor to impose a configuration on a user or machine that the user cannot change.

For Windows NT machines, the System Policy file is called NTConfig.pol. To enable system policy, create the NTConfig.pol file (using System Policy Editor) and place it in the \<winnt_root>\System32\Repl\Import\Scripts folder of the Domain controller's boot partition. This directory is shared as \\PDC_servername\Netlogon$. (Store system policy information for Windows 95 machines in the file Config.pol rather than NTConfig.pol.)

When a Windows NT computer attempts to log on, Windows NT looks for the NTConfig.pol file and checks NTConfig.pol for system policy information that affects the user or computer. Windows NT merges the system policy information with local Registry settings, overwriting the Registry information if necessary.

System policy information can come in several different forms. You can define a system policy for a specific computer, user, or group, or you can define default system policies. Default computer policies apply to any computer that does not have specific policy settings. Default user policies apply to any user that does not have specific policy settings or that isn't part of a group with specific policy settings.

Computer system policies modify the HKEY_LOCAL_MACHINE Registry subtree. User and group policies modify the HKEY_CURRENT_USER Registry subtree.

The types of settings you can define through System Policy Editor's Policy File mode are similar to the settings you can define through Registry mode, but system policy settings override Registry settings. Also, because you can apply system policy settings to groups, you can simultaneously set policies for several users, or even for an entire domain.

A complete set of all system policy information for a given configuration is stored in one big system policy file. You can create different system policy files to test different system policy configurations. The active file (for NT machines), however, must be saved as NTConfig.pol. (As mentioned in a previous section, Windows 95 system policies must be saved in Config.pol.)

Windows NT Server includes some System Policy templates, which contain system policy settings and categories. The template files present on Windows NT are as follows:

▶ **c:\<winnt_root>\inf\common.adm.** Settings common to both Windows NT and Windows 95 (and not present on the following two files)

▶ **c:\<winnt_root>\inf\winnt.adm.** Windows NT settings

▶ **c:\<winnt_root>\inf\windows.** Windows 95 settings

To add a System Policy template, choose Options, Policy Template from the System Policy Editor and choose a template from the list.

The System Policy templates are written in a proprietary scripting language. (See the Windows NT Resource kit for more information on the policy template scripting language.)

To define a system policy, perform these steps:

1. Choose File, New Policy in the System Policy Editor.

2. The Default Computer and Default User icons appear. Double-click on one of these icons to set the default computer or default user policy. (The policy settings appear in a tree structure with check boxes at the leaf level.)

3. Use the Edit menu to add specific users, computers, or groups to the policy file (see fig. 3.25). When you add a computer, user, or group, an icon for whatever you choose appears with the Default Computer and Default User icons in the System Policy Editor main window.

4. Double-click on that icon to set or change system policy settings. (Select an icon and choose Edit, Remove to remove that item from the policy file.)

Figure 3.25

The System Policy Editor Edit menu.

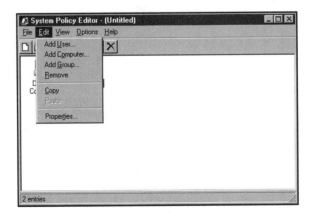

5. After you finish making changes to the Policy file, choose File, Save As. Save the file as the following:

```
\<winnt_root>\System32\Repl\Import\Scripts\NTconfig
```

System Policy Editor appends the POL extension.

Or, if you are only experimenting with the Policy file and don't want to use it yet, save it under a different name. After you save the Policy file, you can open it by choosing File, Open Policy in the System Policy Editor.

Managing Windows NT Server from Client Machines

The Network Client Administrator tool, located in the Administrative Tools program group, makes a set of Windows NT administration tools available to Windows NT clients. The Administration tools enable you to perform network administration functions from a client machine.

Microsoft lists the following objective for the Windows NT Server exam:

Administer remote servers from various types of client computers. Client computer types include Windows 95 and Windows NT Workstation.

There are two packages of client-based network administration tools: one for Windows 95 clients and one for Windows NT Workstation clients.

The Windows 95 client-based network administration tools are as follows:

▶ Event Viewer

▶ File Security tab

▶ Print Security tab

- ▶ Server Manager

- ▶ User Manager for Domains

- ▶ User Manager Extensions for Services for NetWare

- ▶ File and Print Services for NetWare

Before you can use the Windows 95 client-based network administration package, you must have a 486DX/33 or better Windows 95 computer with 8 MB of RAM (highly recommended) and a minimum of 3 MB of free disk space in the system partition. Client for Microsoft Networks must be installed on the Windows 95 computer.

The Windows NT Workstation client-based network administration tools are as follows:

- ▶ DHCP Manager

- ▶ Remote Access Administrator

- ▶ Remoteboot Manager

- ▶ Services for Macintosh

- ▶ Server Manager

- ▶ System Policy Editor

- ▶ User Manager for Domains

- ▶ WINS Manager

Before you can use the client-based network administration package, the Windows NT Workstation must be a 486DX/33 or better with 12 MB of RAM and a minimum of 2.5 MB of free disk space in the system partition. The Workstation and Server services must be installed on the Windows NT Workstation.

To create a share for the client administration tools (so you can access them from the client machine), choose Start, Programs, Administrative Tools, and then click on the Network Client Administrator icon. The Network Client Administrator dialog box appears (see fig. 3.26). Select the Copy Client-based Network Administration Tools radio button, and then click on Continue.

Figure 3.26

The Network Client Administrator dialog box.

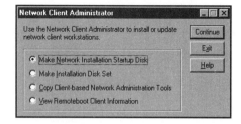

Managing Disk Resources

A big part of an NT administrator's job is managing file resources for the network. This might include such things as assigning permissions, creating directory shares, troubleshooting file name problems, and copying or moving files and directories.

The following sections take a close look at working with file resources and working with file permissions and security.

> Microsoft lists the following objective for the Windows NT Server exam:
>
> Manage disk resources. Tasks include copying and moving files between file systems, creating and sharing resources, implementing permissions and security, and establishing file auditing.

Working with Windows NT File Resources

File resources are an important aspect of Windows NT administration and, consequently, the file resources topic is an important step in the objective list for the Windows NT Server exam. One significant part of managing file resources is managing NTFS security, which you will get a closer look at later in this chapter. But first, the following sections examine some other important topics you need to understand for the Windows NT Server exam, as follows:

▶ The Universal Naming Convention (UNC)

▶ Copying and moving files

▶ Long file names

▶ Converting a FAT partition to NTFS

▶ NTFS compression

▶ Sharing files

▶ Synchronizing files

The Universal Naming Convention (UNC)

Actually, this is the Microsoft Naming Convention, but when you are Microsoft you can get away with a little hubris. UNC is a common method for referring to servers on a network and the shares published on these servers. A UNC path begins with a double-backslash immediately followed by a server name, like so:

`\\NTServer`

To view the shared directories on a computer named NTServer, type the following command from the Windows NT command prompt:

`net view \\NTServer`

When you want to refer to a specific shared resource, you refer to the system name, followed by the share name. To map a new drive letter (for example, G) to the documents shared on NTServer, you could type the following command from the Windows NT command prompt:

`net use G: \\NTServer\Documents`

You can extend the path even further; from this point forward it looks like an MS-DOS path. To refer to the file README.TXT contained within the PUBLIC subdirectory of the Documents share on NTServer, you could use the following syntax:

```
\\NTServer\Documents\PUBLIC\README.TXT
```

Don't worry about the capitalization; it isn't important here.

To make the connection persistent, (in other words, if you want Windows NT to reconnect you to this drive every time you log on), use the /PERSISTENT switch:

```
net use F: \\NTServer\Documents /PERSISTENT:YES
```

To disconnect a network drive, use the /DELETE switch:

```
net use F: /DELETE
```

You can use UNC throughout Windows NT. To view the contents of the documents shared on NTServer, for example, you could type the following:

```
dir \\NTServer\Documents
```

To copy README.TXT from its original location on NTServer to a new location on another server, you could type:

```
copy \\NTServer\Documents\PUBLIC\README.TXT \\ServerTwo\Archive\
```

You don't have to go to the SCS to use UNC, however; you can use UNC as a time-saver from within the Windows NT GUI. A shortcut can use a UNC as a target address, for example. From Network Neighborhood, you can create a shortcut to a file or directory on a network device just as you would to a file or directory on your local machine.

In Explorer, if you know the name of the server to which you need to connect, you don't need to waste time browsing. Choose Tools, Go To and type the UNC path in the Go To Folder dialog box (see fig. 3.27). Then click on OK.

Microsoft operating systems use UNC to connect to network resources, regardless of the type of server in use. You can use UNC to connect from a Windows NT Workstation to a NetWare server, for example, just as easily as you can connect to a Windows NT Server.

Figure 3.27

The Go To Folder dialog box.

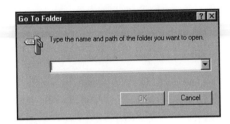

Copying and Moving Files

When you copy a file within or between partitions with the Copy command, a new instance of that file is created, and the new file inherits the compression and security attributes of the new parent directory. (You will learn more about compression and security later in this chapter.)

The same effect results if a file is moved between partitions by using the Move command. (Remember that a move between partitions is really a copy followed by a delete.) When a file is moved within a partition, the file retains its original attributes. The attributes do not change, because the file itself is never altered. Only the source and target directories change.

Long File Names

For an exercise testing this information, see end of chapter.

Although all the Windows NT-supported file systems support long file names, you should be aware of certain issues.

FAT Long File Names

Although, as explained earlier, the file name length limitations of the FAT file system has been overcome, one limitation that remains is that only 512 directory entries are permitted in the root directory of any partition. Because each long file name requires a directory entry for every thirteen characters (or portion thereof) in its name and an additional entry for its 8.3 alias, you are in danger of quickly reaching the entry limit if you use excessively long file names in a root directory.

Also, if you are dual-booting between Windows NT and Windows 95, you should be aware that although the long file names are compatible with both operating systems, Windows 95 has a path limitation of 260 characters, including the drive letter. If you use a deep hierarchy of subdirectories with long file names, therefore, you may find that Windows 95 cannot access a file buried deep within that directory tree.

The two operating systems also differ in the way they create the 8.3 alias. Both Windows NT and Windows 95 begin by taking the first six legal characters in the LFN (in other words, stripping spaces and punctuation and converting to uppercase) and following them by a tilde (˜) and a number. If the first six legal characters result in a unique identifier for that file, the number following the tilde is 1. If a file in that directory already has the same first six legal characters, the numeric suffix will be 2. For an extension, Windows NT uses the first three legal characters following the last period in the LFN. To give you an idea of what this looks like, here is a sample directory listing:

```
Team Meeting Report #3.Doc        TEAMME˜1.DOC
Team Meeting Report #4.Doc        TEAMME˜2.DOC
Team Meeting Report #5.Doc        TEAMME˜3.DOC
Team Meeting Report #6.Doc        TEAMME˜4.DOC
Nov. 1995 Status Report.Doc       NOV199˜1.DOC
```

Both Windows 95 and Windows NT generate aliases in this fashion until the fifth iteration of the same first six legal characters. At this point, Windows 95 continues to do so, but Windows NT does something altogether different; it takes only the first two legal characters, performs a hash on the file name to produce four hexadecimal characters, and then appends a ˜5. The ˜5 remains for all subsequent aliases of those same initial six characters. If additional reports were saved in the directory used in the preceding example, for example, here is how Windows 95 would and Windows NT might generate the aliases:

	Windows 95	Windows NT
Team Meeting	TEAMME~5.DOC	TEA4F2~5.DOC Report #7.Doc
Team Meeting	TEAMME~6.DOC	TE12B4~5.DOC Report #8.Doc
Team Meeting	TEAMME~7.DOC	TE833E~5.DOC Report #9.Doc

Windows NT does this for performance reasons. It takes a long time to search a directory list for a unique file name if it has to go six or more characters in to find a unique match. Windows 95 eschews this technique, probably assuming that the performance gains are not worth the calls from consumers who can't make heads or tails of their file names from their 16-bit applications.

There are not any problems switching back and forth between Windows 95 and Windows NT on LFN-enabled FAT partitions. Each time you save the file, the LFN remains intact, but you may find that the alias is renamed, depending on the operating system and the file names currently in use in the directory.

If you choose to disable long file name support altogether on a FAT partition, be careful when copying files from a partition that does support LFNs because both the COPY and XCOPY commands always default to using the LFN for their operations. When these commands attempt to write an LFN to an LFN-disabled FAT partition, this error message appears:

```
The file name, directory name, or volume label syntax is incor-
rect.
```

If you are copying from an LFN-enabled FAT partition or from an NTFS partition, you can use the /n switch with both COPY and XCOPY. The /n switch directs the command to use the alias rather than the LFN.

Beware of third-party MS-DOS-based disk utilities. When run under Windows NT, they are harmless because they cannot access the hard disk directly. Run under MS-DOS on a dual-boot system, however, they can wreak havoc on your LFN-enabled FAT partitions. See the sidebar earlier in this chapter for more details. You can use Windows 95-specific disk utilities safely, again, when running Windows 95 on a multiboot system.

NTFS Long File Names

NTFS generates an alias for each LFN the same way that FAT does. This auto-generation takes time, however. If you won't be using 16-bit MS-DOS or Windows 3.x-based applications, you might consider disabling the automatic alias generation by adding a value called NtfsDisable8dot3NameCreation with a type of REG_DWORD and a value of 1 to HKEY_LOCAL_MACHINE\ System\CurrentControlSet\Control\FileSystem. To re-enable alias generation, set the value to 0, or delete the value altogether.

Converting a FAT Partition to NTFS

You can convert a FAT partition to NTFS at any time. You cannot, however, convert an NTFS partition to a FAT partition. Therefore, if you aren't certain about what type of file system to use for a partition, you might want to start with FAT and convert after you are sure there will be no ill effects.

To convert from FAT to NTFS, issue this command from the command prompt (there is no GUI utility for this):

```
CONVERT <drive_letter>: /FS:NTFS
```

The reason for specifying the file system when there has never been more than one choice probably is to accommodate future expansion, perhaps when the new OFS file system is added to Windows NT in the Cairo release.

When you perform a conversion, you do not have to back up your data (although you always should, just in case something goes awry); the conversion is done on the fly. You usually don't even need to shut down and restart the computer, unless another process currently is using the partition you are converting. If so, Windows NT performs the conversion after the system reboots using a special boot-time utility called autoconv. You see it happen when the screen turns blue immediately following the CHKDSK output.

)

NTFS Compression

Individual files and directories can be marked for compression on NTFS partitions only. (An entire drive can be compressed, too, but all you are really doing is compressing the root directory and the files within it; everything is handled at the file level.)

Compression occurs on the fly. All this is transparent to applications and the rest of the operating system.

> Stacker, DoubleSpace, DriveSpace, and the other disk compression products are great products, but you never really know how much disk space you have left. Everything is based on an estimated compression ratio, and because the entire drive is compressed (these products allow no granularity), that compression ratio is applied to all files, DOCs, and ZIPs alike. Sometimes you run out of disk space even though a directory listing says you should have several megabytes remaining.
>
> With NTFS, each file is compressed individually, so you always know the exact amount of disk space you have left. You can also choose which files to compress, so you don't have to waste time compressing the entire drive if you only want keep your Word documents down to size.

NTFS compression does not free up as much disk space as most MS-DOS-compatible compression products. This is not because Microsoft could not write a tight compression algorithm; in fact, they did just that with DriveSpace in Windows 95. The reason for the loose compression in Windows NT is actually to ensure that performance is not affected adversely.

Typically, disk compression products sacrifice performance for extra compression. In Windows NT, you can get a compression ratio almost as good as the MS-DOS 6.22 DriveSpace compression engine, without sacrificing any noticeable performance. When a user marks files to compress, NTFS analyzes the files to see how much disk space will be saved and the amount of time it will take to compress and decompress the file. If NTFS determines that it is not a fair trade, it does not compress the file, no matter how many times the user issues the compress command. NTFS compression is not at all configurable; all parameters are handled exclusively by the file system.

You can compress any file or directory on an NTFS partition, even if it is the system or boot partition. NTLDR, a hidden, system, read-only file in the root of your system partition, is the only file that you cannot compress. NTLDR is the first file loaded when Windows NT boots. NTLDR controls the rest of the boot process, including the loading of a mini-NTFS driver used when the system boots. Until NTLDR loads the NTFS minidriver, compressed files are inaccessible. NTLDR must, therefore, always remain uncompressed.

Not all files compress equally. Document files tend to compress the most. Text-based documents and bitmapped graphics, in particular, can shrink to less than one-eighth of their original size. Program files compress about forty or fifty percent, and already compressed files such as JPG and AVI graphics and videos tend not to compress at all.

Compressing and Uncompressing Files, Directories, and Drives

One of a few ways to compress a file or directory on an NTFS partition is to select the directories and files, and choose File, Compress.

To compress NTFS files, follow these steps:

1. Select the files you want to compress. Use the Ctrl key to select multiple files.

2. Choose File, Properties. The Properties dialog box appears.

3. In the Attributes frame, select the Compressed check box (see fig. 3.28).

Figure 3.28

File Properties dialog box for a file on an NTFS partition.

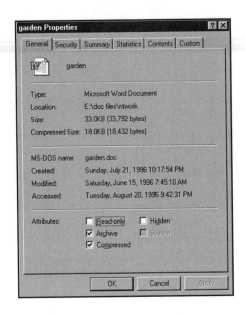

If you select a directory rather than or along with a file, you are asked whether you want to compress all the files and subdirectories within that directory.

To uncompress files or directories, select them and disable the Compressed check box in the Properties dialog box.

When files and directories are compressed, a new Compression attribute is set for those objects. Note that the Compression attribute does not display for non-NTFS partitions.

If you are curious about the amount of disk space NTFS actually is saving you, compare Size to Compressed Size in the General tab of the file Properties dialog box (refer to fig. 3.28).

The procedure for compressing a drive is similar to the procedure for compressing a file or directory. Select the drive in My Computer or Explorer, and then choose File, Properties. Select the Compress check box at the bottom of the General tab of the Properties dialog box (see fig. 3.29).

Figure 3.29

General tab of the drive Properties dialog box.

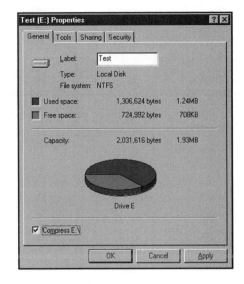

COMPACT.EXE

You also can use a command-line utility to compress files. The COMPACT.EXE command enables a user to compress files and directories from the command prompt. The following table lists switches you can use with the COMPACT command.

Use	To
COMPACT <filelist> /C	Compress
COMPACT <filelist> /U	Uncompress
COMPACT <filelist> /S	Compress an entire directory tree
COMPACT <filelist> /A	Compress hidden and system files
COMPACT <filelist> /I	Ignore errors and continue compressing
COMPACT <filelist> /F	Force compression even if the objects are already compressed
COMPACT <filelist> /Q	Turn on quiet mode; that is, display only summary information

Keep the COMPACT /F command in the back of your mind as a troubleshooting tool because when files are marked for compression, their Compressed attribute is determined and set before the actual file is compressed. Although not usually a big deal, all the selected files would be marked as compressed even though the operation had not been completed if the system were to crash during a compression operation. You could try compressing the files again with the /C switch, but the files would all be skipped because their Compressed attribute has already been set. Using the /F switch forces all files in the list to be recompressed, which should solve the problem.

You also can use the COMPACT command without any switches, in which case it just reports on the compression status, size, and ratio for each file in the file list.

Special Notes About Compressed Directories

Directories do not truly get compressed; the Compressed attribute for a directory just sets a flag to tell Windows NT to compress all current files and all future files created in this directory.

With that in mind, it may be easier to understand that when you copy or move compressed files, the files do not always stay compressed.

When a new file is created in an NTFS directory, it inherits the attributes set for that directory. When a file is created in a "compressed" directory, for example, that file will be compressed. When a file is created in an uncompressed directory, the file will not be compressed. So when a compressed file is copied to an uncompressed directory, the new copy of the file will not be compressed. Likewise, if an uncompressed file is copied to a "compressed" directory, the copy of the file will be compressed even though the original is not.

This much probably makes sense. Windows NT includes a MOVE command, however, that, when used within a single partition, swaps directory pointers so that a single file appears to move from one directory to another. Note the word "appears." The file does not actually go anywhere; it is the source and target directories that actually record a change. When files are moved, attributes do not change. In other words, a compressed file moved into an uncompressed directory stays compressed, and an uncompressed file moved into a compressed directory stays uncompressed.

If you don't think that is complicated enough, Windows NT enables you to use the MOVE command even when the source and target directories are on two different partitions. In this scenario, it is not possible for a directory on one partition to point to a file on another partition. Instead, Windows NT copies the file to the target partition and deletes the original file. Because the target partition now contains a brand-new file, that file inherits the attributes of its new parent directory.

When you copy a file within or between partitions, or move a file between partitions, therefore, the compression attribute of the new copy is inherited from its new parent directory. When you move a file within a single partition, the attributes on the file remain unchanged.

Sharing Directories

Sharing refers to publishing resources on a network for public access. When you share a resource, you make it available to users on other network machines. The Windows NT objects most commonly shared are directories and printers. You learned how to share printers in Chapter 2. This section (and the following subsections) look at how to share directories.

If you are familiar with NetWare but not with Windows NT, you need to understand the concept that, by default, absolutely no Windows NT resources are available to remote users; resources must be explicitly published (shared) on the network to host network users.

If you are familiar with Windows for Workgroups or Windows 95 but not with Windows NT, you also should understand that Windows NT users cannot share directories on their computers; only administrators and power users have this privilege.

Because shares are computer-specific, and because users cannot modify anything that affects the entire computer, shares are off-limits. This restriction is not a default; granting this capability to users is impossible, as is revoking this capability from administrators and power users.

Even if you are an administrator, you must have at least List permissions to the directory before you can share a directory. Any user who has locked you out of a share probably does not want you to publish it on the network.

Three ways to create shared directories are as follows:

▶ Using Explorer or My Computer

▶ Using the command prompt

▶ Using Server Manager

The following sections look at these methods for sharing directories and take a look at two special kinds of shares: hidden shares and administrative shares. You also will get a look at how you can view shared resources and monitor access to them by using the Server Manager and the Control Panel Server application.

Sharing with Explorer and My Computer

You can share directories in Windows NT in a number of ways. The easiest, and usually the most efficient, uses Explorer or My Computer.

Right-click on the directory you want to share and choose Sharing from the shortcut menu to open the Sharing tab of the Properties dialog box (see fig. 3.30). You also can reach the Sharing tab by choosing File, Properties. Or, My Computer enables you to choose Sharing directly from the File menu after you select a directory.

Figure 3.30

The Sharing tab of the directory Properties dialog box.

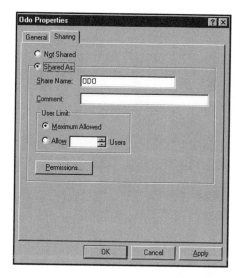

The Share Name defaults to the name of the directory. You can change it; it does not affect the actual directory name at all, it just defines the way the directory appears to network users.

You should never have to change the path. As long as you select the appropriate directory before you choose the Sharing command, the Path box should be set correctly.

The comment is optional. It is nothing more than a free-text tag line that appears next to the share name when browsing in Explorer or Network Neighborhood. (Choose View, Details if you want to see the comments.)

Click on the Permissions button to open the Access Through Share Permissions dialog box, from which you can build an Access Control List for the share to prevent unauthorized network access (see fig. 3.31).

The ATS permissions are completely independent from the local NTFS permissions. In fact, ATS permissions can even be applied to FAT partitions. Because they apply to the entire share, however, you cannot assign granular file-level permissions unless the partition on which the share resides is NTFS.

Figure 3.31

The Access Through Share Permissions dialog box.

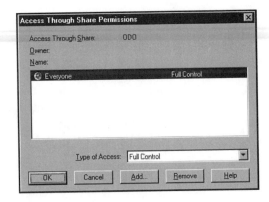

The ATS permissions themselves are not that granular. Here are your choices:

- ▶ **No Access.** Users with No Access to a share can still connect to the share, but nothing appears in File Manager except the message You do not have permission to access this directory.

- ▶ **Read.** Assigns R and X permissions to the share and its contents.

- ▶ **Change.** Assigns R, X, W, and D permissions to the share and its contents.

- ▶ **Full Control.** Assigns R, X, W, and D permissions to the share and its contents. In addition, for NTFS shares, P and O permissions are added.

Just as with local NTFS permissions, user and group permissions accumulate, with the exception of No Access, which instantly overrides all other permissions.

Remember, however, that ATS permissions are completely independent of local NTFS permissions. If both sets of permissions are assigned, only the most restrictive permissions are retained. A user who has Full Control over a file within a share to which only Read access has been granted cannot modify that file. Likewise, a user who has Read access to a file within a Full Control share cannot modify the file.

If you don't require security, you don't have to touch the ATS permissions. The default permissions grant the Everyone group Full Control (just as the default NTFS permissions do).

Choose the OK button to enact sharing of the directory. To modify the share configuration, right-click on the directory again and choose Sharing from the shortcut menu.

The Sharing tab looks identical to the New Share dialog box, with the addition of the New Share button (see fig. 3.32). Click on the New Share button to share the directory again, with a different name and ACL. It does not remove the original share, it just shares the directory again. You can share a single directory an unlimited number of times.

Figure 3.32

The Sharing tab after sharing has been enabled. Note the New Share button.

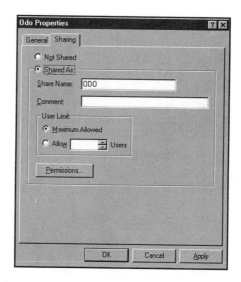

Sharing from the Command Prompt

To share from the Windows NT command prompt, use the NET SHARE command, using this syntax:

```
NET SHARE <share_name>=<drive_letter>:<path>
```

To share the C:\PUBLIC directory as Documents, use the following command:

```
NET SHARE Documents=C:\PUBLIC
```

To add a comment for browsers, use the /REMARK switch:

```
NET SHARE Documents:=C:\PUBLIC /REMARK:"Public Documents"
```

To set the user limit to Maximum allowed, use the /UNLIMITED switch (although this is the default):

```
NET SHARE Documents:=C:\PUBLIC /REMARK:"Public Documents" /
UNLIMITED
```

To set a specific user limit, use the /USERS switch:

```
NET SHARE Documents:=C:\PUBLIC /REMARK:"Public Documents" /
USERS:5
```

To stop a share using the NET SHARE command, use the /DELETE switch:

```
NET SHARE Documents /DELETE
```

Hidden Shares

Regardless of how you created it, you can hide a share by ending the share name with a dollar sign ($):

```
NET SHARE Documents$=C:\Public
```

Users can still connect to these shares, but they must explicitly supply the entire path to do so. And of course, the shares can still be protected using Access Through Share Permissions.

Administrative Shares

Any Windows NT-based computer that has hard-coded ACLs that grant Full Control to Administrators and No Access to everyone else has at least the following two hidden shares:

▶ **C$ shares the root of the computer's drive C.** If other partitions exist on the drive, those partitions also will have similar shares (but not for CD-ROM or disk drives).

Consequently, administrators can easily connect to other computers on the network.

▶ **ADMIN$ shares the root of the Windows NT installation, regardless of where it may have been installed.** It gives administrators easy access to the operating system directory on any Windows NT-based computer.

You can stop these shares if you want to, but they come back the next time you restart your system. You cannot permanently disable them.

Monitoring and Managing Shares

To see a list of all the shares on the system, open the Server application in the Control Panel. Although you cannot stop sharing a resource from the Server application, you can see a complete list of shared resources as well as a list of connected users and other server-related items.

The Server application (SRVMGR.CPL) is a subset of Windows NT Server's Server Manager application. It is a front end for administering connections to your computer. In the Server dialog box, you can view the Usage Summary for your server (see fig. 3.33). The Usage Summary tracks the following statistics:

Figure 3.33

The Control Panel Server application.

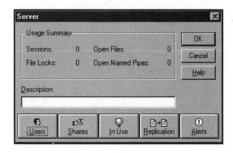

▶ **Sessions.** The number of computers connected to this server.

▶ **Open Files.** The total number of files currently open for access by remote users.

- ▶ **File Locks.** The total number of file locks placed against this computer by remote users.

- ▶ **Open Named Pipes.** The total number of named pipes between this computer and connected workstations. (Named pipes are an interprocess communication (IPC) mechanism.)

The Server dialog box also acts as the launch pad for five other server-configuration dialog boxes, as follows:

- ▶ **Users Sessions.** (Click on the Users button.) Shows detailed information about current user sessions on your Windows NT-based server.

- ▶ **Shared Resources.** (Click on the Shares button.) Displays detailed information about current shares on your server.

- ▶ **Open Resources.** (Click on the In Use button.) Displays the resources of your computer currently being used by remote users.

- ▶ **Directory Replication.** (Click on the Replication button.) You can configure the Directory Replicator service in this window.

- ▶ **Alerts.** (Click on the Alerts button.) Enables an administrator to enter a list of users or workstations to whom messages will be sent in the event of a significant server event.

To view the shared resources on your system, click on the Shares button in the Server application's Server dialog box. The Shared Resources dialog box that appears shows a list of all shares presently configured for your system and the path to each share (see fig. 3.34).

Server Manager, in the Administrative Tools group, offers a similar view of shared resources on the local system and on other network computers as well (see fig. 3.35). Click on a computer icon in the Server Manager main screen to open a dialog box that is similar to the dialog box used for the Control Panel Server application.

Figure 3.34

The Shared Resources dialog box.

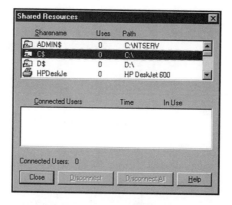

Figure 3.35

The Server Manager main screen.

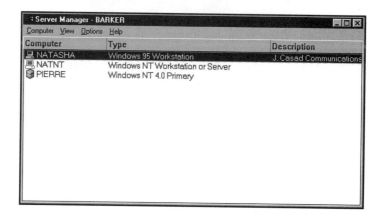

In the Server Manager, not only can you view the share information for a remote PC, you can actually create a new shared directory. Select a computer in the Server Manager and choose Computer, Shared Directories. The Shared Directories dialog box appears (see fig. 3.36). The Shared Directories dialog box shows the shared directories for the computer you selected. Click on the New Share button to add a new share. The New Share dialog box that appears asks you to specify a share name, a path, and an optional comment that will appear in descriptions on the share (see fig. 3.37). You also can limit the number of simultaneous users who can access the share. The Permissions button enables you to specify Access Through Share (ATS) permissions, described earlier in this chapter.

Figure 3.36

The Shared Directories dialog box.

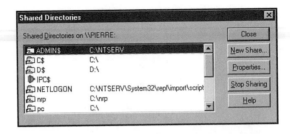

Figure 3.37

The New Share dialog box.

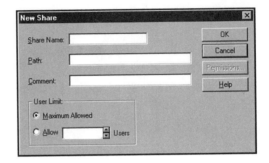

The Stop Sharing button in the Shared Directories dialog box enables you to terminate a share. The Properties button opens the Share Properties dialog box, which is similar to the New Share dialog box.

See Chapter 2 for a discussion of Server Manager's powerful Directory Replication feature.

Synchronizing Files

Windows NT 4, like Windows 95, includes a utility called My Briefcase. My Briefcase helps you synchronize and update files.

My Briefcase is designed to act as a virtual briefcase; you fill it with documents and take it with you when you leave for the office or airport. Of course, you can copy the documents to a disk without the aid of a high-tech virtual briefcase, but as anyone in business knows, keeping multiple copies of important files poses grave dangers. You might forget which version of the file is current and make changes to the non-current version. You might also forget about an update to one of the versions and use an older version as the final document.

My Briefcase solves these problems. Assume, for example, that you copy a document to My Briefcase and take it with you on a business trip. When you return, My Briefcase compares the traveling copy with the original, and tells you whether either or both of the files have changed. Then, you can choose one of the following options:

▶ **Replace.** Replaces the old version with the changed version. (Or you can tell My Briefcase to replace the changed version with the unchanged version, and thereby cancel the changes.)

▶ **Skip.** Skips the update because both versions have changed. (My Briefcase cannot automatically merge the changes when both files have changed unless the application supports the Briefcase merge feature.)

▶ **Merge.** If the application supports the Briefcase merge feature, My Briefcase merges the changes and updates the files so that both copies get the merged version.

▶ **Delete.** If either the original or the Briefcase copy has been deleted, Briefcase synchronizes the files by deleting the remaining copy.

To open My Briefcase, double-click on the My Briefcase icon located on the Desktop.

The following steps show you how My Briefcase is typically used:

1. Open My Briefcase (see fig. 3.38).

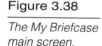

Figure 3.38

The My Briefcase main screen.

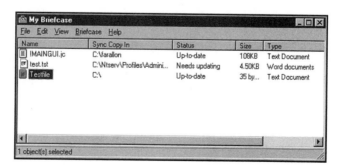

2. Copy a file or a group of files to My Briefcase using Explorer or My Computer. My Briefcase is designed for drag and drop, so drag a file from Explorer to the My Briefcase window or to the My Briefcase icon. You also can use the Clipboard to copy and paste a file to My Briefcase.

3. Put a disk in your disk drive and drag the My Briefcase icon from the Desktop to the disk drive, using Explorer or My Computer.

4. Insert the disk into a different computer. (You can use the same computer if you are just doing this as a test.)

5. Open My Briefcase (on the disk), and then open the copy of the file in My Briefcase and make a change to the file. Close the file.

6. In My Briefcase, choose Briefcase, Update All.

7. The Update My Briefcase dialog box appears, asking whether you want to update the unmodified version (see fig. 3.39). Click on the Update button to synchronize the files, or right-click on a file icon to choose a different action from a shortcut menu (see fig. 3.40).

Figure 3.39

The Update My Briefcase dialog box.

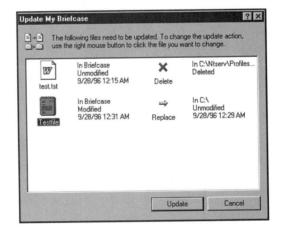

Figure 3.40

*Right-click on the
file icon to
choose a differ-
ent update
action.*

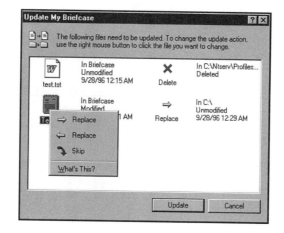

My Briefcase is best known for helping users with portable computers, but you also can use My Briefcase to synchronize files on a
network.

My Briefcase is part of the user profile for a particular user. This
means that each user can have his or her own briefcase, and that a
user's personal briefcase appears on-screen when he or she logs
on. My Briefcase files are stored in the directory:

```
C:\<winnt_root>\Profiles\<username>\Desktop\My Briefcase
```

Working with NTFS File Permissions and Security

The NTFS file system supports a complex arrangement of directory and file security for which there is no equivalent in the FAT file
system.

The following sections examine important aspects of NTFS
security.

Ownership of NTFS Resources

Every NTFS file and directory has one account designated as its
owner. The owner of a resource is the only account that has the

right to access a resource, modify its properties, and secure it from outside access.

By default, the owner of a resource is the user who created the resource. Only one user can own a resource at any given time, except that a user who is a member of the Administrators group cannot be the sole owner of any resource. Any resource created by an administrator, for example, is co-owned by the entire Administrators group. This is part of a checks-and-balances security model in Windows NT that ensures that an administrator cannot irrevocably hoard power and resources—yet another reason administrators should not use administrator-level accounts for day-to-day operations.

To identify the owner of any file or directory, follow these steps:

1. Select the file or directory in My Computer or Windows NT Explorer.

2. Choose File, Properties. The Properties dialog box appears.

3. Click on the Security tab (see fig. 3.41).

Figure 3.41

The file Properties Security tab.

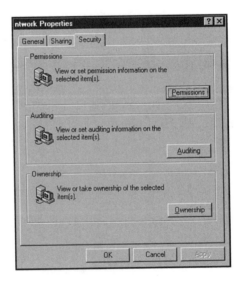

4. Click on the Ownership button. The Owner dialog box appears (see fig. 3.42).

Figure 3.42

The Owner dialog box.

Remember that only NTFS resources have owners.

You also can take ownership away from the current owner by choosing the Take Ownership button in the Owner dialog box. Normally, only administrators can do this—they can take ownership of any resource because they have been granted the Take Ownership of File and Directories user right. You can use User Manager for Domains to revoke the right of administrators to take ownership of files and directories that they did not create or to add another user or group to the list of accounts with the "take ownership" right. It is best, however, not to change this right at all; administrators must have this right if the system is to achieve a C2 security rating.

If you are not an administrator, you may still be able to take ownership if the current owner has granted you permission to take ownership. The important concept to grasp for now, however, is that ownership is taken, never given. Ownership involves responsibility, and that responsibility can never be forced on anyone, even by an administrator. Implications to this rule will surface shortly.

Auditing NTFS Resources

One of the most important aspects of Windows NT security is that system administrators can *audit* access to objects such as directories files. In other words, you can configure NT to track all attempts (successful or not) to access NTFS resources for various purposes. The record of all access attempts then appear in the Security log of the Event Viewer (see Chapter 6).

To configure auditing for a file, follow these steps:

1. Right-click on an NTFS file in Explorer of My Computer and choose Properties.

2. Click on the Security tab of the File Properties dialog box (refer to fig. 3.41).

3. Click on the Auditing button. The File Auditing dialog box appears (see fig. 3.43). You can audit either successful or failed attempts at any of the actions listed, and you can specify which specific groups or users you want to audit.

4. Click on the Add button to add a group or user to the audit list. Click on the Remove button to delete a group or user from the audit list.

Figure 3.43

The File Auditing dialog box.

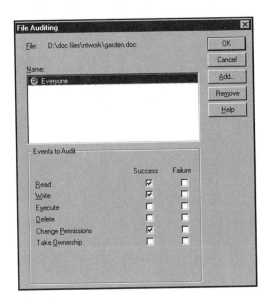

The Directory Auditing dialog box is similar (see fig. 3.44). The procedure for reaching the Directory Auditing dialog box is similar to the procedure for reaching the file Auditing dialog box. Right click on a directory, choose Properties, choose the Directory Properties Security tab, then click on the Auditing button. The Directory Auditing dialog box enables you to choose whether the new auditing arrangement you are configuring will replace the auditing on subdirectories or existing files.

Figure 3.44

*The Directory
Auditing dialog
box.*

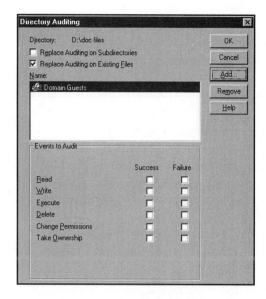

If you copy a file to a directory configured for auditing, the file
inherits the directory's auditing configuration. If you move a file
(dragging a file in Explorer to another directory in the same partition is a move), the file retains its original auditing configuration.

Securing NTFS Resources

The set of permissions on a file or directory is just another attribute (or stream) attached to the file, called an Access Control
List (ACL). Each ACL contains a series of Access Control Entries
(ACEs), and each Access Control Entry references a specific user
or group SID and a type of access to grant or deny that SID. The
end of this section explains how Windows NT checks a user's credentials against the Access Control List. First, this section reviews
how permissions are assigned the ACL to begin with.

Discretionary Access

Who gets to assign permissions to a resource? The owner of the
resource. Who is the owner of the resource? The user who created
it. In other words, unlike other operating systems, security is not
the sole domain of the administrator. If you create a file, you, not

the administrator, get to secure it. You can, in fact, easily lock administrators out of their resources. And that makes sense in many environments.

Picture a typical company network, for example. Along with memos, reports, and routine documents, there are salary information, personnel files, and other sensitive data that the administrator and MIS department should not have access to just because they run the network. The users who created these files and work with them are the best ones to judge who should and should not have access. This type of access control, called discretionary access, is a hallmark of C2-level security.

Because locking administrators out of files and directories is dangerous, there is a spare key. An administrator cannot be blocked from taking ownership of a resource, and after the administrator owns the resource, he or she can modify the permissions on the resource so that he or she can access it. Remember, though, that ownership can be taken but never given, and that goes for giving back too. When the administrator owns the resource, he can never return ownership to the original user without that user explicitly taking ownership. And that is how it should be for legitimate situations in which a user might be absent from work when a critical file needs to be accessed. The administrator could get into a sticky situation by accessing files without a legitimate reason.

Permissions Versus User Rights

You may remember that resource permissions are not the same thing as user rights. User rights are tasks stored with your account information in the Registry, which you can perform on the system as a whole. NTFS permissions are stored with the resource itself, in the ACL property discussed earlier.

It is important to understand the difference between rights and permissions, because that understanding brings light to why the resource permissions assigned to a user cannot be viewed the way trustee assignments in other operating systems such as Novell NetWare are viewed. Displaying all the permissions assigned to a user would require searching all the NTFS files and directories on all the NTFS partitions on the workstation and on shared directories of any other workstation or server on the network. It also requires searching for incidence of the user's SID or group SIDs on the ACL of each of those files.

Directory-Level Permissions

Permissions can be placed on both directories and files. When they are, you need to resolve the permissions to figure out the effective permissions for a user.

The owner of a directory may grant a user the following permissions:

▶ **No Access.** Restricts the user from accessing the directory by any means. The directory appears in the directory tree, but instead of a file list, you see the message You do not have permissions to access this directory.

▶ **List.** Restricts the user from accessing the directory, although the user may view the contents list for the directory.

▶ **Read.** The user may read data files and execute program files from the directory, but can make no changes of any sort.

▶ **Add.** The user may not read or even view the contents of the directory, but may write files to the directory. If you write a file to the directory, you receive the message You do not have permissions to access this directory, but you still may save or copy files to it.

▶ **Add & Read.** The user may view and read from the directory and save new files into the directory, but may not modify existing files in any way.

▶ **Change.** The user may view and read from the directory and save new files into the directory, may modify and even delete existing files, and may change attributes on the directory and even delete the entire directory. This, by the way, is the most extensive permissions you would ever want assign anyone.

▶ **Full Control.** The user may view, read, save, modify, or delete the directory and its contents. In addition, the user may change permissions on the directory and its contents, even if he or she does not own the resource. The user also has permission to take ownership at any time.

What actually happens with all these levels of permissions is a combination of six basic actions that can be performed against a resource:

▶ Read (R)

▶ Write (W)

▶ Execute (X)

▶ Delete

▶ Change Permissions (P)

▶ Take Ownership (O)

The following table breaks down these permissions by permissions level:

Level	Directory Permissions	File Permissions
No Access	None	None
List	RX	Unspecified
Read	RX	RX
Add	WX	Unspecified
Add & Read	RXWD	RX
Change	RXWD	RXWD
Full Control	RXWDPO	RXWDPO

The two custom levels of permissions are Special Directory Access and Special File Access, both of which enable the owner (or any user granted the "P" permission) to custom build an access control entry by using any combination of the six basic actions mentioned here.

To custom build an access control entry for a group or user, follow these steps:

1. Click on the Permissions button on the Security tab of the File or Directory Properties dialog box.

2. In the File Permissions dialog box that appears, select the group or user (see fig. 3.45).

3. Choose Special Directory Access from the Type of Access combo box.

Figure 3.45

The file Permissions dialog box.

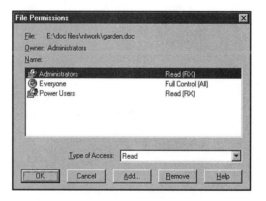

4. Choose the appropriate permissions in the Special Directory Access dialog box that appears (see fig. 3.46).

When an NTFS partition is created, the default permissions are set so that the Everyone group has Full Control. You may want to change this at the root directory level, but see the section, "Special Considerations for the Boot and System Partitions," at the end of this chapter before you do so.

When a new directory or file is created on an NTFS partition, the resource inherits the permissions on its parent directory, the same way it inherits the compression attribute. (See the section, "NTS File Compression," earlier in this chapter.)

File-Level Permissions

Although permissions for files are not as varied as they are for directories, NTFS can store permissions for files also. The owner of a file may grant a user the following permissions:

Figure 3.46

The Special Directory Access dialog box.

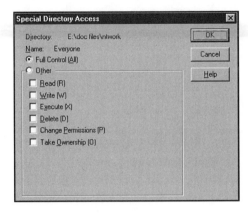

> ▶ **No Access.** The user may not access this file at all, although the file name and basic attributes still appear in File Manager.

> ▶ **Read.** The user may read this file if it is a data file, or execute it if it is a program file, but may not modify it in any way.

> ▶ **Change.** The user may read, execute, modify, or delete this file.

> ▶ **Full Control.** The user may read or execute, write to, or delete this file, may change permissions on it, as well as take ownership away from the current owner.

The following table breaks down these file permissions:

Level	Permissions
No Access	None
Read	RX
Change	RXWD
Full Control	RXWDPO

As with Directory permissions, a Special Access level allows anyone who has the capability to change permissions to custom build an access control entry for a user or group.

Setting Permissions

To set permissions on a file or directory, first select the resource in Explorer or My Computer, and then choose File, Properties. Click on the Permissions button on the Security tab of the File Properties dialog box to open the File Permissions dialog box (refer to fig. 3.45).

To remove a user or group from the ACL, select the user and click on the Remove button. To add a user or group to the ACL, click on the Add button. Clicking on the Add button opens the Add Users and Groups dialog box, which includes a list of all the groups in your account database (see fig. 3.47).

Figure 3.47

The Add Users and Groups dialog box.

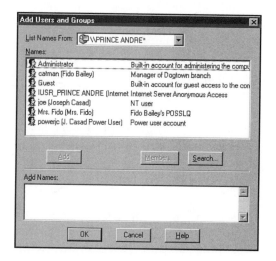

If you want to grant access to a specific user, click on the Show Users button. Otherwise, only the group names are displayed. Choose the users and groups you want to add to the ACL individually or collectively and click on the Add button to enter their names in the Add Names list box at the bottom of the dialog box. Don't try to set their access level here, unless all of these accounts are going to be granted the same access level (this type of access setting is all or nothing). When you click on the OK button, you get another chance to modify the permission level for each individual account on the ACL.

Setting permissions for a directory brings up a slightly different dialog box (see fig. 3.48).

Figure 3.48

*The Directory
Permissions
dialog box.*

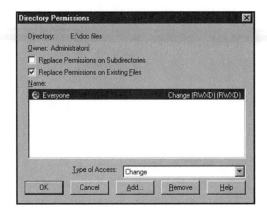

In the Directory Permissions dialog box, you can enable Replace Permissions of Subdirectories or Replace Permissions on Existing Files, the default. If you enable the Replace Permissions on Existing Files check box, the permissions that apply to the directory also apply to the files within the directory, but not to subdirectories or files within subdirectories.

Enabling only the Replace Permissions on Subdirectories check box modifies the permissions on all directories in the directory tree, but not on any files within those directories, even in the top-level directory.

Selecting both check boxes applies these permissions to the entire directory tree and its contents. Enabling neither check box changes the permissions on the top-level directory only.

Local Groups

When working with user rights, assigning rights to user and built-in groups usually suffices. When assigning resource permissions, however, adding individual users may be too time-consuming, and adding built-in groups may be too inclusive. Imagine having a directory that contains meeting minutes for a project on which you are working. You would like to grant permissions to the people on the project team, but the team is more than thirty people strong. Assigning permissions to everybody would take a long time, and assigning permissions to the Users group would give access to too many people.

It is time to introduce local groups, a separate level of user management in Windows NT. Local groups can be created by any user for any purpose (Headquarters, Marketing, Vice Presidents, Portland, Engineering), and once created, can be reused repeatedly. By creating a local group called MyProject and including all the project team members, you need to grant only a single set of permissions for each meeting report.

Local Groups versus Built-In Groups

A *local group* is a group used to assign rights or permissions to a local system and local resources. Local groups are similar to built-in groups in that both can contain many users to address a single purpose. In fact, technically, the built-in groups in Windows NT Workstation are local groups.

Local and built-in groups also have similar structures. Both can contain local users, domain users, and global groups, and users and global groups from trusted domains. The only type of account that cannot be placed inside a local group is another local group.

The difference between local and built-in groups lies in their intended purposes. The built-in groups are predefined and preassigned to specific rights and capabilities for system management. They are not intended for use in managing access to resources. Local groups are impractical for managing the system, but are ideal for assigning permissions to files and directories.

The only other difference between the two types of groups is that built-in groups are permanent members of a computer's account database, whereas local groups can be created and deleted at will.

Defining Local Groups

As with any type of account, you create local groups in User Manager for Domains. To create a local group in User Manager for Domains, follow these steps:

1. Select the user accounts you want to include in the local group (remember to hold down the Ctrl key to select multiple accounts).

2. Choose User, New Local Group to open the New Local Group dialog box (see fig. 3.49).

Figure 3.49

The New Local Group dialog box.

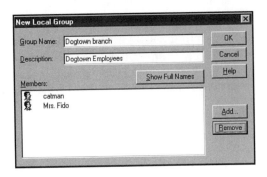

3. Enter a name (required) and a description (optional) for the group. The users you selected before issuing the New Local Group command should already be listed in the Members list.

4. If you want to add additional users, choose the Add button. The Add Users and Groups dialog box appears (refer to fig. 3.47).

   Notice that only users and global groups are displayed, not local groups. Again, local groups cannot be nested, so User Manager does not even tempt you.

5. Choose the users (individual or collective) that you want to add, and click on the Add button to enter their names in the Add Names list at the bottom of the dialog box.

6. Choose OK when you are ready to return to the New Local Group dialog box.

7. If you accidentally choose a user who does not belong in the group, click on the Remove button to delete the account from the group. Otherwise, click on OK to add the local group to the account database.

Managing Local Groups

After you create your local groups, you can manage them much as you manage your user accounts. You should, however, be aware of the following idiosyncrasies concerning local groups:

▶ You cannot rename a group after it has been created. Groups are referenced throughout the system by their Security Identifiers (SIDs), just as users are. Most likely, Microsoft's programmers just never got around to adding this feature to the code. You can copy a local group and give the new group a new name (in fact, you would have to), but that really is not the same as renaming. None of the permissions granted to the original group would apply to the new copy. There just is not a solution for this one.

▶ You cannot disable a group after it has been created. If a group were disabled, some implications would be unclear. Whether members of that group should be unable to log on, or whether the group's permissions and rights just should not apply while it is disabled would be a thorny issue. If you must temporarily disable the effects of a group on the system, remove all the users from the group. Do not delete the group and re-create it later, or your new group will have a new SID and a brand new set of default rights and permissions. All the old properties will be irrevocably lost.

▶ If you do want to delete a group, just select the group in User Manager and choose Delete from the User menu. Be aware that you are deleting only the group itself, not the users within the group. The effect stops here.

▶ You can add or remove members from the group by selecting the group in User Manager and choosing User, Properties.

How User and Group Permissions Interact

At this point, you have probably realized that users are likely to be in many different groups. Abigail's user account, for example, may be a member of the Users group, but also the Marketing group, the Department Managers group, the Philadelphia group, and the Project X group. Each of these user and group accounts are likely to be granted permissions to resources at one time or another, and it is quite likely that some of the accounts might occasionally appear on the same Access Control List. In such scenarios, how should the permissions granted to both a user's user account and group accounts be resolved?

Quite simply, user and group permissions are cumulative; neither takes precedence over the other. If the Marketing group has Read access to a file and the Department Managers group has Change access to the same file, Abigail (a member of both groups) has both—or in other words, Change access, because Change already includes the R and X permissions that Read incorporates.

The one exception to this rule is the No Access permission. No Access overrides all other permissions granted to a user or the user's groups, regardless of where the No Access was assigned. If Abigail were granted Read access to a file but Marketing was granted No Access, for example, Abigail would not be able to access the file. You cannot—and this cannot be emphasized enough—override a No Access permission.

This might seem worrisome at first. Consider a situation in which Beth is thinking about leaving the company and is updating her resume. She doesn't want anyone else to have access to this file, so she assigns the following permissions to the file:

Beth: Full Control

Everyone: No Access

You have probably guessed the result—Beth now can't access her resume because she is a member of the Everyone group, and the No Access she assigned to Everyone overrides the Full Control she assigned to her own account. Can Beth somehow easily retain sole access to her resume, or does she need to create a group called Everyone But Me and assign it No Access?

Yes, there is an easy way, and it involves making the ACL read as follows:

Beth: Full Control

You don't have to specify No Access for a user or group to exclude them from an ACL. The rule in Windows NT is that if you are not on the list, you don't get in. So why does Windows NT include the

No Access command at all if it isn't even necessary to exclude access? Because No Access is intended as a "negator" to remove permissions from a user or group that may already have been implicitly added to the ACL through membership in another group. Beth may not care if her coworkers in the Marketing department know she's thinking about leaving the company, for example, but she would rather her supervisor remain ignorant. She can set the following permissions on her resume's ACL:

Beth: Full Control

Marketing: Read

Abigail: No Access

Because Abigail is a member of the Marketing group, she would have received Read access to Beth's resume if she had not been excluded by a direct No Access.

How Directory and File Permissions Interact

When you have permissions on both directories and files—such is the case on an NTFS partition—things get just a bit more complicated. Fortunately, you can resolve this situation pretty easily, although a few odd circumstances might surround the situation.

Simply put, file permissions override directory permissions. Even if Abigail had Full Control over the directory that contained Beth's resume, she could not read Beth's resume if her account had been granted No Access to that file. Likewise, it is possible to grant a user Read access to a directory and yet still grant Full Control over a single file within that directory.

This can lead to some odd scenarios. Sam may not want anyone to view the contents of his private directory, for example, so he assigns the directory this ACL:

Sam: Full Control

If Beth tries to view this directory, she gets the You do not have permission to access this directory message. Yet Sam may still want to occasionally grant Beth access to one or two of his files. One day, he grants Beth Read access to a document in his private directory. Beth can read that file, but how can she access it? She can't view the directory contents in Explorer, and when she does a File/Open in an application, she cannot view the directory contents there either. Before she can access the file, Beth must type the full path to the file, from the application in which she wants to view it.

File Delete Child

Consider another odd scenario. Sam decides to grant Everyone Full Control to his private directory, and just apply Read permissions to Everyone for the individual files within the directory. Sam knows that although users might be able to copy and save files in his directory, they can't change the ones already present, because those files have only Read permissions. Sam also knows that no one else can change permissions on the existing files, because those files have only Read permissions. Sam, however, thinks that no one can delete his existing files because they only have Read permissions. On this last count, he is wrong.

In addition to the six basic permissions (RXWDPO) granted with Full Control, there is a seventh, implicit permission, called File Delete Child (FDC). FDC is included for POSIX compatibility, and it grants a user who has Full Control over a directory the capability to delete a top-level file within that directory, even if that user does not have delete permissions to the file itself! Only top-level files can be deleted, not subdirectories or files within subdirectories.

There is a workaround, but you must grant Special Directory Access before you can use it. If you grant Special Directory Access and choose all six permissions rather than grant Full Control to a directory, the user granted this level of access won't have the FDC permission. It looks like you are really just assigning the equivalent of Full Control, but you are doing so minus File Delete Child. By the way, don't waste time searching for File Delete Child in the Explorer interface—it is not there. It's an implicit permission granted only when Full Control is granted over a directory.

An even better workaround is to never grant anyone Full Control over anything, unless you grant it to yourself as the owner. After all, you probably don't want anyone else to have the power to change permissions on the file and lock you out. And you certainly don't want someone to have the capability to take ownership of the file at the same time so that you can't even change permissions back to what they were. A good rule of thumb is never to grant anyone any permissions higher than Change. That is high enough, because a user with Change access can delete the resource itself.

Special Considerations for the Boot and System Partitions

When you install Windows NT on an NTFS partition, it is tempting to prevent necessary files from being deleted or overwritten, to try to exclude users from accessing the Windows NT installation directory tree. If you examine the Access Control List for that directory, however, you won't see the customary Everyone/Full Control that you normally find on NTFS resources.

The critical entry on the ACL is the SYSTEM/Full Control ACE. Do not, under any circumstances, remove this ACL from the list, or modify it. Otherwise, Windows NT crashes and you cannot restart the operating system.

If this does happen, don't panic. You can use the Emergency Repair Disk to strip the permissions from the Windows NT installation directory tree. See Chapter 6 for more information on this procedure.

Putting It Together

How does Windows NT make the decision whether to grant access to an NTFS resource?

As you may recall, when a user logs on to a Windows NT-based computer, the security accounts manager generates an access token for the user's current session. The access token contains, among other things, the user's user SID and group SIDs.

When a user requests access to an NTFS resource, the Security Reference Monitor (a component of the security subsystem) examines the SIDs contained in the user's access token. The Security Reference Monitor then parses the Access Control List looking for references to any of the SIDs contained in the user's access token. The search continues until one of the following conditions is met:

▶ The Security Reference Monitor encounters a Deny (the internal representation of No Access) for any SID in the user's access token. At this point, the search stops and access is denied.

▶ The Security Reference Monitor encounters an Allow for any SID in the user's access token. If the Allow specifies the type of access the user seeks, the search stops and access is granted. If the Allow specifies some, but not all the permissions requested, the search continues until all permissions are accumulated, at which point access is granted. If the Allow specifies none of the permissions the user requests, the search continues.

▶ The Security Reference Monitor reaches the end of the Access Control List without accumulating all the requested permissions. Access is denied. No partial access is granted.

What is interesting about this process is that it works only if Denies are placed at the top of the ACL. If any Allows precede a Deny on the ACL, a user can achieve access even if No Access has been granted to one of the SIDs in the user's access token, because the search stops after the requested permissions have been accumulated and before the No Access is encountered.

Luckily, Windows NT does place all Denies before all Allows, at least, in all its built-in applications and interfaces. It is possible for a programmer—to provide maximum compatibility and flexibility in porting existing custom applications to Windows NT—to write a program so that Denies can be placed anywhere within an ACL. You should not have anything to worry about with any professionally sold Windows NT application, but you definitely want to make certain that any programmer hired for custom development knows how structure affects Access Control Lists.

Handles

After the Security Reference Monitor has approved your access to the file resource, the system creates a handle to that resource. (Remember that no user-mode process in Windows NT can access a resource directly.) The handle is entered in the object table of the process that requested the access. The object table contains the list of handles to all resources that process is using, as well as the permissions granted through each handle. When transactions are performed against an open resource, the security subsystem checks the permissions in the object table rather than parsing the entire ACL again, a process which provides both a slight performance boost and guarantees a user's permissions over a file will not refresh until the file is closed and reopened, generating a new handle.

Consider a situation in which you might grant a user Change permissions to a file. The user opens the file that contains the requested and granted Change permissions, and while the file is in use, you decide to change the user's permissions to Read. Although the ACL changes immediately, the security subsystem is not checking the ACL anymore, because the user has an open handle to the file. The user must close and reopen the file before the new permissions can take hold.

Access Tokens Don't Refresh

As is the case with handles, access tokens are generated only when a user logs on. Any changes to a user's rights and group memberships, for example, do not take effect until the user logs off and back on again. You cannot prevent a user logged on as a member of the Marketing group from accessing a resource just by removing him from the group. His access token still reflects Marketing membership until the next time he logs on.

Exercise Section

Exercise 3.1: Creating a User Account

Exercise 3.1 shows you how to configure Windows NT to audit changes to the user account database, create a user account, and then view the audit log.

Estimated time: 20 minutes

1. Log on to the domain as an administrator.

2. Choose Start, Programs, Administrative Tools, and click on User Manager for Domains.

3. In the User Manager for Domains main window, Choose Policies, Audit.

4. In the Audit Policy dialog box that appears, select the Success and Failure check boxes for User and Group Management (refer to fig. 3.11).

5. Click on OK.

6. In the User for Domains main window, choose User, New User. The New User dialog box appears.

7. In the Username text box, type **Exer1**.

8. In the Full Name text box , type **Exercise 1**.

9. For a Description, type **MCSE Training Guide test account**.

10. For the Password, type **exer1**. Type the password again in the Confirm box.

note

You can, of course, make up your own username, password, and description for this test account.

11. Click on the Add button, and then click on the Close button.

continues

Exercise 3.1: Continued

The new user account should appear in the user list in the top panel of the User Manager for Domains main window.

12. Double-click on the account icon in the user list (or select the account and choose User, Properties) to open the User Properties dialog box.

13. Browse through each of the buttons at the bottom of the User Properties dialog box. In the Group button, notice that the new account is a member of the Domain Users group. Add the account to other groups by selecting a group in the right panel and clicking on the Add button. Click on Cancel (or OK if you made changes) to return to the User Manager for Domains main window.

14. Choose Start, Programs, Administrative Tools, and select Event Viewer.

15. In the Event View main window, choose Log, Security. Look for three security log entries related to creating the new account at or near the top of the list. The Category column for each of the three entries will be marked Account Manager.

16. Double-click on each of the entries for a detailed look at the audit information.

17. Close Event Viewer.

18. In the User Manager for Domains main window, choose Policies, Audit.

19. Deselect the User and Group Management check boxes (unless you want to keep auditing User and Group Management events).

20. If you plan to continue with Exercise 3.2, close User Manager for Domains. If you don't plan to continue with Exercise 3.2, double-click on the icon for the Exer1 account and select the Account Disabled check box in the User Properties dialog box. The next time you need to set up a user account, you can rename the Exer1 account by choosing User, Rename in the User Manager for Domains main window.

As this chapter describes, it is generally a better policy to disable a user account rather than to delete it. Because the Exer1 account created in this exercise was never used, advantages for disabling it are less significant. You also could delete the account by choosing User, Delete in the User Manager for Domains main window.

Exercise 3.2: System Policies

Exercise 3.2 will show you how to use the System Policies Editor to configure a user's Desktop environment.

Estimated time: 20 minutes

1. Log on as an administrator.

2. Choose Start, Programs, Administrative Tools, and then click on System Policy Editor.

3. Choose File, Open Policy.

4. Browse to the <winnt_root.\system32\repl\import\scripts folder and look for an ntconfig.pol file. If the file exists, select the file and click on OK. If the ntconfig.pol file does not exist, click on Cancel, and choose File, New Policy.

5. In the System Policy Editor, choose Edit, Add User.

6. In the Add User dialog box, enter **Exer1** (or whatever name you used for the account you created in Exercise 3.1). Click on OK.

7. The name of the user (Exer1 or whatever name you used) should now appear with an icon in the main window. Double-click on the Exer1 icon.

8. Expand the Shell policy category; then expand the Restrictions subcategory.

9. Select the Remove Run command from the Start menu check box and click on OK.

continues

Exercise 3.2: Continued

10. Choose File, Save.

11. If you started with a New Policy in step 4, Windows NT prompts you to enter a file name. Type **ntconfig** in the File Name text box (NT appends the POL extension) and save the file to the <winnt_root>\system32\Repl\Import\Scripts directory.

12. Log on to the domain from a workstation by using the Exer1 account (or whatever account name you established the policy for in step 6). Use the password you created in step 10 of Exercise 3.1.

13. When the Start button appears, click on the Start button and examine the Start menu. The Run command will be missing from the Start menu.

14. Log off the workstation. Disable or delete the Exer1 account as described in step 21 of Exercise 3.1.

Exercise 3.3: Copying and Moving

Exercise 3.3 will show you how to test the differences between copying and moving for NTFS file.

Estimated Time: 10 minutes

1. Start Windows NT Explorer.

2. Right-click on a directory on an NTFS partition.

3. Choose File, New/Folder.

4. Create a new subdirectory called **compressed**.

5. Right-click on the "compressed" subdirectory and choose Properties. In the directory Properties General tab, select the Compress attribute check box.

6. Right-click on a file in another directory on the NTFS partition and select Properties.

7. Select the file and choose Edit, Copy; then choose Paste. A file called Copy of <filename> will be created.

8. Select this new file and choose File, Rename.

9. Change the file name to **Copy**. Create another copy of the original file and change the name of the new copy to **Move**.

10. Examine the Compress attribute of the Copy and Move files. Make certain the files are not compressed. (Right-click on the file and choose Properties to select the Compress attribute.)

11. Select the file called Copy and choose Edit, Copy.

12. Double-click on the "compressed" directory and choose Edit, Paste. A file called Copy will appear in the "compressed" subdirectory.

13. Drag the file called Move to the "compressed" directory. (Dragging the file within the same partition is a move.)

14. Check the Compress attributes of the Copy and Move files in the "compressed" directory. The Copy file is now compressed. (It inherited the Compress attribute from the parent directory.) The Move file retains its uncompressed state.

Review Questions

The following questions will test your knowledge of the information in this chapter. For additional questions, see MCP Endeavor and the Microsoft Roadmap/Assessment exam on the CD-ROM that accompanies this book.

1. You are the administrator of a Windows NT workgroup. You need to devise a group strategy for the following scenario:

   You have a group of several marketing employees who need access to the contact management database; a second group of people who need to access the accounts receivable program; and a third group of people who need to be able to modify the inventory database and run general programs.

   Keep in mind that you are trying to minimize your account administration time. Management has just informed you that the number of people in your area is expected to double over the next quarter. How would you set up group management for each group?

   Select the best answer from the following:

   A. Create user accounts for each user and assign access permissions based on the requirements laid out in the question.

   B. Create global groups for each unique group, assign the necessary permissions to each group, and then place the users in the appropriate groups.

   C. Create a local group for each unique group, assign the needed permissions to each group, and then place the users in the appropriate groups.

2. Which of the following correctly describes the relationship between deleting and disabling user accounts?

   A. Deleting a user account removes the SID from the directory database, whereas disabling the user account does not remove the SID; it changes the naming property of the user.

   B. Disabling a user account removes the SID from the directory database, whereas deleting the account does not remove the SID; it changes the naming property of the user.

    C. After deleting an account, to re-establish the user's permissions and access rights, you just have to re-create the user ID using the same name as it had before, and thus restore the system SID.

3. Which one of the following best describes the differences between local and global groups?

    A. A global group is one that resides in an NT Workstation user accounts database and a local group is one that is local to the computer where the resources reside.

    B. A local group is a group that resides in an NT Workstation computer and is used to grant access permissions to resources on the workstation. A global group is a group created in an NT domain and used to group domain users into groups with common access needs.

    C. Global groups contain local groups that have access to resources on NT Workstation and Windows 95 computers.

    D. Local groups are created on NT domain controllers and are used to grant access to domain users to resources in the domain. Global groups are used to give users access to resources in other domains.

4. If you suspect that a user is attempting to gain access to directories that contain sensitive information, which feature can you enable in Windows NT Workstation to create a log of attempted accesses?

    A. You can use the System Option in Control Panel to enable the auditing feature of Windows NT.

    B. You can use the Windows NT Accounting System.

    C. You can use Directory Logging.

    D. You can use the User Manager program to enable the Windows NT Audit Policy.

5. A user calls and complains that the system time on his NT Workstation is incorrect and when he tries to fix the time, he gets a message that he doesn't have sufficient permissions.

What is the best way to allow him to change the time on his system?

   A. Give him the administrator password and have him log on as administrator and change the system time.

   B. Make his userid a member of the Administrator group to give him the permissions he needs to change the time.

   C. Grant his user ID the Change system time right in User Manager.

   D. Tell him to restart his computer in MS-DOS and change the time and date in DOS.

6. You want to appoint a user the responsibility of backing up all the Windows NT Workstation computers in your workgroup. What is the best way to give the user the permissions necessary to perform this function?

   A. Make the user a member of the Administrator group, and thereby give him access to all resources on the NT Workstation computers.

   B. Give the user the administrator password and tell him to log on as administrator to perform the backups.

   C. Grant the user's account Full Control permissions to all the directories and files that the user needs to back up and restore.

   D. Make the user a member of the Backup Operators group, and thereby give him access to all files and directories on the NT Workstation computer without regard to regular NT permissions.

7. You have installed NT Workstation on several computers in your company for use by several temporary employees. You want to prevent the users from changing their passwords. Which step(s) should you take to perform this?

   A. Create mandatory profiles on the domain controller.

   B. Configure directory, share, and file permissions.

   C. Create user accounts that have the correct permissions.

   D. Assign appropriate user rights on a user-by-user basis.

    E. Enable the User Cannot Change Password option in User Manager.

8. You are the primary user of your NT Workstation computer, but you occasionally share your computer with a couple other users in your department. What is the best way to let them use your computer?

    A. Create a user account for each user.

    B. Create one account and give each user the password for the new account.

    C. Let the users use your account and ask them not to change anything on your computer.

    D. Tell them the password to the administrator account on your computer.

9. You share you computer with another user. You need to install Microsoft Word so that it is available to both of you. What type of program group should you create so that the program is available to you and the other user?

    A. Personal

    B. Local

    C. Global

    D. Common

10. Your company routinely hires temporary employees around the holidays each year. These temps typically work the last two weeks in November and the entire month of December. How would you design an account policy to maximize the security of your network? Select all correct answers.

    A. Set the account policy to lock out users after three bad logon attempts.

    B. Set the account policy so that users' passwords never expire.

    C. Set the account policy so that users are logged out of the workstation when their time restrictions are exceeded.

    D. Modify the temporary users' accounts so that their accounts are disabled after January first.

11. A user calls you and tells you that she accidentally deleted a group that contains several users on her computer. She is worried that this may have affected the users' rights to certain resources on her computer. She knows the name of the group and the users that were members of the group. How can she restore the group and the permissions back to the way they were?

    A. Choose the Undelete option in User Manager to recover the deleted group.

    B. Create a new group with the same name and SID as the deleted group.

    C. Create a new group with the same name, assign the users to the group, and then reassign the permissions to the group.

    D. Re-create the users and group, and reassign the permissions to the group.

12. What are the names of the four special groups in NT Workstation?

    A. Network, Special, Administrators, and Interactive

    B. Administrators, Backup Operators, Network, and Local

    C. Global, Power Users, Macintosh Users, and Network

    D. Network, Creator Owner, Interactive, and Everyone

13. When you connect to a shared directory on another Windows NT Workstation computer, which group do you automatically become a member of?

    A. Network

    B. Administrators

    C. Creator Owner

    D. Interactive

14. You want a user to be able to create user and group accounts, but don't want the user to be able to assign user rights. Of what groups should you make the user a member?

    A. Account Operators

    B. Server Operators

C. Administrators

D. Power Users

15. What is the difference between a user account that is locked out and an account that is disabled?

    A. A disabled userid keeps its SID, whereas a locked out user account does not.

    B. The system administrator can lock out a user account, whereas the system administrator cannot disable a user account.

    C. The system administrator can disable a user account, whereas the system administrator cannot lock out a user account.

    D. A locked out userid keeps its SID, whereas a locked out user account does not.

16. You need to create several user accounts that all have the same properties. What is the best method to use?

    A. Create a user who has the correct parameters and use the Replicate option to create as many users as necessary.

    B. Create a user who has the correct parameters and use the Copy function in User Manager to create as many as necessary.

    C. Use the REPLUSER.EXE program to copy a user template that has the correct properties.

    D. Run the RDISK.EXE program to make duplicate user accounts for as many users as necessary.

17. You are using a template to create several user accounts with similar properties. You want to assign home directories, however, to each user based on his or her userid. Which path should you specify for the home directory in the User Environment Profile dialog box?

    A. C:\USERS\DEFAULT

    B. C:\USERS\%HOMEDRIVE%

    C. C:\USERS\%DOMAINUSERS%

    D. C:\USERS\%USERNAME%

18. A user calls you and complains that he cannot log on. Yesterday, he changed his password and now cannot remember it. What can you do to get this user logged on?

    A. Create a new user account with no password and tell him to log on.

    B. Change the user's password and set his account policy so that his password never expires and the password cannot be changed.

    C. Run User Manager and change his password. Set his account policy so that he must change his password at the next logon. Tell the user the password and tell him that he must change it during the logon process.

    D. Tell the user to attempt to log on guessing his password at each attempt and hopefully he will remember it sooner or later.

19. A user is going to be on leave for the next two months. How would you keep anyone from using this account without having to re-create it when the user returns?

    A. Use Server Manager to disable the user's account from logging on to the workstation.

    B. Remove the user's right to log on locally.

    C. Disable the user's account in User Manager.

    D. Delete the user account.

20. Your boss's secretary complains that she cannot log on to her NT Workstation computer. You make a site visit and the user informs you that even though she is entering the correct password, the system tells her that she is either using the incorrect account, or that her password is incorrect. You question her further and find out that yesterday when she logged on she was required to change her password. Which one of the following probably is the cause of her problems?

    A. She is entering her userid in lower case and does not realize that the userid is case-sensitive.

    B. She is entering her password in lower case and does not realize that the password is case-sensitive.

21. You have a user who uses a laptop computer in a docking station at work and uses the laptop at home without the docking station. The laptop is configured with Windows NT Workstation. What is the best way to configure the laptop for each of the different environments.

    A. Use the Control Panel, System, Hardware Profiles tab to create separate hardware profiles for each location. The user can then choose which configuration at bootup time.

    B. There is no way to configure NT with multiple hardware configuration because the operating system does not support Plug and Play.

    C. You don't have to configure the laptop manually. The plug-and-play features of NT automatically detect the difference.

    D. Tell the user to reconfigure the settings for when he is away from the office (before he leaves the office). The next time he reboots, he will have the correct configuration.

22. The easiest way to make a group of users' desktop environments look the same is to use which of the following tools?

    A. Use Registry Editor and then place a copy of the configured Registry in their home directories.

    B. Use User Profile Editor and then place a copy of the configured profile in the user's home directory. Give the profile a MAN extension and it becomes a mandatory profile that the users cannot change.

    C. Use System Policy Editor and create a POL file that all users will use. Place this POL file in the <winnt root>\System32\Repl\Import\Scripts directory, and then assign the policy file for whichever users you want to be able to use it.

    D. You cannot configure a standard desktop automatically, but you can configure each machine manually so that the next time your users log on, they have the configured settings.

23. Which statement is true regarding system policy files between Windows 95 and Windows NT?

    A. The policies are not the same and can't be interchanged.

    B. The policies are the same and can be interchanged.

    C. Windows 95 doesn't have system policies.

    D. Windows 95 policies are local to the machine, whereas Windows NT policies can be stored only on a server.

24. A user calls and complains that every time she changes her desktop, it reverts to its state prior to her changes the next time she logs on. How can you explain what is happening?

    A. Tell the user to choose the Save Settings on Exit option from the Start menu properties.

    B. Tell the user that she doesn't have sufficient rights to save her desktop settings and that she should contact Microsoft to obtain a license to change her desktop.

    C. Her userid probably is set up to use a mandatory profile that she cannot modify.

    D. Tell her she needs to make the changes and save them by using the System Policy Editor. The next time she logs on, the settings should be the same.

25. A user wants to know why when he logs on to a different workstation, his desktop settings are different than when he logs on to his workstation. Which statement best explains this situation?

    A. The user must be set up to use a local policy. This policy is stored on his machine and hence is not available when he moves to a different computer.

    B. The computer policy of the other machine is configured to override his server-based policy.

    C. The user must be logging on with the Ignore Policy setting enabled in the logon dialog box. Tell him to disable this option.

26. You need to copy files from an NT-based computer to a Windows 95 computer. You don't have a direct network connection. Your only option is to copy the files to a disk. The NT-based computer does not have any FAT partitions. Can you copy the file?

    A. Yes, if you format the disk as NTFS and convert it to the FAT file system by using the CONVERT.EXE utility.

    B. No, it cannot be done because Windows 95 doesn't read NTFS formatted floppies.

    C. Yes, copy the files to a FAT formatted disk and the Windows 95 computer can read the files.

    D. Yes, first you must restart the NT-based computer in MS-DOS and then copy the files over from DOS to the disk.

27. The manager of the MIS department comes to you and informs you that you need to connect the graphics department's Macintosh computers to the NT network. Which type of file system enables the Macintosh users to share files and directories with the rest of the NT users?

    A. NTFS

    B. FAT

    C. CDFS

    D. AFP

28. A user calls you in a panic. He says that he cannot create any files on his C drive. You probe further and find out that the user is trying to create a file on the root of his C drive. You also discover that his C drive is formatted as FAT. He executes DIR and tells you that the system is reporting only 235 files in the root directory. What could be causing this problem and what should the user do to fix it?

    A. This particular problem has no fix. The problem is with Windows NT and the only thing that can be done is to install a new hard drive and save the files on the new drive.

   B. No problem here. Just tell the user to save the files to disk and then use File Manager to copy them over to the C drive.

   C. Tell the user that his hard drive must be full and the only solution is to purchase a new hard drive.

   D. The user must be using long file names. He probably has used all the directory entries in the root of the drive. The solution is to move some of these files to subdirectories. Remember that the FAT system is limited to a maximum of 512 directory entries at the root of every drive.

29. A user calls you and tells you that she is getting a syntax error while trying to copy a file from her FAT partition to a disk. She has booted the computer under MS-DOS and is using the DOS COPY command. The file that she is trying to copy has the file name C:\DOCS\THISISAFILE.TXT. The command that the user is entering is COPY C:\DOCS\THISISAFILE.TXT A:. Which one of the following command-line switches should she be using with the COPY command?

   A. /N

   B. /B

   C. /L

   D. -P

30. You want to further secure your system by storing all your files on an NTFS partition. How can you do this without losing all the data currently stored on your FAT partition?

   A. You cannot.

   B. Using Disk Administrator, format the FAT partition as NTFS.

   C. Back up the current FAT partition and delete it in Disk Administrator. Then re-create the partition and restore the files from the backup.

   D. Use the CONVERT.EXE utility to convert the partition to NTFS without losing the data already on the drive.

31. Recently, you have noticed that your server is running low on disk space. You do not have the budget to go out and purchase a new drive. What can you do as a temporary measure to give your users more disk space?

    A. Nothing.
    B. Reformat the drives and restore the data from a backup to minimize disk fragmentation, reducing the amount of wasted clusters on the drive.
    C. Convert your partitions to NTFS and then implement disk compression.
    D. Convert your partitions to FAT and then install the DriveSpace utility to compress the drive, giving your users more usable disk space.

32. To compress the files on your NTFS partition, you can use which of the following two utilities?

    A. COMPRESS.EXE and File Manager
    B. COMPACT.EXE and Windows NT Explorer
    C. COMPRESS.EXE and Windows NT Explorer
    D. DriveSpace and Windows NT Explorer

33. You copy a file from a folder that has its compression attribute checked to a new folder on the same drive. What attributes will the destination file have?

    A. The destination file will be compressed.
    B. The destination file will not be compressed.
    C. You cannot copy a compressed file without first uncompressing it.
    D. The destination file will inherit the compression attributes of its new parent directory.

34. You have been promoted to manager of a new project in another part of the country. Your replacement has asked you to turn over the current project files to him. Which of the following best describes the process for changing ownership of files and directories?

A. E-mail the files to him as attachments and have him save the files in a directory of his choice.

B. Have the system administrator make the new user the owner of the files and directories.

C. Give the user the Take Ownership permission and then have him take ownership of the files and directories.

D. It is not possible to change the ownership of files and directories.

35. Which of the following statements best describes what happens when ownership of files and directories is changed?

A. The user taking ownership of the files or directories becomes the current owner of the files and directories.

B. The groups to which the user taking ownership belongs become the current owner of the files and directories.

C. The user taking ownership of the files and directories becomes the current owner of the files and directories, as well as any groups to which the user belongs.

D. The user taking ownership of the files and directories becomes the current owner of the files and directories, except when the user is a member of the Administrators group. In this case, the Administrators group becomes the owner of the files and directories.

36. The default file and directory permissions on an NTFS partition are:

A. Everyone has Read.

B. Everyone has No Access.

C. Everyone has Full Control.

D. Administrators have Full Control.

37. The name of the Teachers group needs to be changed to Professors. Which statement best describes the process for changing the name of the group?

A. The name of the group cannot be changed.

B. Select the Rename option from the User menu in User Manager and enter the new group name.

C. Create a new group called Professors and then move the users from the Teachers group to the Professors group.

D. Create a new group called Professors and then delete the users from the Teachers group and add them to the Professors group.

38. A user belongs to the Sales group and the Marketing group. The user has the Read permission to a directory named DIR1. The Sales group has the Change permission to DIR1 and the Marketing group has no permissions to DIR1. What are the user's effective rights to DIR1?

A. The user has the Read and Change permission to DIR1.

B. The user has no permissions to DIR1, because the Marketing group has no permissions to the directory.

C. The user has only Read, because the user only gets what is assigned to the user directly.

D. The user has Full Control, because Read and Change added together equals Full Control.

39. A user belongs to the Sales group and the Marketing group. The user has the Read permission to a directory named DIR1. The Sales group has the Change permission to DIR1 and the Marketing group has No Access to DIR1. What are the user's effective rights to DIR1?

A. The user has the Read and Change permission to DIR1.

B. The user has no permissions to DIR1 because the Marketing group has no permissions to the directory.

C. The user has only Read, because the user only gets what is assigned to the user directly.

D. The user has No Access because the Marketing group has No Access.

40. Which one of the following statements best describes what happens to file permissions when files are copied and moved on NTFS partitions?

A. When you copy a file on an NTFS partition, the file inherits the permissions of the destination directory. When you move a file on an NTFS partition, the file retains the permissions that it had originally.

B. When you copy a file on an NTFS partition, the file retains the permissions that it had originally. When you move a file on an NTFS partition, the file inherits the permissions of the parent directory.

C. Whenever you move or copy a file on an NTFS partition, it always retains its original permissions.

D. Whenever you move or copy a file on an NTFS partition, it always inherits the permissions of the parent directory.

41. A user calls you and states that while running a disk diagnostic utility on his FAT partition, it was reporting errors relating to lost chains and clusters. Which of the following is most likely the problem?

A. The user is running a disk utility that does not recognize the existence of long file names and is incorrectly reporting errors.

B. The user is running a disk utility that does not recognize the existence of NT and its use should be discontinued immediately.

C. The user should restart the computer in DOS and then run the utility.

D. The user should contact the manufacturer of the utility and request a version that is compatible with NT.

Review Answers

1. C	10.A C D	19. C	28. D	37. D
2. A	11. C	20. B	29. A	38. A
3. B	12. D	21. A	30. D	39. D
4. D	13. A	22. C	31. C	40. A
5. C	14. A	23. A	32. B	41. A
6. D	15. C	24. C	33. D	
7. E	16. B	25. A	34. C	
8. A	17. D	26. C	35. D	
9. D	18. C	27. A	36. C	

Test Yourself

Stop! Before reading this chapter, test yourself to determine how much study time you will need to devote to this section.

1. A Microsoft Network computer that uses _____ can access NetWare resources through a GSNW gateway.

   A. SMB

   B. GSNW

   C. NWLink

   D. TCP/IP

2. A Windows NT computer must use _____ to access a client/server application on a NetWare server.

   A. GSNW

   B. CSNW

   C. FPNW

   D. None of the above

3. Windows NT Remote Access Service (RAS) uses _____ to combine several physical pathways into a single communications link.

   A. Link

   B. MultiConnect

   C. Multilink

   D. RASlink

4. To change the information in a Dial-up Networking phonebook entry, _____.

   A. click on the Edit button in the Dial-up Networking main screen.

   B. click on the More button in the Dial-up Networking main screen.

   C. right-click on the shortcut icon for the phonebook entry and choose Properties.

   D. Either A or C

Answers

1. A (see "Gateway Services for NetWare (GSNW)")
2. D (see "Server and Client/Server Applications")
3. C (see "Configuring Remote Access Service (RAS)")
4. B (see "Editing a Phonebook Entry and Other Options")

Chapter

Connectivity

4

This chapter will help you prepare for the "Connectivity" section of Microsoft's Exam 70-67, "Implementing and Supporting Microsoft Windows NT Server." The "Connectivity" section includes the following objectives:

Test Objectives

> ▶ Configure Windows NT Server for interoperability with NetWare servers by using various tools. Tools include Gateway Services for NetWare and Migration Tool for NetWare.
>
> ▶ Install and configure Remote Access Service (RAS). Configuration options include configuring RAS communications, configuring RAS protocols, Configuring RAS security, and configuring Dial-up Networking clients.

Microsoft believes Windows NT is the best network operating system available, but Microsoft is aware of a strong NetWare presence. One of the driving forces behind the rapid acceptance of Windows NT is the ease with which it integrates into a NetWare environment.

Microsoft has gone to considerable trouble to make Windows NT compatible with Novell NetWare. Windows NT's NetWare-compatibility features include the NWLink network protocol, which is a clone of Novell's IPX/SPX, and a number of special services designed to help Windows NT and NetWare networks link up smoothly. This chapter describes the services you'll need to interoperate with NetWare. NetWare connectivity is extremely important to Microsoft, and you can bet they'll make it important to you when you sit down with the Windows NT Server exam.

Windows NT Remote Access Service (RAS) also offers some important connectivity features. This chapter will describe Windows

NT RAS, show you how to install and configure RAS, and show you how to configure Dial-Up Networking.

Interoperating with NetWare

Chapter 2 described how to install and configure NWLink, Microsoft's version of the once-secret IPX/SPX protocol suite. It is important to remember that NWLink by itself does not necessarily provide connectivity with NetWare resources. Microsoft provides a set of services that help Windows NT and NetWare systems interoperate. This section outlines the services and components you'll need to interoperate with NetWare for various purposes. You'll learn about these NetWare-related Windows NT services and tools:

▶ Gateway Services for NetWare (GSNW)

▶ Client Services for NetWare (CSNW)

▶ File and Print Services for NetWare (FPNW)

▶ Directory Service Manager for NetWare (DSMN)

▶ Migration Tool for NetWare

You then get a quick look at the components required for NT-based and NetWare-based client/server applications. This section finishes with a quick summary of NetWare connectivity issues.

As you prepare for the Windows NT Server exam, try to imagine these NetWare connectivity issues in the context of real networking situations.

Gateway Services for NetWare (GSNW)

Gateway Services for NetWare (GSNW) is available only with Windows NT Server. GSNW performs the following functions:

▶ Enables Windows NT Server systems to access NetWare file and print resources directly. (GSNW includes the functionality of Windows NT Workstation's Client Services for NetWare service, CSNW, described later in this chapter.)

▶ Enables a Windows NT Server to act as a gateway to NetWare resources. Non-NetWare clients on a Windows NT network then can access NetWare resources through the gateway as if they were accessing Windows NT resources (see fig. 4.1).

Figure 4.1

GSNW enables a Windows NT Server to act as a gateway to NetWare resources.

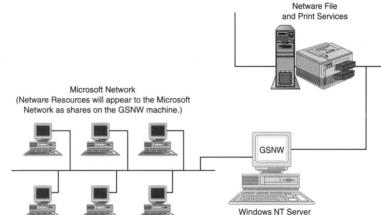

A GSNW gateway can provide Windows NT networks with convenient access to NetWare resources, but it isn't designed to serve as a high-volume solution for a busy network. Because all Windows NT clients must reach the NetWare server through a single connection, performance diminishes considerably with increased traffic. GSNW is ideal for occasional NetWare access—not for large-scale routing.

Network clients with operating systems that use Server Message Block (SMB)—Windows NT, Windows 95, and Windows for Workgroups—can access a share through a GSNW gateway. GSNW supports both NDS-based and bindery-based NetWare systems.

NetWare Directory Service (NDS) is a distributed database of network resources primarily associated with NetWare 4.x systems. Bindery-based NetWare networks are primarily associated with NetWare 3.x.

GSNW is a network service; you install it using the Services tab of the Control Panel Network application (see fig. 4.2). Before installing GSNW, you must remove any NetWare redirectors presently on your system (such as Novell' NetWare services for Windows NT) and reboot. To install GSNW, follow these steps:

1. Choose Start, Settings/Control Panel. Double-click on the Control Panel Network application icon.

2. In the Network application's Network dialog box, select the Services tab. Click on the Add button to open the Select Network Services dialog box.

3. Select Gateway (and Client) Services for NetWare in the Network Service list; then click on OK.

4. Windows NT prompts you for the location of the files (typically, the installation CD-ROM).

5. Windows NT asks if you want to restart your system. You must restart the system to enable the new service.

Figure 4.2

The Services tab of the Network dialog box.

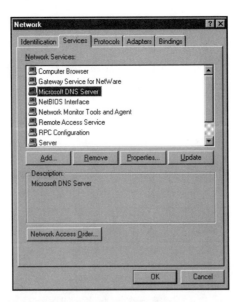

The NetWare client features of GSNW are similar to the features of the CSNW service and are described in the next section.

For an exercise testing this information, see end of chapter.

To enable GSNW to act as a gateway to NetWare resources, you must perform the following steps:

1. Create a group called NTGATEWAY on the NetWare server.

2. Create a user account on the NetWare server for the gateway and add the gateway user account to the NTGATEWAY group.

> You can use the NetWare Syscon utility to create the NTGATE-WAY group and the gateway's user account.

3. Double-click on the GSNW icon in the Control Panel. The Gateway Service for NetWare dialog box appears (see fig. 4.3). The Preferred Server, Default Tree and Context, Print Options, and Login Script Options frames are discussed in the following section.

4. To configure Windows NT to act as a gateway, click on the Gateway button. The Configure Gateway dialog box appears (see fig. 4.4).

Figure 4.3

The Gateway Services for NetWare dialog box.

Gateway Service for NetWare

Username: Administrator

- Preferred Server
  - Current Preferred Server: <None>
  - Select Preferred Server: <None>

- Default Tree and Context
  - Tree:
  - Context:

- Print Options
  - ☐ Add Form Feed
  - ☑ Notify When Printed
  - ☑ Print Banner

- Login Script Options
  - ☐ Run Login Script

OK
Gateway...
Cancel
Help
Overview

Figure 4.4

The Configure Gateway dialog box.

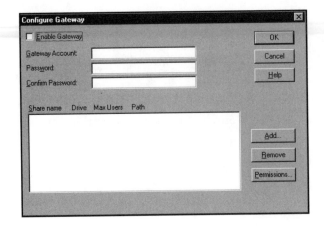

5. Select the Enable Gateway check box. In the Gateway Account text box, enter the name of the account you created on the NetWare server. Below the account name, enter the password for the account and retype the password in the Confirm Password text box.

GSNW essentially enables you to create a Windows NT share for a resource on a NetWare server. Microsoft network machines that use Server Message Block (SMB), such as Windows NT, Windows 95, and Windows for Workgroups, can then access the share even if they don't have NetWare client software. NetWare directories and volumes presently shared through a gateway appear in the Share name list at the bottom of the Configure Gateway dialog box.

To create a new share for a NetWare directory or volume, click on the Add button in the Configure Gateway dialog box. You are asked to enter a share name and a network path to the NetWare resource. You then can enter a drive letter for the share. The share appears to Windows NT, Windows 95, and Windows for Workgroups machines as a network drive on the gateway machine.

The Remove button in the Configure Gateway dialog box removes a gateway share. The Permissions button lets you set permissions for the share.

Client Services for NetWare (CSNW) and the GSNW Client

Client Services for NetWare (CSNW) enables a Windows NT Workstation to access file and print services on a NetWare server (see fig. 4.5). CSNW is incorporated into Windows NT Server's (described in the preceding section). GSNW and CSNW support both NDS-based and bindery-based NetWare servers.

Figure 4.5

CSNW, which is incorporated in GSNW, enables a Windows NT computer to access file and print services as a client on a NetWare network.

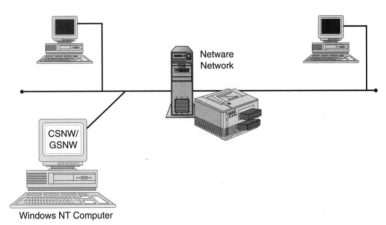

GSNW and CSNW support Novell's NetWare Core Protocol (NCP) and Large Internet Protocol (LIP).

CSNW, like GSNW, is a network service; you install it using the Services tab of the Control Panel Network application (refer to fig. 4.2). If you're running Windows NT Server, CSNW functions are installed automatically when you install GSNW.

To enable your Windows NT Server comptuer to act as a NetWare client, install GSNW (see the preceding section) and restart your system.

The first time you log on after you install CSNW or GSNW, Windows NT prompts you to enter a preferred server and attempts to validate your credentials for the NetWare network.

The Select Preferred Server for NetWare dialog box shows the name of the user attempting to log on and a drop-down list of available NetWare servers. As implied by the username parameter, this is a per-user configuration parameter. The selected server is stored in HKEY_CURRENT_USER, not HKEY_LOCAL_MACHINE.

Choose <None> in the Select Preferred Server for NetWare dialog box if you don't want to have a preferred server authenticate your logon request. Choosing the Cancel button just defers the decision until the next time you log on.

After you select a preferred server, Windows NT always tries to have that server authenticate the user. If the server is unavailable, the user is prompted for a new preferred server. A user can change his or her preferred server at any time via the new CSNW icon in Control Panel (which was added during installation of CSNW).

note

When Windows NT attempts to authenticate a user against the preferred server, the Windows NT-based computer passes the current username and password to the NetWare server. If both the server and the Windows NT-based computer contain the same username/password combination for that user, the user is authenticated immediately. If the preferred server cannot find a match, the user is prompted for a new username and password for the NetWare server.

At first, this is an easy problem to prevent; simply create identical accounts and passwords on each computer. CSNW does not synchronize NetWare passwords with Windows NT passwords, however. As time goes on and Windows NT users change their passwords, the only way users can keep their passwords in sync is to use the Novell SETPASS command to change their NetWare passwords each time they change their Windows NT passwords. This requires some user education on the part of the administrator and good practice on the part of the users.

Double-clicking on the GSNW icon in Control Panel opens the Gateway Service for NetWare dialog box (refer to fig. 4.3), which lets you select a preferred server and a default tree and context for the NetWare network.

You also can set printing options using the Gateway Service for NetWare dialog box, as follows:

▶ Add Form Feed completely ejects the last page from the printer when a job has completed.

▶ Notify When Printed causes a pop-up to appear on the user's display when the job has successfully completed.

▶ Print Banner prints a separator page before each job. The page includes the username of the person who sent the job to the printer as well as the date and time the job was submitted.

You also can choose to run a NetWare logon script.

Connecting to NetWare Servers

CSNW (and the client portion of GSNW) is a redirector implemented as a file system driver, just as is the traditional Windows NT redirector (RDR). As such, it is seamlessly integrated into the Windows NT environment. To connect to a NetWare server's directories, use Explorer or Network Neighborhood.

To connect to a NetWare server's printers, use the Add Printer Wizard in the Printers folder. Select Network Printer Server in the first screen. A display similar to Network Neighborhood then appears, and you can locate the printer on the appropriate server.

You also can use the traditional Windows NT NET USE command to connect to NetWare servers.

When you install GSNW or CSNW, it becomes the default network provider. To change the default back to Microsoft Windows Network, use the Network Access Order button on the Services tab of the Control Panel Network application (this button appears only when you have multiple network providers installed). Network Access Order button invokes the Network Access Order dialog box (see fig. 4.6).

Figure 4.6

*The Network
Access Order
dialog box.*

The default provider is listed at the top of the Network Access Order dialog box. You can expand any network provider's servers simply by double-clicking on its entry in Network Neighborhood.

NetWare servers don't appear under the umbrella of a workgroup or domain. That's intentional; after all, workgroups and domains are Microsoft network concepts.

When you double-click on a NetWare server, you will notice the final difference between the two type of networks. On a Windows NT server, directories must be explicitly shared for users to access them. On NetWare servers, however, all directories are public. When you expand a volume on a NetWare server, all the directories and subdirectories in that volume are accessible. If you continue to double-click down the hierarchy of directories, the tree continues to expand.

NetWare users are authenticated as soon as the server itself is selected. If the server's directories are accessible, the user has been authenticated. If the user's Windows NT password and NetWare password don't match, an Enter Network Credentials dialog box appears to give the user a chance to enter the correct NetWare password.

Command Prompt

You can browse the NetWare Network from the command prompt using the NET VIEW command almost as easily as you can browse the Microsoft Windows Network. You just need one extra switch:

```
NET VIEW /NETWORK:NW
```

This command returns a list of available NetWare servers.

To connect to a NetWare server's resource, use the NET USE command. This time, no additional parameters are necessary:

```
NET USE F: \\NWServer\Sys\Public
```

The preceding example would map drive F to the SYS\PUBLIC directory on NWServer. By design, the syntax is identical, whether connecting to a Windows NT server or a NetWare server (which underscores '"Universal"' in the Universal Naming Convention (UNC) syntax).

You can use the NET USE command as the equivalent of the NetWare CAPTURE command, too:

```
NET USE LPT1: \\NWServer\Queue
```

Compatibility Issues

Although NetWare commands now can be accessed from the command prompt, some executables cannot function unless a drive is mapped. For example, although you can access SYSCON by typing \\NWSERVER\SYS\PUBLIC\SYSCON at the command prompt, the program terminates with an error message unless you map a drive so that supporting files can be found as well.

You can run most NetWare utilities from a Windows NT Workstation running GSNW or CSNW, including SYSCON, PCONSOLE, and SETPASS. There are some specific application compatibility problems, however, and you should consult the documentation for GSNW or CSNW if you encounter problems.

File and Print Services for NetWare (FPNW)

File and Print Services for NetWare (FPNW) is an add-on utility that enables NetWare clients to access Windows NT file, print, and application services (see fig. 4.7).

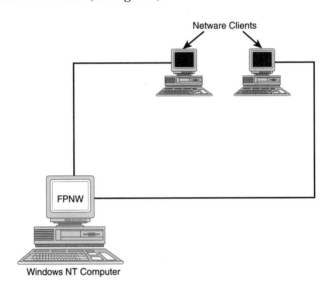

Netware Clients

FPNW

Windows NT Computer

FPNW doesn't require any additional software (such as Server Message Block support) on the NetWare client. In effect, FPNW enables the Windows NT Server to act like a NetWare 3.12 Server. The NetWare client can access the FPNW machine as it would a NetWare server.

Directory Service Manager for NetWare (DSMN)

Directory Service Manager for NetWare (DSMN) is an add-on utility that integrates NetWare and Windows NT user and group account information (see fig. 4.8).

DSMN copies NetWare user and group information to the Windows NT computer. You can use DSMN to manage NetWare accounts from Windows NT. DSMN also can merge server-based

NetWare accounts into a single account database, which the Windows NT computer can then propagate back to the NetWare servers. This enables a single network logon for server-based NetWare accounts.

Figure 4.8

DSMN integrates NetWare and Windows NT user and group accounts.

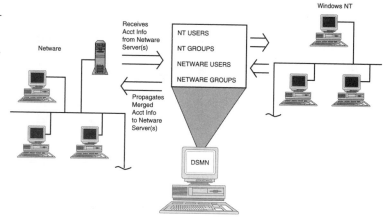

DSMN allows all network accounts (including NetWare accounts) to be managed from User Manager for Domains (see Chapter 3, "Managing Resources").

Migration Tool for NetWare

Microsoft is so eager for NetWare users to migrate to Windows NT that it developed a tool to automate the migration process. The Migration Tool for NetWare transfers file and directory information and user and group account information from a NetWare server to a Windows NT domain controller. The Migration Tool for NetWare also preserves logon scripts and directory and file effective rights. If you want, you can specify which accounts, files, or directories you want to migrate. Migration Tool for NetWare cannot preserve the original NetWare password, but it provides the capability of setting a new password from within the tool.

The Migration Tool for NetWare can migrate NetWare resources to the domain controller on which it is running, or it can execute from a separate NT Server or Workstation and migrate the Net-Ware resources to a domain controller somewhere else on the network (see fig. 4.9). NWLink and Gateway Services for NetWare must be running on both the computer running Migration Tool for NetWare and on the domain controller receiving the migration.

Figure 4.9

The Migration Tool for NetWare dialog box.

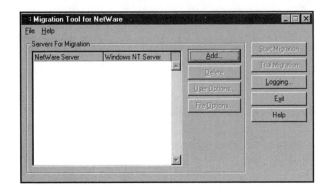

To run the Migration Tool for NetWare, choose Start, Run, and type **nwconv** in the Run dialog box.

The Migration Tool for NetWare provides a number of options for transferring file and account information. Always migrate files and directories to an NTFS partition if possible, because NTFS file and directory permissions provide an equivalent to the trustee rights specified for these resources in the NetWare environment.

Server and Client/Server Applications

A NetWare client that is equipped with Named Pipes, Windows Sockets, or IPX for NetBIOS can access a server-based application (such as Microsoft SQL Server) that is running on a Windows NT computer as long as the Windows NT computer has the NWLink protocol installed.

A Windows NT computer using NWLink can access a client/server application on a NetWare server without requiring any of the connectivity services described in this chapter.

NetWare Connectivity

For the Windows NT Server exam, you should have a good idea of what NetWare-connectivity components you'll need to interoperate with NetWare in various situations. The following list summarizes the preceding discussion of NetWare connectivity. You would do well to memorize this list and be ready to apply it:

▶ The NWLink protocol provides compatibility with Novell Netware IPX/SPX networks.

▶ A Windows NT Workstation computer running CSNW and the NWLink protocol or a Windows NT Server computer running GSNW and the NWLink protocol can connect to file and print services on a NetWare server.

▶ A Windows NT computer using the NWLink protocol can connect to client/server applications on a NetWare server (without requiring additional NetWare-connectivity services).

▶ Any Microsoft network client that uses Server Message Block (Windows NT, Windows 95, or Windows for Workgroups) can access NetWare resources through a NetWare gateway on a Windows NT Server computer that is running GSNW. The NetWare resources will appear to the Microsoft network client as Windows NT resources.

▶ A Windows NT Server system running the add-on utility DSMN can effectively integrate NetWare Server and Windows NT domain account information by copying NetWare account information to Windows NT and propagating the merged information back to the Windows NT Server system. This allows a single network login (across all servers) for NetWare accounts and management of all accounts from User Manager for Domains.

▶ A Windows NT computer running NWLink, GSNW, and the Migration Tool for NetWare can transfer user and group accouts, directories, files, and login scripts from NetWare servers to a Windows NT domain controller.

▶ A NetWare client running IPX can access a Windows NT Server system that is running the add-on utility FPNW.

▶ A NetWare client that supports Named Pipes, Windows Sockets, or IPX with NetBIOS can access a NWLink-enabled Windows NT computer running a server-based application, such as Microsoft SQL Server.

Configuring Remote Access Service (RAS)

Windows NT *Remote Access Service* (RAS) extends the power of Windows NT networking to anywhere you can find a phone line. Using RAS, a Windows NT computer can connect to a remote network via a dial-up connection and fully participate in the network as a network client. RAS also enables your Windows NT computer to receive dial-up connections from remote computers.

Microsoft specifies the following objective for the Windows NT Server exam:

Install and configure Remote Access Service (RAS). Configuration options include configuring RAS communications, configuring RAS protocols, Configuring RAS security, and configuring Dial-up Networking clients.

RAS supports SLIP and PPP line protocols, and NetBEUI, TCP/IP, and IPX network protocols. Because so many Internet users access their service providers using a phone line, RAS often serves as an Internet interface.

The dial-up networking application (in the Accessories program group) lets you create phonebook entries, which are preconfigured dial-up connections to specific sites. The Telephony application in the Control Panel enables the remote user to preconfigure dialing properties for different dialing locations.

RAS can connect to a remote computer using any of the following media:

- ▶ **Public Switched Telephone Network (PSTN).** (Also known as the phone company.) RAS can connect using a modem through an ordinary phone line.

- ▶ **X.25.** A packet-switched network. Computers access the network via a Packet Assembler Disassembler device (PAD). X.25 supports dial-up or direct connections.

- ▶ **Null modem cable.** A cable that connects two computers directly. The computers then communicate using their modems (rather than network adapter cards).

- ▶ **ISDN.** A digital line that provides faster communication and more bandwidth than a normal phone line. (It also costs more—that's why not everybody has it.) A computer must have a special ISDN card to access an ISDN line.

Windows NT 4 also includes a new feature called Multilink. Using Multilink, a Windows NT computer can form a RAS connection using more than one physical pathway. One Multilink connection, for example, could use two modems at once (or one modem line and one ISDN line) to form a single logical link. By using multiple pathways for one connection, Multilink can greatly increase bandwidth. Of course, the computer has to have access to more than one pathway (that is, it must have two modems installed) or you can't use it.

RAS Security

Like everything else in Windows NT, RAS is designed for security. Here are some of RAS's security features:

- ▶ **Auditing.** RAS can leave an audit trail, enabling you to see who logged on when and what authentication they provided.

- ▶ **Callback security.** You can enable RAS server to use callback (hang up all incoming calls and call the caller back), and you can limit callback numbers to prearranged sites that you know are safe.

▶ **Encryption.** RAS can encrypt logon information, or it can encrypt all data crossing the connection.

▶ **Security hosts.** In case Windows NT isn't safe enough, you can add an extra dose of security by using a third-party intermediary security host—a computer that stands between the RAS client and the RAS server and requires an extra round of authentication.

▶ **PPTP filtering.** You can tell Windows NT to filter out all packets except ultra-safe PPTP packets (described later in this chapter in the section "PPTP").

This chapter describes how to configure and use RAS server and dial-up networking.

RAS Line Protocols

RAS supports the following line protocols:

▶ SLIP

▶ PPP

The following sections describe these protocols.

SLIP

Serial Line Internet Protocol (SLIP) is a standard protocol for serial line connections over TCP/IP networks. SLIP is relatively old for the computer age—it was developed in 1984—and, though it hasn't "timed out" yet, it does lack some of the features that are available in PPP. Each node in a SLIP connection must have a static IP address; that is, you can't use nifty Windows NT features such as DHCP and WINS. Unlike PPP, SLIP does not support Net-BEUI or IPX; you must use TCP/IP with SLIP. Also, SLIP cannot encrypt logon information.

PPP

Point-to-Point Protocol (PPP) was originally conceived as a deluxe version of SLIP. Like SLIP, PPP is an industry standard for point-to-point communications, but PPP offers several advantages over SLIP. Most notably, PPP isn't limited to TCP/IP. PPP also supports IPX, NetBEUI, and several other network protocols, such as AppleTalk and DECnet.

Because PPP supports so many protocols, it allows much more flexibility in configuring network communications. Windows NT automatically binds RAS to TCP/IP, NetBEUI, and IPX if those protocols are installed at the same time as RAS.

Another advantage of RAS is that it supports encrypted passwords.

PPTP

Point-to-Point Tunneling Protocol (PPTP) is related to PPP, but is different enough, and important enough, to deserve its own section. PPTP is a protocol that lets you transmit PPP packets over a TCP/IP network securely. Because the Internet is a TCP/IP network, PPTP enables highly private network links over the otherwise highly public Internet. PPTP connections are encrypted, making them a nearly impenetrable to virtual voyeurs.

In fact, PPTP is part of an emerging technology called Virtual Private Networks (VPNs). The point of VPN is to provide corporate networks with the same (or close to the same) security over the Internet that they would have over a direct connection.

Another exciting advantage of PPTP (and another reason that it fits nicely into the scheme of the virtual private network) is that PPTP doesn't discriminate among protocols. Because PPP supports NetBEUI, IPX, and other network protocols, and because a PPTP operates on PPP packets, PPTP actually lets you transmit non-TCP/IP protocols over the Internet.

Because PPTP provides intranet privacy over the open Internet, it can significantly reduce costs in some situations. Networks that once would have depended on extravagant direct connections now can hook up via a local Internet service provider.

Routing with RAS

Windows NT RAS can perform some interesting routing functions. These functions are likely to make their way into the Windows NT Server exam, either as part of the connectivity section or as part of the protocols objective in the planning section.

RAS comes with a NetBIOS gateway. A RAS client using the NetBEUI protocol can connect to a RAS server and, using the NetBIOS gateway on the RAS server, can gain access to the remote LAN beyond the gateway regardless of what protocol the LAN is using (see fig. 4.10).

Figure 4.10

RAS can act as a NetBIOS gateway, connecting NetBEUI clients with networks using other protocols.

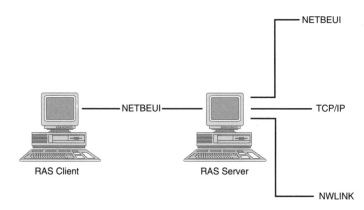

RAS can act as a TCP/IP or IPX router. RAS also is capable of serving as a Service Advertising Protocol (SAP) agent. (*SAP* is a NetWare protocol that lets servers advertise their services to the network.)

The Telephony API

The *Telephony Application Program Interface* (TAPI) provides a standard interface with telephony applications. (Telephony applications are applications that enable a computer to interact with telephone services, such as a network fax service or an online answering machine). TAPI oversees communication between the computer and the phone system, including initiating, answering, and ending calls. In effect, TAPI is a device driver for the phone system.

Windows NT's basic TAPI settings are set up in the Dialing Properties dialog box (see fig. 4.11). The Dialing Properties dialog box maintains location and area code settings, as well as calling card settings and a setting for the dialing type (tone or pulse). The first time you run a TAPI-aware application, you have a chance to set dialing properties. Or, you can reach the Dialing Properties dialog box directly in several ways, including through the Control Panel Telephony and Modems applications.

Figure 4.11

The Dialing Properties dialog box.

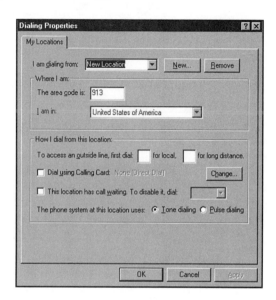

Installing and Configuring RAS

RAS is a network service, and, like other network services, is installed and removed using the Services tab of the Control Panel Network application.

Install RAS as follows:

1. In the Control Panel, double-click on the Network application icon.

2. In the Network dialog box that appears, click on the Services tab and then click on the Add button. The Select Network Service dialog box appears.

3. In the Select Network Service dialog box, choose Remote Access Service from the Network Service list and click on OK (see fig. 4.12). Windows NT prompts you for the path to the Windows NT Installation CD-ROM.

Figure 4.12

The Select Network Service dialog box.

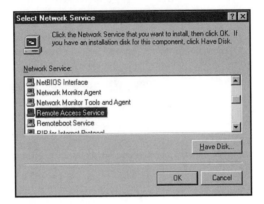

4. Windows NT prompts you for name of an RAS-capable device and an associated communications port (see fig. 4.13). A modem installed on your system typically appears as a default value. Click on OK to accept the modem, or click on the down arrow to choose another RAS-capable device on your system. You also can install a new modem or an X.25 Pad using the Install Modem and Install X25 Pad buttons.

Figure 4.13

Selecting a RAS-capable device.

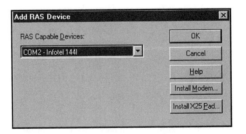

5. The Remote Access Setup dialog box appears (see fig. 4.14). Click on the Configure button to specify whether to use the port for dial-out connections, dial-in connections, or both (see fig. 4.15). The Port Usage options in figure 4.15 apply only to the port. In other words, you could configure COM1 for Dial out only and COM2 for Receive only. In the Remote

Access Setup dialog box, you also can add or remove a port entry from the list. The Clone button lets you copy a port configuration.

Figure 4.14

The Remote Access Setup dialog box.

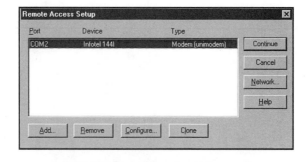

Figure 4.15

The Configure Port Usage dialog box.

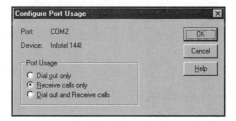

6. Click on the Network button in the Remote Access Setup dialog box to specify the network protocols for your Remote Access Service to support (see fig. 4.16). The Server Settings options in the lower portion of the Network Configuration dialog box appear only if you configure the port to receive calls. Select one or more dial-out protocols. If you want RAS to take care of receiving calls, select one or more server protocols, and choose an encryption setting for incoming connections. You also can enable Multilink. Multilink allows one logical connection to use several physical pathways.

Note in figure 4.15 that a Configure button follows each of the Server Settings protocol options. Each Configure button opens a dialog box that lets you specify configuration options for the protocol, as follows:

▶ The RAS Server NetBEUI Configuration dialog box lets you specify whether the incoming caller will have access to the entire network or to only the RAS server.

Figure 4.16

*The Network
Configuration
dialog box.*

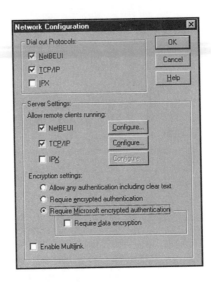

By confining a caller's access to the RAS server, you improve security (because the caller can access only one computer), but you reduce functionality because the caller can't access information on other machines.

▶ The RAS Server TCP/IP Configuration dialog box lets you define how the RAS server assigns IP addresses to dial-up clients (see fig. 4.17). You can use DHCP to assign client addresses, or you can configure RAS to assign IP addresses from a static address pool. If you choose to use a static address pool, input the beginning and ending addresses in the range. To exclude a range of addresses within the address pool, enter the beginning and ending addresses in the range you're excluding in the From and To boxes, then click on the Add button. The excluded range appears in the Excluded ranges box.

The RAS Server TCP/IP Configuration dialog box lets you specify whether a client can access the entire network or only the RAS server. By confining a caller's access to the RAS server, you improve security (because the caller can access only one computer), but you reduce functionality because the caller can't access information on other machines.

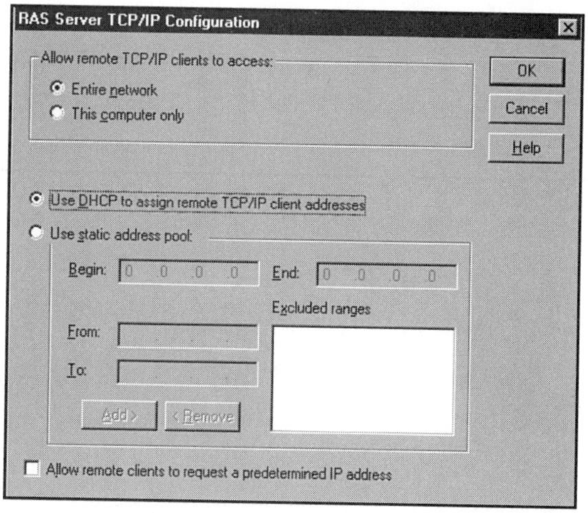

Figure 4.17

*The RAS Server
TCP/IP Configu-
ration dialog box.*

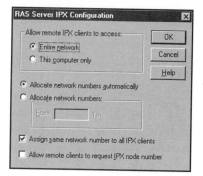

▶ The RAS Server IPX Configuration dialog box lets you
specify how the RAS server assigns IPX network numbers (see fig. 4.18).

Figure 4.18

*The RAS Server
IPX Configuration
dialog box.*

You also can specify whether a client can access the
entire network or only the RAS server. By confining a
caller's access to the RAS server, you improve security
(because the caller can access only one computer), but
you reduce functionality because the caller can't access
information on other machines.

7. After you define the RAS settings to your satisfaction, click
on OK.

8. The Network application's Services tab appears in the foreground. You should see Remote Access Service in the list of services. Click on the Close button.

9. Windows NT asks whether you want to Restart your computer. Choose Yes.

Changing the RAS Configuration

To view or change your RAS configuration, follow these steps:

1. Double-click on the Network icon in the Control Panel and select the Network application's Services tab.

2. Select Remote Access Service from the services list and click on the Properties button.

3. The Remote Access Setup dialog box appears (refer to fig. 4.13). Specify your new RAS configuration as described in steps 5 to 7 in the preceding section.

Dial-Up Networking

The Dial-Up Networking application lets you establish remote connections with other computers. The most common uses for Dial-Up Networking are as follows:

▶ Accessing an Internet service provider

▶ Accessing a remote Windows NT computer or domain

You can open the Dial-Up Networking application as follows:

1. Choose Start, Programs, Accessories.

2. Click on the Dial-Up Networking icon. Figure 4.19 shows the Dial-Up Networking dialog box.

Figure 4.19

The Dial-Up Networking dialog box.

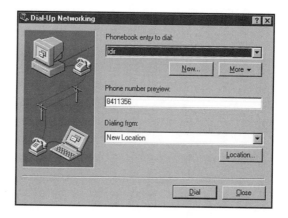

Dial-Up Networking maintains a list of phonebook entries. A *phonebook entry* is a bundle of information that Windows NT needs to establish a specific connection. You can use the Dial-Up Networking application to create a phonebook entry for your access provider, your Windows NT domain, or any other dial-up connection. When it's time to connect, select a phonebook entry from the drop-down menu at the top of the screen and click on the Dial button. If you access the phonebook entry often, you can create a Desktop shortcut that lets you access the phonebook entry directly.

You can create a new phonebook entry as follows:

1. Click on the New button in the Dial-Up Networking dialog box to open the New Phonebook Entry dialog box (see fig. 4.20).

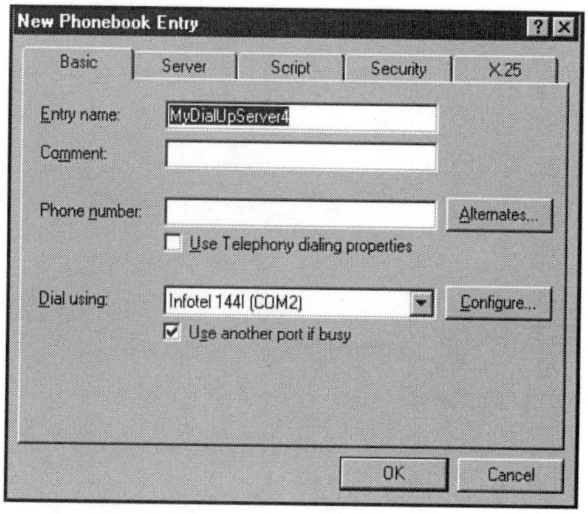

Figure 4.20

The New Phonebook Entry Basic tab.

2. In the New Phonebook Entry Basic tab, specify a name for the entry, an optional comment, and the phone number you want Windows NT to dial to make the connection. The Alternates button beside the phone number box lets you specify a prioritized list of alternative phone numbers. You also can specify a different modem or configure a modem from the Basic tab.

3. In the New Phonebook Entry Server tab, specify the communications protocol for the dial-up server (in the Dial-Up server type combo box) and the network protocol (see fig. 4.21). If you select the TCP/IP network protocol, click on the TCP/IP Settings button to configure TCP/IP settings (see fig. 4.22).

Figure 4.21

The New Phonebook Entry Server tab.

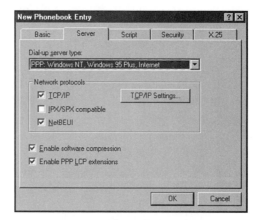

Figure 4.22

The PPP TCP/IP Settings dialog box.

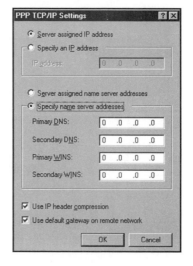

4. The New Phonebook Entry Script tab defines some of the connection's logon properties (see fig. 4.23). You can tell Windows NT to pop up a terminal window after dialing or to run a logon script after dialing. A terminal window enables you to interactively log on to the remote server in terminal mode. The Run this script radio button option automates the logon process. For more information on dial-up logon scripts, click on the Edit script button, which places you in a file that provides instructions and sample logon scripts, called SWITCH.INF. The Before dialing button lets you specify a terminal window or a logon script to execute before you dial.

Figure 4.23

The New Phonebook Entry Script tab.

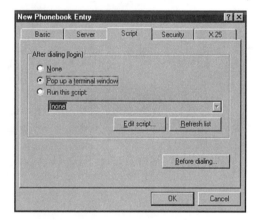

5. In the New Phonebook Entry Security tab, you can require encrypted authentication, or you can elect to accept any authentication including clear text (see fig. 4.24). You also can specify data encryption.

6. The New Phonebook Entry X.25 tab serves only for X.25 service (described earlier in this chapter). Select an X.25 access provider from the Network combo box and enter the requested information (see fig. 4.25).

Figure 4.24

*The New
Phonebook Entry
Security tab.*

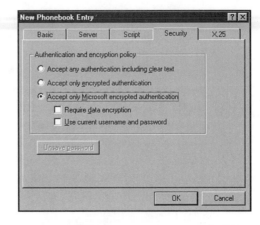

Figure 4.25

*The New
Phonebook Entry
X.25 tab.*

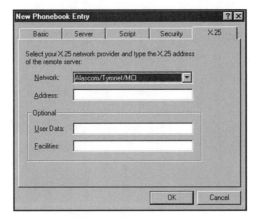

7. After you make changes to the New Phonebook Entry tab,
   click on OK. The new phonebook entry appears in the Dial-
   Up Networking dialog box.

Editing a Phonebook Entry and Other Options

The More button in the Dial-Up Networking dialog box offers
several options. Figure 4.26 shows the More menu.

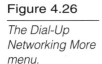

Figure 4.26

The Dial-Up Networking More menu.

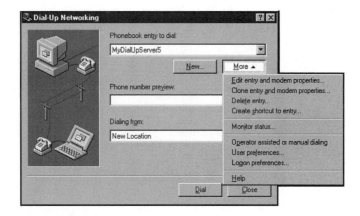

The following list describes the More menu options.

- ▶ **Edit entry and modem properties.** Returns you to the set-up tabs you configured in the preceding section (refer to figures 4.20 to 4.25).

- ▶ **Create shortcut to entry.** Creates a shortcut to the active phonebook entry (the Phonebook entry to dial drop-down list box in figure 4.19).

- ▶ **Monitor status.** Opens the Control Panel Dial-Up Networking Monitor.

- ▶ **User preferences.** Opens a User Preferences dialog box that presents the following four tabs:

    - ▶ **Dialing.** Lets you specify dialing options, such as the number of redial attempts and the time between redial attempts. You also can use the Dialing tab to enable or disable Autodial (see the following section). Figure 4.27 shows the Dialing tab.

    - ▶ **Callback.** Tells Windows NT what to do if the server you connect to offers callback. You can specify a number, you can elect to skip callback, or you can tell NT to prompt at the time callback is offered.

    - ▶ **Appearance.** Offers some dial-time interface options (see fig. 4.28).

Figure 4.27

The User Preferences Dialing tab.

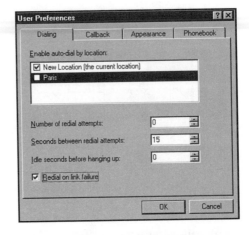

Figure 4.28

The User Preferences Appearance tab.

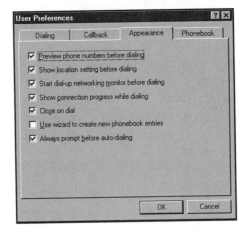

▶ **Phonebook.** Lets you specify a Dial-Up Networking phonebook. Phonebook entries are stored in a file with the .pbk extension. The default phonebook is the system phonebook. Using the Phonebook tab, you can place an entry in your personal phonebook (a user-specific phonebook), or you can choose a different phonebook.

▶ **Logon preferences.** Configures Dialing, Callback, Appearance, and Phonebook settings for a remote Windows NT logon. The Logon preferences options are very similar to the User preferences options in the previous discussion. The difference is that the User preferences options apply to a

user who is already logged on to Windows NT and is trying
to connect to a remote machine. The Logon preferences
apply to a user who isn't yet logged on to Windows NT and
wants to log on directly to a Windows NT domain via a remote connection. The Windows NT Ctrl+Alt+Del logon dialog box includes the Logon using dial-up networking check
box. If you enable this check box and log on using Dial-Up
Networking, the preferences you set in the Logon preferences dialog box apply.

> The Logon preferences dialog box doesn't appear unless you
> log on as an Administrator.

The Location button in the Dial-Up Networking dialog box lets
you set a dialing prefix or suffix or specify a Telephony dialing
location (refer to fig. 4.18).

AutoDial

*For an exercise
testing this
information, see
end of chapter.*

Windows NT includes a feature called AutoDial. AutoDial automatically associates network connections with Phonebook entries.
This means that if you attempt to access a file or directory that
can be accessed only via a dial-up connection, Windows NT attempts to make the dial-up connection automatically.

AutoDial supports IP addresses, Internet host names, and Net-
BIOS names. By default, AutoDial is enabled. You can enable/
disable AutoDial for specific calling locations using the Dialing
tab of the User Preferences dialog box (refer to fig. 4.24).

Exercise Section

Exercise 4.1:   Creating a Share with Gateway Services for NetWare

In Exercise 4.1, you learn how to create a gateway to a NetWare directory using GSNW.

Estimated time: 20 minutes

This chapter described how to create a gateway to a NetWare directory using Gateway Services for NetWare. If you have access to both a NetWare network and an NT network, it is helpful to try the process yourself as a learning exercise. If you don't have access to a NetWare network, take a moment to review the following procedure (also described in the chapter). Do as much as you can from the Windows NT end. For example, install the Gateway Services for NetWare service and start the GSNW application in control panel. Become familiar with the features of the Gateway Services for NetWare dialog box and the Configure Gateway dialog box.

1. Click on the Add button in the Services tab of the Control Panel Application and select Gateway (and Client) Services for NetWare in the Network Service list; then click on OK. Windows NT asks for the location of the files (typically, the installation CD-ROM). Windows NT then asks if you want to restart your system. Click on Yes to restart your system.

2. Create a group called NTGATEWAY on the NetWare server.

3. Create a user account on the NetWare server for the gateway and add the gateway user account to the NTGATEWAY group. You can use NetWare's Syscon utility to create the NTGATEWAY group and the gateway's user account.

4. Double-click on the GSNW icon in Control Panel. The Gateway Service for NetWare dialog box appears (refer to fig. 4.22). To configure Windows NT to act as a gateway, click on the Gateway button.

5. The Configure Gateway dialog box appears (refer to fig. 4.23). Click on the Enable Gateway check box. In the Gateway Account text box, enter the name of the account you created on the NetWare server. Below the account name, enter the password for the account and retype the password in the Confirm Password text box.

6. To create a new share for the NetWare directory or volume, click on the Add button. You are asked to enter a share name and a network path to the NetWare resource. You then can enter a drive letter for the share.

7. From another SMB-compatible computer on the Microsoft network (Windows NT, Windows 95, or Windows for Workgroups), access the gateway computer through Network Neighborhood. Look for the drive letter you entered in step 5 for the NetWare directory. Double-click on the drive letter and browse the NetWare files.

Exercise 4.2: AutoDial

Exercise 4.2 shows you how to use Windows NT RAS in a practical situation and lets you try out Windows NT's AutoDial feature.

Estimated time: 20 minutes

1. Logon to a Windows NT domain using dial-Up networking. (Check the Logon using Dial-Up Networking check box below the domain name in the Windows NT Logon dialog box.) If you're already connected directly to the domain, unhook the network cable at the back of your computer so you will truly be remote.

When you logon using Dial-Up Networking, Windows NT will ask for a Dial-Up Networking phonebook entry. Make sure you have a phonebook entry for this connection. Also, be sure the RAS service is working on the domain. (This chapter described how to configure RAS and Dial-Up Networking.)

2. Locate a text file or a word processing document on a shared directory somewhere on the domain using Network Neighborhood icon in Explorer. (Use a file type that your computer is configured to recognize automatically—click on Options in the Explorer View menu and choose the File Types tab for a list or registered file types. A .txt file or a Write file should work.) If Explorer can't find the other computers in the domain, pull down the Explorer menu and click Find with the Computer option. Enter the name of the computer with the shared directory you want to access in the Find: Computer dialog and click on the Find Now button (see fig. 4.29). The computer will appear as an icon in the Find:Computer dialog box. Double-click on the icon for a list of shared resources.

Figure 4.29

The Find: Computer dialog box.

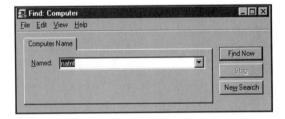

3. When you've located a file on the remote share, right-click on the file and choose Create Shortcut from the shortcut menu that appears. Create a shortcut to the file and drag the shortcut to the Desktop on your own computer.

4. Double-click on the shortcut to make sure it opens the file.

5. Shut down your system.

6. Logon again; this time, don't use dial-up networking. (Deselect the Logon Using Dial-up Networking check box.) You may get a message that says Windows NT could find the domain controller and logged you on using cached account information. Click on OK.

7. Wait until the logon process is finished. Double-click on the shortcut to the file on the remote domain.

8. If you selected the Always prompt before auto-dialing check box in the Appearances tab of the Dial-Up Networking User Preferences dialog box, Windows NT will ask if you want to initiate a connection with the remote file. Click on Yes. Auto-Dial will dial automatically dial the remote network and attempt to initiate a connection to the file referenced in the shortcut.

Review Questions

The following questions will test your knowledge of the information in this chapter. For additional questions, see MCP Endeavor and the Microsoft Roadmap/Assessment exam on the CD-ROM that accompanies this book.

1. Migration Tool for NetWare is not capable of preserving _____.

   A. accounts

   B. passwords

   C. files

   D. directories

   E. effective rights

2. A NetWare client machine running_____ can access Microsoft SQL Server on a Windows NT Server system.

   A. IPX with NetBIOS

   B. Client Services for NetWare (CSNW)

   C. File and Print Services for NetWare (FPNW)

   D. NWLink

3. After creating a NetWare gateway using GSNW, you can then create a share on the gateway machine for NetWare files using_____.

   A. GSNW

   B. Explorer or My Computer

   C. the Control Panel Server application

   D. Any of the above

4. Installing the _____service will enable your Windows NT Server machine to access file and print resources on a NetWare server.

    A. File and Print Services for NetWare (FPNW)

    B. Client Services for NetWare (CSNW)

    C. Gateway Services for NetWare (GSNW)

    D. Directory Service Manager for NetWare (DSMN)

5. What is the name of the utility that enables users to access the network through an NT Workstation or Server?

    A. Remote Control

    B. Remote Access Service

    C. Remote Network Service

    D. The Internet

6. The type of connections that RAS supports are (select all that apply):

    A. PSTN (Public Switched Telephone Network)

    B. X.25

    C. IEEE X.400

    D. Null Modem Cable

    E. ISDN

    F. RadioLan

7. What's the name of the feature that lets RAS use more than one communication channel at a time for the same connection?

    A. Multinet

    B. Multilink

    C. ISDN

    D. Multichannel

8. Identify the two serial protocols that RAS supports.

    A. IEEE 802.2 and X.25

    B. Ethernet and Token Ring

    C. SLIP and PPP

    D. ESLIP and PPTP

9. Which of the serial protocols supports the NetBEUI, IPX/SPX, and TCP/IP transport protocols over RAS?

   A. PPP

   B. SLIP

   C. PPTPS

   D. IEEE 802.2

10. You want to let users connect to your local area network using the Internet; however, you're concerned that security might be a problem. Which protocol should you use to ensure a reliable connection and a secure transmission of information?

   A. PPP

   B. SLIP

   C. IEEE 802.2

   D. PPTP

11. A user calls you and states that he's getting connected to his NT Workstation via RAS, but cannot see any resources on the network. What could be causing the problem?

   A. The user is using a userid that isn't configured to have network access via RAS.

   B. He's dialing in with a protocol configured for "This computer only" when it needs to configured for "Entire network."

   C. He needs to use a different protocol. NetBEUI isn't routable, so he can't see any other devices on the network if he's using it as his dial-in protocol.

   D. He needs to configure his RAS server to use ISDN because the PSTN can support only a limited amount of bandwidth.

12. A user is trying to dial in to the NT Server-based RAS server. The user is connecting but gets disconnected immediately and receives a message that says he isn't an authorized dial-in user. What is the first thing you should do?

A. Restart the NT Server, because one of the modems
   must be disabled.

B. Change the security configuration options on the RAS
   server to enable any authentication method including
   clear text.

C. Check to make sure the user has dial-in permissions in
   User Manager for Domains.

D. Tell the user to restart his remote system and try again.

13. You're trying to run a program from a NetWare server over
    your RAS connection. You have installed the NWLink-
    compatible transport protocol at your remote computer but
    you still cannot connect to the NetWare server. What did you
    forget to do?

    A. You need to install the Client Service for NetWare
       (CSNW) so you can access a NetWare server using file
       and print services.

    B. You need to install the FPNW (File and Print Services
       for NetWare) on the RAS Server to gain access to the
       NetWare servers.

    C. You must dial in to the NetWare server directly.

    D. You have to change your protocol to TCP/IP and install
       TCP/IP on the NetWare server.

14. You have several salespeople who dial in to your network via
    RAS. How can you configure the security options in RAS so
    the users can minimize long distance phone charges?

    A. Configure the user's Dial-Up Networking software to
       use PPTP, which bypasses the PSTN billing computers,
       thus giving the users free long distance service.

    B. Configure the RAS service to perform a callback based
       on the number specified by the user dialing in to the
       RAS server. The server authenticates the logon and
       then disconnects and calls the user back at the specified
       number.

    C. Issue the users long distance calling cards and have
       their RAS calls billed directly to the company.

D. Make sure the users are calling only from public tele-phones and are making collect calls to the RAS server. Then configure the RAS server to accept collect calls.

15. If you're having problems with the RAS server, what can you do to have NT create a log?

A. Under Remote Access Administrator, configure the logging option.

B. Under Control Panel, Network, Services, configure RAS to write all connection information to the System log.

C. In the Registry, set the parameter Logging under the following key to 1 to create a PPP.LOG file in the <winnt root>\system32\Ras directory: `HKEY_LOCAL_MACHINE\System\CurrentControlSet\Services\Rasman\PPP\`

D. Run the program Raslog.exe, to create a RAS log in the <winnt root>\system32\Ras directory.

16. Users would like to be able to connect to the Internet using the company's T1 connection from home. You configure RAS to allow your users to dial in. What protocol must they use to dial in to the RAS server?

A. IEEE 802.2

B. Ethernet

C. NetBEUI

D. TCP/IP

17. Your management is concerned that accessing the network via RAS may open up security problems. What features does RAS support that help alleviate some of these concerns?

A. RAS supports the U.S. Government DES (Data Encryp-tion Standard) and encrypts all data going across the communication channel.

B. RAS, in fact, can be more secure than a LAN connec-tion because of the Callback security, Encryption of userid and password information, and PPTP features.

    C. RAS is not secure over standard PSTN connections unless data scrambling equipment is used on both ends of the connection.

    D. You can obtain a C2 level version the RAS product which meets U.S. Government standards for security.

18. Which statement below correctly identifies the differences between the RAS software running on Windows NT Workstation and RAS software running on Windows NT Server?

    A. When RAS is running on NT Workstation, you can access only the shared resources on that machine. When it is running on NT Server, you can access resources on the entire network.

    B. When RAS is running on NT Workstation you can access shared resources on the entire network, except for resources on NetWare Servers. Before you can do so, you must be running RAS on Windows NT Server.

    C. RAS running on Windows NT Workstation supports only one simultaneous connection whereas, if it is running on NT Server, it can support up to 256 connections.

    D. RAS running on Windows NT Workstation supports up to 256 simultaneous connections whereas if it's running on NT Server, it can support only one simultaneous connection, because the server is running other services that tie up the CPU.

19. You want remote TCP/IP RAS clients to have access to the entire TCP/IP network, but right now they can only connect to the RAS server machine. _____ will enable the client to reach the network.

    A. The Entire Network check box in the Server tab of the Dial-Up Networking Edit Phonebook Entry dialog box

    B. The Entire Network radio button in the Remote Access Permissions dialog box of the Remote Access Admin application

    C. The Entire Network radio button in the TCP/IP Configuration dialog box accessible via the Network button in the Remote Access Setup dialog box

    D. A, B, and C are all necessary

Review Answers

1. B	6. A B D E	11. B	16. D
2. A	7. B	12. C	17. B
3. A	8. C	13. A	18. C
4. C	9. A	14. B	19. C
5. B	10. D	15. C	

Stop! Before reading this chapter, test yourself to determine how much study time you will need to devote to this section.

1. You are attempting to monitor disk performance statistics using Performance Monitor; however, all the statistics are showing 0. Why?

    A. Disk performance counters are not available on 486 computers because of the overhead they impose.

    B. Disk performance counters are usable only on SCSI controllers.

    C. Disk performance counters are usable only on IDE controllers.

    D. By default, disk performance counters are turned off unless you type **diskperf** ×y at the command prompt.

2. By default, Windows NT Server is configured to work best as a file server for _____ users.

    A. 10

    B. 32

    C. 64

    D. 256

3. The Performance Monitor counter Bytes Total/sec measures the performance of _____.

    A. the physical disk

    B. the network segment

    C. the Server service

    D. the processor

Answers

1. D (see "The PhysicalDisk and LogicalDisk Objects")
2. C (see "Optimizing the Server Service")
3. C (see "The Server Object")

Monitoring and Optimization

This chapter will help you prepare for the "Monitoring and Optimization" section of Microsoft's Exam 70-67, "Implementing and Supporting Windows NT Server 4.0." Microsoft provides the following specific objectives:

Test Objectives

> ▶ Monitor performance of various functions by using Performance Monitor. Functions include: processor, memory, disk, network.
>
> ▶ Identify performance bottlenecks.

The discussion of optimizing techniques (preceding the "Performance Monitor" section) provides a better understanding of Windows NT. You may see some of this material, such as the section on "Optimizing the Paging File," for either the "Optimizing" or the "Troubleshooting" sections of the Windows NT Server exam.

As with any computer solution, the performance of your applications on Windows NT depends on the combination of hardware and software on your system. A good match of the two provides a cost-effective computing solution. A mismatch of the two, however, results in inefficient use of resources or inadequate performance. Fortunately, Windows NT has many self-optimizing characteristics that don't require user intervention. With some careful planning, a typical installation can show some decent performance without the need for tinkering with obscure parameters in the Registry. This chapter looks at some of the steps you can take to make your Windows NT system (and your network) run more efficiently. You will also learn about a useful tool called Performance Monitor that will help you monitor and analyze what is going on within your system.

Performance Optimization

Optimal performance seems simple enough to define: completing a task in the shortest amount of time. Optimizing the performance of a system is a matter of arranging the resources of the system in such a way that the desired task is finished as quickly as possible. It means getting the best results with the hardware and software you have.

Optimization of a task on your system, then, consists of measuring and analyzing the resource demands of the task to determine what can be done to make it finish in a shorter period of time.

Before you can get truly optimal performance from your system, however, you need to answer some very important questions:

▶ What task or tasks on the system are most important?

▶ Do you want to optimize the utilization of the hardware, or the speed of a particular application or service?

The answers to these questions determine what you should measure and how to decide whether your performance is "optimal."

Performance Objectives

On a file server, for example, the objective could be to service requests from clients for files as quickly as possible. By measuring the number of bytes transferred to all the server's clients across the network in a given period of time, you can tell whether changes you made to the system's configuration made performance better or worse.

On the other hand, what would be "optimal performance" for a Primary Domain Controller (PDC) responsible for replicating a large account database to many Backup Domain Controllers (BDCs)? In such a case, the objective could be to achieve synchronization of the account database throughout the WAN in a timely manner with the minimum amount of network traffic. To know whether performance was optimal, you would need to measure two things: the amount of time it takes for changes to the account database to be implemented on all domain controllers, and the amount of network traffic that the domain synchronization generates.

Optimizing performance of a database server might include this objective: Provide the fastest response time for queries against the customer service database. If your goal is to make the database task complete as quickly as possible, regardless of the impact on other processes on the system, optimization could result in non-database tasks running more slowly than before.

Yet another performance goal could be to make the most efficient use of resources to get the greatest amount of work completed by all processes on the system. To achieve this goal, you need to optimize overall throughput and efficiency, making certain that processes do not get blocked by bottlenecks created by other processes.

After you optimize performance of your application (that is, get the best performance from the hardware and software you have), the next question is whether that level of performance meets your business goals. You may have the best performance possible with your existing system, but to get adequate performance you may need to upgrade one or more components, such as memory, disk, or processor.

The best way to know what you can do to improve performance is to measure it. Gathering data on how your system performs under various circumstances gives you the information you need to make appropriate changes to your system.

Windows NT Tunes Itself

One of Microsoft's design goals for Windows NT was that it should not require a user to make changes to Registry settings to get good performance. One of the problems with optimizing performance with any operating system is that what passes for "optimal configuration" changes as the demands on the system fluctuate. How large should the paging file be, for example? At one point in the day, a large paging file might be optimal, while a few hours or minutes later, a smaller paging file might be optimal.

Asking users and administrators to make these kinds of frequent configuration changes is not practical, and yet leaving a static configuration would inevitably lead to inefficiencies. So, Microsoft decided to let the operating system itself handle evaluating settings, such as the size of the disk cache and paging file, and adjust them dynamically as resource demands change.

As a result, Windows NT does most of the task of optimizing overall performance of the system without requiring manual changes to Registry parameters. Windows NT dynamically adjusts the balance between the size of the disk cache and the amount of RAM used for applications, for example, in response to resource demands on the system.

Reasons to Monitor Performance

Although there is little to tune in NT itself, you still have several reasons to monitor system performance.

Optimizing Specific Tasks

If you have a particular application on your server that you want to optimize, monitoring system performance can tell you whether changing your hardware would enable your application to run faster. It also can uncover contention by multiple applications for resources.

If you are setting up a database server, for example, performance data can tell you whether you have excess capacity to handle additional work, or whether you have a resource shortage affecting performance. If other applications are competing for the same resources as your database application, you can move the other applications to another server that is not as busy.

Troubleshooting Performance Problems

One of the most difficult kinds of performance problem to troubleshoot is diagnosing transient network problems. A sudden increase in interrupts generated by a malfunctioning network card can bring server performance to a screeching halt as the processor handles all the interrupts. If you monitor key indicators of network performance (number of errors, number of interrupts processed), you can be alerted of problems as they occur.

Planning for Future Needs

Another reason to monitor performance is that it enables you to detect changes in the way that the server is being used by users. If users are using a file server more frequently to store very large files, for example, the increased demands for file services can be measured and documented.

By anticipating changes in demand for the server's resources, you can take appropriate action before performance suffers.

Configuration Changes That Affect Performance

You can, however, change many things that affect overall system performance. All these strategies have the effect of shifting the demands for resources to achieve higher throughput.

Adding or Upgrading Hardware Components

This section furnishes examples of common hardware upgrades that may improve performance of their respective subsystems.

Processor

▶ Upgrade the speed of the processor.

▶ Add another processor (for example, two Pentium processors on an SMP system).

▶ Upgrade the secondary cache.

Memory

▶ You can never have too much RAM. Having adequate RAM reduces the need for paging memory to and from the hard disk.

▶ Shadowing of the ROM BIOS in RAM does not improve performance under Windows NT. Disabling this feature can, therefore, make more memory available to the system. ✓

Disks

▶ Replace slow disks with faster ones.

▶ Use NTFS for partitions larger than 400 MB.

▶ Use a defragmentation tool if disks become fragmented.

▶ Upgrade from IDE to SCSI.

▶ Use a controller with the highest possible transfer rate and best multitasking functionality.

▶ Isolate disk I/O-intensive tasks on separate physical disks and/or disk controllers.

▶ Create a stripe set to gain the advantage of simultaneous writes to multiple disks if your hardware will support it.

Network

▶ Get a network card with the widest data bus available on your system. If your system has a PCI bus, for example, use a PCI network adapter rather than an ISA adapter. This consideration is especially important for network servers.

▶ Divide your network into multiple networks, attaching the server to each network with a different adapter. Allocating the server requests across the two separate interfaces alleviates congestion at the server.

Fault Tolerance

▶ If using software-based fault tolerance (such as striping with parity or RAID-5), use a hardware-based solution instead. Using RAID-5 implemented in hardware takes the burden of calculating the parity information off the processor.

▶ If the goal is the greatest availability of data, you could consider mirroring (via Windows NT fault tolerant drivers) two hardware-based RAID-5 arrays. There are also solutions for Windows NT for mirroring of entire servers, such as Octopus from Octopus Technologies.

Removing Unnecessary Software Components

To optimize your system, you can remove any software components that are using precious processor and memory resources. These software components fall into three categories: device drivers, network protocols, and services.

Device Drivers

Any drivers that are loaded into memory but not used should be removed. If you have a SCSI driver loaded for a non-existent adapter, for example, remove it. If you have an extra network adapter installed, but it is not currently connected to the network, remove the driver.

> Be extremely careful when removing or disabling components in Windows NT. Removing the wrong components can make your system unstable or prevent it from booting. If you remove one of NT's standard drivers by mistake, you can run the Windows NT Setup program (WINNT32.EXE) to refresh the system files.

Network Protocols

Remove any unnecessary network protocols. If all your systems can communicate using NWLink, for example, remove NetBEUI. Loading protocols that are not necessary increases network traffic and processing overhead without improving performance.

You can remove the bindings for a protocol selectively, rather than removing the entire protocol component, by using the Bindings tab of the Control Panel Network application (see fig. 5.1). The Bindings tab in the Control Panel Network application enables you to enable and disable network bindings. In the figure, the circular mark beside NetBEUI Protocol indicates that it has been disabled for the Server service. This server will no longer service file and print requests that come via NetBEUI.

Figure 5.1

The Network dialog box.

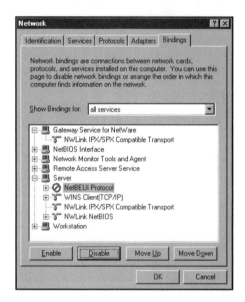

Services

Any services that this server does not need to provide should be disabled, or configured to start manually. If a server will not be providing print services, for example, you can disable the Spooler service.

You can display the list of installed services by choosing the Services application in the Control Panel, as shown in figure 5.2. You can free up wasted processor and memory resources by disabling unneeded services.

Figure 5.2

The Services dialog box.

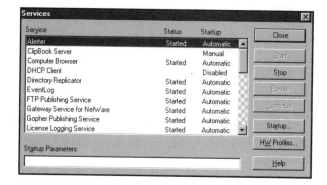

You can start and stop services from the command prompt. To stop the Spooler service, for example, type the following command:

net stop spooler

To start the Spooler service, type this command:

net start spooler

You can combine the NET START command with the AT command to start and stop services as needed, locally or on another system:

at \\myserver 12:00 net start spooler

This technique is useful when you need certain services across slow WAN links only at certain times of the day, such as directory replication.

Replacing Inefficient Software

If your system has applications or drivers that use system resources inefficiently, you may not be able to make a particular application run faster. A poorly coded application or device driver can adversely affect performance of the entire system.

If your performance monitoring uncovers a software component that makes unacceptably large resource demands, the solution is to replace the offending software.

If the slow application is a 16-bit application, you may be able to find a faster 32-bit version.

Changing Windows NT Performance Parameters

Several relatively easy-to-change settings can make a substantial difference in performance.

Optimizing the Paging File

The Virtual Memory Manager in Windows NT is responsible for managing all the memory pages on the system, including physical memory (RAM) and virtual memory (the paging file). Whenever an application makes a reference to a page of memory that isn't currently located in physical RAM, a page fault occurs. Excessive paging activity dramatically affects overall system performance. Adding RAM reduces the need for paging, so when in doubt, add more RAM!

You configure the size of the paging file in the Virtual Memory dialog box (see fig. 5.3). To open the Virtual Memory dialog box, click on the Change button in the Performance tab of the Control Panel System application. When the system starts up, Windows NT creates a paging file (PAGEFILE.SYS) and sets its size to the minimum value in the Virtual Memory dialog box. The Virtual Memory Manager then monitors system activity and can increase the size of the paging file up to the maximum value if it determines that paging would be more efficient.

Figure 5.3

The Virtual Memory Manager.

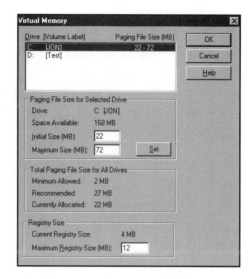

The following are general recommendations regarding the virtual memory settings:

▶ Consider spreading the paging file across multiple disks if your hardware supports writing to those disks at the same time.

▶ Move the paging file to the disk(s) with the lowest amount of total disk activity (see fig. 5.4).

Figure 5.4

Optimizing the paging file.

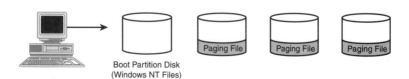

It's better to put the paging file on the disk(s) with the lowest amount of disk activity. If your system has two disks, consider putting the paging file on the disk that isn't the boot disk. (The boot disk contains Windows NT system files.) If you have multiple disks, try distributing the paging file among all disks except the boot disk.

▶ If you plan to use Windows NT's Recovery feature, which writes out debugging information if a stop error occurs to disk, your swap file must be larger than the amount of physical RAM present on the system.

▶ Monitor the size of the paging file under peak usage and then set the minimum size to that value. Making the minimum paging file size large enough eliminates the need for Virtual Memory Manager to increase its size (and saves processor cycles).

▶ To determine the amount of RAM to add to reduce paging activity, use a tool, such as Performance Monitor, to determine the amount of memory each application needs. Then remove applications (noting their working set sizes) until paging activity falls within acceptable limits. The amount of memory freed up by terminating those applications is the amount of physical RAM that the system requires.

Optimizing the Server Service

Another setting that can affect performance is the configuration of the Server service. To access the Server dialog box (see fig. 5.5), choose the Services tab in the Control Panel Network application, select the Server service, and click on the Properties button. By default, Windows NT Server is configured to work best as a file server for 64 or more users. Changing the Server service settings adjusts the amount of RAM and other resources allocated for the Server service to use. Table 5.1 provides a description of each of these settings.

Figure 5.5

The Server dialog box, accessible through the Services tab of the Control Panel Network application.

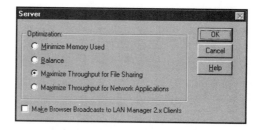

Table 5.1

Server Service Optimization

Setting	Description
Minimize Memory Used	Up to 10 connections
Balance	Up to 64 connections
Maximize Throughput for File Sharing	64 or more connections, large file cache (for file servers)
Maximize Throughput for Network Application	64 or more connections, small file cache (for servers)

Optimizing Other Services

Other services on your system may have Registry settings that you need to adjust for optimal performance. Table 5.2 lists some common values for standard Windows NT services that would be a good starting point for evaluation.

If you have installed additional services on your system, research the Registry parameters associated with those services for performance enhancement opportunities.

Table 5.2

Some Common Registry Values for Standard Windows NT Services

Service	Value
Net Logon	Pulse, Pulse Concurrency, Pulse Maximum, Replication Governor
Directory Replication	Interval, Guard Time
Computer Browser	Hidden, IsDomainMaster, MaintainServerList
Spooler	DefaultSpoolDirectory, PriorityClass

Rescheduling Resource-Intensive Tasks

Demands for resources on a server often fluctuate widely at different times of day. A server running an accounting package meets its greatest demands at the end of an accounting period. A logon server typically experiences a spike in authentication requests at the beginning of the day. Print servers often experience their heaviest demands during late morning and late afternoon. Shifting some of the demand from the peak period to other times can help alleviate the load on the server (see fig. 5.6). In addition, any task that competes for resources with your primary application should be scheduled to non-peak hours.

Figure 5.6

The Scheduling tab of the Printer Properties dialog box enables you to specify when a printer will be available.

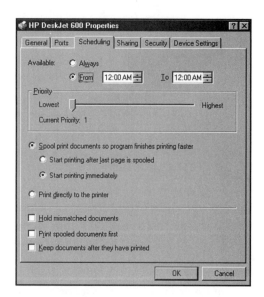

If you have a batch job that is processor-intensive, for example, do not schedule it to run on a domain controller at 8:00 a.m., when most users are logging on and logon authentication demands are at their greatest. Shift demands for resources to times when you have a surplus of the resource available.

Moving Tasks to Another System

If you find that you cannot resolve a resource shortage in an acceptable way on your system, you may be able to move the demand to another machine that has idle resources.

If you have two applications on a server, both of which are I/O-intensive, for example, you may be able to improve performance of both applications by moving one of them to another less busy server (see fig. 5.7).

Figure 5.7

Spreading out the workload.

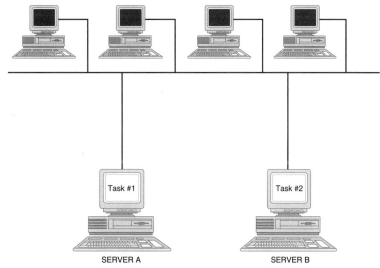

If you have two I/O-intensive applications running on a server, consider moving one application to a different server to even out the workload.

In a client/server application, you might also be able to spread out the load of your application by running portions of it using the idle processing capacity of other systems on the network.

Before You Change Anything

Before you can make any of these changes, you first must do some detective work. You have to be able to isolate which resource on the system has become the bottleneck; then you have to discover the source of the demand for that resource.

Suppose you find that while a certain task is being performed, the processor is busy 100 percent of the time. You cannot conclude that the problem is that you need a faster processor. You have to determine why the processor was busy. If your system has a memory shortage, for example, the processor could be busy handling the increased need to manage virtual memory. Alternatively, your task could have invoked another process that was ill-behaved and consumed the processor.

This kind of investigative work requires a measurement tool that can tell you what is really going on with your system.

Performance Monitor

For an exercise testing this information, see end of chapter.

By far the most useful tool for measuring performance on NT systems is Performance Monitor. Performance Monitor installs to the Administrative Tools program group by default. You can use Performance Monitor for the following tasks:

▶ Measuring the demand for resources on your system

▶ Identifying bottlenecks in your system performance

▶ Monitoring the behavior of individual processes

▶ Monitoring the performance of remote systems

▶ Generating alerts to inform you that an exception condition has occurred

▶ Exporting performance data for analysis using other tools

Figure 5.8 shows an example of a Performance Monitor chart measuring various aspects of a system's performance.

Figure 5.8

Performance Monitor chart.

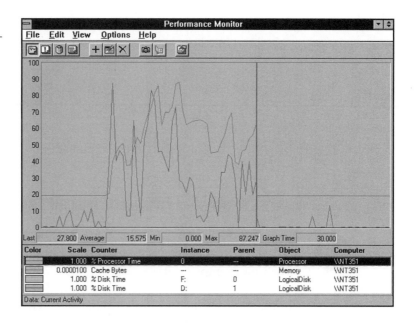

Performance Monitor is an essential tool for monitoring your system. You can use it to gather everything from general indicators of system health to details on individual processes on the system.

You can configure Performance Monitor to record a variety of statistical measurements (called *counters*) for a variety of system hardware and software components (called *objects*). Each object has its own collection of counters. The System object, for example, has counters that measure Processor Queue length, System Calls/sec, and so on. The Paging File object has counters that measure %Usage and %Usage Peak.

Windows NT Server exam objectives specify that you should be familiar with how to use Performance Monitor to measure processor, memory, disk, and network functions. Performance Monitor comes with Processor, Memory, and PhysicalDisk objects (all with associated counters) for measuring processor, memory, and disk functions. The Server object and the Network Segment object are two good indicators of network functions.

This section offers some guidelines on detecting bottlenecks and discusses some of the counters you can use to measure processor, memory, disk, and network activity. The exercises at the end of this chapter provide you with step-by-step instructions on how to use Performance Monitor to create charts, logs, and reports.

Microsoft lists the following objectives for the Monitoring and Optimizing section of the Windows NT Server exam:

▶ Monitor performance of various functions by using Performance Monitor. Functions include processor, memory, disk, network.

▶ Identify performance bottlenecks.

Bottleneck—The Limiting Resource

When you understand the tools you need for measuring your system's performance, you are ready to dig into the data to determine how to improve it.

This section presents a simple strategy for detecting the part of your system that has become the performance bottleneck.

The term *bottleneck* is a descriptive term that comes from a familiar phenomenon. If you take a bottle filled with your favorite beverage and turn it upside down, the rate at which the liquid pours out of the bottle depends on one thing: the width of the neck. In this sense, the limiting characteristic of the bottle, the characteristic that prevents a faster rate, is the neck of the bottle. If the neck were wider, you could pour the contents of the bottle more quickly.

The bottleneck on your system is the resource that limits the rate at which a task can complete. If the resource were faster, or you had more of it, the task would finish sooner. If your task uses processor, network, and disk resources, but mostly spends time using the disk, for example, the disk is the bottleneck. After you identify the bottleneck, you can resolve it by changing or reallocating your resources (such as adding a faster hard disk).

The simplest way to detect the bottleneck on your system is to examine the amount of time that the various components of your system consume in completing a task. The component that uses the most time to complete its portion of the task is the bottleneck.

Suppose that, using Performance Monitor, you determined that Windows NT consumed .5 seconds of processor time, .1 second accessing the network, and .8 seconds accessing the disk in executing your task. During most of the time the task is running, the processor and network are sitting idle waiting for the disk (see fig. 5.9). After you add a faster hard disk, the disk access is down to .4 seconds, but the processor still takes .5 seconds. Now the processor is the bottleneck.

Figure 5.9

Identifying a bottleneck.

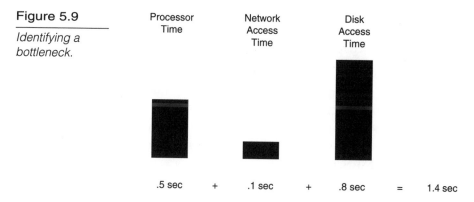

The subtask that consumes the greatest share of execution time is the bottleneck. In figure 5.9, the disk is the bottleneck.

Overall Performance Indicators

A reasonable place to start in monitoring performance for a server in Windows NT is to watch a number of general counters in Performance Monitor. These counters can provide a great deal of insight into the performance of the system as a whole. If you are not certain what to monitor, start with these and then gather more detail as you determine which component is the bottleneck.

Table 5.3 lists four counters that can give you a good indicator of overall system health.

Table 5.3

Counters that Provide an Indicator of Overall Performance	
Object	Counter
Processor	% Processor Time
Memory	Pages/sec
Physical Disk	% Disk Time
Server	Bytes Total/sec
Network Segment	% Network utilization

The following sections describe the counters in table 5.3, as well as some other important counters you may need to measure the performance of the processor, memory, physical disk, and server objects. You should be familiar with these counters for the Windows NT Server exam.

> You can use Performance Monitor to monitor these counters on your system regularly, including logging the activity to disk. If you have multiple servers to monitor, you can monitor all of them from one Performance Monitor session by adding counters from each of the systems.

The Processor Object

The following are useful counters for the processor object. In looking at the processor, be certain to remember that high levels of processor activity can result from two situations other than handling a processor-intensive task:

- A severe memory shortage with the processor busy managing virtual memory (swapping pages of memory to and from the disk).

- The system is busy handling a large number of interrupts.

In either of these cases, replacing the processor with a faster one does not address the real problem.

% Processor Time

This counter measures the amount of time the processor spent executing a non-idle thread. In effect, it is the percent of time that the processor was busy. If the average value exceeds 80 percent, the processor could be the bottleneck.

Interrupts/sec

This counter measures the number of interrupts the processor handles per second. An increase in the number of interrupts can indicate hardware failures in I/O devices such as disk controllers and network cards.

System: Processor Queue Length

This counter measures the number of threads waiting in the queue for an available processor. Generally, if the number of threads in the queue exceeds two, you have a problem with processor performance.

The Memory Object

In general, the symptoms of a memory shortage on the system are a busy processor (managing the virtual memory) and a high level of disk activity on the disk that contains the page file (accessing the disk to read and write memory pages).

Pages/sec

This counter measures the number of times that a memory page had to be paged in to memory or out to the disk. An increase in this value indicates an increase in paging activity.

Available Bytes

This counter measures the amount of physical memory available. When this value falls below 1 MB, you are getting excessive paging.

The PhysicalDisk and LogicalDisk Objects

Before you can use Performance Monitor to monitor disk activity, you must enable the disk performance counters. Otherwise, all values for the disk counters report zeroes in Performance Monitor.

To turn on the disk performance counters, log on as a user with administrative privileges and type the following:

```
diskperf -y
```

> To start the disk counters on a remote computer, add the computer name to the `diskperf` command:
>
> ```
> diskperf -y \\computername
> ```

The PhysicalDisk object measures the performance of a physical disk. The LogicalDisk object records parameters pertaining to a logical disk. A logical disk is a partition or logical drive that is accorded a drive letter (C, D, and so on).

PhysicalDisk: % Disk Time

This counter reports the percentage of time that the physical disk was busy reading or writing.

PhysicalDisk: Avg. Disk Queue Length

The average disk queue length is the average number of requests for a given disk (both read and write requests).

LogicalDisk: % Disk Time

This counter reports the percentage of time that the logical disk (for example, C) was busy. To monitor the total activity of all the partitions on a single disk drive, use the Physical Disk: % Disk Time counter.

LogicalDisk: Disk Queue Length

This counter measures the number of read and write requests waiting for the logical disk to become available. If this counter exceeds two, disk performance is suffering.

The Server Object

The Server component is responsible for handling all SMB-based requests for sessions and file and print services. If the Server service becomes the bottleneck, requests from clients are denied, forcing retries and creating slower response times and increased traffic.

Bytes Total/sec

This counter measures the number of bytes sent to and received from the network. It provides an overall indicator of how much information the Server service is handling. When the combined total of this counter for all your servers nears the maximum throughput for your network medium, you have run out of network capacity and need to subdivide the network.

Pool Nonpaged Failures and Pool Paged Failures

This counter measures the number of times that a request from the server to allocate memory failed. These failures are indicators of a memory shortage.

Establishing Baseline Performance Data

Many of the counters that Performance Monitor provides cannot be interpreted without some baseline data to which to compare it. The number of bytes read per second from the disk varies tremendously depending of the type of drive and controller that you have. The historical data for these counters, however, can provide a basis for comparison.

It is a good idea to log performance from your servers at various times of the day, regularly. Then if you do encounter a performance problem, you can look at the historical data to see how the demands on the server have changed over time. If you see changes in the percent of free space on the disk or the number of bytes that the Server component is handling, for example, you can make appropriate adjustments in the hardware before a performance problem develops.

With the right combination of hardware and software, Windows NT Server requires minimal to no tuning. Determining the right hardware for your needs, however, is critical in getting the best performance. Knowing how to interpret performance data for your system can help you understand how changes to your hardware will affect performance.

Exercise Section

Exercise 5.1: Creating a Chart in Performance Monitor

Exercise 5.1 will help you do the following: become familiar with the process of creating and reading a Performance Monitor chart; understand the basic components of the Performance Monitor main window and the Add to Chart dialog box; and learn how to turn on disk performance counters by using the `diskperf` command.

Estimated Time: 25 minutes

1. Choose Start, Programs, Administrative Tools, and click on Performance Monitor. The Performance Monitor window appears.

2. Choose Edit, Add to Chart (see fig. 5.10). The Add to Chart dialog box appears (see fig. 5.11). You also can open the Add to Chart dialog box by clicking on the plus sign in the toolbar of the Performance Monitor window.

Figure 5.10

The Performance Monitor window.

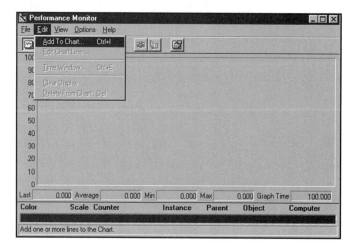

continues

Exercise 5.1:   Continued

Figure 5.11

The Add to Chart dialog box.

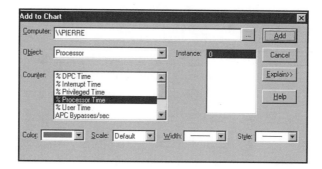

3a. The Computer text box at the top of the Add to Chart dialog box tells Performance Monitor which computer you want to monitor. The default is the local system. Click on the ellipses button to the right of the Computer text box for a browse list of computers on the network.

3b. The Object combo box tells Performance Monitor which object you want to monitor. As you learned earlier in this chapter, an object is a hardware or software component of your system. You can think of an object as a *category* of system statistics. Click on the down arrow to the right of the Object combo box to see a list of object options. Scroll through the list of objects. Look for the Processor, Memory, PhysicalDisk, LogicalDisk, Server, and Network Segment objects described earlier in this chapter. Choose the PhysicalDisk object. If you have more than one physical disk on your system, a list of your physical disks appears in the Instances box to the right of the Object box. The Instances box lists all instances of the object selected in the Object box. If necessary, choose a physical disk instance.

3c. The Counter list box displays the counters (the statistical measurements) available for the object in the Object box. Scroll through the list of counters for the PhysicalDisk object. If you feel like experimenting, select a different object in the Object box. Notice that the different object is accompanied by a different set of counters. Switch back to the PhysicalDisk object and choose the % Disk Time counter. Click on the Explain button. Notice that a description of the % Disk Time counter appears at the bottom of the dialog box.

3d. Click on the Done button in the Add to Chart dialog box. The dialog box closes and you see the Performance main window.

4. In the Performance Monitor main window, you'll see a vertical line sweeping across the chart from left to right. You also might also see a faint colored line at the bottom of the chart recording a % Disk Time value of 0. If so, this is because you have not enabled the disk performance counters for your system. (If the disk performance counters are enabled on your system, you should see a spikey line that looks like the readout from an electrocardiogram. Go on to step 5.)

   If you need to enable the disk performance counters, choose click on the Start button go to the command prompt. Enter the command: diskperf –y. Reboot your system and repeat steps 1–4. (You do not have to browse through the Object and Counter lists this time.)

5. You should now see a spikey line representing the percent of time that the physical disk is busy reading or writing. Choose Edit, Add to Chart. Select the PhysicalDisk object and choose the counter Avg. Disk Queue Length. Click on the Add button; then choose the counter Avg. Disk Bytes/Read. Click on the Add button. Click on the Done button.

6. Examine the Performance Monitor main window. All three of the counters you selected should be tracing out spikey lines on the chart (see fig. 5.12). Each line is a different color. A table at the bottom of the window shows which counter goes with which color. The table also gives the scale of the output, the instance, the object, and the computer.

continues

Figure 5.12

Displaying performance data.

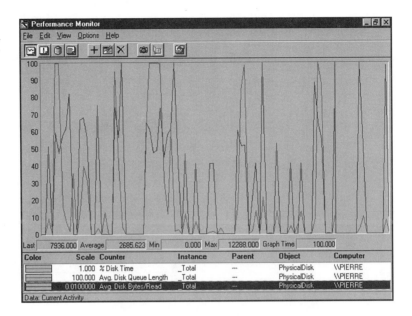

7. Below the chart (but above the table of counters) you will find a row of statistical parameters labeled Last, Average, Min, Max, and Graph Time. These parameters pertain to the counter selected in the table at the bottom of the window. Select a different counter and some of these values will change. The Last value is the counter value over the last second. Graph Time is the time it will take (in seconds) for the vertical line that draws the chart to sweep across the window.

8. Start Windows NT Explorer. Select a file (a graphics file or a word processing document) and choose Edit, Copy. (This will copy the file you selected to the Clipboard.) Go to another directory and choose Edit, Paste. (This will create a copy of the file in the second directory.) Minimize Explorer and return to the Performance Monitor main window. The disk activity caused by your Explorer session will be reflected in the spikes of the counter lines.

9. Choose Options, Chart. The Chart Options dialog box appears (see fig. 5.13), providing a number of options

governing the chart display. The Update Time frame enables you to choose an update interval. The update interval tells Performance Monitor how frequently it should update the chart with new values. (If you choose the Manual Update option, the chart updates only when you press Ctrl+U or choose Options, Update Now.) Experiment with the Chart Options dialog box, or click on the Cancel button.

Figure 5.13

The Chart Options dialog box.

10. Choose File, Exit to exit Performance Monitor. The Save Chart Settings and Save Chart Settings As options in the File menu enable you to save the collection of objects and counters you are using now so you can monitor the same counters later without having to set them up again. The Export Chart option enables you to export the data to a file that you can open with a spreadsheet or database application. The Save Workspace option saves the settings for your chart as well as any settings for alerts, logs, or reports specified in this session. You will learn more about alerts, logs, and reports in Exercise 5.2.

Exercise 5.2: Performance Monitor Alerts, Logs, and Reports

In Exercise 5.2, you will learn about the alternative views (Alert view, Log view, and Report view) available through the View menu of Performance Monitor, and you will learn how to log performance data to a log file.

continues

Exercise 5.2:   Continued

Estimated time: 25 minutes

1. Choose Start, Programs, Administrative Tools, and Performance Monitor. The Performance Monitormain window appears.

2. Open the View menu. You see the following four options:

   ▶ **The Chart option** plots the counters you select in a continuous chart (refer to Exercise 5.1).

   ▶ **The Alert option** automatically alert a network official if a predetermined counter threshold is surpassed.

   ▶ **The Log option** saves your system performance data to a log file.

   ▶ **The Report option** displays system performance data in a report format.

   The setup is similar for each of these view formats. All use some form of the Add to Chart dialog box (refer to Exercise 5.1). All have options configured through the first command at the top of the Options menu. (The name of the first command at the top of the Options menu changes depending on the active view. It was the Chart command in Exercise 5.1.)

3a. Choose View, Alert.

3b. Click on the plus sign in the toolbar or choose Edit, Add to Alert. The Add to Alert dialog box appears; it is similar to the Add to Chart dialog box, except you will notice two additional items at the bottom (see fig. 5.14).

   The options in the Alert If frame enable you to enter a threshold for the counter. The Over and Under radio buttons specify whether you should receive an alert if the counter value is over or under the threshold value. The Run Program on Alert text box enables you to specify a command line that will execute if the counter value reaches the threshold you specify in the Alert If box. Use the Run Program on

Alert text box to execute a command or script that will send a message to your beeper, send you an e-mail message, or notify your paging service.

Figure 5.14

The Add to Alert dialog box.

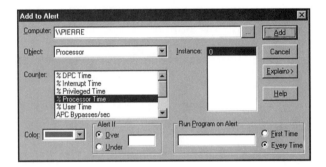

Do not specify a batch file in the Run Program on Alert text box. Performance Monitor uses Unicode format, which can confuse the command-prompt interpreter. (The < and > symbols, which are used in Unicode format, are interpreted as a redirection of input or output.)

3c. The default object in the Object combo box should be the Processor object. The default counter in the Counter list box should be % Processor Time. Enter the value **5%** in the Alert If box and select the Over radio button.

In the Run Program on Alert text box, type **SOL** and select the First Time radio button. This configuration tells Performance Monitor to execute Windows NT's Solitaire program when the % Processor Time exceeds five percent.

It is important to select the First Time radio button; otherwise, Performance Monitor will execute a new instance of Solitaire every time the % Processor Time exceeds five percent, which happens every time Performance Monitor executes a new instance of Solitaire. In other words, if you try this experiment without selecting the First Time radio button, you'll probably have to close Performance Monitor using the X button or reboot your system to stop the incessant shuffling and dealing.

continues

3d. Click on the Add button, and then click on the Done button. The Alert Legend at the bottom of the Performance Monitor window describes the active alert parameters. The Alert Log shows every instance of an alert (see fig. 5.15).

Figure 5.15

The Performance Monitor Alert Log.

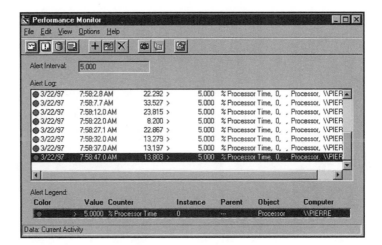

3e. Make some change to your Desktop. (Hide or reveal the taskbar, change the size of the Performance Monitor window—anything that will cause a five percent utilization of the processor.) The Solitaire program should miraculously appear on your screen. In a real alert situation, Performance Monitor would execute an alert application instead of starting a card game.

3f. Choose Edit, Delete Alert.

4a. Choose View, Log. The Log view saves performance data to a log file instead of displaying it on-screen.

4b. Choose Edit, Add to Log. Notice that only the objects appear in the Add to Log dialog box. The counters and instances boxes do not appear because Performance Monitor automatically logs all counters and all instances of the object to the log file.

Select the Memory Object and click on Add. If you want, you can select another object, such as the Paging File object, and then click on Add again. When you are finished adding objects, click on Done.

4c. Choose Options Log. The Log Options dialog box appears (see fig. 5.16), enabling you to designate a log file that Performance Monitor will use to log the data.

In the File Name text box, enter the name **exer2**.

You also can specify an update interval. The update interval is the interval at which Performance Monitor records performance data to the log. The Manual Update radio button specifies that the file won't be undated unless you press Ctrl+U or choose Options, Update Now.

Click on the Start Log button to start saving data to the log. Wait a few minutes, and then return to the Log Options dialog box and click on the Stop Log button.

Figure 5.16

The Log Options dialog box.

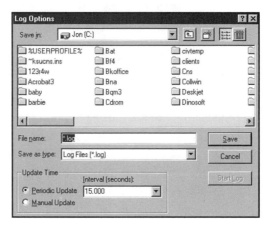

4d. Choose View, Chart.

4e. Choose Options, Data From. The Data From dialog box enables you to specify a source for the performance data that will appear in the chart. Note that the default source is Current Activity. (That is why the chart you created in Exercise 5.1 took its data from current system activity.)

The alternative to the Current Activity option is to use data from a log file. Click on the Log File radio button; click on the ellipses button to the right of Log File; and select the exer2 file you created in step 4c. Click on OK.

continues

4f. Choose Edit, Add to Chart.

Click on the down arrow of the Object combo box. Notice that your only object choices are the Memory object and any other objects you selected in step 4b. Select the Memory object. Browse through the counter list and select Pages/sec. Click on the Add button. Select any other memory counters you want to display and click on the Add button. Click on Done.

4g. The log file's record of the counters you selected in 4f appear in the chart in the Performance main window. Notice that, unlike the chart you created in Exercise 5.1, this chart does not continuously sweep out new data. That is because this chart represents static data from a previous, finite monitoring session.

4h. Choose Edit, Time Window. A time window enables you to focus on a particular time interval within the log file (see fig. 5.17).

In this example (because you only collected data for a few minutes), the Time Window option might seem unnecessary. If you collected data for a longer period, however, and you want to zero in on a particular event, a time window can be very useful.

Set the beginning and end points of your Time Window by adjusting the gray start and stop sliders on the Time Window slide bar. The Bookmarks frame enables you to specify a log file bookmark as a start or stop point. (You can create a bookmark by choosing Options, Bookmark while collecting data to the log file or by clicking on the book in the Performance Monitor toolbar.)

Click on OK to view the data for the time interval.

Figure 5.17

The Input Log File Timeframe dialog box.

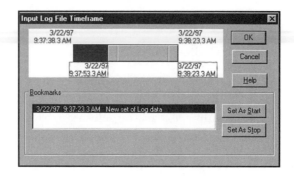

5a. Choose View, Report.

Choose Options, Data From.

In the Data From... dialog box, select the radio button labeled Current Activity. Report view displays the performance data in a report rather than in a graphics format.

5b. Choose Edit, Add to Report.

Select the processor object and choose the % Processor Time, % Interrupt Time, and Interrupts/sec counters (hold down the Ctrl key to select all three), and then click on Add. Select the PhysicalDisk object and choose the % Disk Time, Avg. Disk Queue Length, and Current Disk Queue Length counters. Click on the Add button. Select the Memory object and choose the Pages/sec, Page Faults/sec, and Available Bytes counters. Click on the Add button. Click on Done.

5c. Examine the main report window. Performance Monitor displays a report of the performance data in a hierarchical format, with counters listed under the appropriate object.

6. Choose File, Exit to exit Performance Monitor.

Review Questions

The following questions will test your knowledge of the information in this chapter. For additional questions, see MCP Endeavor and the Microsoft Roadmap/Assessment exam on the CD-ROM that accompanies this book.

1. For the most part, how much time should you spend tuning and optimizing Windows NT?

   A. At least an hour a day.

   B. You should plan on spending most of the first week after the initial installation.

   C. You should never have to.

   D. NT, for the most part, is self-tuning and requires very little user intervention.

2. Name the major tool for gathering information and identifying bottlenecks.

   A. Tune—T

   B. Monitor

   C. Performance Monitor

   D. Server Manager

   E. NT doesn't provide any tools for tuning and performance monitoring

3. Before you can tune a file server for optimum performance, which one of the following questions must you answer?

   A. How much money do you have to spend on new hardware?

   B. What types of tasks is the file server expected to perform?

   C. This question has no answer; simply put, tuning is the process of putting the fastest hardware in your computer.

   D. What type of business is the company using file server in? For certain companies, you cannot tune NT because of U.S. government restrictions.

4. A curious user tells you that while reading a major computer periodical, he came across this statement: "All computer systems have a bottleneck of some type." Why is this so?

   A. All computer systems are only as fast as their slowest component. You may remove one bottleneck, but you always expose another.

   B. The article was incorrect. For example, your file server has absolutely no bottlenecks.

   C. The article was referring to non-Windows NT systems. Microsoft has designed the system to continually self-adjust, thus eliminating bottlenecks.

   D. Because you always upgrade components as soon as new ones are available, you eliminate any potential bottlenecks before they become apparent.

5. Which statement is true regarding the type of hardware you should place in a heavily used file server?

   A. The equipment in the server is not important because nobody actually uses the server to run applications.

   B. You should always spend the most money on the server hardware.

   C. When designing a file server, always pick the hardware that exploits the full bus speed if possible (for example, SCSI hard drives, PCI bus network cards, and so on).

   D. You should use the same type of computer hardware as the workstations, so the users get good response time, because hardware from the same vendor works better together.

6. To optimize the network components in an NT Workstation or Server, which one of the following should you do?

   A. You do not need to do anything. NT automatically optimizes the network components.

   B. You should remove unused adapter cards and protocols.

   C. You should always have TCP/IP, NetBEUI, and NWLink installed, even if your computers are using only one protocol. This leaves more paths open in case one protocol becomes unusable.

7. Select the name of the piece of software that automatically swaps data in physical RAM out to disk and back.

   A. The Virtual Memory Manager

   B. The Virtual Device Driver

   C. Himem.exe

   D. Emm386.exe

8. Name the paging file that Windows NT creates.

   A. RAMPAGE.SYS

   B. SYS$RAM.SYS

   C. PAGEFILE.SYS

   D. VIRAM.SYS

9. What are some of the things you can do to make the system use virtual memory more efficiently? Select all that apply.

   A. Spread out the paging file across multiple hard drives.

   B. Move the paging file to the drive where the Windows NT System files are located.

   C. Move the paging file from the drive where the Windows NT System files are located.

   D. Monitor the size of the paging file under peak usage and then set the minimum size of the paging file to that value, thereby saving time when the system has to expand the paging file.

10. Which Performance Monitor object and counter measures the amount of time that the CPU is busy?

   A. Processor: % Busy Time

   B. Processor: % Processor Time

   C. System: % Processor Time

   D. System: TotalProcessorUsage

11. While monitoring system performance in Performance Monitor, you notice that the number of interrupts per second have doubled. You haven't increased the number of users or added any new applications to the server. What does an increase of this counter mean?

    A. Nothing. It is normal for this counter to increase over time.

    B. It could mean that you have a potential hardware problem, and that a piece of hardware is generating many more interrupts than normal.

    C. It indicates that the network card is the bottleneck in the system and should be replaced.

    D. It indicates that the CPU is the bottleneck in the system and should be replaced or upgraded.

12. You're trying to explain the System: Processor Queue Length counter in Performance Monitor to a coworker. Which statement below best describes the purpose of this counter?

    A. It measures the amount of activity on the CPU.

    B. It indicates the number of threads waiting for CPU time.

    C. It indicates the number of users waiting to log on to the domain.

    D. It indicates the total CPU usage across all CPUs in the system. You see a number for this counter only if your computer has more than one CPU.

13. You're trying to get some statistics that measure the total amount of network traffic. Which Performance Monitor counter can you measure?

    A. Pool Nonpaged Failures

    B. Total Network Bytes/sec

    C. Bytes Total/sec

    D. Network: %Network Bytes

14. You notice an increase in the number of Pool Nonpaged Failures. What does that indicate?

    A. That you need to add more RAM to the server.

    B. That the hard disk is failing, and the system must continually retry to allocate page file space.

    C. That the system is using the RAM installed in the system, and is good sign that the server is running efficiently.

    D. That you need to upgrade the RAM in the system by installing faster EDO memory.

Review Answers

1. D	4. A	7. A	10. B	13. B
2. C	5. C	8. C	11. B	14. A
3. B	6. B	9. A C D	12. B	

Test Yourself

Stop! Before reading this chapter, test yourself to determine how much study time you will need to devote to this section.

1. To boot with the LastKnownGood configuration _____.

   A. press F3 when the hardware profile screen appears.

   B. press Ctrl+Alt+Delete when prompted during the boot process.

   C. press the Escape key when prompted during the boot process.

   D. press the space bar when prompted during the boot process.

2. Which three of the following files are on the Windows NT emergency repair disk?

   A. DEFAULT.LOG

   B. CONFIG.NT

   C. SOFTWARE._

   D. NTUSER.DA_

3. Windows NT Server assigns a priority of _____ to the print spooler service.

   A. 5

   B. 7

   C. 9

   D. 12

4. Near the end of the logon process, your Windows NT Server system starts spontaneously dialing a phone number. The most likely cause for this is _____.

   A. a Dial-up Networking Phonebook entry was left minimized when you shut down your system.

   B. the AutoDial service is configured to start at Startup.

C. a remote user did not properly shut down a RAS connection before system shutdown.

D. Explorer is referencing a shortcut that requires an AutoDial connection.

Chapter

6

Troubleshooting

This chapter will help you prepare for the "Troubleshooting" section of Microsoft's Exam 70-67, "Implementing and Supporting Microsoft Windows NT Server 4.0." Microsoft provides for the Troubleshooting section:

Test Objectives

▶ Choose the appropriate course of action to take to resolve installation failures.

▶ Choose the appropriate course of action to take to resolve boot failures.

▶ Choose the appropriate course of action to take to resolve configuration errors.

▶ Choose the appropriate course of action to take to resolve printer problems.

▶ Choose the appropriate course of action to take to resolve RAS problems.

▶ Choose the appropriate course of action to take to resolve connectivity problems.

▶ Choose the appropriate course of action to take to resolve resource access problems and permission problems.

▶ Choose the appropriate course of action to take to resolve fault-tolerance failures. Fault-tolerance methods include: tape backup, mirroring, stripe set with parity, and disk duplexing.

The subject of Windows NT troubleshooting is as broad as the subject of Windows NT. Almost any task you perform in Windows NT may someday require troubleshooting. All the material in the preceding chapters is thus important to your achieving an understanding of troubleshooting. The more you know, the easier time you will have solving problems. The best tool for troubleshooting is an understanding of the underlying processes within NT. When something trips up, try to figure out what it tripped on, and you will be on your way to knowing why. In that vein, you may want to spend some time with Appendix A, overview of the "Overview of the Certification Process," which discusses Windows NT architecture and the ways that Windows NT supports various kinds of applications. You also may want to review some of the performance optimization techniques in Chapter 5, "Monitoring and Optimization," as you prepare for the "Troubleshooting" section of the NT Server exam.

This chapter describes some of the tips, tools, and techniques you need to find and solve problems in Windows NT.

General Troubleshooting Techniques

The following sections review some good solid general troubleshooting practices. You could consider these your troubleshooting fundamentals. Whatever other specific troubleshooting tips you have encountered are essentially meaningless if you don't integrate these basic habits into the fabric of your administrative being.

Document It

When a problem occurs, write it down. If it happened one time, it can happen again. Include the symptoms of the problem, configuration of the computer, and the diagnosis and resolution of the problem. Good troubleshooters build an incident reference library to save time and effort the next time the same problem occurs.

Back It Up

Experimentation can worsen a problem or introduce a new one. Always back up the system (if possible) before altering system files or configurations.

Test One Thing at a Time

If you suspect several possibilities as the cause of a problem, test only one suspicion at a time. If you change more than one item, you may solve the problem but still not know its exact cause or the exact solution.

Fix the Problem, Don't Remove It

If a component is not functioning correctly, going for the quick fix by just removing the malfunctioning device, driver, service, or application can feel highly enticing. You may, in fact, have to do just that to get the computer back up and running, but don't stop there. Follow through and fix the original problem so that you can restore the computer to its original configuration.

Troubleshooting Installation

 The Windows NT installation process is remarkably easy for the user, but you still may occasionally experience problems (see Chapter 2, "Installation and Configuration"). Microsoft has identified the following common installation problems and solutions:

- ▶ **Media errors.** If there seems to be a problem with the Windows NT Installation CD-ROM or floppy disks, ask Microsoft Sales to replace the disk. Call 800-426-9400.

- ▶ **Insufficient disk space.** Delete unnecessary files and folders, compress NTFS partitions, reformat an existing partition or use Setup to create more space, create a new partition with more space.

- ▶ **Non-supported SCSI adapter.** Boot to a different operating system (that can use the SCSI adapter) and run WINNT from the installation CD-ROM, try a network installation, replace the unsupported adapter with a supported adapter on the Hardware Compatibility List.

▶ **Failure of dependency service to start.** Verify the protocol and adapter configuration in the Control Panel Network application, make certain that the local computer has a unique name.

▶ **Inability to connect to the domain controller.** Verify account name and password, make sure the domain name is correct, make sure the Primary Domain Controller is functioning properly, and verify protocol and adapter configuration settings in the Control Panel Network application. If you just finished installing or upgrading, make sure the domain account for the computer has been reset (added to the network again).

▶ **Error in assigning domain name.** Make certain that the domain name isn't identical to some other domain or computer name on the network.

Microsoft lists the following objective for the Windows NT Server exam:

Choose the appropriate course of action to take to resolve installation failures.

Troubleshooting Boot Failures

You usually know when you have a problem with the boot process: you can't boot. The boot process is one of the most common sources of problems in Windows NT. The cause may be a lost or corrupt boot file. Try booting from the Windows NT boot disk and perform an emergency repair if necessary. (The emergency repair process is described later in this chapter.)

Microsoft lists the following objective for the Windows NT Server exam:

Choose the appropriate course of action to take to resolve boot failures.

To diagnose a boot problem, you must understand the boot process. This section focuses on booting Windows NT and troubleshooting the boot process. It discusses various diagnostic and troubleshooting utilities useful to this end. Before you can use any of these Win32 programs, however, you need to be able to boot into Windows NT. If you can't do that, all Microsoft's tools are useless to you. Therefore, the first type of troubleshooting you should understand is how to deal with problems that you can encounter in booting the computer into Windows NT.

Booting Up

The boot process begins when your computer accesses the hard drive's Master Boot Record (MBR) to load Windows NT. If your system fails during the Power On Self Test (POST), the problem isn't NT-related; instead, it is a hardware issue. What happens after the MBR's program loads depends on the type of computer you are using.

The Intel Boot Sequence

On Intel x86-based computers, the boot sector of the active partition loads a file called NTLDR. Similar to IO.SYS for MS-DOS or Windows 95, NTLDR is a hidden, system, read-only file in the root of your system partition, responsible for loading the rest of the operating system. NTLDR carries out the following steps:

1. Switches the processor to the 32-bit flat memory model necessary to address 4 GB of RAM.

2. Starts the minifile system driver necessary for accessing the system and boot partitions. This minifile system driver contains just enough code to read files at boot time. The full file systems are loaded later.

3. Displays a Boot Loader menu that gives the user a choice of operating system to load, and waits for a response. The options for the Boot Loader menu are stored in a hidden, read-only file in the root of your system partition named BOOT.INI. This file is discussed in greater depth later in this chapter.

4. Invokes, if Windows NT is the selected system, the hardware detection routine to determine the hardware required. NTDETECT.COM (the same program that detects the hardware during NTSETUP) performs the hardware detection. NTDETECT.COM builds the hardware list and returns it to NTLDR. NTDETECT.COM is hidden, system, and read-only in the root of the system partition.

5. Loads the kernel of the operating system. The kernel is called NTOSKRNL.EXE, and you can find it in the <winnt_root>\SYSTEM32 directory. At this point, the screen clears and displays OS Loader V4.00.

6. Loads the Hardware Abstraction Layer (HAL). The HAL is a single file (HAL.DLL) that contains the code necessary to mask interrupts and exceptions from the kernel.

7. Loads SYSTEM, the HKEY_LOCAL_MACHINE\SYSTEM hive in the Registry. You can find the corresponding file in the <winnt_root>\SYSTEM32\CONFIG directory.

8. Loads the boot-time drivers. Boot-time drivers have a start value of 0. These values are loaded in the order in which they are listed in HKEY_LOCAL_MACHINE\SYSTEM\ CurrentControlSet\ Control\ServiceGroupOrder. Each time a driver loads, a dot is added to the series following the OS Loader V4.00 at the top of the screen. If the /sos switch is used in BOOT.INI, the name of each driver appears on a separate line as each is loaded. The drivers are not initialized yet.

9. Passes control, along with the hardware list collected by NTDETECT.COM, to NTOSKRNL.EXE.

After NTOSKRNL.EXE takes control, the boot phase ends and the load phases begin.

The RISC Boot Sequence

On a RISC-based computer, the boot process is much simpler because the firmware does much of the work that NTLDR and company does on the Intel platform. RISC-based computers maintain hardware configuration in their firmware (also called non-volatile RAM), so they don't need NTDETECT.COM. Their firmware also contains a list of valid operating systems and their locations, so they don't need BOOT.INI either.

RISC-based machines don't look for the Intel-specific NTLDR to boot the operating system; instead, they always look for a file called OSLOADER.EXE. This file is handed the hardware configuration data from the firmware. It then loads NTOSKRNL.EXE, HAL.DLL, and SYSTEM, and the boot process concludes.

Booting to Windows 95, MS-DOS, or OS/2

On Intel-based computers, you can install Windows NT over Windows 95 or MS-DOS. The boot loader screen offers the user a choice of Windows NT Workstation 4, Microsoft Windows, and MS-DOS. If the user chooses a non-Windows NT operating system, a file called BOOTSECT.DOS is loaded and executed. BOOTSECT.DOS is a hidden, system, read-only file in the root of the system partition. It contains the information that was present in the boot sector before Windows NT was installed. If a user chooses Windows 95 from the boot menu, for example, BOOTSECT.DOS loads IO.SYS and passes control to it.

BOOT.INI

NTLDR may invoke the Boot Loader menu, but BOOT.INI, an editable text file, controls it. (It is read-only, so you must remove that attribute before editing it.) BOOT.INI is the only INI file that Windows NT uses—if, indeed you can actually say that NT uses it. After all, Windows NT is not loaded when this file is called on.

BOOT.INI has only two sections: [boot loader] and [operating systems]:

ARC Sidebar

Because not all machines use MS-DOS-style paths (for example, c:\winnt) for referring to locations on a hard drive, Windows NT uses a cross-platform standard format called Advanced RISC Computer (ARC), within BOOT.INI. An ARC-compliant path consists of four parameters:

Parameter	Description
scsi(x) or multi(x)	indentifies the hardware adapter
disk(y)	SCSI bus number: always 0 if multi
rdisk(z)	Physical drive number for multi; ignored for SCSI
parition(a)	Logical partition number

The first three parameters are zero-based; that is, the first physical IDE drive is rdisk(0) and the second is rdisk(1). The partition parameter, however, is one-based, so the first partition on the drive is rdisk(0)partition(1).

All of the parameters—even the ones that are ignored—must be present in the path. For instance, multi(0)disk(0) rdisk(0)partition(1) is a valid path even though disk(0) is essentially unnecessary. multi(0)rdisk(0)partition(1) is not valid.

The first parameter almost always is multi, even for a SCSI controller. The only time you even see SCSI in a BOOT.INI file is if the BIOS on the controller is turned off. If this is the case, don't worry; an additional hidden, system, read-only file, NTBOOTDD.SYS, is present in the root of the system partition. NTBOOTDD.SYS is a device driver necessary for accessing a SCSI controller that doesn't have an on-board BIOS or doesn't use INT 13 to identify hard disks. If you have this file present, you probably see a scsi(x) entry in BOOT.INI. If you don't, you probably have upgraded from Windows NT 3.1 (where this setting was more common) without ever deleting the file.

The same holds true for a RISC-based computer; look at the firmware entries for the operating system paths, and you should see the same kind of ARC-compliant paths.

[boot loader]

The [boot loader] section of BOOT.INI defines the operating system that will be loaded if the user doesn't make a selection within a defined period of time. By default, you see something like this:

```
[boot loader]
timeout=30
default=multi(0)disk(0)rdisk(0)partition(1)\WINNT
```

The timeout parameter is the length of time (in seconds) that NTLDR has to wait for the user to make a decision. If timeout is set to 0, the default operating system loads immediately. If it is set to _1, the menu displays until the user makes a decision.

The default parameter defines the actual path, in ARC-compliant form, to the directory that contains the files for the default operating system, which usually is the last operating system installed, unless someone has changed this entry.

The easiest way to change the default operating system and the timeout is by using the Control Panel System application. Select the Startup/Shutdown tab and change the values in the System Startup frame (see fig. 6.1). You can edit BOOT.INI directly, but remember that a mistyped character in NOTEPAD.EXE or EDIT.COM could result in your system not booting properly.

Figure 6.1

Changing the default operating system in the System application's Startup/Shutdown tab.

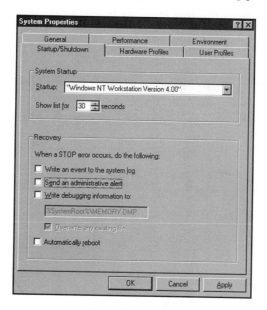

[operating systems]

The [operating systems] section contains a reference for every operating system available to the user from the Boot Loader menu, as well as any special switches necessary to customize the Windows NT environment. One of these entries must match the default= entry in the [boot loader] section. Otherwise, you end up with two entries for the same OS on-screen, one of which has "(default)" following it. In all likelihood, only one of these will work. Trial-and-error should quickly discern which one.

Note that the paths are in ARC format with a label in quotation marks, which displays as an on-screen selection. Here's an example of an [operating systems] section:

```
multi(0)disk(0)rdisk(0)partition(1)\WINNT="Windows NT Workstation
~Version 4.00"
multi(0)disk(0)rdisk(0)partition(1)\WINNT="Windows NT Workstation
~Version 4.00 [VGA mode]" /basevideo /sos
c:\="Windows 95"
```

There are two entries for the same Windows NT Workstation installation, but the second one includes two switches that customize the Windows NT boot and load process.

BOOT.INI Switches

The following sections delineate several useful switches that you can include in the [operating systems] section of BOOT.INI. The only way to include them is to manually edit the BOOT.INI file. If you decide to do so, be certain to take the read-only attribute off of the file before editing it, and be sure that you save the altered file as a text file if you use a word processor that normally saves in another format.

/basevideo

The /basevideo switch tells Windows NT to load the standard VGA driver rather than the optimized driver written for your video card, which is useful, for example, if your monitor breaks and is replaced by one that doesn't support the resolution or the refresh rate that your last one did. If you can't see, it is awfully hard to get into Control Panel to change the video settings. Selecting the VGA mode entry uses the standard VGA 640 × 480, 16-color driver that works with almost every monitor.

/sos

The /sos switch enumerates to the screen each driver as it loads during the kernel load phase. If Windows NT hangs during this phase, you can use the /sos switch to determine which driver caused the problem.

/noserialmice=[COMx|COMx,y,z_]

When Windows NT boots, NTDETECT.COM looks for, among other things, the presence of serial mice. Sometimes this detection routine misfires and identifies modems or other devices as serial mice. Then, when Windows NT loads and initializes, the serial port is unavailable and the device is unusable because Windows NT is expecting a serial mouse. In other instances, the serial mouse detection signal can shut down a UPS connected to the serial port.

The /noserialmice switch by itself tells NTDETECT.COM not to bother looking for serial mice. Used with a specific COM port(s), NTDETECT.COM still looks for serial mice, but not on the port(s) specified.

/crashdebug

The /crashdebug switch turns on the Automatic Recovery and Restart capability, which you can also configure using the Control Panel System application. In fact, when you configure this capability through Control Panel, what you are doing is merely adding this switch to the OS path in BOOT.INI.

/nodebug

Programmers often use a special version of Windows NT that includes debugging symbols useful for tracking down problems with code. This version of Windows NT runs slowly compared to the retail version, owing to the extra overhead in tracking every piece of executing code. To turn off the monitoring in this version of NT, add the /nodebug switch to the OS path in BOOT.INI.

/maxmem:n

Memory parity errors can be notoriously difficult to isolate. The /maxmem switch helps. When followed with a numeric value, this switch limits Windows NT's usable memory to the amount specified in the switch. This switch also is useful for developers using high-level workstations, who want to simulate performance on a lower-level machine.

/scsiordinal:n

If your system has two identical SCSI controllers, you need a way to distinguish one from the other. The /scsiordinal switch is used to assign a value of 0 to the first controller and 1 to the second.

Kernel Initialization Phase

After all the initial drivers have loaded, the screen turns blue and the text height shrinks; the kernel initialization phase has begun. Now the kernel and all the drivers loaded in the previous phase are initialized. The Registry begins to flesh out. The CurrentControlSet is copied to the CloneControlSet, and the volatile HARDWARE key is created. The system Registry hive then is scanned once more for higher-level drivers configured to start during system initialization. These drivers have a start value of 1 (like the keyboard and mouse) and then are loaded and initialized.

Services Load Phase

Here the session manager scans the system hive for a list of programs that must run before Windows NT fully initializes. These programs may include AUTOCHK.EXE, the boot-time version of CHKDSK.EXE that examines and repairs any problems within a file system, or AUTOCONV.EXE, which converts a partition from FAT to NTFS. These boot-time programs are stored in the following:

```
HKEY_LOCAL_MACHINE\SYSTEM\CurrentControlSet\Control\Session
Manager\BootExecute
```

Following these programs, the page file(s) are created based on the locations specified in

```
HKEY_LOCAL_MACHINE\SYSTEM\CurrentControlSet\Control\Session
Manager\Memory Management
```

Next, the SOFTWARE hive loads from <winnt_root>\SYSTEM32\ CONFIG. Session Manager then loads the CSR subsystem and any other required subsystems from

```
HKEY_LOCAL_MACHINE\System\CurrentControlSet\Control\Session
Manager\SubSystems\Required
```

Finally, drivers that have a start value of 2 (Automatic) load.

The Windows NT Resource Kit includes a command-line utility called DRIVERS.EXE that reports the name of all successfully loaded drivers. If you have any doubts about a driver's capability to successfully load and initialize, try DRIVERS> EXE.

Windows Start Phase

After the Win32 subsystem starts, the screen then switches into GUI mode. In other words, it looks like Windows. The Winlogon process is invoked, which starts the Welcome dialog box appears. Although users can go ahead and log on at this point, the system might not respond for a few more moments while the Service Controller initializes Computer Browser, Workstation, Server, Spooler, and other automatic services.

The critical file at this point is SERVICES.EXE, which actually starts Alerter, Computer Browser, EventLog, Messenger, Net-Logon, NT LM Security Support Provider, Server, TCP/IP NetBIOS Helper, and Workstation. A missing or corrupt SERVICES.EXE cripples your Windows NT-based computer.

SERVICES.EXE starts its services by calling the appropriate DLLs:

Alerter	ALRSVC.DLL
Computer Browser	BROWSER.DLL
EventLog	EVENTLOG.DLL

Messenger	MSGSVC.DLL
Net Logon	NETLOGON.DLL
NT LM Security Support Provider	NTLMSSPS.DLL
Server	SRVSVC.DLL
TCP/IP NetBIOS Helper	LMHSVC.DLL
Workstation	WKSSVC.DLL

After a user successfully logs on to the system, the LastKnown-Good control set is updated and the boot is considered good. Until a user logs on for the first time, though, the boot/load process technically remains unfinished, so a problem that Windows NT cannot detect but that a user can see (such as a video problem) can be resolved by falling back on the LastKnownGood configuration.

Control Sets and LastKnownGood

A control set is a collection of configuration information used during boot by Windows NT. A special control set, called Last-KnownGood, plays a special role in troubleshooting the boot process.

After the system boots and a user logs on successfully, the current configuration settings are copied to the LastKnownGood control set in the Registry. These settings are preserved so that if the system cannot boot successfully the next time a user attempts to log on, the system can fall back on LastKnownGood, which, as the name implies, is the last configuration known to facilitate a "good" boot. LastKnownGood is stored in the Registry under

```
HKEY_LOCAL_MACHINE\SYSTEM\CurrentControlSet
```

The key to understanding LastKnownGood lies in recognizing that it updates the first (and only the first) time a user logs on to Windows NT after a reboot. If you notice something dicey—if, for example, you changed the settings for a driver that now refuses to load—you can power down and restart the system using the Last-

KnownGood configuration. If you notice something wrong but still log on to the system, you are telling it that everything is okay, that this is a configuration that facilitates a good boot. The system then overwrites the LastKnownGood, and what you essentially end up with is a "LastKnownBad" configuration.

To boot with the LastKnownGood configuration, press the space-bar when prompted during the boot process. You are presented with the Hardware Profile/Configuration Recovery menu. Select a hardware profile and enter L for the LastKnownGood configuration.

Sometimes Windows NT boots using LastKnownGood of its own volition, but only if the normal boot process produces severe or critical errors in loading device drivers.

LastKnownGood does not do you any good if files are corrupt or missing. You must use the Emergency Repair Process for aid with that.

Troubleshooting the Boot Process

If one of the important boot files is missing or corrupt, Windows NT can't boot correctly. If NTLDR, NTDTECT.COM, BOOTSECT.DOS, or NTOSKRNL.EXE fail, NT displays a message that tells you the name of the missing file. Use the Emergency Repair Process to restore the system.

If BOOT.INI is missing, NTLDR tries to start Windows NT without consulting BOOT.INI or the boot menu. This works as long as Windows NT is installed in the default \Winnt directory. If Windows NT is installed in a different directory, however, NTLDR cannot find it and issues an error message stating that the file, \winnt root\system32\ntoskrnl.exe, is missing or corrupt.

If BOOT.INI contains an invalid path name, or if a BOOT.INI path includes an invalid device, the boot fails. Verify all BOOT.INI paths. If possible, boot from a floppy and edit BOOT.INI to fix the problem. The Emergency Repair Process described later in this chapter can restore BOOT.INI if the error stems from a recent change.

If you need to boot Windows NT from the floppy drive, you can use Setup Boot disks created using the Winnt.exe or Winnt32.exe utilities with the /ox switch (see Chapter 2). You need these disks to invoke the Emergency Repair Process, so it is nice to have them around.

The Emergency Repair Process

As you may recall from Chapter 2, the installation process enables you to create an emergency repair directory and emergency repair disk, both of which are backup copies of Registry information, (which come in handy if you can't boot Windows NT owing to missing or corrupt files). It is now time to take a look at ways in which the Emergency Repair Process can aid a troubled Windows NT installation.

Emergency Repair Directory Versus Emergency Repair Disk

Installation always creates the emergency repair directory. You can find it in <winnt_root>\REPAIR. You can create an emergency repair disk as well. Do you need both? Well, no, not really. The directory serves just as well as the disk unless the directory itself becomes corrupt, or the drive itself dies, in which case you're stuck. The disk serves as a backup in case of an extreme emergency.

Both the directory and disk are computer-specific, at least in part. Although you can sometimes borrow an emergency repair disk from another computer, you generally should assume otherwise. Keep a separate emergency repair disk for each computer and tag it with the serial number of the computer because names and locations change over time. Don't leave these disks in the hands of users. Keep them with an administrator in a secure but accessible location.

Table 6.1 lists and describes the files on the emergency repair disk.

Table 6.1

Files on the Emergency Repair Disk	
Files	Description
SETUP.LOG	A text file that contains the names of all the Windows NT installation files, along with checksum values for each. If any of the files on your hard drive are missing or corrupt, the Emergency Repair Process should detect them with the aid of this hidden, system, and read-only file.
SYSTEM._	A compressed copy of the Registry's SYSTEM hive. This is the Windows NT control set collection.
SAM._	A compressed copy of the Registry's SAM hive. This is the Windows NT user accounts database.
SECURITY.__	A compressed copy of the Registry's SECURITY hive. This is the Windows NT security information, which includes SAM and the security policies.
SOFTWARE._	A compressed copy of the Registry's SOFTWARE hive. This hive contains all Win32 software configuration information.
DEFAULT._	A compressed copy of the system default profile.
CONFIG.NT	The VDM version of the MS-DOS CONFIG.SYS file.
AUTOEXEC.NT	The VDM version of the MS-DOS AUTOEXEC.BAT file.
NTUSER.DA_	A copy of the file NTUSER.DAT (which contains user profile information) from the directory winnt_root\profiles\Defaultuser.

RDISK.EXE

Both the emergency repair disk and directory are created during installation, but neither are updated automatically at anytime thereafter. To update the emergency repair information, use the hidden utility RDISK.EXE. To start RDISK, choose Start, Run and type **RDISK**. Because RDISK.EXE is in the search path

(\<winnt_root>\SYSTEM32), you do not have to specify the full path. Some administrators just add the RDISK program to the Administrative Tools group.

RDISK offers two options for administrators: Update Repair Info and Create Repair Disk (see fig. 6.2).

Figure 6.2

The RDISK utility.

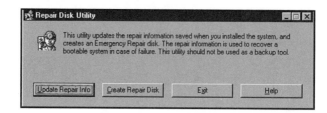

Update Repair Info

The Update Repair Info button updates only the emergency repair directory, although it does prompt for the creation/update of an emergency repair disk immediately following successful completion of the directory update. Always update the directory before creating the disk, because the disk will be created using the information in the directory.

Create Repair Disk

If the information in the repair directory is up-to-date, you may choose to create or update an emergency repair disk. You don't have to use a preformatted disk for the repair disk. RDISK formats the disk regardless.

A significant limitation of RDISK that you should definitely know about is that it will not update DEFAULT._, SECURITY, or SAM, in the repair directory (or disk). In other words, you may update your repair disk week-to-week, but none of your account changes are being backed up. To do a complete emergency repair update, you must run RDISK.EXE using the undocumented /S switch. This takes a while, especially if your account database is quite large. It is better, however, than losing all your accounts when disaster strikes. By the way, if you are wondering what happens if the emergency repair information requires more than one disk, rest easy, RDISK asks for an additional disk (or disks).

Starting the Emergency Repair Process

Whether you use the emergency repair directory or the emergency repair disk, you need to recognize that you can't boot from either or use either from within Windows NT. To actually invoke the Emergency Repair Process, you must access the original three Windows NT Setup disks. If you don't have the original disks handy, you generate them from the CD by using the WINNT /O or /OX switch. Chapter 2 includes more information on the WINNT.EXE program.

If you think way back to installation, you might recall that the Setup process actually gives you the initial choice either to install Windows NT or repair an existing installation. Pressing R on this screen invokes the Emergency Repair Process. Don't be concerned when the Setup process then continues apace through the rest of the three setup disks. This is normal.

The emergency repair process gives you several options. You can select any or all of the options in the emergency repair menu. (The default is to undertake all repair options.) After you select your repair options, Setup attempts to locate your hard drive. After Setup locates your hard drive, it asks you whether you want to use an emergency repair disk or whether you want Setup to search for your repair directory. You then encounter a series of restoration choices based on the repair options you selected and the problems Setup uncovers as it analyzes your system. The next few sections discuss the emergency repair options.

Inspect Registry Files

At this point, the process gets computer-specific. If your registry becomes corrupt, only your own emergency repair disk can save you—no one else's can. You granularly select to repair any combination of the SYSTEM, SOFTWARE, DEFAULT, and SECURITY/ SAM hives, and these are copied directly from the repair directory/disk. You don't need the original source CD or disks for this procedure.

Inspect Startup Environment

The files required to boot Windows NT are discussed earlier in this chapter. If any of these files go AWOL or become corrupted, choose Inspect Startup Environment to repair them. You can use anyone's emergency repair disk for this option because these files are generic across all Windows NT installations (for the same platform, anyway). You do need to produce the original installation CD, however, before the repair process can replace the files.

Verify Windows NT System Files

This option often takes time, but systematically inspects every file in the Windows NT directory tree and compares them with the checksum values in SETUP.LOG. If it determines that any files are missing or corrupt, the repair process attempts to replace them. Again, you need the original disks or CD before you can do so.

Inspect Boot Sector

If you upgrade to a new version of DOS and suddenly find that you cannot boot to Windows NT anymore, your boot sector probably has been replaced. Using the MS-DOS or Windows 95 SYS command is notorious for trashing the Windows NT boot sector. The emergency repair disk solves this problem, and you don't even need a computer-specific ERD—you can borrow anybody's.

Troubleshooting Configuration Errors

Configuration errors are another common source of hardship for network professionals. Configuration errors are often introduced by a user or an administrator installing new software or a new device.

Microsoft lists the following objective for the Windows NT Server exam:

Choose the appropriate course of action to take to resolve configuration errors.

Some common device problems are resource conflicts (such as interrupt conflicts) and SCSI problems. Sometimes these problems manifest themselves at boot time. Sometimes they don't appear until you try to access the misconfigured device. Device error reports appear in the Event Log (described later in this chapter). Use Windows NT diagnostics to check resource settings. If the error is the result of a recent configuration change, you can reboot the system and boot to the LastKnownGood configuration.

If a Windows NT service doesn't start, check Event Viewer; or, check the Control Panel Services application to make sure the service is installed and configured to start.

Windows NT includes some important tools you can use to look for configuration errors. Those tool are as follows:

▶ Event Viewer

▶ Windows NT Diagnostics

▶ System Recovery

You will learn more about these tools in the following sections. You will also learn how to fend off a catastrophic misconfiguration by backing up your Registry.

Event Viewer

If your Windows NT-based computer manages to boot successfully, yet still isn't performing correctly, the first thing to check is the system event log, where all critical system messages are stored.

Windows NT includes the Event Viewer application in the Administrative Tool program group for viewing the messages stored in the system, security, and application log files (see fig. 6.3).

System Log

The system log, the default view in Event Viewer, is maintained by the operating system. It tracks three kinds of events:

> ▶ **Errors.** Symbolized by Stop signs, and indicative of the failure of a Windows NT component or device, or perhaps an inability to start. These errors are common on notebook computers when Windows NT fails to start the network components because PCMCIA network cards are not present.

> ▶ **Warnings.** Symbolized by exclamation points, and indicative of an impending problem. Low disk space on a partition triggers a warning, for example.

> ▶ **Information Events.** Symbolized by the traditional "I" in a blue circle, and indicative of an event that isn't at all bad but is still somehow significant. Browser elections often cause information events.

Figure 6.3

Event Viewer.

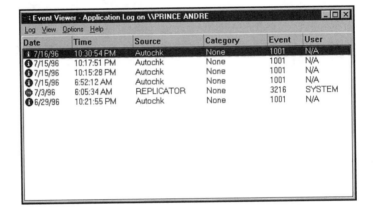

Security Log

The security log remains empty until you enable auditing through User Manager. After enabling auditing, the audited events reside here. The security log tracks two types of events:

> ▶ **Success Audits.** Symbolized by a key, and indicative of successful security access.

> ▶ **Failure Audits.** Symbolized by a padlock, and indicative of unsuccessful security access.

Application Log

The application log collects messages from native Windows NT applications (refer to fig. 6.3). If you aren't using any Win32 applications, this log remains empty. As you move toward native Windows NT programs, check this log occasionally, and certainly check it when you suspect a problem.

Securing Event Logs

Ordinarily, anyone can view the event log information. Some administrators, however, might not want guests to have this sort of access. There is one restriction, enabled through the Registry, that you can place on Event Viewer—you can prohibit guests from accessing the system or application logs from the following Registry location, where <log_name> is either System or Application:

```
HKEY_LOCAL_MACHINE\System\CurrentControlSet\Services\EventLog\~<log_name>
```

You need to add a value called RestrictGuestAccess of type REG_DWORD and set it equal to 1. To re-enable guest access to either log, set the appropriate RestrictGuestAccess value to 0 or just delete the value altogether.

Configuring Event Viewer

By default, log files can reach 512 KB, and events are overwritten after seven days. You can change these settings in the Event Log Settings dialog box, which you open by choosing Log Settings in the Event Viewer Log menu (see fig. 6.4).

Figure 6.4

The Event Log Settings dialog box.

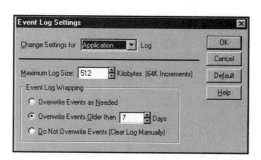

The Save As option in the Log menu enables you to save the log as an event log file (with an EVT extension), making it available for examination on another computer at a future time, or as a comma-separated value text file (also with a TXT extension) for importing into a spreadsheet or database. The format you select depends on the spreadsheet or database program you use for the text file you import. Choose the Select Computer command to view events on another computer (of course, you must have an administrator-level account on the remote Windows NT-based computer to succeed).

> C2 environments require that all log information be retained. No information may be overwritten, because overwriting events may allow a security break to escape unnoticed after it is overwritten. This isn't the default setting, however; using it can result in the log file becoming quite large and unwieldy.

Using Event Viewer

At some point, every Windows NT user receives this infamous message:

```
One or more services failed to start. Please see the Event Viewer
for details.
```

This message appears when the first user logs on to the system after at least one Windows NT component fails to load successfully. As directed, you should immediately proceed to Event Viewer.

To find the source of the problem, look at the system log under the Event heading. Somewhere toward the top of the column, you should find an Event code of 6005. (By default, the logs list the most recent events at the top of the list, so start scanning at the top of the list or you may not find the most recent 6005 event.) If you look under the Source heading for this event, it should read EventLog, and it is an informational message. Event 6005 means that the EventLog service was successfully started. Any events that appear chronologically earlier than 6005 are events logged during system boot. Investigate these events, particularly the errors, because they may reveal the source of your problem.

To examine an event message, double-click on an event to open the Event Detail dialog box (see fig. 6.5).

Figure 6.5

The Event Detail dialog box.

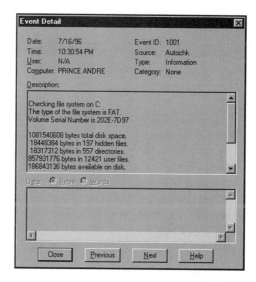

Note the identifying information for the event:

▶ Date of the event

▶ Time of the event

▶ User account that generated the event, if applicable (usually found in the security log)

▶ Computer on which the event occurred

▶ Event ID (the Windows NT Event code)

▶ Source Windows NT component that generated the event

▶ Type of event (Error, Warning, and so on)

▶ Category of event (Logon/Logoff audit, for example)

▶ Description of the event

▶ Data in hexadecimal format, useful to a developer or debugger

A note about the preceding items: the Event Descriptions have come a long way since the cryptic MS-DOS error messages. Some Windows NT messages tell you everything you need to know:

```
The D drive is almost full. The files will need to be backed up
and then deleted from the D drive.
```

Others perhaps tell you too much:

```
Could not look up the assoc block for an NBT association. Check
if the message read is corrupted. WINS looks at bit 11-14 of the
message to determine if the assoc. is from another WINS or from
an NBT node. It is possible that the bits are corrupted or that
there is a mismatch between what the two WINS servers expect to
see in those bits (maybe you changed the value to be put in code
and not increment the version number set during assoc. setup).
```

Sometimes progress seems to work in reverse:

```
A DosDevIoctl or DosFsCtl to NETWKSTA.SYS failed. The data shown
is in the format:DWORD approx CS:IP of call to ioctl or fsctlWORD
error code WORD ioctl or fsctl number.
```

Just write down the error message and call Microsoft's Product Support Services. They know what to do with the information.

note

> If you want to save the hexadecimal data along with the event description, be certain to save the events as EVT files. The hex data doesn't save with TXT files.

You also can filter events so that only certain events report on-screen. Note that doing so doesn't delete messages from the event log, but rather, only controls which of the logged events appear in Event Viewer at any given time. To filter events, choose View, Filter Events. You may filter by the following:

- Event date and time

- Event type (Error, Warning, and so on)

- Source (Atdisk, Browser, and so on)

▶ User

▶ Computer

▶ Event ID

If you are filtering an event log imported from another computer, you can filter only for components installed on your own machine. In other words, the filters are read from your own Registry, not from the event log file itself.

Windows NT Diagnostics

Windows NT Diagnostics provides a tidy front end to much of the information in the HKEY_LOCAL_MACHINE Registry subtree. Like its ancestor, MSD from Windows 3.1, Windows NT Diagnostics can create incredibly detailed and valuable system configuration reports. One thing you cannot do with Windows NT Diagnostics is edit the system configuration. Figure 6.6 shows the Windows NT Diagnostics dialog box.

Figure 6.6

The Windows NT Diagnostics dialog box.

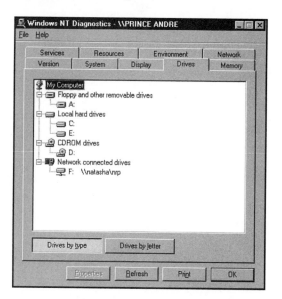

The Windows NT Diagnostics dialog box includes the following nine tabs:

▶ **Version.** Displays information stored under HKEY_LOCAL_ MACHINE\Software\Microsoft\Windows NT\CurrentVersion, including the build number, registered owner, and Service Pack update information.

▶ **System.** Displays information stored under HKEY_LOCAL_ MACHINE\Hardware, including CPU and other device identification information.

▶ **Display.** Displays information on the video adapter and adapter settings.

▶ **Drives.** Lists all drive letters in use and their types, including drive letters for floppy drives, hard disks, CD-ROM and optical drives, and network connections. Double-click on a drive letter to display a drive Properties dialog box. The General tab of the drive Properties dialog box shows byte and cluster information for the drive (see fig. 6.7). The File System tab shows file system information (see fig. 6.8).

Figure 6.7

The drive Properties General tab.

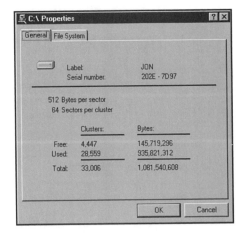

▶ **Memory.** Displays current memory load, as well as physical and virtual memory statistics.

▶ **Services.** Displays service information stored under HKEY_LOCAL_MACHINE\System\CurrentControlSet\Services, including status. Click on the Devices button to display driver information stored under HKEY_LOCAL_MACHINE\ System\CurrentControlSet\Control, including status.

▶ **Resources.** Displays device information listed by interrupt and by port, and also by DMA channels and UMB locations in use.

▶ **Environment.** Displays environment variables for command prompt sessions (set under Control Panel System).

▶ **Network.** Displays network component configuration and status.

Figure 6.8

The drive Properties File System tab.

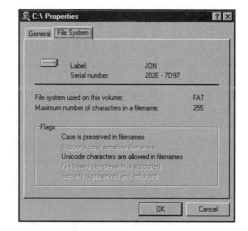

System Recovery

The Recovery utility is a tool you can use to record debugging information, alert an administrator, or reboot the system in the event of a Stop error. (A Stop error causes Windows NT to stop all processes.) To configure the Recovery utility, start the Control Panel System application and click on the Startup/Shutdown tab (see fig. 6.9).

The bottom frame of the Startup/Shutdown tab is devoted to Recovery options. The options are as follows:

▶ Write an event to the system log.

▶ Send an administrative alert.

▶ Write debugging information to (specify a file name). In the event of a Stop error, the Savedump.exe program dumps everything in memory to the pagefile and marks the location of the dump. When you restart your system, Windows NT copies the memory dump from the pagefile to the file specified in the Startup/Shutdown tab. You can then use a program called Dumpexam.exe in the \Support directory of the Windows NT CD-ROM to study the contents of the memory dump and determine the cause of the Stop error.

▶ Automatically reboot. You might not want to have your server sit idle after a Stop error. This option instructs Windows NT to automatically reboot after a Stop error.

Figure 6.9

The System application Startup/Shutdown tab.

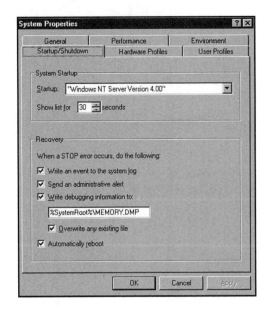

Backing Up the Registry

By now, you're more than aware of the danger of tampering with the Registry. Safety demands you back up the Registry before trying new Registry modification. It is useful to understand which files are involved during a backup of the Registry.

Before discussing Registry files, you should be familiar with the term hive. A hive is a binary file that contains all the keys and values within a branch of the Registry. Not every key is a hive.

Some keys are contained within hives, and others are never written to disk at all (such as HKEY_LOCAL_MACHINE\Hardware, which was examined earlier).

> You may be wondering why these files are called *hives*. Supposedly, one of the Windows NT developers thought the Registry resembled a massive beehive with all its tunnels and chambers, and so coined the term.

Two files are associated with each hive: one file is named after the hive and has no extension, and the other is identically named with a LOG extension (with the exception of SYSTEM, which has a SYSTEM.ALT counterpart for reasons to be explained shortly). Both files reside in the \<winnt_root>\SYSTEM32\CONFIG directory. Most of the hives loaded at any given time are residents of HKEY_LOCAL_MACHINE, and the others belong to HKEY_USERS. Here is a list of the Registry hives:

HKEY_LOCAL_MACHINE\SAM (SAM, SAM.LOG)

HKEY_LOCAL_MACHINE\SECURITY (SECURITY, SECURITY.LOG)

HKEY_LOCAL_MACHINE\SOFTWARE (SOFTWARE, SOFTWARE.LOG)

HKEY_LOCAL_MACHINE\SYSTEM (SYSTEM, SYSTEM.ALT)

HKEY_USERS\.DEFAULT (DEFAULT, DEFAULT.LOG)

HKEY_USERS\<user_sid> (<user_profile>, <user_profile>.LOG)

The LOG files provide fault tolerance for the Registry. Whenever configuration data is changed, the changes are written to the LOG file first. Then the first sector of the actual hive is flagged to indicate that an update is taking place. The data is transferred from the log to the hive, and the update flag on the hive is then lowered. If the computer were to crash after the flag had been raised but before it had been lowered, some, if not all the data, would quite possibly be corrupt. If that happened, when Windows NT restarted it would detect the flag still raised on the hive, and it would use the log to redo the update.

The only exception to this rule is the SYSTEM file. Because the SYSTEM hive contains critical information that must be loaded intact to load enough of the operating system to process the log files, a duplicate of SYSTEM is maintained as SYSTEM.ALT. This file functions identically to a log file, except that the entire file (rather than just the changes) is mirrored. If the computer were to crash during an update to the SYSTEM branch of the Registry, the integrity of the SYSTEM hive is still preserved. If the data had not yet been fully committed to SYSTEM.ALT, the SYSTEM hive is still preserved in its original configuration. If the data had not yet been fully committed to SYSTEM, SYSTEM.ALT would be used to redo the update.

Now that you know which files are involved in the Registry, do you need to back them all up? No. In fact, the LOG files are so transitory that they would be useless by the time the backup completes. You may want to back up the user profile information if you are going to alter user-specific information, but usually these settings are potentially harmless. SAM and SECURITY are off-limits for editing, so you can't hurt them at all.

The files of greatest import are SYSTEM and SOFTWARE, which usually are so small they can fit on a floppy disk. Consequently, just copying the files to a disk is rather tempting. Do not, however, give in to that temptation.

Registry files almost always are in a state of flux and are constantly open for read/write access. The Windows NT Backup program usually skips over these files for that reason. Probably the best way to back up the SYSTEM and SOFTWARE files is to use the Repair Disk application, another hidden application in the \<winnt_root>\SYSTEM32 directory. The section "RDISK.EXE," earlier in this chapter, discussed the Repair Disk utility, otherwise known as RDISK.EXE.

Backing Up Individual Keys

You can create your own hive files by saving an entire branch of the Registry starting from any key you choose. You do so by choosing Registry, Save Key in Registry Editor. To load the hive into the Registry of another Windows NT computer, choose Registry, Restore Key.

If you want to work with the key only temporarily, you can use the Restore Volatile command rather than the Restore Key command. The key still loads into the Registry at the selected location, but it doesn't reload the next time the system restarts.

Troubleshooting Printer Problems

Printing has always been troublesome, regardless of the operating system. Windows NT handles printing better than most systems do, but you still should make a concerted effort to avoid certain potential printing pitfalls.

If you can't print to a printer, try a different printer to see whether the problem also appears there. Try printing from a different account. Make certain that that the printer is plugged in, turned on, and so on. Make sure that the printer has paper. Remove and re-create the printer if necessary.

Microsoft lists the following objective for the Windows NT Server exam:

Choose the appropriate course of action to take to resolve printer problems.

When you try to isolate printing problems, the following guidelines can be helpful:

1. Check the cable connections and the printer port to verify that the printing device is on and the cables are all securely fitted. This precaution may seem rather obvious, but the simplest of things cause some of the most perplexing problems.

2. To verify that the correct printer driver is installed and configured properly, establish the type of printing device (such as PCL, PostScript, and so on) and verify that the correct driver type has been installed. If necessary, reinstall the printer driver. If a printer driver needs updating, use the Printers folder to install and configure the new printer driver.

3. Verify that the printer is selected, either explicitly in the application or as the default printer. Most Windows NT applications have a Printer Setup menu or toolbar button. When printing by means of OLE or some other indirect means, you need to specify a default printer.

4. Verify that enough hard disk space is available to generate the print job, especially on the partition that has the spooler directory specified, which, by default, is the system partition (that is, the winnt_root partition).

5. Run the simplest application possible (for example, Notepad) to verify that printing can occur from other applications within Windows NT. If problems are encountered printing from the application (other than a Win32-based application), check the appropriate application subsystem (for example, DOS, Win16, POSIX, and OS/2).

6. Print to a file (FILE:) and then copy the output file to a printer port. If this works, the problem is the spooler, or is data-transmission related. If this doesn't work, the problem is application- or driver-related.

Spooling Problems

By default, spooled print jobs reside in the \<winnt_root>\ SYSTEM32\SPOOL\PRINTERS directory until completely printed. If a Windows NT-based computer is acting as a print server for the network, make sure plenty of free disk space is available on the partition that contains the default spool directory. Spooled print jobs can be quite large and can eat up disk space more quickly than you might think, especially during peak printing periods. Also, keeping this partition defragmented improves printing performance. Because Windows NT doesn't include a defrag utility, you need to use a third-party utility (or boot to MS-DOS if you are using the FAT file system).

If you have more room on another partition, you may change the default spool directory in the Advanced tab of the Server Properties dialog box (as described earlier in this chapter). You can also change the spool directory in the Registry by adding a value called DefaultSpoolDirectory of type REG_SZ to the following and entering the path to the new spool directory:

```
HKEY_LOCAL_MACHINE\System\CurrentControlSet\Control\Print\
Printers
```

You need to restart the spooler service (or the computer itself) for the change to take effect.

You can also assign a separate spool directory for each individual printer. Enter the path to the new spool directory as the data for the value SpoolDirectory in the following, where <Printer> is the name of the printer you want to redirect:

```
HKEY_LOCAL_MACHINE\System\CurrentControlSet\Control\Print\~Printers\
<Printer>
```

Again, you need to restart the spooler service for this change to take effect.

Printing from Non-Windows-Based Applications

Non-Windows-based applications—for example, MS-DOS-based applications—require their own printer drivers if the application requires any kind of formatted output other than plain ASCII text. WordPerfect for MS-DOS, for example, does not even allow the user to print a document unless there is a WordPerfect-specific and printer-specific driver installed, for example, because non-Windows-based applications are not written to conform to or take advantage of the Windows APIs. Also, remember that you may need to use the NET USE LPT1: \\servername\printername command to enable the DOS-based application to print.

Handling the Computer Crashing

When a document prints, two files are created for the print job in the spool directory (by default, <winnt_root>\SYSTEM32\ SPOOL\PRINTERS). One of the files, which has an .SPL extension, is the actual print job spool file. The other file, which has an .SHD extension, is a shadow file that contains information about the job, including its owner and priority. These files remain in the spool directory until the jobs finish printing, at which point they are deleted.

In the event of a system crash, some spool and shadow files may be left over from jobs that were waiting to be printed. When the spooler service restarts (along with the rest of the system), the printer should process these files immediately. They are, however, sometimes corrupted during the crash and get stuck. Be certain, therefore, to check the spool directory every so often, and delete any spool and shadow files with old date/time stamps. How old is old depends on how long it takes to print a job on your printer. Certainly anything from days, weeks, or months ago should be deleted.

If a print job appears stuck in the printer and you cannot delete it, stop the spooler service in Control Panel Services and delete the SPL and/or SHD file for that job from the spool directory (match the date/time stamp on the files and in Print Manager to determine which files are causing the problem).

Printing Too Slow or Workstation Too Sluggish

Windows NT Workstation assigns priority 7 to the spooler service, which puts printing on an equal footing with other background applications. Windows NT Server, which favors printing over background applications, assigns priority 9 to the spooler, which puts it neck-and-neck with the foreground applications.

If a Windows NT-based workstation moonlighting as a print server appears to print too slowly, consider raising the priority by one or two classes. If the workstation is responding sluggishly to the user while printing, consider lowering the priority by a class or two. Don't alter the priority by more than two levels under any circumstances without a full understanding of the performance consequences involved.

To change the priority class for the Spooler service, add a value called PriorityClass of type REG_DWORD to HKEY_LOCAL_ MACHINE\System\CurrentControlSet\Control\Print and set it equal to the priority class desired. If this value is set to 0 or isn't present, the default is used (7 for Windows NT Workstation, or 9 for Windows NT Server).

Troubleshooting RAS

If RAS isn't working, check the Event Viewer. Several RAS events appear in the system log.

You might also check the Control Panel Dial-Up Networking Monitor application. The Status tab of Dial-Up Networking Monitor displays statistics on current conditions, including connection statistics and device errors.

Microsoft lists the following objective for the Windows NT Server exam:

Choose the appropriate course of action to take to resolve RAS problems.

If you are having problems with PPP, you can log PPP debugging information to a file called PPP.Log in the \<winnt_root>\ System32\Ras directory. To log PPP debugging information to PPP.Log, change the Registry value for the following subkey to 1:

```
\HKEY_LOCAL_MACHINE\System\CurrentControlSet\Services\Rasman\PPP\
Logging
```

Microsoft has identified the following common RAS problems and some possible solutions:

► **Authentication.** RAS authentication problems often stem from incompatible encryption methods. Try to connect using the `Allow any authentication including clear text` option (described earlier in this chapter). It you can connect using clear text and you can't connect using encryption, you know the client and server encryption methods are incompatible.

► **Callback with Multilink.** If a client makes a connection using Multilink over multiple phone lines, with Callback enabled, the server will call back using only a single phone line (in other words, Multilink functionality is lost). RAS can use only one phone number for callback. If the Multilink connection uses two channels over an ISDN line, the server can still use Multilink on the callback.

► **AutoDial at Logon.** At logon, when Explorer is initializing, it might reference a shortcut or some other target that requires an AutoDial connection, causing AutoDial to spontaneously dial a remote connection during logon. The only way to prevent this is to disable AutoDial, or to eliminate the shortcut or other target causing the AutoDial to occur.

Troubleshooting Connectivity Problems

Network problems often are caused by cables, adapters, or IRQ conflicts, or problems with transmission media. Protocol problems also can disrupt the network. Use a diagnostics program to check the network adapter card. Use a cable analyzer to check the cabling. Use Network Monitor (described in the next section) to check network traffic, or use a network protocol analyzer.

Microsoft lists the following objective for the Windows NT Server exam:

Choose the appropriate course of action to take to resolve connectivity problems.

If you are using TCP/IP, you often can isolate the problem by *pinging* the other computers on your network. Exercise 1.2 in Chapter 1 described a common diagnostic procedure:

1. Ping the 127.0.0.1 (the loopback address).

2. Ping your own IP address.

3. Ping the address of another computer on your subnet.

4. Ping the default gateway.

5. Ping a computer beyond the default gateway.

Check the Control Panel Services application to ensure that the Server service and the Workstation service (and any other vital services that might affect connectivity) are running properly. Check the Bindings tab in the Control Panel Network application to ensure that the services are bound to applications and adapters.

Network Monitor

Windows NT Server 4 includes a tool called Network Monitor. Network Monitor captures and filters packets and analyzes network activity. The Network Monitor included with Windows NT Server can monitor only the specific system on which it is installed, unlike the Network Monitor in Microsoft's Systems Management Server package, which can monitor other systems on the network.

To install Windows NT Server's Network Monitor, start the Network application in Control Panel and click on the Services tab. Click on the Add button and select Network Monitor from the network services list. After Network Monitor is installed, it appears in the Administrative Tools program group.

Figure 6.10 shows the Network Monitor main screen.

Figure 6.10

The Network Monitor main screen.

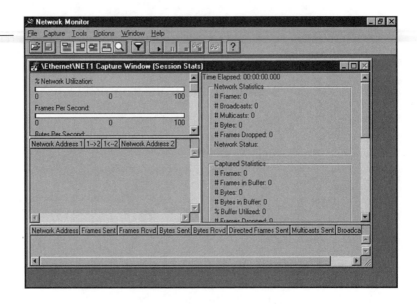

The Network Monitor window is divided into four sections, or *panes*. This section describes each of the four Network Monitor panes and discusses the various parameters and statistics you can monitor with Network Monitor.

The Graph pane (in the upper-left corner) shows the current network activity in a series of five bar charts. Note the scroll bar to the right of the Graph section. To view the bar charts (not shown in fig. 6.10), scroll down or drag the lower border down, exposing the hidden charts. The five bar graphs are as follows:

▶ % Network Utilization

▶ Frames Per Second

▶ Bytes Per Second

▶ Broadcasts Per Second

▶ Multicasts Per Second

Below the Graphs pane you see the Session Stats pane. The Session Stats pane indicates the exchange of information from two nodes on the network, the amount of data, and the direction of travel. This data is limited to a per-session basis.

The Session Stats pane reports only on the first 128 sessions it finds. You can specify a particular session creating a capture filter.

The Session Stats pane collects information on the following four areas:

▶ **Network Address 1.** The first node included in a network session.

▶ **1→2.** The number of packets sent from the first address to the second.

▶ **1←2.** The number of packets sent from the second address to the first.

▶ **Network Address 2.** The second node included in the network session.

On the right side of the display windows is the Total Stats pane, which reveals information relevant to the entire activity on the network. Whether statistics are supported depends on the network adapter. If a given network adapter isn't supported, Unsupported replaces the label.

The Total Stats information is divided into the following five categories:

▶ *Network Statistics*

Total Frames
Total Broadcasts
Total Multicasts
Total Bytes
Total Frames Dropped
Network Status

The Network Status value is always normal if you use an Ethernet network. If you use Token Ring, the Network Status value indicates the status of the ring.

▶ *Captured Statistics*

Captured Frames
Captured Frames in Buffer
Captured Bytes
Capture Bytes in Buffer
Percentage of Allotted Buffer Space in Use
Captured Packets Dropped

▶ *Per Second Statistics*

Frames
Bytes/second
Broadcasts/second
Multicasts/second
% Network Utilization

▶ *Network Card (MAC) Statistics*

Total Frames
Total Broadcasts
Total Multicasts
Total Bytes

▶ *Network Card (MAC) Error Statistics*

Total Cyclical Redundancy Check (CRC) Errors
Total Dropped Frames Due to Inadequate Buffer Space
Total Dropped Packets Due to Hardware Failure(s)

At the bottom of the display window, you see the Station Stats pane. The Station Stats pane displays information specific to a workstation's activity on the network. You can sort on any category by right-clicking on the column label.

The Station pane reports only on the first 128 sessions it finds. You can specify a particular session using a capture filter.

The following eight categories constitute the Station pane:

▶ Network Address

▶ Frames Sent

- ▶ Frames Rcvd

- ▶ Bytes Sent

- ▶ Bytes Rcvd

- ▶ Directed Frames Sent

- ▶ Multicasts Sent

- ▶ Broadcasts Sent

Troubleshooting Access and Permission Problems

If you can't log on, you may be using an incorrect username or password. Also, enable the check box beneath the password to make certain that you are logging on to the correct domain or workgroup (or the local machine). If you still can't log on, try logging on using another account. If other accounts are working normally, check the settings for your account in User Manager for Domains. If you can't log on from any account, repair the accounts database by using the emergency repair process. One of the worst culprits for logon problems is the Caps Lock key. Make certain that the user isn't typing the password in all caps.

Microsoft lists the following objective for the Windows NT Server exam:

Choose the appropriate course of action to take to resolve resource access problems and permission problems.

If a user can't access a file, a share, a printer, or some other resource, check the resource permissions. Try connecting using a different account. Try accessing a similar resource to see whether the problem also appears there. Make certain that the user has spelled the name of the resource correctly.

Check the Control Panel Services application to ensure that the NetLogon service, the Server service, and the Workstation service are running properly, and check the Bindings tab in the of the Control Panel Network application to ensure that the services are bound to applications and adapters.

You can also check User Manager for Domains to ensure that the user's group memberships haven't changed or that a change to a group rights setting hasn't inadvertently denied the user access to the resource.

Check System Policy Editor for restrictions on the user's access to computers or other resources.

Recovering from Fault-Tolerance Failures

Even if you are employing a high-tech RAID fault-tolerance system, a well planned backup routine is still your best defense against lost data. Windows NT includes a backup utility (NTBACKUP.EXE). Backup is part of the Administrative Tools group; figure 6.11 shows the Backup utility.

Figure 6.11

The Backup window.

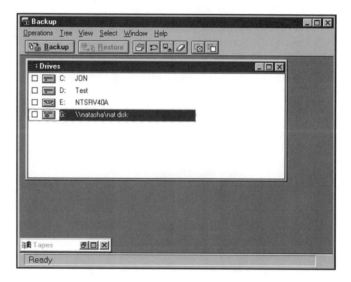

Microsoft lists the following objective for the Windows NT Server exam:

Choose the appropriate course of action to take to resolve fault-tolerance failures. Fault-tolerance methods include: tape backup, mirroring, stripe set with parity, disk duplexing.

Backing Up Files and Directories

The Backup main window shows the disk drives presently accessible to the Backup utility. Double-click on a drive and to see an Explorer-type directory tree (see fig. 6.12). Note that every directory or file has a small box beside it. Click on the box to back up the file or directory and all child files/directories beneath it.

Figure 6.12

Selecting a file or directory for backup.

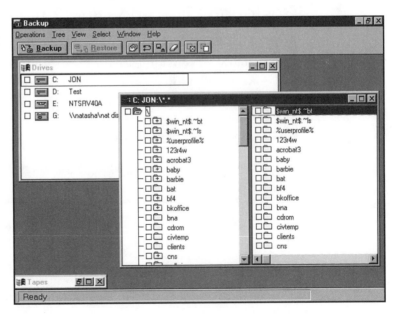

To start a backup, click on the Backup button in the toolbar or choose Operations, Backup. The Backup Information dialog box appears, offering a number of backup options (see fig. 6.13). Note the Log Information frame at the bottom of the Backup Information dialog box. You can write a summary or a detailed description of the backup operation to a log file.

Figure 6.13

The Backup Information dialog box.

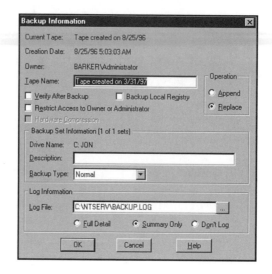

Restoring Files and Directories

To restore a file or directory using the Backuputility, open the Tapes window (if you don't see the Tapes window on your screen, pull down the Window menu and choose Tapes) and select the backup set you want to restore. Like the Drives window, the Tapes window enables you to expand directories and select individual files for restoration (see fig. 6.14).

Figure 6.14

The Tapes window.

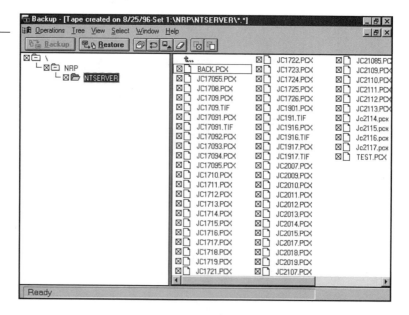

Select the files/directories you want to restore and click on the Restore button in the toolbar (or choose Operations, Restore). The Restore Information dialog box appears (see fig. 6.15). Select the desired restore options and click on OK to restore the files/directories.

Figure 6.15

The Restore Information dialog box.

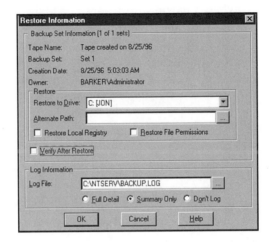

You also can run the NTBACKUP utility from the command prompt. This enables you to automate the backup process through batch files, so you can perform backups at regular intervals. You can only back up directories with the ntbackup command (not individual files). The syntax is as follows:

ntbackup *operation path*

where *operation* is the name of the operation (backup, restore, and so on), and *path* is the path to the directory you're backing up. The NTBACKUP command includes a number of switches, including the following:

/a cause the backup set to be appended after the last backup set. (If you don't specify /a will overwrite existing backup sets on the tape.)

/v verifies the backup operation.

/d "text" enables you to add a description of the data in the backup set.

/t {option} enables you to specify the backup type (normal, incremental, daily, differential, copy).

For a complete description of NTBACKUP options, see Windows NT Online Help.

Breaking a Mirror Set

When a partitionin a mirror set fails, it becomes an orphan. To maintain service until the mirror is repaired, the fault-tolerant device directs all I/O requests to the healthy partition. If the boot and/or system partitions are involved, a fault tolerant boot disk is required to restart the system. To create a fault tolerance boot disk, follow these steps:

1. Format a floppy disk using Windows NT.

2. If you are using an I386 system, copy NTLDR, NTDETECT.COM, NTBOOTDD.SYS (for SCSI disks not using SCSI BIOS), and BOOT.INI to the disk.

   If you're using a RISC-based computer, copy OSLOADER.EXE and HAL.DLL.

3. Modify the BOOT.INI file so that it points to the mirrored copy of the boot partition.

To fix a mirror set, you must first break it by choosing Fault Tolerance, Break Mirror. This action exposes the remaining partition as a separate volume. The healthy partition is given the drive letter that was previously assigned to it in the set, and the orphaned partition is given the next logical drive letter, or one that you manually selected for it.

After the mirror has been re-established as a primary partition, a new relationship can be formed by selecting additional free space and restarting the process of creating a mirror set.

Regenerating a Stripe Set with Parity

Like a mirror set, the partition that fails in a stripe set with parity becomes an orphan. Also, the fault-tolerant device redirects I/O requests to the remaining partitions in the set to enable reconstruction. So that this can be done, the data is stored in RAM by using the parity bits (which may affect the system's performance).

To regenerate a stripe set with parity, follow these steps:

1. Select the stripe set with parity by clicking on it.

2. Select an area of free space as large or larger than the stripe set.

3. Choose Fault Tolerance, Regenerate.

You must close the Disk Administrator and restart the system before the process can begin. After the system restarts, the information from the existing partitions in the stripe set are read into memory and re-created on the new member. This process completes in the background, so the stripe set with parity isn't active in the Disk Administrator until it finishes.

Troubleshooting Partitions and Disks

When you install Windows NT, your initial disk configuration is saved on the emergency repair disk and in the directory \<winnt_root>\Repair. The RDISK utility does update the disk configuration information stored on the repair disk and in the Repair directory. You can also save or restore the disk configuration by using Disk Adminstrator (see the section "Saving and Restoring Configuration Information," earlier in this chapter).

You should periodically update emergency configuration information in case you ever need to use the Emergency Repair Process or you ever want to you upgrade to a newer version of Windows NT. Otherwise, NT restores the original configuration that was saved when you first installed Windows NT.

Exercise Section

Exercise 6.1: Booting with SOS

In Exercise 6.1, you learn how to initiate a Windows NT boot by using the /sos switch, which enumerates each driver as the drivers load during the kernel load phase.

Estimated time: 20 minutes

1. Start the Notepad accessory application and open the boot.ini file in the root directory of the system partition. In the Notepad Open dialog box, don't forget to select All Files in the box labeled Files of type. The extension may not appear in the browse list. (The file name may appear as *boot*, without the extension. If you aren't sure you have the right file, right-click on the file and select Properties.) Examine the MS-DOS name setting in the file Properties dialog box.

2. Figure 6.16 shows the boot.ini file in Notepad. Find the line with the text string "Windows NT Server Version 4.00 [VGA]." Make sure the string is followed by the switches /basevideo and /sos. If you're confident your system uses a VGA video driver, skip to step 6; otherwise, continue with step 4.

3. Save the boot.ini file to a different file name (such as boot.tmp) by using the File, Save As command.

4. Delete the /basevideo switch in the line with the text string "Windows NT Server Version 4.00 [VGA]." The /sos switch should remain. Change the text in the square brackets from "VGA" to "sos."

5. Save the file as boot.ini.

   You may have to use the Save As command to save boot.ini. Verify the file name in the File name box. Step 3 may have changed the default file name.

6. Close Notepad and shut down your system.

continues

Exercise 6.1: Continued

7. Reboot Windows NT. When the boot menu appears, choose the "sos" option (or the VGA option if you skipped steps 3–5).

8. Watch the drivers display on-screen as they load. (Watch carefully, they will disappear quickly from the screen.) The drivers, like the boot.ini entries, will appear in ARC format. If you experience a boot failure, you can use this technique to determine which driver crashed or hung the system.

9. Log on to Windows NT. Restore the boot.ini file to its original state, either by inserting "VGA" and "/basevideo" using Notepad or by copying the boot.tmp file back to boot.ini. When you're finished, open boot.ini and make sure it is back to normal.

Figure 6.16

A boot.ini file.

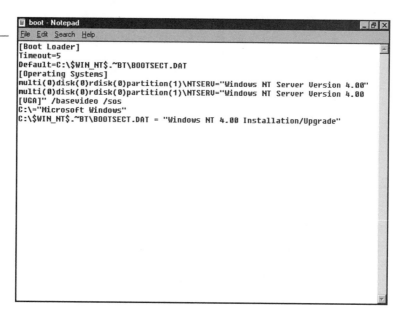

```
[Boot Loader]
Timeout=5
Default=C:\$WIN_NT$.~BT\BOOTSECT.DAT
[Operating Systems]
multi(0)disk(0)rdisk(0)partition(1)\NTSERV="Windows NT Server Version 4.00"
multi(0)disk(0)rdisk(0)partition(1)\NTSERV="Windows NT Server Version 4.00
[VGA]" /basevideo /sos
C:\="Microsoft Windows"
C:\$WIN_NT$.~BT\BOOTSECT.DAT = "Windows NT 4.00 Installation/Upgrade"
```

Step 9 is very important. You may not use the VGA boot option for months or even years, and when you do, you may not remember that you tried this exercise.

Review Questions

The following questions will text your knowledge of the information in this chapter. For additional questions, see MCP Endeavor and the Microsoft Roadmap/Assessment exam on the CD-ROM that accompanies this book.

1. A user calls and says that he can't log on to the system. He is getting a message that says NT cannot log you on. Check your userid and password information and try again, or something to that effect. What would you check?

    A. Make sure that the user types in the correct password and userid combination. Also check that the user has entered the password in the correct case and is specifying the correct domain name.

    B. Nothing. It's a normal message that the user would get when the server is down for maintenance.

    C. Log on as administrator and restart the domain controller to clear out any unused connections. When the server comes back up, the user should be able to log on.

2. You received a message during the boot process that a dependency service failed to start. Where should you check for more information?

    A. The file server error log

    B. In Event Viewer under the security log

    C. In Event Viewer under the system log

    D. In Server Manager, under the system log

3. You have turned on auditing, but cannot remember where the system puts the audit information. Where do you need to look?

    A. In Event Viewer under the security log

    B. In Event Viewer under the system log

C. In Auditcon under the security section

D. At the command prompt, type **NET** Show Audit

4. You're looking for a particular message in the system log under Event Viewer, but there are so many messages that you can't find the one you're looking for. How can you display messages of a certain type?

A. You cannot. Event Viewer shows all the messages in the system log.

B. You must set up Event Viewer to store only messages of the type you're looking for and then restart the system.

C. You can filter the log by choosing View, Filter Events.

D. You must first export the data to an ASCII file and then use the Edit program to find the specific data you seek.

5. Your manager informs you that an inventory of all company Computers running NT Workstation and NT Server needs to be done. Which NT utility can you use to safely determine the amount of RAM, type of CPU, and other information about the computers in question?

A. You must purchase the 32-bit version of PC Tools. This program gives you the required information.

B. No tools will run under NT because they would have to access the hardware directly, which isn't allowed under NT.

C. You must manually edit the Registry and search for the information you need.

D. Use the Windows NT Diagnostics utility.

6. A user calls you and says that while he was running Windows NT Diagnostics, he attempted to change the type of CPU that was reported but could not. Why?

    A. NT Diagnostics only shows information. You cannot make any modifications using this tool.

    B. The type of CPU cannot be changed with NT Diagnostics. The user must use Registry Editor to make the change manually.

    C. The user must make the CPU change in CMOS setup, not in NT Diagnostics.

7. While on a telephone call with Microsoft, the support engineer asks you which version of the operating system you're running. How can you find this out? Choose all that apply.

    A. You cannot. You must contact your network administrator for the information.

    B. The support engineer should be able to look up your product registration information.

    C. Run Windows NT Diagnostics and choose Version.

    D. Check the Registry under the HKEY_LOCAL_MACHINE subtree.

8. You're having problems with Stop errors on a computer running Windows NT Server. How can you set the recovery options that tell the system what action to perform in the event of a Stop error?

    A. You can set these options under Control Panel, System.

    B. You cannot. The system automatically places an event in the system log and then restarts the computer.

    C. You must configure a process to start whenever a Stop error is encountered by using the command-line utility AT.

    D. Use the Control Panel, Network option to configure the action to be taken when a Stop error is encountered.

9. Which set of files are required to boot Windows NT on an Intel-x86 based computer?

    A. NTLDR
       BOOT.INI
       NTDETECT.COM
       NTOSKRNL.EXE
       NTBOOTDD.SYS

    B. NTLDR
       BOOT.MNU
       NTDETECT.EXE
       OSLOADER
       NTBOOTDD.SYS

    C. OSLOADER
       NTOSKRNL.EXE
       NTDETECT.COM
       NTBOOTDD.SYS

10. Which file is used on an Intel-x86 based computer for computers that have SCSI hard drive controllers with the BIOS disabled?

    A. OSLOADER.EXE

    B. BOOTSCSI.SYS

    C. NTBOOTDD.SYS

    D. NTBOOTSCSI.SYS

11. What is the best explanation of the function of the NTDETECT.COM program?

    A. It reads the hardware configuration data from a RISC-based computer and passes it on to the OSLOADER program.

    B. It reads the hardware configuration information from a computer with a Plug-and-Play BIOS and updates the Registry.

    C. It scans the hardware in the computer and reports the list back to NTLDR for later inclusion in the Registry.

    D. It initializes the hardware on a computer with a Plug-and-Play BIOS.

12. You receive a phone call from a user asking you whether she can somehow reduce the amount of time her computer takes to boot. She also would like to change the default operating system from MS-DOS to NT Workstation. Which utility would you advise her to use to accomplish this?

    A. Control Panel, Boot

    B. Control Panel, System

    C. Server Manager

    D. Configure on a user-by-user basis in the users' profiles

13. You receive a phone call from a user who accidentally changed the SCSI controller card driver and now the computer won't boot NT. It stops at the blue screen and gives him a system error. What would you suggest?

    A. Tell the user to boot into DOS and rerun the Windows NT Setup program.

    B. Suggest that the user go out and purchase and install the SCSI device that he selected.

    C. Tell the user that he now needs to reinstall NT.

    D. Suggest that the user select the LastKnowGood configuration during NT booting. Then have the user remove the incorrect driver.

14. You're trying to understand the ARC-naming conventions in your BOOT.INI file. What would the ARC name look like if your computer had an IDE drive as the boot device?

    A. scsi(0)disk(1)rdisk(0)partition(1)

    B. scsi(1)disk(1)rdisk(0)partition(1)

    C. multi(1)disk(0)rdisk(1)partition(1)

    D. multi(1)disk(1)rdisk(0)partition(2)

15. What does the /basevideo switch in the BOOT.INI file specify?

    A. To load NT, but not to use any upper memory blocks.

    B. To load NT, using the resolution specified by your last driver configuration for the display.

    C. To load NT, but to select the standard VGA mode 640 × 480.

    D. To load NT, but not in graphics mode. Load only the command-line version of NT.

16. You're having a problem loading NT on your workstation. It appears that a driver may not be loading correctly, but you can't tell which drivers are loading and which ones aren't. What command-line switch can you add to the BOOT.INI file to see a list of the drivers loading during the boot process?

    A. /sos

    B. /basevideo

    C. /crashdebug

    D. /listdrivers

17. Which utility enables you to create an emergency repair disk?

    A. Disk Administrator

    B. ERD.EXE

    C. BOOTNT.COM

    D. RDISK.EXE

18. If you receive the message I/O Error accessing boot sector file multi(0)disk(0)rdisk(0)partition(1):\bootsect.dos, which one of the critical boot files is missing?

     A. NTLDR

     B. NTDETECT.COM

     C. BOOTSECT.DOS

     D. MSDOS.SYS

19. What is the BOOTSECT.DOS file?

     A. A copy of the information that was originally on the boot sector of the drive before NT was installed. You use it to boot an operating system other than NT.

     B. A copy of the information needed to boot a RISC-based computer.

     C. The file that detects the hardware installed on a PC with a Plug-and-Play BIOS.

     D. The file that contains the boot menu selections.

20. If your BOOTSECT.DOS file becomes corrupted, can you copy this file from another NT-based computer?

     A. Yes

     B. No

     C. Yes, if the computer is configured exactly like yours

     D. No, but you can create it from DOS using the RDISK.EXE utility

21. The boot process is considered complete when?

     A. The WinLogon dialog box appears

     B. The user presses Ctrl+Alt+Del

     C. When the user logs on

     D. After the NTDETECT.COM program runs

22. You're concerned that your boot partition is filling up with print jobs and the disk may soon run out of disk space. What can you do?

    A. Change the Registry parameter DefaultSpoolDirectory to point to a hard disk partition that has more free disk space.
    B. There is nothing that you can do. You cannot change where NT puts the spooled print jobs.
    C. Install a larger hard disk in the system.
    D. Install another hard disk in the system and span the boot partition over the newly installed disk.

23. After you make changes to the disk partitioning scheme with the Disk Administrator program, what utility should you use to update the emergency repair disk?

    A. Disk Administrator
    B. BOOTUP.EXE
    C. FDISK
    D. RDISK

Review Answers

1. A	6. A	11. C	16. A	21. C
2. C	7. C D	12. B	17. D	22. A
3. A	8. A	13. D	18. C	23. D
4. C	9. A	14. C	19. A	
5. D	10. C	15. C	20. B	

To become a Microsoft Certified Professional, candidates must pass rigorous certification exams that provide a valid and reliable measure of their technical proficiency and expertise. These closed-book exams have on-the-job relevance because they are developed with the input of professionals in the computer industry and reflect how Microsoft products are actually used in the workplace. The exams are conducted by an independent organization—Sylvan Prometric—at more than 700 Sylvan Authorized Testing Centers around the world.

Currently Microsoft offers four types of certification, based on specific areas of expertise:

▶ **Microsoft Certified Product Specialist (MCPS).** Qualified to provide installation, configuration, and support for users of at least one Microsoft desktop operating system, such as Windows 95. In addition, candidates may take additional elective exams to add areas of specialization. MCPS is the first level of expertise.

▶ **Microsoft Certified Systems Engineer (MCSE).** Qualified to effectively plan, implement, maintain, and support information systems with Microsoft Windows NT and other Microsoft advanced systems and workgroup products, such as Microsoft Office and Microsoft BackOffice. The Windows 95 exam can be used as one of the four core operating systems exams. MCSE is the second level of expertise.

▶ **Microsoft Certified Solution Developer (MCSD).** Qualified to design and develop custom business solutions using Microsoft development tools, technologies, and platforms, including Microsoft Office and Microsoft BackOffice. MCSD also is a second level of expertise, but in the area of software development.

▶ **Microsoft Certified Trainer (MCT).** Instructionally and technically qualified by Microsoft to deliver Microsoft Education Courses at Microsoft authorized sites. An MCT must be employed by a Microsoft Solution Provider Authorized Technical Education Center or a Microsoft Authorized Academic Training site.

You can find complete descriptions of all Microsoft Certifications in the Microsoft Education and Certification Roadmap on the CD-ROM that comes with this book. The following sections describe the requirements for each type of certification.

For up-to-date information about each type of certification, visit the Microsoft Training and Certification World Wide Web site at http://www.microsoft.com/tran_cert. You must have an Internet account and a WWW browser to access this information. You also can call the following sources:

▶ Microsoft Certified Professional Program: 800-636-7544

▶ Sylvan Prometric Testing Centers: 800-755-EXAM

▶ Microsoft Online Institute (MOLI): 800-449-9333

How to Become a Microsoft Certified Product Specialist (MCPS)

Becoming an MCPS requires you pass one operating system exam. Passing the "Implementing and Supporting Microsoft Windows NT Server" exam (#70-67), which this book covers, satisfies the MCPS requirement.

Windows 95 is not the only operating system you can be tested on to get your MCSP certification. The following list shows the names and exam numbers of all the operating systems from which you can choose to get your MCPS certification:

▶ Implementing and Supporting Microsoft Windows 95 #70-63

▶ Implementing and Supporting Microsoft Windows NT Workstation 4.02 #70-73

▶ Implementing and Supporting Microsoft Windows NT Workstation 3.51 #70-42

▶ Implementing and Supporting Microsoft Windows NT Server 4.0 #70-67

▶ Implementing and Supporting Microsoft Windows NT Server 3.51 #70-43

▶ Microsoft Windows for Workgroups 3.11-Desktop #70-48

▶ Microsoft Windows 3.1 #70-30

▶ Microsoft Windows Operating Systems and Services Architecture I #70-150

▶ Microsoft Windows Operating Systems and Services Architecture II #70-151

How to Become a Microsoft Certified Systems Engineer (MCSE)

MCSE candidates need to pass four operating system exams and two elective exams. The MCSE certification path is divided into two tracks: the Windows NT 3.51 track and the Windows NT 4.0 track. The "Implementing and Supporting Microsoft Windows 95" exam covered in this book can be applied to either track of the MCSE certification path.

Table A.1 shows the core requirements (four operating system exams) and the elective courses (two exams) for the Windows NT 3.51 track.

Table A.1

Windows NT 3.51 MCSE Track			
Take These Two Required Exams (Core Requirements)	Plus, Pick One Exam from the Following Operating System Exams (Core Requirement)	Plus, Pick One Exam from the Following Networking Exams (Core Requirement)	Plus, Pick Two Exams from the Following Elective Exams (Elective Requirements)
Implementing and Supporting Microsoft Windows NT Server 3.51 #70-43	Implementing and Supporting Microsoft Windows 95 #70-63	Networking Microsoft Windows for Workgroups 3.11 #70-46	Microsoft SNA Server #70-12
AND Implementing and Supporting Microsoft Windows NT Workstation 3.51 #70-42	*OR* Microsoft Windows for Workgroups 3.11-Desktop #70-48	*OR* Networking with Microsoft Windows 3.1 #70-47	*OR* Implementing and Supporting Microsoft Systems Management Server 1.0 #70-14
	OR Microsoft Windows 3.1 #70-30	*OR* Networking Essentials #70-58	*OR* Microsoft SQL Server 4.2 Database Implementation #70-21
			OR Microsoft SQL Server 4.2 Database Administration for Microsoft Windows NT #70-22
			OR System Administration for Microsoft SQL Server 6 #70-26
			OR Implementing a Database Design on Microsoft SQL Server 6 #70-27

Take These Two Required Exams (Core Requirements)	Plus, Pick One Exam from the Following Operating System Exams (Core Requirement)	Plus, Pick One Exam from the Following Networking Exams (Core Requirement)	Plus, Pick Two Exams from the Following Elective Exams (Electtive Requirements)
			OR Microsoft Mail for PC Networks 3.2-Enterprise #70-37
			OR Internetworking Microsoft TCP/IP on Microsoft Windows NT (3.5-3.51) #70-53
			OR Internetworking Microsoft TCP/IP on Microsoft Windows NT 4.0 #70-59
			OR Implementing and Supporting Microsoft Exchange Server 4.0 #70-75
			OR Implementing and Supporting Microsoft Internet Information Server #70-77
			OR Implementing and Supporting Microsoft Proxy Server 1.0 #70-78

Table A.2 shows the core requirements (four operating system exams) and elective courses (two exams) for the Windows NT 4.0 track. Tables A.1 and A.2 have many of the same exams listed, but there are distinct differences between the two. Make sure you read each track's requirements carefully.

Table A.2

Windows NT 4.0 MCSE Track			
Take These Two Required Exams (Core Requirements)	Plus, Pick One Exam from the Following Operating System Exams (Core Requirement)	Plus, Pick One Exam from the Following Networking Exams (Core Requirement)	Plus, Pick Two Exams from the Following Elective Exams (Elective Requirements)
Implementing and Supporting Microsoft Windows NT Server 4.0 #70-67	Implementing and Supporting Microsoft Windows 95 #70-63	Networking Microsoft Windows for Workgroups 3.11 #70-46	Microsoft SNA Server #70-12
AND Implementing and Supporting Microsoft Windows NT Server 4.0 in the Enterprise #70-68	*OR* Microsoft Windows for Workgroups 3.11-Desktop #70-48	*OR* Networking with Microsoft Windows 3.1 #70-47	*OR* Implementing and Supporting Microsoft Systems Management Server 1.0 #70-14
	OR Microsoft Windows 3.1 #70-30	*OR* Networking Essentials #70-58	*OR* Microsoft SQL Server 4.2 Database Implementation #70-21
	OR Implementing and Supporting Microsoft Windows NT Workstation 4.02 #70-73		*OR* Microsoft SQL Server 4.2 Database Administration for Microsoft Windows NT #70-22
			OR System Administration for Microsoft SQL Server 6 #70-26
			OR Implementing a Database Design on Microsoft SQL Server 6 #70-27

Take These Two Required Exams (Core Requirements)	Plus, Pick One Exam from the Following Operating System Exams (Core Requirement)	Plus, Pick One Exam from the Following Networking Exams (Core Requirement)	Plus, Pick Two Exams from the Following Elective Exams (Elective Requirements)
			OR Microsoft Mail for PC Networks 3.2-Enterprise #70-37
			OR Internetworking Microsoft TCP/IP on Microsoft Windows NT (3.5-3.51) #70-53
			OR Internetworking Microsoft TCP/IP on Microsoft Windows NT 4.0 #70-59
			OR Implementing and Supporting Microsoft Exchange Server 4.0 #70-75
			OR Implementing and Supporting Microsoft Internet Information Server #70-77
			OR Implementing and Supporting Microsoft Proxy Server 1.0 #70-78

How to Become a Microsoft Certified Solution Developer (MCSD)

MCSD candidates need to pass two core technology exams and two elective exams. Unfortunately, the Microsoft Windows Server exam does NOT apply toward any of these requirements. Table A.3 shows the required technology exams, plus the elective exams that apply toward obtaining the MCSD.

Warning	The "Implementing and Supporting Microsoft Windows NT Server" exam (#70-67) does NOT apply toward any of the MCSD requirements.

Table A.3

MCSD Exams and Requirements

Take These Two Core Technology Exams	Plus, Choose from Two of the Following Elective Exams
Microsoft Windows Operating Systems and Services Architecture I #70-150	Microsoft SQL Server 4.2 Database Implementation #70-21
AND Microsoft Windows Operating Systems and Services Architecture II #70-151	*OR* Developing Applications with C++ Using the Microsoft Foundation Class Library #70-24
	OR Implementing a Database Design on Microsoft SQL Server 6 #70-27
	OR Microsoft Visual Basic 3.0 for Windows-Application Development #70-50
	OR Microsoft Access 2.0 for Windows-Application Development #70-51
	OR Developing Applications with Microsoft Excel 5.0 Using Visual Basic for Applications #70-52

Take These Two Core Technology Exams	Plus, Choose from Two of the Following Elective Exams
	OR Programming in Microsoft Visual FoxPro 3.0 for Windows #70-54
	OR Programming with Microsoft Visual Basic 4.0 #70-65
	OR Microsoft Access for Windows 95 and the Microsoft Access Development Toolkit #70-69
	OR Implementing OLE in Microsoft Foundation Class Applications #70-25

Becoming a Microsoft Certified Trainer (MCT)

To understand the requirements and process for becoming a Microsoft Certified Trainer (MCT), you need to obtain the Microsoft Certified Trainer Guide document (MCTGUIDE.DOC) from the following WWW site:

http://www.microsoft.com/train_cert/download.htm

On this page, click on the hyperlink MCT GUIDE (mctguide.doc) (117k). If your WWW browser can display DOC files (Word for Windows native file format), the MCT Guide displays in the browser window. Otherwise, you need to download it and open it in Word for Windows or Windows 95 WordPad. The MCT Guide explains the four-step process to becoming an MCT. The general steps for the MCT certification are as follows:

1. Complete and mail a Microsoft Certified Trainer application to Microsoft. You must include proof of your skills for presenting instructional material. The options for doing so are described in the MCT Guide.

2. Obtain and study the Microsoft Trainer Kit for the Microsoft Official Curricula (MOC) course(s) for which you want to be

certified. Microsoft Trainer Kits can be ordered by calling 800-688-0496 in North America. Other regions should review the MCT Guide for information on how to order a Trainer Kit.

3. Pass the Microsoft certification exam for the product for which you want to be certified to teach.

4. Attend the Microsoft Official Curriculum (MOC) course for which you want to be certified. This is done so you can understand how the course is structured, how labs are completed, and how the course flows.

> You should use the preceding steps as a general overview of the MCT certification process. The actual steps you need to take are described in detail in the MCTGUIDE.DOC file on the WWW site mentioned earlier. Do not misconstrue the preceding steps as the actual process you need to take.

If you are interested in becoming an MCT, you can receive more information by visiting the Microsoft Certified Training (MCT) WWW site at http://www.microsoft.com/train_cert/mctint.htm; or call 800-688-0496.

Appendix

Study Tips

B

Self-study involves any method that you employ to learn a given topic, with the most popular being third-party books, such as the one you hold in your hand. Before you begin to study for a certification book, you should know exactly what Microsoft expects you to learn.

Pay close attention to the objectives posted for the exam. The most current objectives can always be found on the WWW site http://www.microsoft.com/train_cert. This book was written to the most current objectives, and the beginning of each chapter lists the relevant objectives for that chapter. As well, you should notice a handy tear-out card with an objective matrix that lists all objectives and the page you can turn to for information on that objective.

If you have taken any college courses in the past, you have probably learned what study habits work best for you. Nevertheless, consider the following:

▶ Study in bright light to reduce fatigue and depression.

▶ Establish a regular study schedule and stick as close to it as possible.

▶ Turn off all forms of distraction, including radios and televisions; or try studying in a quiet room.

▶ Study in the same place each time you study so your materials are always readily at hand.

▶ Take short breaks (approximately 15 minutes) every two to three hours or so. Studies have proven that your brain assimilates information better when this is allowed.

There are three ways in which humans learn information: visually, audially, and through tactile confirmation. That's why, in a college class, the students who took notes on the lectures had better recall on exam day; they took in information both audially and through tactile confirmation—writing it down.

Hence, use study techniques that reinforce information in all three ways. For example, by reading books, you are visually taking in information. By writing down the information when you test yourself, you are giving your brain tactile confirmation. Last, have someone test you outloud, so you can hear yourself giving the correct answer. Having someone test you should always be the last step in studying.

Pre-testing Yourself

Before taking the actual exam, verify that you are ready to do so by testing yourself over and over again in a variety of ways. Within this book, there are questions at the beginning and end of each chapter. On the accompanying CD-ROM, there are a number of electronic test engines that emulate the actual Microsoft test and enable you to test your knowledge of the subject areas. Use these over and over and over again, until you are consistently scoring in the 90 percent range (or better).

> This means, of course, that you can't start studying five days before the exam begins. You will need to give yourself plenty of time to read, practice, and then test yourself several times.

The New Riders' TestPrep electronic testing engine, we believe, is the best one on the market. While described in Appendix D, "All About TestPrep," here it's just important for you to know that TestPrep will prepare you for the exam in a way unparalleled by most other engines.

Hints and Tips for Doing Your Best on the Tests

In a confusing twist of terminology, when you take one of the Microsoft exams, you are said to be "writing" the exam. When you go to take the actual exam, be prepared. Arrive early and be ready to show your two forms of identification and sit before the monitor. Expect wordy questions. Although you have 90 minutes to take the exam, there are 70 questions you must answers. This gives you just over one minute to answer each question. This may sound like ample time for each question, but remember that most of the questions are lengthy word problems, which tend to ramble on for paragraphs. Your 90 minutes of exam time can be consumed very quickly.

It has been estimated that approximately 85 percent of the candidates taking their first Microsoft exam fail it. It is not so much that they are unprepared and unknowledgeable. It is more the case that they don't know what to expect and are immediately intimidated by the wordiness of the questions and the ambiguity implied in the answers.

For every exam that Microsoft offers, there is a different required passing score. The Windows 95 score is 714, or 71.4 percent. Because there are 70 questions on the exam (randomly taken from a pool of about 150), this means you must correctly answer 50 or more to pass.

Things to Watch For

When you take the exam, look closely at the number of correct choices you need to make. Some questions require that you select one correct answer; other questions have more than one correct answer. When you see radial buttons next to the answer choices, you need to remember that the answers are mutually exclusive and there is but one right answer. On the other hand, check boxes indicate that the answers are not mutually exclusive and there are multiple right answers. On the Windows 95 test, as opposed to several others, the number of correct choices is always stated on the screen. Be sure to read the questions closely to see how many correct answers you need to choose.

Also, read the questions fully. With lengthy questions, the last sentence often dramatically changes the scenario. When taking the exam, you are given pencils and two sheets of paper. If you are uncertain of what the question is saying, map out the scenario on the paper until you have it clear in your mind. You're required to turn in the scrap paper at the end of the exam.

Marking Answers for Return

You can mark questions on the actual exam and refer back to them later. If you get a wordy question that will take a long time to read and decipher, mark it and return to it when you have completed the rest of the exam. This will save you from wasting time on it and running out of time on the exam—there are only 90 minutes allotted for the exam and it ends when those 90 minutes expire, whether or not you are finished with the exam.

Attaching Notes to Test Questions

At the conclusion of the exam, before the grading takes place, you are given the opportunity to attach a message to any question. If you feel that a question was too ambiguous, or tested on knowledge you did not need to know to work with the product, take this opportunity to state your case. Unheard of is the instance where Microsoft changes a test score as a result of an attached message. However, it never hurts to try—and it helps to vent your frustration before blowing the proverbial 50-amp fuse.

Good luck.

Appendix

What's on the CD-ROM

This appendix is a brief rundown of what you'll find on the CD-ROM that comes with this book. For a more detailed description of the newly-developed TestPrep test engine, exclusive to New Riders, please see Appendix D, "All About TestPrep."

New Riders' Exclusive TestPrep

A new test engine was developed exclusively for New Riders. It is, we believe, the best test engine available, because it closely emulates the actual Microsoft exam, and it enables you to check your score by category, which helps you determine what you need to study further. For a complete description of the benefits of TestPrep, please see Appendix D.

New Riders' Exclusive FLASH! Electronic Flash Card Program

You can use the FLASH! Electronic Flash Card program to convert some of the questions in the test engine database to a fill-in-the-blank format. Run the FLASH! program and select which categories you want to test on. The engine then goes through the database in sequential order and tests your knowledge without multiple choice possibilities.

Transcender Corporation's Certification Sampler

The Transcender Corporation Certification Sampler test engine is the best-selling free-standing self-study certification product on the market today. This demonstration sampler will familiarize you with Transcender's products and help you further prepare for the exam.

MCP Endeavor Sampler

This is a testing application that helps you prepare for MCSE Certification.

Exclusive Electronic Version of Text

Use the electronic version of this book to help you search for terms or areas that you need to study. It comes complete with all figures as they appear in the book.

Copyright Information and Disclaimer

New Riders' TestPrep test engine: Copyright 1997 New Riders Publishing. All rights reserved. Made in U.S.A.

FLASH! Electronic Flash Cards: Copyright 1997 New Riders Publishing. All rights reserved. Made in U.S.A.

MCP Endeavor: Copyright 1995 VFX Technologies, Inc. All rights reserved. Made in the U.S.A.

Appendix

All About TestPrep

D

The electronic TestPrep utility included on the CD-ROM accompanying this book enables you to test your Windows NT Server 4 knowledge in a manner similar to that employed by the actual Microsoft exam. When you first start the TestPrep exam, select the number of questions you want to be asked, and the objective categories you want to be tested in. You can choose anywhere between one and 70 questions, and from one to 12 categories, which the real exam consists of.

While it is possible to maximize the TestPrep application, the default is for it to run in smaller mode so you can refer to your Windows 95 Desktop while answering questions. TestPrep uses a unique randomization sequence to ensure that each time you run the program you are presented with a different sequence of questions—this enhances your learning and prevents you from merely learning the expected answers over time without reading the question each and every time.

Question Presentation

TestPrep emulates the actual Microsoft "Implementing and Supporting Microsoft Windows NT Server" exam (#70-67), in that radial (circle) buttons are used to signify only one correct choice, while check boxes (squares) are used to imply multiple correct answers. Whenever more than one answer is correct, the number you should select is given in the wording of the question.

You can exit the program at any time by choosing the Exit key, or you can continue to the next question by choosing the Next key.

Scoring

The TestPrep Score Report uses actual numbers from the "Implementing and Supporting Microsoft Windows NT Server" exam. For Windows 95, a score of 714 or higher is considered passing; the same parameters apply to TestPrep. Each objective category is broken down into categories with a percentage correct given for each of the 12 categories.

Choose Show Me What I Missed to go back through the questions you incorrectly answered and see what the correct answers are. Choose Exit to return to the beginning of the testing routine and start over.

Non-Random Mode

You can run TestPrep in Non-Random mode, which enables you to see the same set of questions each time, or on each machine. To run TestPrep in this manner, you need to create a shortcut to the executable file, and place the CLASS parameter on the command line calling the application, after the application's name. For example:

```
C:\TESTENG\70_63.EXE CLASS
```

Now, when you run TestPrep, the same sequence of questions will appear each and every time. To change the sequence but stay in Non-Random mode (for example, if you're in a classroom setting, where it is important that everyone see the same questions), choose Help, Class Mode on the main screen. This lets you enter a number from 1 to 8 to select a predefined sequence of questions.

Instructor Mode

To run TestPrep in Instructor mode (seeing the same set of questions each time, or on each machine), create a shortcut to the executable file, and place the INSTR parameter following CLASS on the command line calling the application, after the application's name. For example:

```
C:\TESTENG\70_63.EXE CLASS INSTR
```

Now, when you run TestPrep, the same sequence of questions will appear each and every time. Additionally, the correct answer will be marked already, and the objective category from which the question is coming will be given in the question. To change the sequence of questions that appear, choose Help, Class Mode on the main screen. This prompts you to enter a number from 1 to 8 to select a predefined sequence of questions; increment that by 100 and the sequence will be presented in Instructor mode.

Flash Cards

As a further learning aid, you can use the FLASH! Electronic Flash Cards program to convert some of the questions in the database into a fill-in-the-blank format. Run the FLASH! program and select the categories on which you want to be tested. The engine then goes through the database in sequential order and tests your knowledge without multiple choice possibilities.

I n d e x

Symbols

% Disk Time counter
  LogicalDisk object, 408
  PhysicalDisk object, 408
% Processor Time counter (Processor object), 407

A

/a switch (NTBACKUP command), 476
access
  access tokens, 317
  Client Access License, *see* CAL
  Directory Replication, denials, 138
  NTFS file system, auditing, 299-301
  restricting (Event Viewer), 451
  troubleshooting, 471-472
Access Control Entries (ACEs), 301
Access Control List, *see* ACLs
Access Through Share Permissions dialog box, 287
Access Through Share (ATS), 287
access tokens, 317
Accessories command (Programs menu), 366
Account command (Policies menu), 246
Account Policy dialog box, 243

accounts
  groups, *see* groups
  member servers, 233
  NTFS file system, ownership, 297-299
  User Manager for Domains, 235-237
    auditing, 250
    creating user accounts, 237-240
    policies, 243-248
    properties, 243
    rights, 248-250
    trust relationships, 251
  users, *see* user accounts
  Workstation, 233-234
    Administrator account, 234-235
    Guest account, 235
    local domain, compared, 240
ACEs (Access Control Entries), 301
ACLs (Access Control List), 301
  discretionary access, 302
  NTFS file systems (Security Reference Monitor), 316-317
  see also permissions
active partitions, 17-18
adapter cards
  bindings, *see* bindings
  configuring (Control Panel), 108-109

frame types
 configuring, 112-113
 detecting, 111
 Networking, installation, 69-70
adapters
 DHCP (Dynamic Host Configuration
  Protocol), TCP/IP installation, 120
 network, configuring, 126
 SCSI
  installing, 149, 431
  removing, 150
  troubleshooting, 431
 video display, configuring, 156
Add (directory permissions), 303
Add Key command (Edit menu), 98
Add Key dialog box, 98
Add Printer Wizard, 182
 installing printers, 183-184
 network print servers, 185
Add Users and Groups dialog
 box, 249, 310
Add Value command (Edit menu), 97
Add Value dialog box, 97
addresses (IP), 29, 114
 default gateways, 116
 hostids, 114
 InterNIC (Internet Network
  Information Center), 117
 netids, 114
 NICs, 114
 rules, 117-118
 subnet masks, 115-116
ADMIN$ shares, 291
administration tools, 271-273
 Event Viewer, *see* Event Viewer
 License Manager, 141-142
 Network Monitor, *see* Network
  Monitor, 467
 Registry, 83
 Server Manager, viewing sharing
  statistics, 292
 sharing, 272

System Policy Editor, *see* System
 Policy Editor
Windows 95, 271
Workstation, 272
User Manager for Domains, *see* User
 Manager for Domains
Administrative Tools commands
 (Programs menu), 272
Administrators
 domain local groups, 229-230
 passwords, installation, 68
 Workstation, 234-235
Admins, Domain global group, 231
Advanced IP Addressing dialog box, 120
alerts (crash recovery), 102
Alerts dialog box, 292
Allow (Security Reference Monitor), 316
appearance (computer display
 setting), 155
application log (Event Viewer), 451
applications
 Control Panel, *see* Control Panel
 Event Viewer, *see* Event Viewer
 optimizing performance, 389-390
 services, 127-128
  CAL (Client Access License), 139-142
  Computer Browser, 142-144
  CSNW, see CSNW
  diagnostics, 456
  *Directory Replication, see Directory
   Replication*
  disabling, 394-395
  *DSMN (Directory Service Manager
   for NetWare), 352-353*
  *FPNW (File and Print Services for
   NetWare), 352*
  Gateway, 345
  network services, 130
  optimizing, 399-401
  RAS (Remote Access Service), see RAS
  Server service, 127
  Spooler, 178

UPS, 127

WINS, see WINS

Workstation service, 127

TestPrep utility, 505

FLASH! Electronic Flash Cards, 507

Instructor mode, 506-507

Non-Random mode, 506

question set up, 505

scoring, 506

Windows 95 support, 6

Workstation support, 8

Assign Drive Letter command (Tools menu), 169

ATS (Access Through Share), permissions, 287

attributes (Compression), 282

Audit Policy dialog box, 250

auditing

Event Viewer, 450

NTFS file system, access, 299-301

RAS (Remote Access Service), 357

User Manager for Domains, 250

Auditing command (Policy menu), 250

authentication, RAS (Remote Access Service), 466

AUTOCHK.EXE, booting, 440

AUTOCONV.EXE, booting, 440

autodialing

Dial-Up Networking application, 373

RAS (Remote Access Service), 466

AUTOEXEC.NCF file, 113

AUTOEXEC.NT (emergency repair disk), 445

automatic devices (Control Panel), 146

automatic reboot, crash recovery, 102

availability settings (printers), 194

Available Bytes counter (Memory Object), 407

Available Hardware Profiles list, 102

Avg. Disk Queue Length counter (PhysicalDisk object), 408

B

/B switch (WINNT.EXE), 59

\B\M print escape code, 191

\B\S print escape code, 191

backgrounds, configuring, 155

backing up

fault tolerance, 473-477

Registry, 458-461

troubleshooting, 431

BackOffice, support, 10

backup browsers, 143

Backup Domain Controller (BDC), 55-56

Backup Information dialog box, 473

Backup Operators, 227, 231

/basevideo switch (BOOT.INI), 438

BDC (Backup Domain Controller), 55-56

bindings, 109

configuring (Control Panel), 109

removing (Network application), 394

[boot loader] section (BOOT.INI), 436-437

default parameter, 437

timeout parameter, 437

boot partitions, 18, 165-166

BOOT.INI

setting defaults, 101

switches, 438-440

/basevideo, 438

/crashdebug, 439

/maxmem, 440

/nodebug, 439

/noserialmice, 439

/scsiordinal, 440

/sos, 439

troubleshooting, 435-440

[boot loader] section, 436-437

Emergency Repair Process, 443-444

missing files, 443-444

[operating systems] section, 437-438

booting

boot disks, 444

Devices application (Control Panel), 146

emergency repair, inspecting, 448-449

FAT (File Allocation Table) file system, 20

multiple, installation requirements, 53-55

Registry, 83

setting defaults (Control Panel), 101

troubleshooting, 432-433

BOOT.INI, see BOOT.INI

BOOTSECT.DOS, 435

control sets, 442-443

Intel computers, 433-434

kernel initialization, 440

MBR (Master Boot Record), 433

POST (Power On Self Test), 433

RISC-based computers, 435

services, loading, 440-441

Windows interface, 441-442

BOOTSECT.DOS, troubleshooting, 435

bottlenecks, detecting (Performance Monitor), 404-405

Break Mirror command (Fault Tolerance menu), 476

Briefcase menu commands (Update All), 296

browsers (Computer Browser service), 142-144

built-in groups, *see* groups

Bytes Total/sec counter (Server object), 409

C

/C switch (WINNT.EXE), 61-63

C$ shares, 290

cable connections, print troubleshooting, 461

caching, 10

CAL (Client Access License)

License Manager, 141-142

Licensing application (Control Panel), 140-141

Per Seat mode, 139

Per Server mode, 139

callback, RAS (Remote Access Service), 357, 466

Caps Lock key, troubleshooting, 471

captured statistics (Network Monitor), 469

CD ROM

device drivers

installing, 149

removing, 150

installation, 57

LAN Manager 2.2c systems, 33-35

Network Client 3.0, 33

Resource Guide, 99

troubleshooting, 431

certification process, 489-490

MCPS (Microsoft Certified Product Specialist), 489-491

MCSD (Microsoft Certified Solution Developer), 490, 496-497

MCSE (Microsoft Certified Systems Engineer), 489, 491-495

MCT (Microsoft Certified Trainer), 490, 497-498

Change

ATS permission, 288

directory permissions, 303

file permissions, 306

Change Password dialog box, 238

Characterization File (printing DLL), 176

child windows (Registry Editor), 86-87

HKEY_CLASSES_ROOT, 95

HKEY_CURRENT_CONFIG, 96

HKEY_CURRENT_USER, 96

HKEY_LOCAL_MACHINE, 87-95

HKEY_USERS, 96

values, 87

CHKDSK, 171

Choose Licensing Mode dialog box, 140

class subnet masks, 115-116

Classes subkey (Registry Editor), 91-93

Client Access License, *see* CAL
Client Administrator (Network), 76-80
   installation disk sets, creating, 79-80
   startup disks, creating, 77-79
Client Services for NetWare, *see* CSNW
client software
clients, 32-34
   administration tools, 271-273
     sharing, 272
     Windows 95, 271-272
     Workstation, 272
   configuring (Server), 202-203
   LAN Manager 2.2c systems, 33-35
   Network Client 3.0, 33
   protocols, 34, 203
   Server/Workstation, compared, 9
cluster size, installation, 53
colors, customizing (Disk
  Administrator), 160
Colors and Patterns command (Options
  menu), 160
Colors and Patterns dialog box, 160
command prompt, sharing directories,
  289-290
commands
   Briefcase menu (Update All), 296
   COMPACT.EXE, 283-284
   diskperf, 408
   Edit menu
     Add Key, 98
     Add Value, 97
   Fault Tolerance menu
     Break Mirror, 476
     Create Stripe Set with Parity, 173
     Establish Mirror, 172
     Regenerate, 477
   File menu
     Compress, 281
     Connect, 265
     Document Defaults, 186

New Policy, 270
Open Registry, 264
Log menu (Save As), 451
NET SHARE, 289-290
NET USE, 58, 351
NET VIEW, 351
NTBACKUP switches, 475
Operations menu (Restore), 474
Options menu
   Colors and Patterns, 160
   Region Display, 160
Options menu (Registry Editor)
   Confirm on Delete, 85
   Read Only Mode, 85
Partition menu
   Commit Changes Now, 162, 166
   Configuration, 167
   Create, 161
   Create Extended, 161
   Create Stripe Set, 164
   Create Volume Set, 161
   Delete, 167
   Extend Volume Set, 163
   Mark Active, 166
Policy menu
   Account, 246
   Auditing, 250
   Trust Relationships, 251
   User Rights, 248
Programs menu
   Accessories, 366
   Administrative Tools, 272
Registry menu
   Print Subtree, 99
   Restore Key, 461
   Restore Volatile, 461
   Save Key, 461
   Save Subtree As, 99
Settings menu (Control Panel), 100
Sharing, 287

Tools menu
  Assign Drive Letter, 169
  Format, 168
  Properties, 171
User menu
  New Local Group, 310
  Properties, 247
  Rename, 252
  Select Domain, 235
View menu
  Details, 287
  Find Key, 98
Commit Changes Now command (Partition menu), 162, 166
COMPACT.EXE command, 283-284
components (software), removing, 393-395
Compress command (File menu), 281
compression
  COMPACT.EXE command, 283-284
  directories, 284-285
  file systems, 23
  NTFS file system, 22, 280-282
Compression attribute, 282
Computer Browser,
Computer Browser service, 142-144, 399
computer name registration, installation, 67
CONFIG.NT (emergency repair disk), 445
Configuration command (Partition menu), 167
Configure Gateway dialog box, 345
configuring
  disk configuration, *see* disk configuration
  Event Viewer, 451-452
  hard disks, 158-159, 167-168
    display customization, 159-160
    partitioning, 160-163
  modems (locations), 153
  network adapters (Control Panel), 126
  network computers (System Policy Editor), 265-267

NWLink protocol (Control Panel), 112-113
printers, 186-188
  document settings, 186-188
  forms, 188-189
  ports, 189, 192
  properties, 190-200
  separating print jobs, 190-192
  RAS (Remote Access Service), 363-366
  Registry, *see* Registry
  roaming profiles, 258-259
  screen savers, 155
  Server, 10, 202-203
  video display adapter, 156
  virtual memory, 397-398
  wallpaper, 155
Confirm on Delete command (Options menu; Registry Editor), 85
Connect command (File menu), 265
Connect to Printer dialog box, 185
connectivity
  NetWare, 342, 355-356
    commands, 351
    CSNW (Client Services for NetWare), 347-349
    DSMN (Directory Service Manager for NetWare), 352-353
    FPNW (File and Print Services for NetWare), 352
    GSNW (Gateway Services for NetWare), 342-347
    migration, 353-354
    server access, 354
  RAS, 357
  troubleshooting, 466-467
    Network Monitor, 467-471
Control Panel, 99-100
  Devices application, 145-147
    automatic devices, 146
    boot devices, 146
    manual devices, 146
    system devices, 146

Dial-Up Networking Monitor, 371, 465

Display application, 155-157

Keyboard application, 153-154

Licensing application, 140-141

Modems application, 151-153

Mouse application, 154-155

Multimedia application (MMSYS.CPL), 147

Network application, 106-109
  adapter cards, configuring, 108-109
  adapters, configuring, 126
  bindings, 109, 394
  GSNW installation, 344
  identification settings, 106
  network services settings, 107
  NWLink protocol, 110-113
  protocols, configuring, 108
  RAS, installing, 361-366
  Server service, optimizing, 398-399
  services, 130
  TCP/IP, see TCP/IP

opening, 100

PC Card application, 151

Ports application (PORTS.CPL), 147-148

Printers folder, 181-182

Registry, 82

SCSI Adapters, 149-150

Server application, 291-294

Services application, 128-129
  Directory Replication, see Directory Replication
  hardware profile, 129
  security, 129
  Startup type, 128
  stopping services, 129

System application, 100
  BOOT.INI, 437
  booting, setting defaults, 101
  crash recovery, 101-102
  displaying information, 105
  environment variables, 103-105

hardware profiles, 102-103, 261-262
  performance enhancement, 105
  Recovery utility, 457
  roaming profiles, 258
  Virtual Memory Manager, 396

Tape Devices, 150-151

UPS application (UPS.CPL), 148-149

Control Panel command (Settings menu), 100

Control Panel Ports dialog box, 148

control sets, boot troubleshooting, 442-443
  LastKnownGood, 442-443

ControlSets (Registry Editor), 93-96

converting file systems, 23

Copy Profile dialog box, 102, 261

copying
  files, 276
  user accounts, 253

correct answers (multiple), study tips, 501-502

corruption (hard disks), 66

counters (Performance Monitor), 403, 405-406
  LogicalDisk object
    % Disk Time, 408
    Disk Queue Length, 408
  Memory Object, 407
    Available Bytes, 407
    Pages/sec, 407
  Memory object, 406
  Network object, 406
  Physical Disk object, 406, 408
    % Disk Time, 408
    Avg. Disk Queue Length, 408
  Processor object, 406
    % Processor Time, 407
    Interrupts/sec, 407
    System: Processor Queue Length, 407
  Server object, 406, 408-409
    Bytes Total/sec, 409
    pool failure, 409

crash recovery (Control Panel), 101

/crashdebug switch (BOOT.INI), 439

crashes

crash recovery (Control Panel), 101

/crashdebug switch (BOOT.INI), 439

print troubleshooting, 464

Create command (Partition menu), 161

Create Extended command (Partition menu), 161

Create Extended dialog box, 161

Create Primary Partition dialog box, 161

Create Stripe Set command (Partition menu), 164

Create Stripe Set dialog box, 164

Create Stripe Set with Parity command (Fault Tolerance menu), 173

Create Stripe Set with Parity dialog box, 173

Create Volume Set command (Partition menu), 161

Create Volume Set dialog box, 161

CSNW (Client Services for NetWare), 347-349

installing, 347

passwords, setting, 348

printing, setting, 349

servers

connecting, 349-350

selecting, 347

customizing

directory permissions, 305

hard disks, displays, 159

installation (WINNT.EXE), 59-61

logons (System Policy Editor), 267

see also GSNW

D

\D print escape code, 191

/d switch (NTBACKUP command), 476

database servers, optimizing, 389

date/time, installation settings, 73

debugging

crash recovery, 102

Recovery utility, 457-458

Default Document Properties dialog box, 186

default gateways (IP address), 116

default parameter (BOOT.INI), 437

DEFAULT._ (emergency repair disk), 445

[DefaultIPInfo], Networking protocols installation, 71

DefaultSpoolDirectory value, 463

Delete command (Partition menu), 167

/DELETE switch (NET SHARE command), 290

deleting

disabling (user accounts), compared, 253-255

files (My Briefcase), 295-297

local groups, 311

partitioning changes, 167

Registry keys, 98

denials (Security Reference Monitor), 316

Description subkey (Registry Editor), 88-89

descriptions (user accounts), creating, 238

Details command (View menu), 287

Device dialog box, 146

device drivers

CD-ROM

installing, 149

removing, 150

PCMCIA, 151

printing, 176-177

DLLs (dynamic link libraries), 176

printers, 200

troubleshooting, 462

removing (optimization), 393-395

tape drive

installing, 150

removing, 151

DeviceMap subkey (Registry Editor), 89

devices

    diagnostics, 457

    printing, 174

Devices application (Control Panel), 145-147

    automatic devices, 146

    boot devices, 146

    manual devices, 146

    system devices, 146

DHCP (Dynamic Host Configuration Protocol), 29-30, 118-121

diagnostics, 455-457

Dial-Up Networking dialog box, 366

Dial-Up Networking Monitor (Control Panel), 366-373

    appearance, 371

    autodial, 373

    callback, 371

    dialing options, 371

    logon preferences, 372

    phonebook entries, 367, 372

        creating, 367-369

        editing, 371-375

        shortcuts, creating, 371

    RAS (Remote Access Service), 465

Dialin (user accounts), 240

Dialing Properties dialog box, 361

dialog boxes

    Access Through Share Permissions, 287

    Account Policy, 243

    Add Key, 98

    Add Users and Groups, 249, 310

    Add Value, 97

    Advanced IP Addressing, 120

    Alerts, 292

    Audit Policy, 250

    Backup Information, 473

    Change Password, 238

    Choose Licensing Mode, 140

    Colors and Patterns, 160

    Configure Gateway, 345

    Connect to Printer, 185

    Control Panel Ports, 148

    Copy Profile, 102, 261

    Create Extended, 161

    Create Primary Partition, 161

    Create Stripe Set, 164

    Create Stripe Set with Parity, 173

    Create Volume Set, 161

    Default Document Properties, 186

    Device, 146

    Dial-Up Networking, 366

    Dialing Properties, 361

    Directory Auditing, 300

    Directory Export, 134

    Directory Replication, 134, 292

    Disk Properties, 170

    Display Properties, 155

    Display Type, 156

    Enter Network Credentials, 350

    Event Detail, 453

    Event Log Settings, 451

    File Auditing, 300

    File Permissions, 305

    Format, 168

    Gateway Service for NetWare, 349

    Install New Modem, 151

    Keyboard Properties, 153

    Local Computer Properties, 264

    Logon preferences, 373

    Manage Exported Directories, 135

    Manage Imported Directories, 137

    Modem Properties, 151, 153

    Network Access Order, 350

    Network Card Setup, 126

    Network Client Administrator, 79, 272

    New Global Group, 242

    New Local Group, 242, 310

    New Phonebook Entry, 367

    New User, 237

    NWLink IPX/SPX Properties, 110

Open Resources, 292

Owner, 298

RAS Server IPX Configuration, 365

RAS Server NetBEUI Configuration, 363

RAS Server TCP/IP Configuration, 364

Region Display Options, 160

Remote Access Setup, 362

Replication Configuration, 140

Restore Information, 474

SCSI Adapters, 149

Select Domain, 134

Select Network Adapter, 126

Select Network Service, 130

Select Preferred Server for NetWare, 348

Server, 398

Service, 136

Services, 128

Share Network Client Installation
  Filbox, 78

Shared Directories, 293

Shared Resources, 292

String Editor, 98

System Properties, 100

TCP/IP Properties, 119

Update My Briefcase, 296

User Environment Profile, 240

User Preferences, 371

User Properties, 243, 251

User Rights Policy, 248

Users Sessions, 292

Virtual Memory, 396

Volume Properties, 170

Welcome, 441

Windows NT Diagnostics, 455

disconnecting users (User Manager for
Domains), 247

directories

  auditing, 300

  compression, 284-285

  emergency repair

    disk comparison, 444-445

    see also emergency repair

file systems, 23

naming, installation, 65-66

permissions, 303-305

  customizing, 305

  file conflicts, 313-315

  setting, 307-308

REPAIR, installation, 75

shared

  persistant connections, 275

  referring, 274

  viewing, 274

sharing, 285-286

  ADMIN$ shares, 291

  C$ shares, 290

  command prompt, 289-290

  Explorer, 286-289

  hiding shares, 290

  My Computer, 286-289

Directory Auditing dialog box, 300

Directory Export dialog box, 134

Directory Replication, 131-132

  export servers, 131, 133-136

  import computers, 131

    configuring, 136-137

    Startup Type frame, 136

  locking subdirectories, 135

  optimizing, 399

  parameters, 131-146

  passwords

    non-expiring, 133

  troubleshooting, 137-139

Directory Replication dialog box, 134, 292

Directory Service Manager for NetWare,
see DSMN

disabling

  local groups, 311

  user accounts, 239, 254-255

discretionary access, 302

Disk Administrator (hard disks), 160-163

  configuring, 167-168

  customizing display, 159-160

fault tolerance (RAID), 171-173
  disk mirroring, 172
  stripe set with parity, 172-173
partitioning, 160-163
  active marking, 166
  boot partitions, 165-166
  deleting, 167
  drive letters, assigning, 169-170
  extended partitions, 161
  formatting, 168-169
  hiding, 169
  primary partitions, 160-161
  properties, 170-171
  saving changes, 166-167
  security, 173
  stripe sets, 163-165
  stripe sets with parity, 164
  system partitions, 165-166
  volume sets, 161-163
starting, 158-159
disk configuration, 14-15
  fault tolerance, 24-27
  file systems, 19, 23-24
    FAT (File Allocation Table), 19-21
    NTFS (New Technology File System), 21-23
  partitioning, 15-16
    boot partitions, 18
    extended partitions, 16-17
    primary partitions, 16-17
    system partitions, 18
disk duplexing, 26
Disk Manager, 53
Disk Properties dialog box, 170
Disk Queue Length counter (LogicalDisk object), 408
disk striping with parity, 26-27
diskperf command, 408
disks
  configuration, *see* disk configuration
  drives, diagnostics, 456
  duplexing, 26

emergency repair
  creating, 446
  directory, compared, 444-445
  files, 444-445
  installation, 68
  see also emergency repair
hard disks
  configuring, 158-159
  display, customizing, 159-160
  partitioning, see partitioning
  upgrading, 392
installation
  EIDE drives, 53
  examining, 66
  IDE drives, 53
  space, 431
mirroring, *see* mirrors
Performance Monitor, 407-408
  Physical Disk object, see Physical Disk object
Server requirements (Intel), 52
Display application (Control Panel), 155-157
Display Properties dialog box, 155
Display Type dialog box, 156
DLLs (dynamic link libraries)
  printing device drivers, 176-177
  SERVICES.EXE, 441-442
  SFMPSPRT.DLL, 180
  WINPRINT.DLL, 179-180
DNS (Domain Name System), 29-30, 123
Document Defaults command (File menu), 186
documents, printing
  mismatched, 195
  settings, 186-188
Domain Admins group, 228, 231
domain master browsers, 143
Domain Name System (DNS), 29-30, 123
domains, 11, 13-14

BDC (Backup Domain Controller)

controller connections, troubleshooting, 432

Directory Replication, export servers, 134

global groups, 231

Domain Admins, 231

Guests, 232

Users, 231

local account, 240

local groups, 229

Administrators, 229-230

Backup Operators, 231

Guest groups, 230

Print Operators, 231

Replicator, 231

Server Operators, 231

Users group, 230

member servers, 56

name errors, installation troubleshooting, 432

Networking, installation, 72

PDC (Primary Domain Controller), 55

stand-alone servers, 55

DOS

installation, multi-booting requirements, 54

LAN MAN 2.2c protocols, 34

Network Client protocols, 34

NTFS file systems, 20

primary partitions, 16

printing, 202

drive letters (partitions), assigning, 169-170

drivers, *see* device drivers

DRIVERS.EXE (Resource Kit), 441

DSMN (Directory Service Manager for NetWare), 352-353

dual-booting

FAT file system (File Allocation Table), 20, 277

Dumpexam.exe, 458

DUN, *see* Dial-Up Networking application

duplexing (disks), 26

Dynamic Host Configuration Protocol, *see* DHCP

dynamic link libraries, *see* DLLs

E

\E print escape code, 191

Edit menu commands

Add Key, 98

Add Value, 97

editing

Dial-Up Networking application (phonebook entries), 371-375

Registry (REGEDT32.EXE), 84-87, 97-98

HKEY_CLASSES_ROOT, 95

HKEY_CURRENT_CONFIG, 96

HKEY_CURRENT_USER, 96

HKEY_LOCAL_MACHINE, 87-95

HKEY_USERS, 96

values, 87

System Policy Editor, 262

Policy File mode, 268-271

Registry mode, 262-268

EIDE drives, installation, 53

emergency repair, 444

BOOT.INI, 443-444

boot files, inspecting, 448

directory/disk, compared, 444-445

disk

creating, 446

directory, compared, 444-445

files, 444-445

installation, 68

Registry files, inspecting, 447

RISK.EXE, 445-446

creating disk, 446

updating information, 446

starting, 447

Windows NT files, inspecting, 448

EMF (Enhanced Metafile), 179

encryption, RAS (Remote Access Service), 358

Enhanced Metafile, 179

Enter Network Credentials dialog box, 350

environment variables (Control Panel)

changing, 103-104

creating, 104

deleting, 105

diagnostics, 457

ERD (Emergency Repair Disk), *see* emergency repair; disk

errors, system log view (Event Viewer), 450

escape codes, printing, 191-192

Establish Mirror command (Fault Tolerance menu), 172

Event Detail dialog box, 453

Event Log Settings dialog box, 451

Event Viewer

application log, 451

configuring, 451-452

Directory Replication errors, 138

RAS (Remote Access Service), 465-466

security log, 450-451

system log, 449-450

troubleshooting, 449-457

event descriptions, 453-454

filtering events, 454-455

expiration (user accounts), 239-240

Explorer

ATS permissions, 288-289

NTFS file systems, auditing, 299

sharing directories, 286-289

export servers (Directory Replication), 131, 133-136

Extend Volume Set command (Partition menu), 163

extending

partitions, 16-17, 161

volume sets, 163

F

\F print escape code, 191

/F switch (WINNT.EXE), 61

failure audits (Event Viewer), 450

FAT (File Allocation Table) file system, 19-21

conserving space, 20

converting partition (NTFS), 279

dual-booting, 20

efficiency, 20

long names, 276-278

naming files, 19-20

security, 20

selecting, installation, 65

speed, 20

Windows 95, 6

volume sets, 161

FAT32 file system, 6

fault tolerance (RAID), 24, 171-173

backing up, 473

disk mirroring, 25-26, 172

mirrored partitions, fixing, 476

Registry, 459

restoring, 473-475

stripe set with parity, 26-27, 172-173, 476-477

troubleshooting, 472-477

upgrading hardware, 392-393

Fault Tolerance menu commands

Break Mirror, 476

Create Stripe Set with Parity, 173

Establish Mirror, 172

Regenerate, 477

File Allocation Table, *see* FAT file system

File and Print Services for NetWare, *see* FPNW

File Auditing dialog box, 300

file locks, viewing statistics, 292

File menu commands

Compress, 281

Connect, 265

Document Defaults, 186
New Policy, 270
Open Registry, 264
File Permissions dialog box, 305
file resources, 273-274
  COMPACT.EXE command, 283-284
  copying files, 276
  directory compression, 284-285
  FAT file system, long names, 276-278
  moving files, 276
  NTFS file system
    compression, 280-282
    Fat partition conversion, 279
    long names, 279
    uncompressing, 282
  UNC (Universal Naming Convention), 274-275
file servers, optimizing, 388
file systems, 19, 23-24
  directories, 23
  FAT (File Allocation Table), 19-21
    conserving space, 20
    converting partition (NTFS), 279
    dual-booting, 20
    efficiency, 20
    long names, 276-278
    naming files, 19-20
    security, 20
    selecting, installation, 65
    speed, 20
    Windows 95, 6
    volume sets, 161
  FAT32
    support, 6
  NTFS (New Technology File System), 21-23
    compression, 22
    MS-DOS support, 20
    naming files, 22
    security, 22
    Windows 95 support, 20

security, 23
selecting, installation, 65
transaction tracking, 23
files
  AUTOEXEC.NCF file, 113
  copying, 276
  emergency repair disk, 444-445, 448-449
  moving, 276
  My Briefcase, 294-297
    deleting files, 295
    merging changes, 295-297
    opening, 295
    replacing changes, 295-297
    skipping updates, 295-297
  NTConfig.pol, 268
  ntuser.dat, 256
  open, viewing statistics, 291
  permissions, 305-306
    directory conflicts, 313-315
    setting, 307-308
  REGENTRY.HLP, 99
files system driver, 10
filtering (PPTP), RAS (Remote Access Service), 358
Find Key command (View menu), 98
FLASH! Electronic Flash Cards (TestPrep utility), 507
folders (Printers), 181-182
Format command (Tools menu), 168
Format dialog box, 168
formatting
  partitions
    Disk Administrator, 168-169
    file systems, see file systems
  volume sets, 161-162
forms (printer), creating, 189
FPNW (File and Print Services for NetWare), 352
fragmentation (file systems), 23
frame types (adapter cards)
  configuring, 112-113
  detecting, 111

free space, WINNT.EXE installation check, 61

ftp (file transfer protocol) sites (Microsoft), 99

Full Control
ATS permissions, 288
directory permissions, 304
file permissions, 306

full names (user accounts), creating, 238

G

Gateway service, 345

Gateway Service for NetWare dialog box, 349

Gateway Services for NetWare, *see* GSNW

gateways
Gateway Services for NetWare, *see* GSNW
IP address, 116

global groups, 228
creating (User Manager for Domains), 242-243
domain, 231
Domain Admins group, 228, 231
Guests, 232
Users, 231
member servers, 233
workstations, 233

Graph pane (Network Monitor), 468

groups, 226
Backup Operators, 227
creating (User Manager for Domains), 242-243
global, 228, 231-232
local, 227-228, 240
adding/removing members, 311
built-in groups, comparing, 309
deleting, 311
disabling, 311
domain, 229-231
member servers, 232-234

permissions, assigning, 308-309
renaming, 311
Workstations, 232-234
permissions, *see* permissions
user accounts, creating, 239
User Manager for Domains, 235-237
creating user accounts, 237-240
properties, 243
rights, 248-250
see also accounts

GSNW (Gateway Services for NetWare), 342-347
gateway enabling, 345-346
installing, 344
see also CSNW

GuardTime REG_WORD value (Directory Replicator), 131

Guest account (Workstation), 235

Guest groups (domain local groups), 230, 232

H

\H<code> print escape code, 191

HAL (Hardware Abstraction Layer), boot troubleshooting, 434

handles (Security Reference Monitor), 317

hard disks
configuring, 158-159, 167-168
customizing display, 159-160
partitioning, 160-163
fault tolerance (RAID), 171-173
disk mirroring, 172
stripe set with parity, 172-173
installation
EIDE drives, 53
examining, 66
IDE drives, 53
partitioning
active marking, 166
boot partitions, 165-166

deleting, 167
drive letters, assigning, 169-170
formatting, 168-169
hiding, 169
properties, 170-171
saving changes, 166-167
security, 173
stripe sets, 163-165
stripe sets with parity, 164
system partitions, 165-166
Server requirements (Intel), 52
hardware
    installation
        detecting, 64
        requirements, 53
    Performance Monitor, 403
    upgrading, 391-393
        disks, 392
        fault tolerance, 392-393
        memory, 391-392
        networks, 392
        processors, 391
Hardware Abstraction Layer, *see* HAL
Hardware Compatibility List, 51-52
Hardware key (Registry Editor), 88-95
hardware profiles (Control Panel),
    102-103, 260-262
    creating, 102
    organizing, 103
    Services application, 129
HCL (Hardware Compatibility List), 51-52
help (REGENTRY.HLP file), 99
hiding
    partitions, 169
    shared directories, 290
hives, 458-460
HKEY_CLASSES_ROOT (Registry
    Editor), 95
HKEY_CURRENT_CONFIG (Registry
    Editor), 96
HKEY_CURRENT_USER (Registry
    Editor), 96

HKEY_LOCAL_MACHINE (Registry
    Editor), 87-95
    Hardware key, 88-95
    SAM key, 90
    SECURITY key, 90
    SOFTWARE key, 90-93
    SYSTEM key, 93-95
HKEY_USERS (Registry Editor), 96
home directories
    creating, 241-242
    naming, 242
hostids (IP address), 114
    uniqueness, 118
    zero settings, 117
    see also subnet masks
hosts (security), RAS (Remote Access
    Service), 358
hot fixing (file systems), 23
hours (user accounts), creating, 239

I-J

\l print escape code, 191
ICMP (Internet Control Message
    Protocol), Ping utility, 123-125, 467
IDE drives, installation, 53
identification settings (Control Panel), 106
import computers (Directory
    Replication), 131
    configuring, 136-137
    Startup Type frame, 136
information events, system log view
    (Event Viewer), 450
INI files
    BOOT.INI, *see* BOOT.INI
    see also Registry
Install New Modem dialog box, 151
installing
    CD-ROM
        device drivers, 149
        source, 57

computer name registration, 67

CSNW (Client Services for NetWare), 347

date/time settings, 73

device drivers
  PCMCIA, 151
  tape drive, 150

EIDE drives, 53

emergency repair
  directory, 444
  disk, 68

GSNW (Gateway Services for NetWare), 344

HCL (Hardware Compatibility List), 51-52

IDE drives, 53

Intel platform
  Pentium patch, 74-75
  requirements, 52-53

licensing modes, 67

modems, 151-152

name registration, 67

Network Client Administrator, 76-80
  installation disk sets, creating, 79-80
  startup disks, creating, 77-79

network installs, 57-61

Network Monitor, 467

Networking, 69-73
  adapter cards, 69-70
  domains, 72
  protocols, 70-71
  workgroups, 72

NWLink protocol
  adapter card frame types, 110-113
  Control Panel, 110-112

password setup, 68

pre-installation, 62-66
  file systems, selecting, 65
  hard disk examination, 66
  hardware detection, 64
  partitions, selecting, 64
  rebooting, 66

root directory, naming, 65-66
storage devices, detecting, 63-64

print monitors, 180-181

printers, 182-185

RAS (Remote Access Service), 361-366

REPAIR directory, 75

requirements
  hardware, 53
  multi-booting, 53-55

SCSI adapters, 149

Server, 50-51

server roles, 55-56

TCP/IP
  Control Panel, 118
  DHCP, 118-121
  manually, 121

troubleshooting, 431-432

uninstalling, 75-76

video display, 74

Instructor mode (TestPrep utility), 506-507

Intel computers
  installation
    Pentium patch, 74-75
    requirements, 52-53
  troubleshooting (booting), 433-434
  Windows 95, 6

Internet
  connections, 9
  protocols, *see* protocols

Internet Control Message Protocol, *see* ICMP

Internet Network Information Center, *see* InterNIC

Internet Protocol address, *see* IP address

InterNIC (Internet Network Information Center), 117-118

interoperating (NetWare), 342, 355-356
  commands, 351
  CSNW (Client Services for NetWare), 347-349
  DSMN (Directory Service Manager for NetWare), 352-353

FPNW (File and Print Services for NetWare), 352

GSNW (Gateway Services for NetWare), 342-347

migration, 353-354

server access, 354

Interrupts/sec counter (Processor object), 407

Interval REG_WORD value (Directory Replicator), 131

IP (Internet protocol) address, 29, 114

default gateways, 116

hostids, 114

InterNIC (Internet Network Information Center), 117

netids, 114

NICs, 114

rules, 117-118

subnet masks, 115-116

IPConfig utility (TCP/IP), 123, 125

ISDNs, RAS (Remote Access Service), 357

K

kernels, boot troubleshooting, 434, 440

Keyboard application (Control Panel), 153-154

Keyboard Properties dialog box, 153

keys

hives, 458-459

Registry

adding, 98

backing up, 461

deleting, 98

values, 97-98

L

\L print escape code, 191

LAN Manager 2.2c systems, 33-35

MS-DOS (protocols), 34, 203

OS/2 (protocols), 34, 203

LANs (Local Area Networks), NetBEUI protocol, 32

LastKnownGood control set, boot troubleshooting, 442-443

licences (CAL), *see* CAL

License Manager, 141-142

Licensing application (Control Panel), 140-141

licensing modes, installation, 67

List (directory permissions), 303

loading services, boot troubleshooting, 440-441

local accounts (domain), 240

Local Computer Properties dialog box, 264

local groups, 227-228, 240

built-in groups, comparing, 309

creating (User Manager for Domains), 242-243, 309-310

deleting, 311

disabling, 311

domain, 229

Administrators, 229-230

Backup Operators, 231

Guest groups, 230

Print Operators, 231

Replicator, 231

Server Operators, 231

Users group, 230

member servers, 232-233

members

adding, 311

removing, 311

permissions, assigning, 308-309

power users, 232

renaming, 311

Workstations, 232-233

local profiles, 257-258

Local Security Authority, *see* LSA

locations (modems), 153

locking subdirectories (Directory Replication), 135

lockouts (account), 246-247

log files (Registry), 459

Log menu commands (Save As), 451

LogicalDisk object

% Disk Time counter, 408

Disk Queue Length counter, 408

Logon preferences dialog box, 373

logon scripts (users), 241

logons

account lockout, 246-247

customizing (System Policy Editor), 267

Dial-Up Networking application, 372

domains, 14

troubleshooting, 471-472

user accounts, creating, 239

workgroups, 12-13

loopback addresses (netids), 117

low battery signal (UPS application), 149

LSA (Local Security Authority)

domains, 14

workgroups, 13

M

Manage Exported Directories dialog box, 135

Manage Imported Directories dialog box, 137

manual devices (Control Panel), 146

Mark Active command (Partition menu), 166

Master Boot Record, *see* MBR

master browsers, 142-144

Maximize Throughout settings (Server service optimization)

Network Application, 399

Sharing setting, 399

/maxmem switch (BOOT.INI), 440

MBR (Master Boot Record), troubleshooting, 433

MCPS (Microsoft Certified Product Specialist), 489-491

MCSD (Microsoft Certified Solution Developer), 496-497

MCSE (Microsoft Certified Systems Engineer), 489, 491-495

MCT (Microsoft Certified Trainer), 490, 497-498

MCTGUIDE.DOC Web site, 497

member servers, 56

accounts, 233

groups, 232-234

power users, 232-233

memory

diagnostics, 456

optimizing (Virtual Memory Manager), 396-398

Performance Monitor (Memory object), *see* Memory object

Server requirements (Intel), 52

upgrading, 391-392

virtual memory, configuring, 397-398

Memory Object (Performance Monitor), 406-407

Available Bytes counter, 407

Pages/sec counter, 407

merging files (My Briefcase), 295-297

Microsoft Network Client 3.0, 33

Microsoft Certified Product Specialist, 489-491

Microsoft Certified Solution Developer, 496-497

Microsoft Certified Systems Engineer, 489, 491-495

Microsoft Certified Trainer, 490, 497-498

Microsoft Certified Training Web site, 498

Microsoft ftp site, 99

Microsoft TCP/IP, *see* TCP/IP

Microsoft Training and Certification Web site, 490

migration

NetWare, 353-354

status subkey (Registry Editor), 93

Minimize Memory Used setting (Server service optimization), 399

mirrors
  disks, 25-26
  partitions, 476

mismatched documents, printing, 195

MMSYS.CPL, 147

Modem Properties dialog box, 151, 153

modems
  installing, 151-152
  locations, configuring, 153

Modems application (Control Panel), 151-153

monitoring performance
  optimization, 390-391
  Performance Monitor, *see* Performance Monitor

monitors
  display settings, 156
  print, 180-181

Mouse application (Control Panel), 154-155

MS-DOS
  installation, multi-booting requirements, 54
  LAN MAN 2.2c protocols, 34
  Network Client protocols, 34
  NTFS file systems, 20
  primary partitions, 16
  printing, 202
  WINNT.EXE, installation, 58-61

multiprocessing, 7, 9

<multifunction_adapter> entry, 89

multilinking, RAS (Remote Access Service), 466

Multimedia application (Control Panel), 147

multitasking (Windows 95), 6

My Briefcase, 294-297
  deleting files, 295
  merging changed files, 295-297
  opening, 295

replacing changes, 295-297
  skipping updates, 295-297

My Computer
  ATS permissions, 288-289
  NTFS file systems, auditing, 299
  sharing directories, 286-289

N

\N print escape code, 191

name registration, installation, 67

named pipes, viewing statistics, 292

naming
  FAT file system, 19-20, 276-278
  local groups, renaming, 311
  NTFS file system, 22, 279
  UNC (Universal Naming Convention), 274-275
  user accounts
    full names, 238
    renaming, 252-253
    usernames, 237-238

NDS (NetWare Directory Service), 343

Net Logon service, optimizing, 399

NET SHARE command, 289-290

NET USE command, 58, 351

NET VIEW command, 351

NetBEUI protocol, 32

NetBIOS
  name registration, 67
  WINS, 121-123

NetBT, 122

netids (IP address), 114
  loopback address, 117
  matching, 118
  see also subnet masks

NetLogon (domains), 14

NetWare
  connectivity, 355-356
  CSNW (Client Services for NetWare), 347-349

installing, 347
passwords, 348
printing, 349
servers, 347, 349-350
DSMN (Directory Service Manager for NetWare), 352-353
FPNW (File and Print Services for NetWare), 352
GSNW (Gateway Services for NetWare), 342-347
gateway enabling, 345-346
installing, 344
interoperating, 342
migration, 353-354
NET SHARE command, 289-290
NET USE command, 351
NET VIEW command, 351
NWLink protocol, 31
protocols, SAP (Service Advertising Protocol), 360
server access, 354-355
NetWare Directory Service, *see* NDS
Network Access Order dialog box, 350
network adapters (Control Panel), configuring, 126
Network application (Control Panel), 106-109
adapter cards, configuring, 108-109
adapters, configuring, 126
bindings, 109, 394
GSNW (Gateway Services for NetWare), installing, 344
identification settings, 106
network services settings, 107
NWLink protocol
adapter card frame types, 110-113
configuring, 112-113
installing, 110-112
protocols, configuring, 108
RAS (Remote Access Service), installing, 361-366
Server service, optimizing, 398-399

services, 130
TCP/IP, installing, 118
Network Card Setup dialog box, 126
Network Card statistics (Network Monitor), 470
Network Client 3.0, 33
Administrator, 76-80, 271-273
installation disk sets, creating, 79-80
startup disks, creating, 77-79
protocols, 34, 203
Network Client Administrator dialog box, 79, 272
network interface cards, *see* NICs
Network Monitor, 467-471
Graph pane, 468
installing, 467
Session Stats pane, 469
Station Stats pane, 470-471
Total Stats pane, 469-470
Network object (Performance Monitor), counters, 406
Networking, installation, 69-73
adapter cards, 69-70
domains, 72
protocols, 70-71
workgroups, 72
networks
diagnostics, 457
disk configuration, *see* disk configuration
NetWare (NWLink protocol), 31
optimizing performance, monitoring, 390-391
protocols, *see* protocols
services, 130, 107
statistics (Network Monitor), 469
troubleshooting, 466-467
Network Monitor, 467-471
upgrading hardware, 392
workgroups, 11, 12-13
New Global Group dialog box, 242
New Local Group commands (User menu), 310

New Local Group dialog box, 242, 310
New Phonebook Entry dialog box, 367
New Policy command (File menu), 270
New Technology File System, *see* NTFS
file system
New User dialog box, 237
NICs (network interface cards)
IP address, 114
TCP/IP installation, 119
No Access
ATS permission, 288
directory permissions, 303
file permissions, 306
No Master (Directory Replication), 138
No Sync (Directory Replication), 138
/nodebug switch (BOOT.INI), 439
non-browsers, 143
non-expiring passwords (Directory
Replication), 133
Non-Random mode (TestPrep utility), 506
/noserialmice switch (BOOT.INI), 439
Novell NetWare, *see* NetWare
Novell SETPASS command, 348
NT (Windows), *see* Windows NT
NT File System, *see* NTFS file system
NTBACKUP command, switches, 475
NTConfig.pol, 268
NTDETECT.COM, boot
troubleshooting, 434
NTFS
volume sets, 161
NTFS (New Technology File System) file
system, 19, 21-23
access tokens, 302-303, 317
compression, 22, 280-282
directories, 284
uncompressing, 282
converting, FAT partition, 279
long names, 279
MS-DOS support, 20
naming files, 22
permissions, 301-302

directory level, 303-305
file level, 305-306
setting, 307-308
security, 22, 297
account ownership, 297-299
auditing access, 299-301
discretionary access, 302
Security Reference Monitor, 316-317
selecting installation, 65
support, 6
User Manager for Domains, revoking
ownerships, 299
Windows 95 support, 20
NTFSDOS, 20
NTLDR file, boot troubleshooting, 433-434
NTOSKRNL.EXE, boot
troubleshooting, 434
NTUSER.DA_ (emergency repair
disk), 445
ntuser.dat file, 256
Null modem cables, RAS (Remote Access
Service), 357
\<number> print escape code, 191
NWLink IPX/SPX Properties dialog
box, 110
NWLink protocol
adapter card frame types
configuring, 112-113
detecting, 110-112
Control Panel
configuring, 112-113
installing, 110-112
NWLink/SPX protocol, 31

O

objects (Performance Monitor), 403
open files, viewing statistics, 291
Open Registry command (File menu), 264
Open Resources dialog box, 292

operating systems
   Windows 95, *see* Windows 95
   Windows NT, *see* Windows NT
[operating systems] section (BOOT.INI),
437-438
   /basevideo switch, 438
   /crashdebug switch, 439
   /maxmem switch, 440
   /nodebug switch, 439
   /noserialmice switch, 439
   /scsiordinal switch, 440
   /sos switch, 439
Operations menu commands
(Restore), 474
optimizing performance, 388
   applications, 389
   automatic, 389-390
   database servers, 389
   device drivers, removing, 393-395
   file servers, 388
   hardware, upgrading, 391-393
   memory (Virtual Memory Manager),
   396-398
   monitoring
     applications, 390
     networks, 390-391
     server demands, 391
   network protocols, removing, 393-395
   PDC (Primary Domain Controller), 388
   researching trouble, 401-402
   resources, 389, 400
   Server service, 398-399
   services, 394-395, 399
   software, upgrading, 395-396
   tasks, dividing, 400-401
   see also Performance Monitor
Options menu commands
   Colors and Patterns, 160
   Confirm on Delete, 85
   Read Only Mode, 85
   Region Display, 160
orphans (partition mirrors), 476

OS/2
   installation, multi-booting
   requirements, 54
   LAN MAN 2.2c, protocols, 34
OSLOADER.EXE, boot
troubleshooting, 435
Owner dialog box, 298
/OX switch (WINNT.EXE), 61

P-Q

Pages/sec counter (Memory Object), 407
Paging File object (Performance
Monitor), 403
paging file, *see* virtual memory
panes (Network Monitor), 468
   Graph, 468
   Session Stats, 469
   Station Stats pane, 470-471
   Total Stats pane, 469-470
parameters
   BOOT.INI
     default, 437
     timeout, 437
   Directory Replication, 131
parity stripe blocks, 26-27
parity striping, *see* stripe set with parity
Partition menu commands
   Commit Changes Now, 162, 166
   Configuration, 167
   Create, 161
   Create Extended, 161
   Create Stripe Set, 164
   Create Volume Set, 161
   Delete, 167
   Extend Volume Set, 163
   Mark Active, 166
partitioning, 15-16
   active marking, 166
   boot partitions, 18, 165-166
   deleting, 167

drive letters, assigning, 169-170

extended partitions, 16-17

fault tolerance

   mirrors, fixing, 476

   stripe set with parity, fixing, 476-477

file systems, *see* file systems

formatting, 168-169

hard disks, 160-163

   extended partitions, 161

   primary partitions, 160-161

   volume sets, 161-163

hiding, 169

NTFS (New Technology File System) file system, 21-23, 279

primary partitions, 16-17

   action, 17

   MS-DOS, 16

saving changes, 166-167

security, 173

selecting, installation, 64

stripe sets, 163-165

stripe sets with parity, 164

system partitions, 18, 165-166

volume sets

   comparing, 162

   properties, 170-171

passwords

CSNW (Client Services for NetWare), 348

domains, 13

installation, 68

non-expiring (Directory Replication), 133

troubleshooting, 471-472

user accounts

   creating, 237

   expiration, 238-239

   forcing change, 238

User Manager for Domains, 243-244

   account lockout, 246-247

   changing, 248

   maximum time, 244-245

   minimum time, 245

   uniqueness, 246

   word length, 245

workgroups, 12

patches (Intel Pentium), installation, 74-75

paths (user profiles), 240-241

PC Card application (Control Panel), 151

PCMCIA device drivers, 151

PDC (Primary Domain Controller), 55

local groups

optimizing, 388

Per Seat mode, CAL (Client Access Licenses), 67, 139

per second statistics (Network Monitor), 470

Per Server mode, CAL (Client Access Licenses), 67, 139

Performance Monitor, 402-404

bottlenecks, detecting, 404-405

counters, 403, 405-406

LogicalDisk object

   % Disk Time counter, 408

   Disk Queue Length, 408

Memory Object, 407

   Available Bytes counter, 407

   Pages/sec counter, 407

Memory object, 406

memory optimization, 398

Network object, 406

objects, 403

organizing data, 409

Paging File object, 403

Physical Disk object, 406

Processor object, 406

   % Processor Time counter, 407

   Interrupts/sec counter, 407

   System: Processor Queue Length counter, 407

PhysicalDisk object, 408

   % Disk Time counter, 408

   Avg. Disk Queue Length counter, 408

Server object, 406, 408-409
  Bytes Total/sec counter, 409
  pool failure counters, 409
System object, 403
performance optimization, 388
  applications, 389
  automatic, 389-390
  database servers, 389
  device drivers, removing, 393
  file servers, 388
  hardware, upgrading, 391-393
  memory (Virtual Memory Manager), 396-398
  monitoring, 390-391
    applications, 390
    networks, 390-391
    server demands, 391
  network protocols, removing, 393-394
  PDC (Primary Domain Controller), 388
  researching trouble, 401-402
  resources, 389, 400
  Server service, 398-399
  services, 394-395, 399
  software, upgrading, 395-396
  task, dividing, 400-401
  see also Performance Monitor
permissions
  ATS (Access Through Share), 287
  directory level, 303-305
  directory/file conflicts, 313-315
  file level, 305-306
  local groups, assigning, 308-309
  NTFS file systems, 301-302
  printing, 197-199
  rights, compared, 249, 302-303
  setting, 307-308
  troubleshooting, 471-472
  users, obtaining, 226
  users/groups conflicts, 311-313
persistent connections, shared directories, 275

phonebook entries (Dial-Up Networking application), 367, 372
  creating, 367-369
  editing, 370-373
  shortcuts, creating, 371
Physical Disk object (Performance Monitor), 406
Ping utility (TCP/IP), 123-125, 467
platforms
  Intel, 52-53
  Windows 95, 6
  Workstation support, 8
Plug and Play (Windows 95), 6
Plus!, computer display setting, 155
Point-to-Point Protocol, *see* PPP
Point-to-Point Tunneling Protocol, *see* PPTP
policies
  System Policy Editor, 262
    Policy File mode, 268-271
    Registry mode, 262-268
    templates, 269-270
  User Manager for Domains (passwords), 243-244
    account lockout, 246-247
    changing passwords, 248
    disconnecting remote users, 247
    maximum time, 244-245
    minimum time, 245
    uniqueness, 246
    word length, 245
Policies menu commands
  Account, 246
  User Rights, 248
Policy File mode (System Policy Editor), 268-271
Policy menu commands
  Auditing, 250
  Trust Relationships, 251
pool failure counters (Server object), 409
ports (printers), 189, 192
Ports application (Control Panel), 147-148

PORTS.CPL, 147-148

POST, *see* Power On Self Test, 433

potential browsers, 143

Power failure signal (UPS application), 148

Power On Self Test, 433

Power User group, 232-233

PPP (Point-to-Point Protocol)

    RAS (Remote Access Service), 359

    troubleshooting, 465

PPTP (Point-to-Point Tunneling Protocol)

    filtering, 358

    RAS (Remote Access Service), 359

preemptive multitasking

    Windows 95, 6

    Workstation, 7

preinstallation

    file systems, selecting, 65

    hard disk examination, 66

    hardware detection, 64

    partitions, selecting, 64

    rebooting, 66

    root directory, naming, 65

    setup disks, 62-63

    storage devices, detecting, 63-64

Primary Domain Controller, *see* PDC

primary partitions, 16-17

    action, 17

    creating (Disk Administrator), 160-161

    MS-DOS, 16

Print Subtree command (Registry menu), 99

Printer Graphics Driver DLL, 176

Printer Interface Driver, 176

Printers folder (Control Panel), 181-182

printing, 174

    CSNW (Client Services for NetWare), 349

    devices, 174

    document settings, 186-188

    escape codes, 191-192

mismatched documents, 195

MS-DOS, 202

ports, configuring, 192

print jobs, separating, 190-192

print monitors, 180-181

print queue, 175

printer pools, 175, 200-201

printers, 174

    availability settings, 194

    configuring, 186-188

    device drivers, 176-177, 462

    device settings, 200

    installing (Add Printer Wizard), 182-185

    NetWare, connecting, 349

    security, 197-199

    sharing, 184, 196, 200

Printers folder, 181-182

priorities, 193, 194

process, 175-176

processor, 179-180, 192

rendering, 179-180

routers, 179

servers

    forms, 188-189

    ports, 189

spoolers, 177-179, 194-195

troubleshooting, 461-462

    crashes, 464

    isolating problems, 461-462

    non-Windows, 463

    speed (priority levels), 464-467

    spooler, 462-463

Processor object (Performance Monitor), 406

    % Processor Time counter, 407

    Interrupts/sec counter, 407

    System: Processor Queue Length counter, 407

processors

    printing, 179-180, 192

    Server requirements (Intel), 52

    upgrading, 391

profiles, 256-257

hardware, 102-103, 260-262

local, 257

roaming, 257-260

changing to local, 258

configuring, 258-259

user accounts

creating, 239

path specification, 240-241

Program Groups subkey (Registry Editor), 93

Programs menu commands

Accessories, 366

Administrative Tools, 272

properties

printers, 190-200

User Manager for Domains, 243

volume sets (partitioning), 170-171

Properties command (Tools menu), 171

Properties command (User menu), 247

protocols, 27-28

bindings, *see* bindings

clients, 34, 203

configuring (Control Panel), 108

Lan MAN 2.2c for MS-DOS, 203

Lan MAN 2.2c for OS/2, 203

NetBEUI, 32

Network Client for MS-DOS, 203

Networking, installation, 70-71

NWLink

adapter card frame types, 110-113

configuring, 112-113

installing, 110-112

NWLink/SPX, 31

PPP (Point to Point), troubleshooting, 359, 465

PPTP (Point-to-Point Tunneling Protocol), 358-359

RAS (Remote Access Service), 358-359

SAP (Service Advertising Protocol), 360

TCP/IP, 28-30, 113-114

DHCP (Dynamic Host Configuration Protocol), 29, 30

Dial-Up Networking settings, 368

DNS (Domain Name System), 29-30, 123

installing, 118-121

IP address, see IP address

IPConfig utility, 123, 125

Microsoft TCP/IP, 29

NetBT, 122

Ping utility, 123-125

TRACERT utility, 124-126

WINS (Windows Internet Name Service), 29-30, 121-123

Windows 95, 203

Workstation, 203

PSTN (Public Switched Telephone Network), 357

PhysicalDisk object (Performance Monitor), 408

% Disk Time counter, 408

Avg. Disk Queue Length counter, 408

questions (TestPrep utility), 505

Queue Length counter

LogicalDisk object, 408

PhysicalDisk object, 408

Processor object, 406

R

RAID (Redundant Array of Inexpensive Disks), 24, 171-173

disk mirroring, 25-26, 172

stripe set with parity, 26-27, 172-173

stripe sets, 164

RAM, optimizing, 396

RAS (Remote Access Service), 356-357

configuring, 363-366

connecting, 357

Dial-Up Networking application, 366-373

appearance, 371-383

autodial, 373-383

callback, 371-383

    dialing options, 371-383

    logon preferences, 372-383

    phonebook entries, see phonebook entries

installing, 361-366

NWLink protocol, installing, 110

protocols, 358-359

routing, 360

security, 357-358

TAPI (Telephony Application Program Interface), 360-361

troubleshooting, 465-466

    authentication, 466

    autodialing, 466

    callback, 466

    multilinking, 466

RAS Server IPX Configuration dialog box, 365

RAS Server NetBEUI Configuration dialog box, 363

RAS Server TCP/IP Configuration dialog box, 364

Read

    ATS permission, 288

    directory permissions, 303

    file permissions, 306

Read Only Mode command (Options menu; Registry Editor), 85

Recovery utility, 457-458

    memory optimization, 398

    Control Panel, 101

Redundant Array of Inexpensive Disks, *see* RAID

REG_BINARY (Registry Editor), 87

REG_DWORD (Registry Editor), 87

REG_EXPAND_SZ (Registry Editor), 87

REG_MULTI_SZ (Registry Editor), 87

REG_SZ (Registry Editor), 87

REG_WORD values (Directory Replicator)

    GuardTime, 131

    Interval, 131

REGEDIT.EXE, REGEDT32.EXE comparison, 84

REGEDT32.EXE, 84-87

    HKEY_CLASSES_ROOT, 95

    HKEY_CURRENT_CONFIG, 96

    HKEY_CURRENT_USER, 96

    HKEY_LOCAL_MACHINE, 87-95

        Hardware key, 88-90

        SAM key, 90

        SECURITY key, 90

        SOFTWARE key, 90-93

        SYSTEM key, 93-95

    HKEY_USERS, 96

    values, 87

Regenerate command (Fault Tolerance menu), 477

REGENTRY.HLP file, 99

Region Display command (Options menu), 160

Region Display Options dialog box, 160

Registry, 80-96

    Administrative Tools, 83

    backing up, 458-460

    booting, 83

    Control Panel, 82

    editing, 97-98

    Editor (REGEDT32.EXE), 84-87

        HKEY_CLASSES_ROOT, 95

        HKEY_CURRENT_CONFIG, 96

        HKEY_CURRENT_USER, 96

        HKEY_LOCAL_MACHINE, 87-95

        HKEY_USERS, 96

        printing spooler directories, changing, 178

        values, 87

    emergency repair, *see* emergency repair

    fault tolerance, 459

    hives, 458-460

    keys

        adding, 98

        backing up, 461

        deleting, 98

        values, 97-98

LastKnownGood control set, 442

searching, 98-99

services, optimizing, 399

Setup, 83

Registry menu commands

Print Subtree, 99

Restore Key, 461

Restore Volatile, 461

Save Key, 461

Save Subtree As, 99

Registry mode (System Policy Editor), 262-268

changing settings, 263-264

configuring network computers, 265-267

customizing logons, 267

/REMARK switch (NET SHARE command), 290

Remote Access Service, *see* RAS

Remote Access Setup dialog box, 362

remote shutdown (UPS application), 149

remote users, disconnecting, 247

Rename command (User menu), 252

renaming, user accounts, 252-253

rendering (printing), 179-180

REPAIR directory, 75; *see also* emergency repair

Repl$, 132

replication

PDC (Primary Domain Controller), 388

see also directory replication

Replication Configuration dialog box, 140

Replicator (domain local groups), 231

requests, server failures, 409

requirements

installation

hardware, 53

HCL, 51-52

Intel platform requirements, 52-53

multi-booting, 53-55

Server, 11

Windows 95, 6

Workstation, 7

Resource Guide (CD-ROM), 99

Resource Kit (DRIVERS.EXE), 441

ResourceMap subkey (Registry Editor), 90

resources

diagnostics, 457

optimizing, 389

peak time scheduling, 400

task division, 400-401

Restore command (Operations menu), 474

Restore Information dialog box, 474

Restore Key command (Registry menu), 461

Restore Volatile command (Registry menu), 461

RestrictGuestAccess value (Event Viewer), 451

rights

permissions, compared, 249, 302-303

User Manager for Domains, 248-250

RISC computers, troubleshooting (booting), 435

RISK.EXE (emergency repair), 445-446

creating disk, 446

updating information, 446

roaming profiles, 257-260

changing to local, 258

configuring, 258-259

root directory, naming, 65-66

routers

NetBEUI protocol, 32

printing, 179

TCP/IP, 29

routing, RAS (Remote Access Service), 360

S

/S switch (WINNT.EXE), 59

SAM (Security Accounts Manager), 14

SAM key (Registry Editor), 90

SAM._ (emergency repair disk), 445

SAP (Service Advertising Protocol), 360

Save As command (Log menu), 451

Save Key command (Registry menu), 461

Save Subtree As command (Registry menu), 99

SAVEDUMP.EXE, crash recovery, 102

Savedump.exe, 458

scoring (TestPrep utility), 506

screen savers, configuring, 155

scripts (Directory Replication), 139

SCSI adapter, installation troubleshooting

SCSI Adapters (Control Panel), 149-150

   installing, 149, 431

   removing, 150

SCSI Adapters dialog box, 149

/scsiordinal switch (BOOT.INI), 440

searching (Registry), 98-99

seat license, installation, 67

Secure subkey (Registry Editor), 93

security

   Event Viewer, 451

   FAT file system, 20

   NTFS file system, 22, 297

     account ownership, 297-299

     auditing access, 299-301

     discretionary access, 302

   partitioning, 173

   permissions, *see* permissions

   printers, 197-199

   RAS, 357-358

   Registry, 81

   Services application (Control Panel), 129

   workgroups, 12

   Workstation, 7

Security Accounts Manager, *see* SAM

Security Identifier, *see* SID

SECURITY key (Registry Editor), 90

security log (Event Viewer), 450

Security Reference Monitor, 316-317

SECURITY.__ (emergency repair disk), 445

Select Domain command (User menu), 235

Select Domain dialog box, 134

Select Network Adapter dialog box, 126

Select Network Service dialog box, 130

Select Preferred Server for NetWare dialog box, 348

Serial Line Internet Protocol, *see* SLIP

Server (Windows NT), 5, 9

   caching, 10

   client software, configuring, 202-203

   disk configuration, 15

   installing, 50-51, 54

   local groups (power users), 232-233

   servers, configuring, 10

   workgroups, 12

   Workstation, compared, 6-11

     BackOffice support, 10

     client sessions, 9

     files system driver, 10

     Internet connections, 9

     multiprocessing, 9

     Remote Access, 9

     requirements, 11

Server application (Control Panel), 291-294

Server dialog box, 398

server license, installation, 67

Server Manager

   Directory Replicator parameters, 131

   export servers, configuring, 133

   viewing sharing statistics, 292

Server Message Block, *see* SMB

Server object (Performance Monitor), 406, 408-409

   Bytes Total/sec counter, 409

   pool failure counters, 409

Server Operators (domain local groups), 231

server roles, installation, 55-56

Server service, 127, 398-399

servers

  configuring, 10

  CSNW (Client Services for NetWare)

    connecting, 349-350

    selecting, 347

  database servers, optimizing, 389

  file servers, optimizing, 388

  monitoring, 391

  NetWare access, 354

  Performance Monitor (Server object),
    see Server object

  printers

    forms, 188-189

    ports, 189

  TCP/IP installation, 118

  WINS, *see* WINS

Service Advertising Protocol, *see* SAP

Service dialog box, 136

services, 127-128

  CAL (Client Access License), 139-142

  Computer Browser, 142-144, 399

  CSNW, *see* CSNW

  diagnostics, 456

  Directory Replication, *see* Directory
    Replication

  disabling, optimization, 394-395

  DSMN (Directory Service Manager for
    NetWare), 352-353

  FPNW (File and Print Services for
    NetWare), 352

  Gateway, 345

  loading, boot troubleshooting, 440-441

  Net Logon, optimizing, 399

  network services, 130

  optimizing, 399-401

  RAS (Remote Access Service) , *see* RAS

  Server service, 127, 398-399

  Services application (Control Panel),
    128-129

    hardware profiles, 129

    security, 129

    Startup type, 128

    stopping services, 129

  Spooler, 178, 399

  UPS, 127

  WINS, 127

  Workstation service, 127

Services application (Control Panel),
128-129

  Directory Replicator, 131-132

    export servers, 131, 133

    import computers, 131, 136-137

    parameters, 131

    troubleshooting, 137-139

  hardware profiles, 129

  security, 129

  Startup type, 128

  stopping services, 129

Services dialog box, 128

SERVICES.EXE (DLLs), 441-442

session manager, 440-441

sessions statistics, viewing, 291

Session Stats pane (Network
Monitor), 469

Settings menu commands (Control
Panel), 100

Setup

  Administrator password, 68

  CD ROM installation, 57

  computer name registration, 67

  date/time settings, 73

  emergency repair, *see* emergency repair

  Intel Pentium patch, 74-75

  licensing modes, 67

  name registration, 67

  Networking, 69-73

    adapter cards, 69-70

    domains, 72

    protocols, 70-71

    workgroups, 72

pre-installation
  disks, 62-63
  file systems, selecting, 65
  hard disk examination, 66
  hardware detection, 64
  partitions, selecting, 64
  rebooting, 66
  root directory, naming, 65-66
  storage devices, detecting, 63-64
  print device drivers, 176
  Registry, 83
  REPAIR directory, 75
  video display, 74
Setup Boot disks, 444
Setup Wizard, *see* Setup
SETUP.LOG (emergency repair disk), 445
SFMPSPRT.DLL, 180
Share Network Client Installation Files
  dialog box, 78
Shared Directories dialog box, 293
Shared Resources dialog box, 292
sharing, 285
  ADMIN$ shares, 291
  administration tools, 272
  C$ shares, 290
  directories, 285-286
    command prompt, 289-290
    Explorer, 286-289
    hiding shares, 290
    My Computer, 286-289
    persistent connections, 275
    referring, 274
    viewing, 274
  printers, 184, 196, 200
  statistics, viewing, 291-294
Sharing command, 287
SID (Security Identifier), 253
signatures (Disk Administrator), 158
sites
  ftp (Microsoft), 99

Web
  MCTGUIDE.DOC, 497
  Microsoft Certified Training, 498
  Microsoft Training and Certification, 490
SLIP (Serial Line Internet Protocol), 358
SMB (Server Message Block), 343
Social Security Numbers, *see* SSNs
software
  components, removing, 393-395
  detecting, installation, 64
  optimizing, 395-396
  Performance Monitor, 403
  troubleshooting, 431
SOFTWARE key (Registry Editor), 90-93
SOFTWARE._ (emergency repair
  disk), 445
/sos switch (BOOT.INI), 439
Spooler service, 178
spoolers (printing), 177-179, 194-195
  optimizing, 399
  troubleshooting, 462-463
SRV.SYS, 10
SRVMGR.CPL, 145
SSNs (Social Security Numbers), 253
stand-alone servers, 55
startup disks, creating, 77-79
Startup type
  Directory Replication
    import computer, 136
    Startup Type frame, 136
  Services application, 100-101, 128
Station Stats pane (Network Monitor),
  470-471
statistics
  Network Monitor
    captured, 469
    network, 469
    Network Card, 470
    per second, 470
  Performance Monitor, 403
  sharing, viewing, 291-294

storage devices, detecting, 63-64

String Editor dialog box, 98

stripe set with parity (partitions),
26-27, 164

creating, 172-173

fault tolerance, 476-477

stripe sets (partitioning), 163-165

study tips

attaching notes to questions, 502

habits, 499-500

marking difficult questions, 502

multiple correct answers, 501-502

pretesting, 500

timing, 501

subdirectories, locking (Directory
Replication), 135

subnet masks (IP address), 115-116

subtrees (Registry Editor), 86-87

HKEY_CLASSES_ROOT, 95

HKEY_CURRENT_CONFIG, 96

HKEY_CURRENT_USER, 96

HKEY_LOCAL_MACHINE, 87-95

HKEY_USERS, 96

values, 87

success audits (Event Viewer), 450

switches

BOOT.INI, 438

/basevideo, 438

/crashdebug, 439

/maxmem, 440

/nodebug, 439

/noserialmice, 439

/scsiordinal, 440

/sos, 439

NTBACKUP command, 475

NET SHARE command

/DELETE switch, 290

/REMARK switch, 290

/USERS switch, 290

/UNLIMITED switch, 290

WINNT.EXE, installation, 59-61

SYSTEM account (Services
application), 129

System application (Control Panel), 100

booting

BOOT.INI, 437

setting defaults, 101

crash recovery, 101-102

displaying information, 105

environment variables

changing, 103-104

creating, 104

deleting, 105

hardware profiles, 261-262

creating, 102

organizing, 103

memory, optimizing (Virtual Memory
Manager), 396

performance enhancement, 105

Recovery utility, 457

roaming profiles, 258

system devices (Control Panel), 146

system diagnostics, 456

SYSTEM hive (Registry), 460

SYSTEM key (Registry Editor), 93-96

system log, crash recovery, 101

system log view (Event Viewer), 449-450

System object (Performance Monitor), 403

system partitions, 18, 165-166

System Policy Editor, 262

Policy File mode, 268-271

Registry mode, 262-268

changing settings, 263-264

configuring network computers, 265-267

customizing logons, 267

templates, 269-270

System Properties dialog box, 100

SYSTEM._ (emergency repair disk), 445

System: Processor Queue Length counter
(Processor object), 407

T

\T print escape code, 191

/T switch (WINNT.EXE), 60

/t switch (NTBACKUP command), 476

Tape Devices (Control Panel), 150-151

tape drive device driver

installing, 150

removing, 151

TAPI (Telephony Application Program Interface), 360-361

TCP/IP (Transmission Control Protocol/Internet Protocol), 28-30, 113-114

client software, 203

DHCP (Dynamic Host Configuration Protocol), 29, 30

Dial-Up Networking settings, 368

DNS (Domain Name System), 29, 30, 123

installing

Control Panel, 118

DHCP, 118-121

manually, 121

IP address, 29, 114

default gateways, 116

hostids, 114

InterNIC (Internet Network Information Center), 117

netids, 114

NICs, 114

rules, 117-118

subnet masks, 115-116

IPConfig utility, 123, 125

Microsoft TCP/IP, 29

NetBT, 122

Networking, installation, 70-71

Ping utility, 123-125, 467

TRACERT utility, 124-126

WINS (Windows Internet Name Service), 29-30, 121-123

TCP/IP Properties dialog box, 119

Telephony Application Program Interface, see TAPI

templates (System Policy), 269-270

testing

computer display settings, 156

study tips, see study tips

troubleshooting, 431

TestPrep utility, 505

FLASH! Electronic Flash Cards, 507

Instructor mode, 506-507

Non-Random mode, 506

question set up, 505

scoring, 506

TEXT data type (WINPRINT.DLL), 179

This account (Services application), 129

time, installation settings, 73

timeout parameter (BOOT.INI), 437

tolerance (fault), see fault tolerance

tools

administration tools, 271-273

sharing, 272

Windows 95, 271-272

Workstation, 272

migration (NetWare), 353-354

Tools menu commands

Assign Drive Letter, 169

Format, 168

Properties, 171

Total Stats pane (Network Monitor), 469-470

TRACERT utility (TCP/IP), 124-126

transaction tracking (file systems), 23

Transmission Control Protocol/Internet Protocol, see TCP/IP

troubleshooting, 429-430

backing up, 431

booting, 432-433

BOOT.INI, see BOOT.INI

BOOTSECT.DOS, 435

control sets, 442-443

Intel computers, 433-434

kernel initialization, 440

MBR (Master Boot Record), 433

POST (Power On Self Test), 433
RISC-based computer, 435
services, loading, 440-441
Windows interface, 441-442
diagnostics, 455-457
Directory Replication, 137-139
documenting problems, 430
emergency repair, 444
 boot files, inspecting, 448
 directory/disk, compared, 444-445
 Registry files, inspecting, 447
 RISK.EXE, 445-446
 starting, 447
 Windows NT files, inspecting, 448
Event Viewer, 449-457
 application log, 451
 event descriptions, 453-454
 filtering events, 454-455
 security log, 450
 system log view, 449-450
fault tolerance, 472-477
 backing up, 473-477
 mirrored partitions, 476
 restoring, 473-475
 stripe set with parity, 476-477
installation, 431-432
logon access, 471-472
network connections, 466-467
Network Monitor, 467-471
permissions
 directory/file conflicts, 313-315
 users/groups conflicts, 311-313
printing, 461-462
 crashes, 464
 isolating problems, 461-462
 non-Windows, 463
 speed (priority levels), 464-465
 spooler, 462-463
RAS (Remote Access Service), 465-466
 authentication, 466
 autodialing, 466

 callback, 466
 multilinking, 466
Recovery utility, 457-458
Registry, backing up, 458-460
removing problems, 431
TCP/IP, pinging, 467
testing, deduction method, 431
Trust Relationships command (Policy menu), 251

U

\U print escape code, 191
/U switch (WINNT.EXE), 59-60
UDF (Uniqueness Database File), installation, 60
/UDF switch (WINNT.EXE), 60
UNC (Universal Naming Convention), 274-275
uncompressing NTFS file system, 282
undo (My Briefcase), 295-297
uninstalling (Windows NT), 75-76
Uninterruptible Power Supply, *see* UPS application
Uniqueness Database File (UDF), 60
Universal Naming Convention, 274-275
/UNLIMITED switch (NET SHARE command), 290
Update All command (Briefcase menu), 296
Update My Briefcase dialog box, 296
updating (emergency repair), 446
updating files (My Briefcase), 295-297
upgrading
 hardware, 391-393
  disks, 392
  fault tolerance, 392-393
  memory, 391-392
  networks, 392
  processors, 391
 software, optimizing, 395-396

UPS (Uninterruptible Power Supply) application (Control Panel), 127, 148-149

UPS.CPL, 148-149

Usage Summary, viewing, 291-294

user accounts, 226

  copying, 253

  deleting, 253-255

  disabling, 239, 253-255

  renaming, 252-253

  see also groups

User Environment Profile dialog box, 240

user environment variables (Control Panel)

  changing, 103-104

  creating, 104

  deleting, 105

User Manager for Domains, 235-237

  assigning rights, 248-250

  auditing accounts, 250

  creating user accounts, 237-240

    access time settings, 239

    descriptions, 238

    Dialin, 240

    expiration date setting, 239-240

    full names, 238

    groups, 239

    logon settings, 239

    passwords, 238-239

    profiles, 239

    usernames, 237

  groups, creating, 242-243

  home directories

    creating, 241-242

    naming, 242

  local groups, creating, 309-310

  logon scripts, 241

  NTFS file system, revoking ownerships, 299

  policies (passwords), 243-244

    account lockout, 246-247

    changing passwords, 248

    disconnecting remote users, 247

    maximum time, 244-245

    minimum time, 245

    uniqueness, 246

    word length, 245

  profiles, setting paths, 240

  properties, 243

  rights, removing, 249-250

  trust relationships, 251

  user accounts

    copying, 253

    deleting, 253-255

    disabling, 239, 253-255

    renaming, 252-253

User menu commands

  New Local Group, 310

  Properties, 247

  Rename, 252

  Select Domain, 235

User Preferences dialog box, 371

User Properties dialog box, 243, 251

User Rights command (Policies menu), 248

User Rights Policy dialog box, 248

usernames, creating, 237

users

  domain

    global groups, 231

    local groups, 230

  home directories

    creating, 241-242

    naming, 242

  logon scripts, 241

  permissions

    groups conflicts, 311-313

    obtaining, 226

  profiles, 256-257

    local, 257

    path specification, 240-241

    roaming, 257-260

User Manager for Domains, 235-237
creating user accounts, 237-240
properties, 243
rights, 248-250
Users Sessions dialog box, 292
/USERS switch (NET SHARE command), 290
utilities (TCP/IP), 125
  IPConfig, 123, 125
  Ping, 123-125
  TRACERT, 124-126

V

/v switch (NTBACKUP command), 476
values (Registry)
  Editor, 87
  keys
    adding, 97
    deleting, 98
variables (environment)
  Control Panel, 103-105
  diagnostics, 457
VDM (Virtual DOS Machine), 10
version diagnostics, 456
video display adapter
  configuring, 156
  installation settings, 74
View menu commands
  Details, 287
  Find Key, 98
Virtual DOS Machine, *see* VDM
virtual memory (paging file), configuring, 397-398
Virtual Memory dialog box, 396
Virtual Memory Manager, optimizing, 396-398
Virtual Private Networks, *see* VPNs
Volume Properties dialog box, 170
volume sets (partitioning), 162-163
  creating, 161
  extending, 163

formatting, 161-162
normal partitions, comparing, 162
properties, 170-171
VPNs (Virtual Private Networks), 359

W-X-Y-Z

\W<width> print escape code, 191
wallpaper, configuring, 155
WANs (Wide Area Networks)
  Directory Replication, 139
  TCP/IP, *see* TCP/IP
warnings, system log view (Event Viewer), 450
Welcome dialog box, 441
Wide Area Networks, *see* WANs
Windows 95, 6
  administration tools, 271
  application support, 6
  FAT file system, 6, 277-278
  installation, 54
  multitasking, 6
  NTFS file systems, 20
  platforms, 6
  Plug and Play, 6
  protocols, 34, 203
  requirements, 6
  workgroups, 6
Windows Internet Name Service, *see* WINS
Windows NT, 5
  Control Panel, *see* Control Panel
  installing
    CD-ROM source, 57
    computer name registration, 67
    date/time settings, 73
    emergency repair, see emergency repair
    hardware requirements, 53
    HCL (Hardware Compatibility List), 51-52
    Intel Pentium patch, 74-75
    Intel platforms, 52-53

licensing modes, 67
multi-booting requirements, 53-55
name registration, 67
network installs, 57-61
Networking, 69
password setup, 68
pre-installation, 62-66
REPAIR directory, 75
server roles, 55-56
video display, 74
Registry, *see* Registry
Server, *see* Server
uninstalling, 75-76
workgroups, 11-13
Workstation, *see* Workstation
Windows NT Diagnostics dialog box, 455
Windows NT Setup Wizard, *see* Setup
WinLogon
domains, 14
workgroups, 13
WINNT.EXE, installation, 58-61
WINPRINT.DLL (print processor), 179
WINS (Windows Internet Name Service), 29-30, 121-123, 127
wizards
Add Printer Wizard, 182
installing printers, 183-184
network print servers, adding, 185
Setup Wizard, *see* Setup
workgroups, 11, 12-13
Networking, installation, 72
stand-alone servers, 55
Windows 95, 6
Workstation, 5-8
accounts, 234
Administrator, 234-235
Guest account, 235
administration tools, 272
applications support, 8
caching, 10

multiprocessing, 7
platforms, 8
protocols, 34, 203
requirements, 7
security, 7
Server, compared, 6-11
BackOffice support, 10
client sessions, 9
files system driver, 10
Internet connections, 9
multiprocessing, 9
Remote Access, 9
requirements, 11
VDM (Virtual DOS Machine), 10
Workstation service, 127
accounts, 233
groups
hard-coded characteristics, 234
local groups, 232-233
World Wide Web sites
MCTGUIDE.DOC, 497
Microsoft Certified Training, 498
Microsoft Training and Certification, 490

X.25 connection, 357

REGISTRATION CARD

MCSE Training Guide: Windows NT Server 4

Name _____ Title _____

Company _____ Type of business _____

Address _____

City/State/ZIP _____

Have you used these types of books before? ☐ yes ☐ no

If yes, which ones? _____

_____

How many computer books do you purchase each year? ☐ 1–5 ☐ 6 or more

How did you learn about this book? _____

Where did you purchase this book? _____

Which applications do you currently use? _____

_____

Which computer magazines do you subscribe to? _____

_____

What trade shows do you attend? _____

_____

Comments: _____

_____

_____

Would you like to be placed on our preferred mailing list? ☐ yes ☐ no

---

☐ **I would like to see my name in print!** You may use my name and quote me in future New Riders products and promotions. My daytime phone number is: _____

New Riders Publishing   201 West 103rd Street ◆ Indianapolis, Indiana 46290 USA

Fax to **317-817-7448**

Fold Here

BUSINESS REPLY MAIL
FIRST-CLASS MAIL PERMIT NO. 9918 INDIANAPOLIS IN

POSTAGE WILL BE PAID BY THE ADDRESSEE

NEW RIDERS PUBLISHING
201 W 103RD ST
INDIANAPOLIS IN 46290-9058

A VIACOM SERVIC

The Information SuperLibrar

Bookstore

Search

What's New

Reference Desk

Software Library

Newsletter

Yellow Pages

Internet Starter Kit

HTML Workshop

Win a Free T-Shirt!

Macmillan Computer Publishing

Site Map

CHECK OUT THE BOOKS IN THIS LIBRARY

You'll find thousands of shareware files and over 1,600 computer books designed for both technowizards and technophobes. You can browse through 700 sample chapters, get the latest news on the Net, and find just about anything using our massive search directories.

All Macmillan Computer Publishing books are available at your local bookstore.

We're open 24-hours a day, 365

You don't

We don't charge fines.

And you can be as **LOUD**

The Information S

http://www.mcp.com/mcp/